AN INTRODUCTION
TO THE TRINITY

Over the last decade there has been a resurgence of writing on the Trinity, indicating a renewal of ideas and debate concerning this key element of Christian theology. This introduction challenges the standard account of a decline and revival in Trinitarian theology, taking into account recent, alternative readings of the theological tradition by Lewis Ayres and Michel Barnes amongst other scholars. By clearly analysing the scope of these new approaches, the authors establish the importance of a considered understanding of the Trinity, resisting the notion of separating faith and reason and identifying theology's link to spirituality. Their account also eschews the easy stereotypes of Western Christianity's supposedly more Unitarian approach, as opposed to the more Trinitarian view of the East. Offering an overview of the main people and themes in Trinitarian theology past and present, this book thus provides an accessible, comprehensive guide for students and scholars alike.

DECLAN MARMION is Head of the Department of Systematic Theology and History at the Milltown Institute of Theology and Philosophy, Dublin. He is the author of *A Spirituality of Everyday Faith: A Theological Investigation of the Notion of Spirituality in Karl Rahner* (1998) and is the editor of *The Cambridge Companion to Karl Rahner* (Cambridge, 2005) and *Christian Identity in a Postmodern Age* (2005).

RIK VAN NIEUWENHOVE is Lecturer in Theology at Mary Immaculate College, Limerick. He is the author of *Jan van Ruusbroec: Mystical Theologian of the Trinity* (2003) and is co-editor (with J. Wawrykow) of *The Theology of Thomas Aquinas* (2005) and *Late Medieval Mysticism of the Low Countries* (2008).

AN INTRODUCTION
TO THE TRINITY

DECLAN MARMION

AND

RIK VAN NIEUWENHOVE

CAMBRIDGE
UNIVERSITY PRESS

CAMBRIDGE UNIVERSITY PRESS

Cambridge, New York, Melbourne, Madrid, Cape Town, Singapore,
São Paulo, Delhi, Dubai, Tokyo, Mexico City

Cambridge University Press
The Edinburgh Building, Cambridge CB2 8RU, UK

Published in the United States of America by Cambridge University Press, New York

www.cambridge.org
Information on this title: www.cambridge.org/9780521879521

First published 2011

Printed in the United Kingdom at the University Press, Cambridge

A catalogue record for this publication is available from the British Library

Library of Congress Cataloguing in Publication Data
Marmion, Declan.
An introduction to the Trinity / Declan Marmion and
Rik Van Nieuwenhove.
p.   cm. – (Introduction to religion)
Includes bibliographical references and index.
ISBN 978-0-521-87952-1 – ISBN 978-0-521-70522-6 (pbk.)
1. Trinity – History of doctrines.   I. Van Nieuwenhove, Rik, 1967–   II. Title.
BT109.M37   2011
231'.044–dc22
2010030610

ISBN 978-0-521-87952-1 Hardback
ISBN 978-0-521-70522-6 Paperback

Contents

Abbreviations

ABD	*The Anchor Bible Dictionary*, ed. David Noel Freedman, 6 vols. (New Haven: Yale University Press, 1992).
BC	John Zizioulas, *Being as Communion: Studies in Personhood and the Church* (London: Darton, Longman and Todd, 1985).
Brevil.	Bonaventure, *Works of St Bonaventure*, vol. IX. *Breviloquium*, trans. D. Monti, Bonaventure Texts in Translation Series (New York: The Franciscan Institute, 2005).
CCCM	*Corpus Christianorum Continuatio Mediaevalis* (Turnhout: Brepols, 1988–2005).
CD	Karl Barth, *Church Dogmatics* (Edinburgh: T&T Clark, 1956–75).
CF	Friedrich Schleiermacher, *The Christian Faith* (Edinburgh: T&T Clark, 1994).
CG	Jürgen Moltmann, *The Crucified God* (London: SCM Press, 1974).
CO	John Zizioulas, *Communion and Otherness: Further Studies in Personhood and the Church*, ed. Paul McPartlan (London and New York: T&T Clark, 2006).
De Trin.	Saint Augustine, *The Trinity*, trans. S. McKenna, The Fathers of the Church (Washington, DC: The Catholic University of America Press, 1963); Saint Augustine, *The Trinity*, trans. E. Hill (New York: New City Press, 1991); Richard of St Victor, *La Trinité* ed. Gaston Salet. Sources Chrétiennes no. 63 (Paris: Cerf, 1998).
DS	*Enchiridion Symbolorum definitionum et declarationum de rebus fidei et morum*, 37th edn, ed. Heinrich Denzinger (Freiburg: Herder, 1991).

FCF	Karl Rahner, *Foundations of Christian Faith: An Introduction to the Idea of Christianity*, trans. W. Dych (New York: Crossroad, 1997).
GfU	Catherine Mowry LaCugna, *God for Us: The Trinity and the Christian Life* (San Francisco: HarperCollins, 1991).
GL	Hans Urs von Balthasar, *The Glory of the Lord: A Theological Aesthetics*, 7 vols. (San Francisco: Ignatius Press, 1982–9).
Hex.	Bonaventure, *The Works of Bonaventure: Collations on the Six Days [Collationes in Hexaemeron]*, trans. J. De Vinck (Paterson, NJ: St Anthony Guild Press, 1970).
Instit.	John Calvin, *Institutes of the Christian Religion*, trans. H. Beveridge, rev. edn (Peabody, MA: Hendrickson Publishers, 2008).
Itin.	Bonaventure, *Itinerarium Mentis in Deum*. ET: *The Soul's Journey into God*, ed. Ewert Cousins, The Classics of Western Spirituality (Mahwah, NJ: Paulist Press, 1978).
LW	Jaroslav Pelikan and Helmut T. Lehman, eds., *Luther's Works*, 55 vols. (St. Louis: Concordia; Philadelphia: Fortress Press, 1955–1986).
Meta.	Aristotle, *Metaphysics*.
MP	Hans Urs von Balthasar, *Mysterium Paschale* (Edinburgh: T&T Clark, 1990).
Myst. Trin.	Bonaventure, *Works of St Bonaventure*, vol. iii. *Disputed Questions on the Mystery of the Trinity*, trans. Z. Hayes, Bonaventure Texts in Translation Series (New York: The Franciscan Institute, 2000).
N/D	Josef Neuner and Jacques Dupuis, eds., *The Christian Faith* (London: Collins, 1982).
NPNF	*A Select Library of the Nicene and Post-Nicene Fathers of the Christian Church*, Second Series, ed. Henry Wace and Philip Schaff, 14 vols. (Oxford: Parker and Company; New York: The Christian Literature Company, 1886–1900).
PG	*Patrologiae cursus completus: Series graeca*, ed. J. P. Migne (Paris, 1857–66).
PR	G. W. F. Hegel, *Lectures on the Philosophy of Religion*, 3 vols., 2nd German edn (1840) trans. Ebenezer B. Speirs (London: Routledge, 1974).
SC	*Sources Chrétiennes* (Paris: Les Éditions du Cerf, 1941–).

ScG	Thomas Aquinas, *Summa contra Gentiles*, trans. A. Pegis et al., 4 vols. (Notre Dame, IN: University of Notre Dame Press, 1975).
Sent.	Bonaventure, *Commentaria in quatuor libros sententiarum*, *Opera Omnia*, vols. I–IV, ed. the Fathers of the Collegium S. Bonaventurae (Ad Claras Aquas, Quarrachi, 1882–1902).
ST	Thomas Aquinas, *Summa Theologiae*, 5 vols., trans. Fathers of the English Dominican Province (Notre Dame, IN: Ave Maria Press, 1981).
TD	Hans Urs von Balthasar, *Theo-Drama: Theological Dramatic Theory*, 5 vols. (San Francisco: Ignatius Press, 1988–98).
TKG	Jürgen Moltmann, *The Trinity and the Kingdom of God* (London: SCM Press, 1991).
TL	Hans Urs von Balthasar, *Theo-Logic*, 3 vols. (San Francisco: Ignatius Press, 2000–5).
Trin.	Karl Rahner, *The Trinity*, rev. edn, trans. J. Donceel, introduction Catherine Mowry LaCugna (New York: Crossroad, 1998).
WA	*D. Martin Luthers Werke kritisch Gesamtausgabe* (Weimar, 1884 vv).

Acknowledgements

There are a number of people we would like to thank and who have helped and supported us in our work.

Declan Marmion would like especially to thank Dr Gesa Thiessen for her support and encouragement and for reading several drafts of chapters. Other friends and colleagues who read portions of the text include: Dr Thomas Dalzell, Dr Kevin Duffy, Dr David Kelly, and Dr Kieran O'Mahony. Many thanks to you all.

Rik Van Nieuwenhove would like to express his gratitude to his wife for her love, support, and patience. He also would like to thank his colleagues and friends in the Theology Department at Mary Immaculate College, Limerick: Professor Eamonn Conway, Dr Patrick Connolly, Dr Eugene Duffy, Dr Jessie Rogers, and Fr Michael Wall.

CHAPTER I

Introducing trinitarian theology

Much current writing on the Trinity refers to a renaissance of trinitarian theology. Certainly the last two decades have seen a surge in publications on the Trinity – incorporating historical, contemporary, and interdisciplinary perspectives. It is as if theologians want to compensate for a legacy of marginalisation, particularly of pneumatology, within theology. Not that theology was ever entirely unaware of its trinitarian foundations and structure. But this framework remained to a large extent implicit, rather than explicit. The generalised and somewhat caricatured description of this state of affairs is that the doctrine of the Trinity developed in an abstract and speculative direction. It was preoccupied with talk about the inner life of God (the immanent or eternal Trinity) to the neglect of God as revealed in the biblical narratives of salvation history (the economic Trinity).[1]

While this might describe how the Trinity was taught in seminaries with the tracts *De Deo Uno* followed by *De Deo Trino*, and its trinitarian axioms, it does not do justice to the theological giants who transcend easy categorisation. Thus those who accuse Augustine of a basically introspective trinitarian theology – focussing on psychological analogies to explicate the trinitarian life – overlook that, in the first part of his *De Trinitate*, Augustine searches, admittedly rather imaginatively, for trinitarian analogies in Scripture. Even Thomas Aquinas, at whose door many of the problems with an abstract and intellectualist approach to theology have been put, evinces an impressive integration of theology and spirituality, even though this is not immediately apparent in his *Summa Theologiae*. Yet, for Thomas, the theologian is not only engaged in philosophical speculation but is a *magister in sacra pagina*, a commentator on Sacred Scripture. Theology is a *sacra doctrina*, whether practised in the academy or in the pulpit. If God is

---

[1] God's saving activity and presence in history is described as the 'economic' Trinity referring to God's plan of salvation. Distinct from the economic Trinity, but inherently related to it, is the 'immanent' Trinity, immanent because it refers to the divine persons in relationship to one another 'within' God.

the first subject of theology, then the theologian's task also has a contemplative dimension. Like Augustine, the revelation of the Trinity is a matter of faith. For Thomas, the doctrine cannot be proved by the natural powers of reason. Reason may point us to the existence of divinity, but not to the distinction of persons (*ST* Ia.32.1). In subsequent chapters we hope to offer 'congruent reasons' for approaching the Trinity as an explication of the self-revelation of God. Both Augustine and Thomas wanted to show that trinitarian faith is not unreasonable. It might not be rationally demonstrable, but it can be rationally discussed.[2]

THEOLOGY AND SAPIENTIA

Many Christians would be hard pressed to indicate the significance, never mind the implications, of belief in a *triune* God. Indeed, many, when hearing the name 'God', would not think of Trinity. The temptation to appeal to mystery – while containing an important truth – avoids the task of engaging with the doctrine and its development. One goal of this introduction is to show how belief in the Trinity is not simply speculation about the inner nature of God, but is intimately connected with salvation. In short, what God does is directly related to who God is, or more classically formulated, we know God only from God's effects, that is, from God's activity in creation and in the history of salvation. Further, believing in and worshipping a God who is triune has important implications for anthropology, ecclesiology, and society. The Christian vision of God should redound on all of life. Following Rahner and Barth, the Trinity is a mystery of salvation. Otherwise it would not have been revealed. And if salvation incorporates all aspects of life – personal, social, cosmic – then the doctrine of the Trinity has more than intra-ecclesial significance. The link between theology and life, between doctrine and practice, needs to be made more explicit. *Orthodoxy*, in the sense of correct understanding about God, goes hand in hand with *orthopraxis*, the right living out of trinitarian faith. The doctrine of the Trinity teaches that God as triune communion extends outwards into history to include and draw in all of creation. As with any Christian doctrine, this salvific or soteriological principle must be to the fore. As one contemporary theologian of the Trinity has put it:

The life of God – precisely because God is triune – does not belong to God alone. God who dwells in inaccessible light and eternal glory comes to us in the face of

[2] Brian Davies, *The Thought of Thomas Aquinas* (Oxford: Clarendon Press, 1992), 191.

Christ and the activity of Holy Spirit. Because of God's outreach to the creature, God is said to be essentially relational, ecstatic, fecund, alive as passionate love. Divine life is therefore *our* life.[3]

If, within God, there is *communion* and *relationship*, the human person, created in the image of God, is called to share in this dynamic. The Eastern Fathers of the Church, such as Athanasius, described the Christian vocation in terms of 'deification', being drawn into the community of God – Father, Son, and Spirit. The assumption here is the connection between theology and spirituality. If theology has been classically described as faith seeking understanding, spirituality has to do more with the practice of faith in prayer, worship, and service. Today, however, the term 'spirituality' has taken on new meanings – including that of an academic discipline in its own right.[4] Notwithstanding this development, we are convinced that any genuine Christian spirituality must have an explicit trinitarian foundation and orientation.

For its part, theology has an 'existential' and practical aspect; to do theology implies some form of faith-experience which serves as a foundation for reflection. In the patristic era, theology was not solely intellectual, but also a spiritual activity, an *affaire d'amour*, inseparable from prayer.[5] Philosophy and theology often served as synonyms for *theoria* or contemplation. The Greek philosophers comprehended things 'with their eyes' (Gk *theorein* = to look at). They 'theorised' in the literal sense of the word. We arrive at understanding through participation, through uniting with the object – a way of perceiving that transforms the perceiver, not what is perceived. Perception confers communion: we know in order to participate, not in order to dominate. Knowledge, then, is an act of love: we can only know to the extent to which we are capable of loving what we see, and are able, in love, to let it be wholly itself.[6]

In the West, Augustine and Gregory the Great (*c*.540–604) serve as powerful symbols of this current which never separated knowledge from

---

[3] Catherine Mowry LaCugna, *God for Us: The Trinity and Christian Life* (San Francisco: HarperCollins, 1991), 1 (henceforward abbreviated to *GfU*).

[4] Kees Waaijman, *Spirituality: Forms, Foundations, Methods*, Studies in Spirituality, Supplement 8, trans. J. Vriend (Leuven: Peeters, 2002).

[5] Declan Marmion, *A Spirituality of Everyday Faith: A Theological Investigation of the Notion of Spirituality in Karl Rahner*, Louvain Theological and Pastoral Monographs 23 (Leuven: Peeters/ Eerdmans, 1998), 29–33.

[6] See Jürgen Moltmann, *The Spirit of Life: A Universal Affirmation* (London: SCM, 1992), 198–213. For an endorsement of a sapiential approach to theology and the 'aretegenic' ('conducive to virtue') function of doctrine, see Ellen T. Charry, *By the Renewing of your Minds: The Pastoral Function of Christian Doctrine* (New York and Oxford: Oxford University Press, 1997).

love, *theologia* from *eusebeia* (piety). And, in the East, two names that stand out are Origen (*c.*185–254) and Gregory of Nyssa (*c.*330–95). Such unity continued into the High Middle Ages, finding expression in the spiritual treatises of monastic theology, a harmony that lasted into the thirteenth century. Bonaventure (*c.*1217–74), Aquinas, and the other great scholastics knew that theology could not be divorced from experiential knowledge of God. But, little by little, after the period of the great scholastic theologians, the gradual dissociation of theology from spirituality began. Towards the end of the thirteenth century, the term 'theology' began to develop in the West in a more systematic, speculative, and abstract direction. There emerged, in effect, two parallel 'theologies': one, a more scientific and theoretical speculation; the other, a more pious, affective theology rarely nourished by theological doctrine:

> The theologian became a specialist in an autonomous field of knowledge, which he could enter by the use of a technique independent of the witness of his own life, of its personal holiness or sinfulness. The spiritual man [*sic*], on the other hand, became a *dévot* who cared nothing for theology; one for whom his own experience ultimately became an end in itself, without reference to the dogmatic content to be sought in it.[7]

This separation of theology and spirituality was not without its effect on trinitarian theology. The link between Trinity, salvation, and spirituality was not always evident. As we will detail in Chapter 4, from around 1300 theology and spirituality, and faith and reason became increasingly severed from one another, resulting in an impoverished theological imagination. Throughout the book we will argue for a retrieval of a theological perspective which is both theological and spiritual, in which theology is not just speculative but also sapiential. In other words, the task of theology is not only to teach, but also to delight and to move; to do not only with *scientia* – scientific and analytic knowledge – but also with *sapientia* – the more contemplative knowledge of love and desire (Lat. *sapor* = taste). This sapiential understanding of theology was shared by Augustine and his medieval successors until the beginning of the fourteenth century.

It is ironic that alongside the widespread decline in traditional religious practice in the West, interest in spirituality – in both its academic and existential dimensions – has increased. Moreover, in contrast to previous eras, there exists a kind of doctrinal vacuum within and outside Christian

---

[7] Eugene Megyer, 'Theological Trends: Spiritual Theology Today', *The Way* 21 (1981): 56.

communities. There is no longer consensus about the language of faith, and there is a diminishing adherence to Christian doctrines. Former religious certainties have given way to the claim that our grasp of truth is always partial. Our age has been characterised as 'postmodern' in contrast to a previous epoch termed 'modernity'. Modernity espoused a number of myths that, until recently, went unchecked: the myth of unending progress, the myth of clear and distinct ideas of universal reason, the myth of the individual, and the myth of the ascendancy of human control over nature. Theologians who are conscious of the postmodern situation acknowledge that the notion of unending progress is not necessarily something positive, that our reason is limited, that unbridled individualism is inimical to human development, and that our attempts to control and subdue nature have had disastrous effects on the environment. In our final chapter we will turn to a number of theologians who, drawing insights from trinitarian theology, have entered into critical dialogue with postmodernity.

THEOLOGY, DOXOLOGY, AND THE LIMITS OF LANGUAGE

Theology is accountable speech (*logos*) about God (*theos*). It is sometimes described as the science or study of God, specifically, of God's relationship to creation. It is not a question of attaining direct knowledge of God, in the sense of the creature rising above the Creator in an act of comprehension. Nor can theology claim insight into God's inner life apart from God's self-revelation. In Chapter 2 we will look at aspects of the biblical picture of God as they pertain to subsequent trinitarian theology. These include: the conviction that God is the exclusive object of worship: 'I am Yahweh your God ... you shall have no other gods before me' (Exod. 20:23; Deut. 5:6–7) and the use of anthropomorphic images of God: God is described in human terms – having a countenance, arms, eyes, ears, voice, and so on, and feelings of anger, jealousy, and vengeance, alongside compassion, mercy, and love. Biblical anthropomorphic images, however, are qualified by descriptions of God as transcendent, inscrutable and beyond human understanding: 'For as the heavens are higher than the earth [says the Lord], so are my ways higher than your ways and my thoughts higher than your thoughts' (Isa. 55:9). The *pathos* and compassion of God is not at the expense of God's transcendent Otherness.

Notwithstanding the important influence played by the biblical symbol of God across various religious traditions and cultures, the term 'God' itself is ambiguous. It has been subject to a variety of ideological abuses and used to justify violence and oppression.[8] Religious wars and sectarianism have a long history. On the other hand, God has been the inspiration for movements of resistance to injustice and tyranny and the promotion of more humane patterns of life. Subsequent chapters will explore how political and liberation theologians (such as Jürgen Moltmann and Leonardo Boff) have developed a new paradigm for Church and society inspired by the Trinity.

Aside from the biblical conception, other influences and cultures – Greek, Hebrew, and Roman – have shaped the Christian understanding of God.[9] Scripture (e.g., the use of the term *Logos* in John's Gospel) is influenced by Greek philosophy, while the word 'Trinity', not found in the Bible, gradually emerged from a theological and political context permeated by Greek and Latin philosophical ideas. The same is true for many of the terms associated with trinitarian theology, including *ousia, hypostasis*, substance, essence, person, and so on. To play off the 'God of the philosophers' against the 'God of the Bible', as Pascal (1623–62) did, does not do justice to the complicated interconnections between these different strands of influence. Not that the early Christian appropriations of Greek philosophy (e.g., the idea of God's oneness), or of Jewish monotheism, was uncritical or seamless. In the latter case, the challenge was to posit a link or continuity between the *shema Yisrael* (Deut. 6:4–5) and the revelation of God in Jesus Christ. This meant, firstly, affirming God's oneness in the Hebrew Scriptures, not as transcendent and remote from creation, but as an immanent principle in history. Israel's monotheism had a strong soteriological focus: 'There is no other God except me, no saving God, no Saviour except me!' (Isa. 45:21). Secondly, it meant confessing that the Christian understanding of God is grounded in God's self-disclosure in Christ, the parable and face of God, and in the power and activity of the Spirit. The earliest (Jewish) followers of Jesus had, therefore, to reconcile their monotheistic roots with their belief in a God who was present and active in the person of Jesus and in the transforming power of the Spirit. The assumption that

---

[8] '[God] is the most heavy-laden of all human words. None has become so soiled, so mutilated ... Generations of men have laid the burden of their anxious lives upon this word and weighed it to the ground; it lies in the dust and bears their whole burden. The races of men with their religious factions have torn the word to pieces; they have killed for it and died for it, and it bears their fingerprints and their blood ... They draw caricatures and write "God" underneath; they murder one another to say "in God's name" ... We must esteem those who interdict it because they rebel against the injustice and wrong which are so readily referred to "God" for authorisation.' Martin Buber, *Meetings*, trans. M. Friedman (La Salle, IL: Open Court Publishing, 1973), 50–1.

[9] For what follows, see Francis Schüssler Fiorenza and Gordon D. Kaufmann, 'God', in Mark C. Taylor, ed., *Critical Terms in Religious Studies* (Chicago and London: University of Chicago Press, 1998), 136–59.

monotheism and trinitarian theology were mutually exclusive would be questioned. More positively, it would be affirmed that Christian monotheism is a trinitarian monotheism.[10] That Christians believe in one God, not three, and that they therefore assert God's singularity, uniqueness, and unity would not be at odds with the Jewish and Islamic recognition that there are many names for God reflecting the different ways God relates to the world.

The New Testament response to the question of God is the claim: 'God is love' (1 John 4:8). This is not a sentimental metaphor, but is interpreted from the life, death, and resurrection of Jesus as the theological foundation of a properly Christian understanding of God.[11] This would later be expressed in more abstract and metaphysical terms where the one God was characterised by relationality, and seen as the origin, sustainer, and end of all reality. The Western theological tradition developed this line of thinking in a trinitarian direction by describing how God has 'person-like' characteristics, including intelligence and love. One of the earliest and classical examples was Augustine's so-called 'psychological analogy', where Augustine looked 'inside himself' to discover a vestige or trace of the Trinity, specifically, in the operation of the memory, understanding and will as a threefold activity of the human soul or mind. For Augustine, the journey of the soul toward God is a journey inward – the search for the self and the search for God are ultimately the same.

In the medieval period this Augustinian legacy lives on. Anselm of Canterbury (1033–1109) defined God as 'that than which nothing greater can be thought', and developed an argument for the existence of God which was not meant as a rationalistic, purely philosophical, proof for God's existence (although later authors, including Descartes, used it that way), but which should be seen as an attempt to better understand the unfathomable mystery that God is. For Anselm, theology is 'faith seeking understanding', and his philosophical arguments are used within a broader theological setting, which implies a harmony of faith and reason. Similarly, as we will see, Richard of St Victor, although developing a theology of the Trinity with a different emphasis to the Augustinian

---

[10] Yet, monotheistic distortions of the Christian understanding of God were evident from the beginnings of Christianity, for instance, in the Roman Empire, where the one emperor on earth mirrored the one divine ruler in heaven. These distortions persisted, culminating politically in European absolutism, and philosophically and theologically in German Idealism and the notion of God as the absolute subject.

[11] David Tracy, *On Naming the Present: Reflections on Catholicism, Hermeneutics, and the Church* (New York: Orbis Books, 1994), 33–4.

model (Richard's so-called interpersonal model, as distinct from the intrapersonal one), held a theological vision which integrated faith and reason, and theology and spirituality. It is only after the condemnation of secular learning in 1277 that philosophy and theology become severed, resulting in an impoverished view of theological understanding.

In the late thirteenth century theology, increasingly separated from philosophy, becomes progressively more sceptical of the claims of reason, and less sapiential, reflecting the growing chasms between theology and philosophy (faith and reason), and theology and spirituality. Thus, William of Ockham's (*c*.1285–1347) radically empiricist approach to knowledge sharply separated the realms of reason and faith and gave each a certain autonomy over the other. It provided the background for the Reformers' rejection of philosophical knowledge of God. Human nature is radically corrupted by sin; revelation is the only source of theological truth. Thus, Martin Luther (1483–1546) sought to know God solely in Jesus, the Crucified One: 'in Christ crucified is true theology and the knowledge of God'.[12] The Reformers combined existential and personalist language with a concept of God as a divine monarch with absolute power and sovereign will.

What we might call the religious-aesthetic mindset, typical of the patristic and medieval period, had faded by the sixteenth century, and this had implications in terms of how people viewed the world throughout modernity. Rather than seeing it in sacramental terms, reflecting the beauty of the triune God (as in Bonaventure), the modern person viewed it in mechanistic terms. Likewise, it became increasingly difficult to read the Scriptures through the lens of tradition, and understand them also in an allegorical manner. All these elements led to an alienation of some of the more radical Reformers from traditional trinitarian approaches. After the challenge of Kant, which further reinforced the separation of faith and reason, Hegel would attempt to recapture a broader understanding of human rationality. His innovative approach to the doctrine of the Trinity, understanding trinitarian doctrine in terms of subjectivity and self-consciousness, would also force theologians to revisit the way God relates to history, and vice versa. Major theologians in the twentieth century, such as Karl Barth, Karl Rahner, and Jürgen Moltmann, would each assimilate this modern legacy in their own right. Chapters 5 and 6 will

---

[12] *Luther: Early Theological Works*, ed. and trans. James Atkinson, Library of Christian Classics, vol. XVI (Philadelphia: Westminster Press, 1962), Thesis XX, 291.

treat these contributions and those of other important thinkers in more detail. At present, a preliminary outline of the main developments will suffice.

One of the defining characteristics of modernity is the view that reason is autonomous, and not subject to tradition or faith. The certitude of one's own consciousness, one's own act of being aware, becomes the essential basis of knowledge. René Descartes (1596–1650) based all knowledge on the secure foundation of the thinking self who could otherwise call everything into question. God is the infinitely perfect being who cannot deceive, while the idea of the infinite is the condition of knowledge of the finite (since we only know finite objects against a backdrop of the infinite). The quest for epistemological certainty, for truths that were absolutely certain, gave rise not only to a conception of the self as fundamentally rational and autonomous, but to a view of reason as the means to objectify and to gain mastery over the world.

The emphasis on religious subjectivity continued throughout the Enlightenment period and in its religious counterpart the Pietist and Puritan movements, taking the form either of an analysis of consciousness or a focus on the believer's religious faith experience. At the same time, there emerged a scientific worldview that posited an underlying intelligible structure in nature which could be studied, that is, observed and measured, without reference to God. David Hume's (1711–76) naturalistic view of the world would effectively eliminate God from a world that no longer reflected its divine ground. Instead, the locus for God was restricted to the inner self, preoccupied with personal conversion and sanctification. The emerging scientific worldview, exemplified in the discoveries of Johann Kepler (1571–1630), Galileo Galilei (1564–1642), and above all Isaac Newton (1643–1727), culminated in a deistic 'clockmaker' God, who set the universe in motion, but who did not otherwise intervene. Immanuel Kant (1724–84) ultimately sealed the fate of natural theology when he limited human cognition to the phenomenal realm. We can have no knowledge of 'noumena' – objects lying beyond experience – by way of pure reason.[13] Philosophers and theologians would subsequently find it difficult to argue from sense experience to a transcendent reality such as God. Religion was in danger of being reduced to morality and God to a guarantor of happiness for the religiously virtuous.

---

[13] 'We can ... have no knowledge of any object as thing in itself, but only in so far as it is an object of sensible intuition, that is, an appearance.' Immanuel Kant, *Critique of Pure Reason*, trans. N. K. Smith (New York: St Martin's, 1929), 27.

Enlightenment rationalism thus undermined the possibility of any kind of speculative theology, including the doctrine of the Trinity. An example of this was the epistemological modesty of Friedrich Schleiermacher (1768–1834), 'the father of modern theology', who eschewed speculation about differentiations within God. Schleiermacher's philosophy of religion focussed on intuition and feeling, that is, on the immediate self-consciousness of the subject and his or her direct cognitive relation to an object, without the mediation of concepts. Schleiermacher wanted to highlight the soteriological significance of the Trinity, and to show how the doctrine came about as a *consequence* of reflection on the experience of redemption in Christ and the Spirit. So, while the Trinity itself is not an object of immediate experience, it is founded on the Christian consciousness of the divinity of Christ and the Spirit.[14]

Although some of Schleiermacher's heirs (e.g., Albrecht Ritschl) shared his reticence about the inner divine being, an alternative approach was forged by G. W. F. Hegel (1770–1831), who wanted to overcome the dichotomies between God and world, the infinite and the finite, the universal and the particular. Hegel depicted God in terms of a process of historical becoming by way of his dialectical philosophical method and its reconciliation of opposites. Schleiermacher and Hegel will be discussed in Chapter 5, but it is worth noting here the legacy that Schleiermacher and, in particular, Hegel have bequeathed to twentieth-century trinitarian theology. In the wake of Schleiermacher, speculation on the immanent Trinity had receded in favour of grounding the doctrine in biblical revelation, that is, in the economy of salvation. For his part, Hegel introduced the notion of historicity into the conception of God. His point was that the being of God cannot be separated from the unfolding of history. Wolfhart Pannenberg, Jürgen Moltmann, and Eberhard Jüngel have all developed the theme of the Trinity in history with particular reference, in the case of Moltmann and Jüngel, to the cross as a trinitarian event.[15]

Hegel also recast the Trinity in terms of divine subjectivity: God is a single subject, an eternal act of self-consciousness. Both Barth and Rahner would explore the category of subjectivity and how it could shed light on the triune God's relation to the world. Barth is known for his revelational

---

[14] For a sympathetic appraisal of Schleiermacher's trinitarian theology, see Francis Schüssler Fiorenza, 'Schleiermacher's Understanding of God as Triune', in Jacqueline Marina, ed., *The Cambridge Companion to Friedrich Schleiermacher* (Cambridge: Cambridge University Press, 2005), 171–88.

[15] For Pannenberg, see his *Systematic Theology*, vol. 1. trans. G. Bromiley (London and New York: T&T Clark International, 2004), 327–36; for Jüngel, see his *God as the Mystery of the World*, trans. D. Guder (Edinburgh: T&T Clark, 1983), 35–42.

trinitarianism – his conviction that the starting-point for the doctrine must be God's historical self-disclosure in Christ and the Spirit: 'We can know about God only because and to the extent that He gives Himself to us to be known' (*CD* I/1, 371). But, like Hegel, he also insists there is only one divine subject. Father, Son, and Spirit constitute three 'modes of being', eternally subsisting within God. And Barth's specific contribution was to show how God's revelation or Word has a trinitarian shape – subsisting in three forms: revelation, the Bible, and proclamation (*CD* I/1, 120–1).

Rahner too helped set the parameters for much of contemporary trinitarian theology. His 'axiom', which brought together the immanent and economic Trinity, highlighted how much trinitarian theology had become disconnected from the biblical and historical narratives of salvation.[16] He felt that the Trinity had become too speculative and abstract, with little impact on the faith life of the ordinary believer. The doctrine had to be more than the science of God's own inner-relatedness, and this could not be considered independently of God's self-revelation in history. As he put it:

> The isolation of the treatise of the Trinity *has* to be wrong. There *must* be a connection between Trinity and humanity. The Trinity is a mystery of *salvation*, otherwise it would never have been revealed. (*Trin.*, 21)

Of course, there is only *one* Trinity, only one trinitarian self-communication with both eternal and temporal aspects. Rahner's point was to connect the economic and the immanent Trinity, to show that the Trinity in the history of salvation is the active revelation of the immanent Trinity. He was critical of the rigid and unhistorical neo-scholastic context in which he was trained, where less attention was paid to the economic Trinity, and the doctrine had come to be viewed as an arcane description of the inner life of God. Inspired by Vatican II, he took up the Council Fathers' stress on *ressourcement* and *aggiornamento* by exploring the scriptural and patristic sources of the doctrine. Rahner's axiom, his economic starting-point, and his claim that the *mysterium Trinitatis* is primarily a *mysterium salutis*, represent a decisive reorientation of trinitarian theology.

To recap, if theology is speech about God, then the doctrine of the Trinity represents the *specifically Christian* way of speaking about God. The doctrine is a primary and summary affirmation of faith in the God of Jesus Christ, identifying the God whom Christians believe in and worship. Knowledge of the Trinity is derived from the historical form of God's

---

[16] 'The "economic" Trinity is the "immanent" Trinity and the "immanent" Trinity is the "economic" Trinity.' Karl Rahner, *The Trinity*, rev. edn, trans. J. Donceel, introduction Catherine Mowry LaCugna (New York: Crossroad, 1998), 22 (henceforward abbreviated as *Trin.*).

self-communication in Jesus Christ and the Holy Spirit. These are the two ways in which God communicates to humankind – God's Word and God's Spirit are 'the two hands of God', as Irenaeus of Lyons (d. AD 202) put it. Trinitarian understanding and insight only emerged after a long process of reflection on the experience of salvation – past and present:

> The Church gradually and painstakingly came to certain conclusions about the inner reality of God on the basis of its experience of God within its own human experience and within human history ... [It] came to the knowledge of God as triune as it progressively reflected on its experience of the triuneness of God's dealings with us in history. And then the Church concluded that the God whom we experience as triune in history (the 'economic Trinity') must also be triune in essence, i.e., within the inner life of God (the 'immanent Trinity').[17]

Such conclusions derived not from human cognitive effort alone, but from what God has revealed about God's self:

> God, East and West have agreed, is not known by us because he is amenable to the exercise of our cognitive powers. He is known by us in that he grants us what we could never reach ... he takes us into his own knowledge of himself.[18]

Doctrines are not formulated as ends in themselves, nor are they simply ideas to which we give merely notional assent. They are intended to have some influence on the life of the believing community. Yet the doctrine of the Trinity brings us up against the limitations and final inadequacy of language about God. There is a paradox at the root of all theological knowledge that is particularly evident when it comes to the Trinity. On the one hand, the economic Trinity highlights God's self-involvement in history. God is not a solitary remote deity but outgoing, revealing love manifested in God's personal relationship with people. On the other hand, we affirm not only God's relatedness and nearness to us, but also the *difference* between God and creation. The great theologians from Augustine to Aquinas never tired of pointing to the ineffable mystery of God and implying that a degree of modesty does not go amiss in theology. In the end, theology does not yield a comprehensive grasp of the divine, but rather shows up the radical inadequacy of all ideas and language about God.

Theology has become more aware of the limits of language – especially language about God. Even in the New Testament, where we see the climax of God's self-revelation to humanity in Jesus, God in Godself still remains a mystery: Christ is the image of the invisible God (Col. 1:15). This has

---

[17] Richard McBrien, *Catholicism* (London: Chapman, 1994), 322–3.
[18] Robert Jenson, *Systematic Theology*, vol. 1. *The Triune God* (Oxford: Oxford University Press, 1997), 227.

implications for how we speak of God. Is it appropriate, for instance, to use solely masculine language for God? Without pursuing this matter now, we can say that no image or symbol provides an adequate picture of God. Nor is our understanding of God reducible to words. All our knowledge of God is analogical: we gain some knowledge of God from the world by analogy 'since through the grandeur and beauty of creatures, we may, by analogy, contemplate their Author' (Wis. 13:5). The etymology of the word 'analogy' has to do with correspondence, similarity, and proportion. Yet there is not only similarity, but also dissimilarity in every analogy. When it is said that God is a Father, it must be conceded that God is more unlike a father than like one, since God is neither male nor female.[19] The mystical theologian Dionysius the Pseudo-Areopagite (*c*.500) maintained that in dealing with God, negations are true and affirmations inadequate. Analogies are more unlike than like in their comparison of aspects of human reality or creation with God, and are premised on the fundamental ontological difference between Creator and creature.

Throughout the tradition a variety of analogies and images have been used to depict the triune nature of God. Some of the images employed are rather tenuous instances of how three things or operations can also be one. These include materialist ones: a source or wellspring, a stream, and a river; or a root, a stem, and fruit. Another example points to a triadic structure in human consciousness and the intellectual activities of remembering (memory), understanding (intellect), and desiring (will). A further approach uses the notion of love to interpret the Trinity with the image of the lover, his beloved, and their mutual love. Some of these analogies were developed by Augustine (354–430) and, later, by Aquinas and others. A very fundamental image in the tradition is that of *communion* (*koinonia*), which tries to capture both the diversity and the equality and interdependence of the divine Persons. As one contemporary writer puts it:

To think of God as Trinity is fundamentally to assert, among other things, that within God there is society or relationship. To affirm that human beings are created in the image of that God implies that they are called to share more and more in the deep communion that is divine life itself.[20]

---

[19] It is the divine dimension of the analogy that is determinative: it is from God the Father that earthly fatherhood is derived (Eph. 3:14–15) not the other way around. See Geoffrey Wainwright, 'Trinitarian Worship', in Alvin Kimel, ed., *Speaking the Christian God: The Holy Trinity and the Challenge of Feminism* (Grand Rapids, MI: Eerdmans, 1992), 214–15.

[20] Philip Sheldrake, *Spirituality and Theology: Christian Living and the Doctrine of God*, Trinity and Truth Series (London: Darton, Longman and Todd, 1998), 16.

Trinitarian theology in more recent times, then, exhibits an explicitly relational focus and develops out of God's activity past and present. The triune God is no longer viewed along the lines of a (Hegelian) absolute subject, but rather as a network of relationships inclusive of humanity.

The approach to speaking about God, which entails a moment of affirmation as well as negation, was expressed in the confession of faith of the Fourth Lateran Council (1215). The Council stated that 'between Creator and creature there can be noted no similarity so great that a greater dissimilarity cannot be seen between them'.[21] Such a mode of speaking about God that is conscious of how God transcends all created conceptions is called the negative or apophatic (*apophasis* = negation) way. It prefers to speak about what God is not and stresses God's incomprehensibility and ineffable nature.[22] The apophatic way is more than just a process of epistemological scepticism or negation, however. It must also be possible to speak positively about God. The 'emptiness' of the apophatic way is a prelude to *worship*: God is not only 'a third party *about whom* we speak', but 'a "Thou" *to whom* we speak' (*GfU*, 359)[23] – as all the outstanding apophatic mystics and theologians have shown. The name 'God', to paraphrase Aquinas, is an appellative not a proper name (*ST* 1a.13.8, 9).

Christian worship is trinitarian by its nature: we do not worship an undifferentiated deity, but a trinitarian God as Paul's invocation (2 Cor. 13:13) makes clear. In Chapter 3 we will see how the Church's early trinitarian conception of God grew out of its liturgical practice, including baptism, short creeds, and doxologies. Worship and the understanding of God were intimately bound up with the experience of salvation: praise and thanksgiving were offered to God for the salvific deeds God has accomplished. Liturgy was the primary theology: the law of prayer established the law of belief (*lex orandi, lex credendi*). Doxology was a precondition of speech about God. The Eastern Churches in particular have maintained this patristic emphasis, this link between theological reflection and the life of prayer and worship, while in the West Karl Rahner has emphasised that

---

[21] Norman P. Tanner, ed., *Decrees of the Ecumenical Councils*, vol. 1 (London: Sheed & Ward, 1990), 232.

[22] A classic example of the negative way is the fourteenth-century classic, *The Cloud of Unknowing*, where the author aims to draw his readers into praying with a love that is devoid of all concepts, images, and thoughts.

[23] For their part, the Eastern Fathers favour the term 'union' to 'knowledge' in their apophatic approach to God. See Dumitru Staniloae, *Orthodox Dogmatic Theology*, vol. 1. *Revelation and Knowledge of the Triune God: The Experience of God*, trans. and ed. I. Ionita and R. Barringer (Brookline, MA: Holy Cross Orthodox Press, 1994), 101.

theology is the science of mystery, transcending the formulation of human words and culminating in doxology – the acknowledgement and praise of the ever-greater reality of God.[24] A theology that does not acknowledge this dimension of mystery, the *reductio in mysterium* or, more precisely, the *reductio in mysterium Dei*, of theological propositions has, in his view, failed to recognise their analogical nature and remained stuck on the conceptual level. In short, the tension between negative and affirmative theological approaches, between silence and predication, can only be overcome in doxology.[25]

On the other hand, Christian worship too often exhibits Pelagian and unitarian characteristics rather than a participatory trinitarian focus. On this view, worship is something *we* (with the help of the minister) do. A trinitarian perspective, on the other hand, brings out how liturgy is a participation in the trinitarian *koinonia*. We come to the Father through Christ in the power of the Spirit. Christ leads us in our prayer and praise as 'the one true minister of the sanctuary' (Heb. 8:1–2), while the Spirit draws us in to participate in the Son's communion with the Father and his mission from the Father to the world.[26] Worship is a gift of grace animating and bringing us into right relationship with God and each other. Or, as the Orthodox theologian, Dumitru Staniloae, puts it, 'The revelation of the Trinity, occasioned by the incarnation and earthly activity of the Son, has no other purpose than … to draw us through the Holy Spirit into the filial relationship the Son has with the Father.'[27] Although most of the ancient liturgical prayers were offered to the Father, through the Son, in the Spirit, we also have precedents in Scripture and tradition to pray to each of the three Persons (*Maranatha, Veni Creator Spiritus*, etc.). As the theological tradition developed, care was taken in prayers to reflect the equality among the three Persons (rather than subordinating one to another), and to stress their unity, while not blurring the distinctiveness of each.[28]

---

[24] Karl Rahner, 'Reflections on Methodology in Theology', in *Theological Investigations*, vol. XI (London: Darton, Longman and Todd, 1974), 101–14.

[25] 'The positive intention of apophasis is to give God the glory by claiming nothing for ourselves. The positive intention of kataphasis is to speak and proclaim this glory' (*GfU*, 361).

[26] James B. Torrance, *Worship, Community and the Triune God of Grace* (Downers Grove, IL: InterVarsity Press, 1996), 19–41. See also John Thompson, *Modern Trinitarian Perspectives* (New York: Oxford University Press, 1994), 94–105.

[27] Staniloae, *Orthodox Dogmatic Theology*, 249.

[28] Ruth C. Duck and Patricia Wilson-Kastner, *Praising God: The Trinity in Christian Worship* (Louisville, KY: Westminster/John Knox Press, 1999), 27.

APPROACHING THE TRINITY – BETWEEN
THE EXTREMES

It has not always been easy to see the connection between belief in a triune God and the dynamics of Christian life. In the first half of the twentieth century, in the face of the perceived threats of atheism and agnosticism, much theological energy went into establishing the foundations of belief in God, while the specifically triune nature of God was not accorded the same priority. The thinking was that if one could assent first of all to the existence of God, one could more easily accept God's trinitarian nature. And when it did come to the doctrine of the Trinity, this tended to be presented within an abstract and speculative neo-scholastic framework. Bernard Lonergan is reputed to have caricatured clerical students' memorising the essential elements of the Thomistic doctrine of the Trinity in terms of the 5–4–3–2–1 formula (five notions, four relations, three persons, two processions, and one nature) to which he added 'and zero comprehension!' Many pastors still balk at the prospect of preaching on Trinity Sunday. It is as if they feel embarrassed to celebrate a timeless dogma, or they feel obliged to disclose something arcane of the mysteries of the inner life of God, rather than depicting how God is a God of loving involvement and fidelity to people. At its heart, the doctrine of the Trinity affirms that it belongs to God's very nature to be committed to humankind and its history.[29] This claim is based on what God has revealed of God's self in history, namely, that God's covenant with humanity is constant and irrevocable. But before looking at the biblical roots of the doctrine in the next chapter, it might be helpful to indicate what views we are excluding when we say that God is triune.

On the one hand is the attempt to preserve the oneness or singularity of God. This is called *monarchianism* ('monarchy' literally means 'the rule of the one'). Monarchianism is a general term that can be applied to several movements in the second and third centuries which were concerned with safeguarding God's unity. Examples include such Roman thinkers as Noetus and Praxeas, who feared the introduction of a plurality of Godheads into Christianity. However, by so stressing God's oneness, the distinctions between Father, Son, and Holy Spirit were not fully appreciated. By the third century, the name monarchianism was applied to those

---

[29] Catherine Mowry LaCugna and Michael Downey, 'Trinitarian Spirituality', in *The New Dictionary of Catholic Spirituality*, ed. Michael Downey (Collegeville, MN, The Liturgical Press, 1993), 969.

who denied distinct persons in God. A variant of monarchianism is *modalism* – the Father, Son, and Holy Spirit are simply 'modes' or 'masks' of God's appearing within history. These distinctions, it was claimed, have nothing to say about the intradivine life, that is, about the eternal being of God. An important representative of this trend in the third century was the Roman priest Sabellius (modalism is sometimes called *Sabellianism*). Against modalism it was stated that the Son and Spirit were true (and salvific) revelations of the Father. God does not take on three 'roles' but, as Origen stated, Father, Son, and Spirit are three distinct hypostases.

On the other hand, the attempt to make the threefoldness of God comprehensible led to a tendency towards *subordinationism*. In this theory, the Son was less than, or 'subordinate' to, the Father (and later the Holy Spirit was subordinate to both). The best example of extreme subordinationism was the priest/theologian Arius (*c.*250–*c.*336) who maintained that the Father alone is God and that the Son, despite his exalted status, is a creature like us. Christ is presented as a kind of mediator between God and creation – situated above all worldly reality but nevertheless clearly subordinated to God (the Father). *Pace* subordinationism, the Church clarified that Son and Spirit were not created, but co-creators, co-agents of salvation, and that in them God communicates God's very self to humanity.

Another term found in the literature and tradition is *tritheism* – referring to three Gods who have separate powers or spheres of influence. Early Church creeds and declarations (e.g., the fifth-century Symbol of Faith known as the *Quicumque*) refuted the notion of three independent Gods, any of whom could exist without the other, or act independently of the others. The fear was that, by emphasising the differences between the Persons, the threefold unity of the Trinity is reduced to a kind of collective – analogous to the way many persons are said to be one people. In condemning an instance of this tendency, namely, the trinitarian teaching of Abbot Joachim of Fiore (d. 1202), the Fourth Lateran Council (1215) insisted that Father, Son, and Holy Spirit are not different realities, but share an identity in nature (*DS* 803ff.). In 1628 Pope Urban VIII prohibited artistic depictions of the Trinity in terms of three heads (*tricephali*), while in 1745 Pope Benedict XIV ruled out representations of three persons placed side by side as valid depictions of the Trinity.[30] Within contemporary trinitarian theology, theologians (e.g., Moltmann) who have emphasised the distinctness of

---

[30] Gesa Thiessen, 'Images of the Trinity in Visual Art', in Declan Marmion and Gesa Thiessen, eds., *Trinity and Salvation: Theological, Spiritual and Aesthetic Perspectives*, Studies in Theology, Society and Culture 2 (Oxford and Bern: Peter Lang, 2009), 119–40.

the three persons, and who have reacted against a view of God as a single divine subject, have at times been accused of tritheism.

The above-mentioned tendencies are perennial difficulties for trinitarian theology and highlight the paradoxical claim that something can be *three* and *one* simultaneously, a problem that, as we have seen, goes back to the beginnings of Christianity. The background and context of these 'heresies' will become clearer in subsequent chapters as we trace how the doctrine emerged and developed – from an initial 'salvation-history' or 'economic' perspective to a more pronounced consideration of the 'immanent' Trinity. Within Christianity today the doctrine of the Trinity is not an object of ecumenical dispute – it is held by all major denominations – even if its full implications (in terms of our understanding of God, our vision of Church, and relationships within society) continue to be explored.

PARTICIPATING IN GOD – 'PARTAKERS OF THE DIVINE NATURE'

The starting point of any Christian anthropology is that the human person is made in the image and likeness of God (Gen. 1:26–7). Discourse about God illuminates what humanity is. Theology and anthropology are intimately connected. If we view God primarily in personal and relational categories, then our anthropology will also be relational. Thus far, we have been hinting that any theology (or spirituality) claiming to be trinitarian will emphasise community rather than individualism. Such a theology will be critical of previous tendencies to view the human being or God along the lines of an autonomous, rational individual.[31] Instead, a more relational anthropology is proposed: to be is to be in relation, or there is never an 'I' without a 'Thou'. Made in the image of God, we have the capacity to know and love our Creator and to enter into a personal relationship with God. But God did not create us as solitary creatures. We are created male and female and therefore as essentially social beings. In Gen. 2–3 we see how the image of God is to be found in the relationship between male and female, that is, beyond the solitary self. This description of the human person as being-in-relation-to-another is first of all a statement about the triune nature of God – a God whose primary characteristic is that of a communion of love. And the Christian's call into an ever-deeper

---

[31] The description of person as an individual endowed with reason derives from Boethius (*c.*480–*c.*524) and was reinforced by Descartes and the Enlightenment tradition. Boethius drew on Aristotle to define person as 'an individual substance of a rational nature' but this definition obscured the social, communal, and relational dimensions of personhood. For further discussion of Trinity and person-hood, see Chapter 6.

communion with God is at the same time a call to an ever-deeper communion with others. The Christian vocation has not simply to do with inwardness and the perfection of oneself – understood in an isolated sense – but in giving oneself for others and growing in communion with them. We reach wholeness and integration not in autonomy and self-sufficiency, but in self-donation, that is, through our *relationships* (communion) with others, thus imaging a triune God who is pure self-gift.

The emphasis on a God who is relational, then, is a corrective to the idea that God is a universal monarch in heaven – remote, self-sufficient, and invulnerable. It is more this distant God of deism that many Christians have rejected, though they may not have replaced it with a personal, providential God active in the history of creation and salvation. Consequently, theologians have for some time been proposing a renewed vision of the trinitarian God as the Christian response to the challenge of modern atheism and unbelief. Moreover, this new picture of God as three persons who relate to each other in love, and where there is a mutual giving and receiving, challenges the more aggressive and individualistic elements of contemporary Western culture.

The theme of God as triune, as community or relation, has also been explored in visual art, a famous example of which is the icon of the Holy Trinity by the fifteenth-century Russian Orthodox monk/artist Andrei Rublev. In the Orthodox tradition, icons are a kind of 'spiritual window' between heaven and earth through which the community worships and contemplates the heavenly beings and establishes a spiritual link with them.[32] The Holy Spirit is the 'divine iconographer'. It is by the Spirit that the icon is painted, consecrated for liturgical use, and venerated as a medium of worship.[33] Veneration of icons was upheld as long as they were given a relative love; adoration was to be reserved to God alone. It is not so much the icon itself that is venerated as the person whose image is represented. As a contemporary Orthodox theologian puts it, 'an icon remembers its prototype'.[34] The Orthodox tradition emphasises that God's self-revelation is not only by words, but also by images: Christ is not just the Word of God (John 1:1), but also the Image of God (Col. 1:15). Icons are placed on a par with the Scriptures – revelation in visual form.[35]

---

[32] Dan-Ilie Ciobeta and William H. Lazareth, 'The Triune God: The Supreme Source of Life. Thoughts Inspired by Rublev's Icon of the Trinity', in Gennadios Limouris, ed., *Icons, Windows on Eternity: Theology and Spirituality in Colour* (Geneva: World Council of Churches, 1990), 202–4.

[33] Paul Evdokimov, *L'art de l'icône: Théologie de la beauté* (Paris: Desclée de Brouwer, 1972), 13.

[34] Pavel Florensky, *Iconostasis*, trans. D. Sheehan and O. Andrejev (Crestwood, NY: St Vladimir's Seminary Press, 1996), 71.

[35] George Pattison, *Art, Modernity and Faith: Towards a Theology of Art* (London: Macmillan, 1991), 123.

Rublev's icon, 'The Hospitality of Abraham', is kept today in the Tretyakov Gallery in Moscow. It was originally painted at the monastery of the Holy Trinity and St Sergius, north of Moscow, between 1408 and 1410. It is considered the high point of an iconographic tradition which goes back to the earliest days of Christianity and developed over a thousand years in the Eastern Church. The icon itself was inspired by the scene depicted in Gen. 18 where three visitors came to Abraham at the oak of Mamre and experienced his hospitality:

> Yahweh appeared to him at the Oak of Mamre while he was sitting by the entrance of the tent during the hottest part of the day. He looked up, and there he saw three men standing near him. As soon as he saw them he ran from the entrance of the tent to greet them, and bowed to the ground. 'My lord', he said, 'if I find favour with you, please do not pass your servant by. Let me have a little water brought, and you can wash your feet and have a rest under the tree. Let me fetch a little bread and you can refresh yourselves before going further, now that you have come in your servant's direction.' They replied, 'Do as you say.' (Gen. 18:1–5)

In the iconographic tradition these 'visitors' were considered as angels or messengers of God. This tradition works on the typological level: Abraham's three visitors are seen as a representation, figure, or 'type' of the Trinity. Early patristic theology initially gave these kinds of theophanies in the Old Testament a Christological interpretation, but by the fourth century, partly as a result of the Arian heresy (see Chapter 3), a more trinitarian interpretation began to emerge.[36] In Gen. 18 the three men visit Abraham to promise the birth of Isaac, who, in the typological understanding, prefigures Christ. Yet, over time Abraham and Sarah are depicted not so much as hosts, but as servants or worshippers of the three divine guests; in other depictions they are relegated to the role of bystanders or, as in Rublev's icon, left out altogether.[37] There is a gradual move away from the particulars of the biblical narrative and into the realm of symbol.

Turning to the icon, we notice that the three 'divine' visitors appear in rather youthful and androgynous form. Rublev leaves aside anything non-essential to the event in Genesis. Abraham and Sarah are missing, and there is no reference to all the food. There is little by way of movement, no action, just complete 'silence'.[38] The visitors are related to one another in an

---

[36] Gabriel Bunge, *The Rublev Trinity: The Icon of the Trinity by the Monk-Painter Andrei Rublev*, trans. A. Louth (Crestwood, NY: St Vladimir's Seminary Press, 2007), 45–52.

[37] In the older icons with a Christological focus, Christ as the central angel is usually bigger than the other angels, whereas later icons with a trinitarian theme depicted each of the angels similar in size.

[38] As Oliver Davies, following V. N. Lazarev, has noted, 'action and history are removed to be replaced by symbolic meanings'. Oliver Davies, *A Theology of Compassion: Metaphysics of Difference and the Renewal of Tradition* (Grand Rapids, MI: Eerdmans, 2001), 256.

attitude of mutual deference with the heads of the Spirit and Christ slightly bowed towards the Father (see Fig. 1). The overall effect is one of silent communion. Any subordination or separation of the Persons is ruled out – no angel is given greater prominence than the others. The figures seem more female than male in appearance; each seems lost in his or her thoughts while also sharing a common characteristic of humility. The three 'divine' figures appear elongated, floating, evincing a melancholic beauty, gazing, as it were, into eternity.[39] The Orthodox tradition, however, is very circumspect in what it says about the immanent or theological Trinity; at most it will claim that Rublev's icon offers a reflection of the intra-trinitarian life. The sacraments of initiation are also represented. If baptism incorporates the believer into the life of the Trinity and membership of the community of believers, the Eucharist, the hospitality of God, sustains the life of the Spirit in the Christian. The compositional centre of the icon is the chalice with the head of the slaughtered calf. The calf was an Old Testament prototype of the New Testament lamb, while the chalice was viewed as a symbol of the Eucharist, the gateway to the Trinity. The central figure is usually taken to be Christ who, with head bowed to the left, blesses the chalice indicating his willingness to be the sacrifice that takes away the sin of the world. The outgoing love of the Trinity is at the same time a sacrificial love.[40] The Father who is on the left inspires him to do this. If the Father gives the cup, and the Son blesses it, the Holy Spirit, on the right, transmits this gift of divine life to the world. Rublev here retains some of the earlier Christological iconographic focus in that the central angel is still Christ and still looks at the viewer. More striking, however, is how both the central angel and the angel on the right incline towards the Father on the left, in this way preserving a key Eastern stress on the 'monarchy' or primacy of the Father, source or fount of the Trinity.

Rublev's main concern is not only to draw out the distinctiveness of each of the Persons, but their relationship to each other, that is, their unity or mutual indwelling. Orthodox theology uses the term *perichoresis* to describe this mutual indwelling of the three Persons. The term was introduced into trinitarian theology in the eighth century by John of Damascus in his reflection on such texts as 'Know that the Father is in me and I am in the Father' (John

---

[39] The icon is essentially a monastic art. The 'spiritualisation' of Rublev's icon seems 'to imply an abstract rather than a concrete engagement with the world of matter and sense'. The icon reflects 'a spirituality of ascesis, of solitude, of the celibate, undistracted life, of a life of total conversion and sanctification ... Its world is a thoroughly religious world.' Pattison, *Art, Modernity and Faith*, 131–2.

[40] Kallistos of Diokleia draws out the anthropological corollary: 'To be human, after the image and likeness of God the Holy Trinity, means to love others with a love that is costly and self-sacrificing.' See his, 'The Human Person as an Icon of the Trinity', *Sobornost* 8 (1986): 20.

10:38). Damascene's concern is to avoid a fusion or confusion of the persons, on the one hand – the Persons 'neither mingle nor coalesce' – and tritheism, on the other – the Persons are 'inseparable and cannot part from one another' and 'cleave to each other' (*De fide orthodoxa* 1.14). Each divine Person encompasses the others and is co-inherent with the others, not in a static sense, but in a dynamic, cyclical and eternal movement of giving and receiving.

There is also a fourth place in front of the table – for the beholder. An icon draws us in, in this case, into the triune harmony. An icon regards us; we are not detached observers. The foreground is an open space inviting the viewer to enter and to become a participant in the rhythm of the trinitarian life. Typically, the face in an icon looks out; it is rarely shown in profile. This focus on the face invites a face-to-face, that is, personal, encounter when the viewer looks at the icon.[41] The icon shows how God is God by self-giving and that the communion that God is, is an all-inclusive one – at once self-contained and opening out to others. Put otherwise, there is room in God for others and 'the opening of that room is the act of creation'.[42]

For Rublev, then, the Trinity is a circle of love. Russian mystics as well as St John Climacus (*c.*570–649), who spoke in such terms, may have influenced him. The divine communion is an open circle. Certainly, Rublev's icon should be seen against the backdrop of the revival of the tradition of mystical and experiential prayer in the Eastern Orthodox Church known as hesychasm. At issue was how the monk or devout Christian can participate in the dynamic of the Trinity, given the Orthodox strictures on the ineffability of God, who 'dwells in unapproachable light' (1 Tim. 6:16). Eastern trinitarian mysticism saw the answer in Scripture, where the Holy Spirit, whom the Son has sent from the Father, makes us children of God and 'partakers of the divine nature' (2 Pet. 1:4). 'A life in communion with the All-holy Trinity in and through the Holy Spirit is the meaning and end of the Christian life.'[43] This trinitarian mysticism about the conscious acquisition of the Holy Spirit occurs par excellence in the celebration of the Liturgy. It should not surprise that the feast of Pentecost in the East is a feast of the Holy Trinity.

Rublev's icon shows us in a new light how the Trinity is a communion of love.[44] Moreover, trinitarian life is a model for communion in the Church.

---

[41] 'The Greek word for face, *prosopon*, is also the word for person.' Andrew Louth, 'Tradition and the Icon', *The Way* 44 (2005): 157.
[42] Jenson, *Systematic Theology*, vol. 1. *The Triune God*, 226. [43] Bunge, *The Rublev Trinity*, 77.
[44] Tony Castle, *Gateway to the Trinity: Meditations on Rublev's Icon* (Middlegreen, Slough: St Paul's, 1988), 68–84. See also Anthony Kelly, *The Trinity of Love: A Theology of the Christian God*, New Theology Series 4 (Wilmington, DE: Michael Glazier, 1989), xii; Henri J. M. Nouwen, *Behold the Beauty of the Lord: Praying with Icons* (Notre Dame, IN: Ave Maria Press, 1987), 11–25.

Figure 1. Andrei Rublev, *Holy Trinity*, c. 1400, Tretyakov Gallery, Moscow

It is only a communal life of self-giving love that will keep the Christian community united:

> May they all be one, just as, Father, you are in me and I am in you, so that they also may be in us, so that the world may believe it was you who sent me. (John 17:21)

It leaves a lasting impression even today because it is a symbol of divine and human love. The three angels, exhibiting a shy tenderness, are one of the most poetic images in all of Russian art. An aesthetic of restraint is evident, while the overall impact is one of *peace*. The beholder is drawn out of him- or herself, to pray, to contemplate, to be enriched.[45] Rublev's icon not only testifies to the transformation made possible through participating in the life of the Trinity, but provides a means through which this can be experienced.

CONCLUSION: THE 'REVIVAL' OF TRINITARIAN THEOLOGY?

In this chapter we have tried to 'set the scene' in relation to the doctrine of the Trinity, pointing out some of the difficulties inherent in a triune conception of God while also exploring the Trinity's significance for the life of the Christian community. One influential recent voice advocating a greater pastoral and practical resonance for the doctrine has been the American theologian, Catherine LaCugna. Her premises are, firstly, that the doctrine of the Trinity is 'not about the abstract nature of God, but a teaching about God's life with us and our life with each other', and, secondly, that as the mystery of God is revealed in the mystery of salvation, so statements about the nature of God must be rooted in the reality of salvation history. She continues:

> Trinitarian theology could be described as par excellence a theology of relationship, which explores the mysteries of love, relationship, personhood and communion within the framework of God's self-revelation in the person of Christ and the activity of the Spirit. (*GfU*, 1)

LaCugna's criticism of the historical development of the doctrine is that it had become too abstract and remote, focussed on the inner life of God, that is, on the self-relatedness of Father, Son, and Spirit (the immanent Trinity).

---

[45] Jim Forest, 'Through Icons: Word and Image Together', in Jeremy Begbie, ed., *Beholding the Glory: Incarnation through the Arts* (London: Darton, Longman and Todd, 2001), 83–97. Icons *primarily* intend to communicate religious truths and elicit veneration. As the Second Council of Nicea (787) put it: 'Indeed, the honour paid to an image traverses it, reaching the model; and he who venerates the image, venerates the person represented in that image.'

While we are in full agreement that doctrine of the Trinity should not be abstract and remote, it is one of our aims to show that the major representatives of the Western theological tradition did not develop trinitarian doctrine exclusively along those lines.[46]

LaCugna's approach, however, is not new. Karl Rahner had already taken up the challenge with his axiom on the identity of the economic and the immanent Trinity. Indeed LaCugna saw in Rahner's axiom 'a sound starting point for revitalizing the doctrine of the Trinity', and restoring its soteriological ramifications, yet standing 'in need of careful qualification' (*GfU*, 231).[47] While the axiom preserves a distinction as well as a correlation between the historical self-communication of God and God *ad intra*, the distinction is a conceptual not an ontological one; there are not two Trinities.[48] Rather, we have here two ways of conceiving the trinitarian mystery of God. For LaCugna, the starting point for reflection will always be the economy, or what she calls *oikonomia*, since the Trinity is a revealed mystery.

Two further difficulties with Rahner's axiom are noted by LaCugna, following Yves Congar, Walter Kasper, and others. Firstly, the axiom risks jeopardising God's freedom. It does not convey that there is 'something new' about God because of God's self-communication in history. As Kasper maintains, in order to allow the economic Trinity its full historical distinctiveness, we must 'take seriously the truth that through the incarnation the second divine person *exists in history in a new way*'.[49] A second danger is to dissolve the immanent Trinity in the economic Trinity of salvation history. The immanent Trinity, however, is not constituted by the economic Trinity. Rather, God freely decided to open God's self to history. Kasper thus rephrased Rahner's axiom:

In the economic self-communication, *the intra-trinitarian self-communication is present in the world in a new way*, namely, under the veil of historical words, signs, and actions, and ultimately in the figure of the man Jesus of Nazareth.[50]

---

[46] Following Augustine, medieval thinkers were in agreement that the historical missions of Son and Holy Spirit reveal the inner processions. Thus, it can be argued that Rahner's axiom recaptures a traditional approach, and does not necessarily imply a critique of the broader theological tradition (although it is at odds with neo-scholastic textbooks of the early twentieth century).

[47] See also her 'Re-conceiving the Trinity as the Mystery of Salvation', *Scottish Journal of Theology* 38 (1985): 1–23.

[48] For the limitations of the economic-immanent paradigm, see Elizabeth T. Groppe, 'Catherine Mowry LaCugna's Contribution to Trinitarian Theology', *Theological Studies* 63 (2002): 731–41. Rahner's trinitarian theology is discussed in Chapter 5.

[49] Walter Kasper, *The God of Jesus Christ* (London: SCM Press, 1983), 275.

[50] Kasper, *The God of Jesus Christ*, 276.

LaCugna would agree with Kasper's modification of Rahner's paradigm. She too is concerned that the axiom could undermine God's freedom. It cannot be a question of God, and God's actions *ad extra*, being placed under a necessity. Hence, LaCugna stresses that the economic Trinity is neither identical with, nor necessarily consequent upon, the immanent Trinity. Instead, in her account, 'divine freedom is the freedom of persons who act out of love for the sake of communion', (*GfU*, 355) and creation is the fruit of this divine love.

One criticism of LaCugna's project, however, is that in her bolstering of the divine economy, and her reluctance to speculate about the intra-divine realm, she runs the risk of collapsing God into the economy.[51] It seems, in the words of one commentator, that she 'has lost any conception of God beyond the economy of salvation'.[52] There is some truth in these criticisms. She certainly affirms the 'essential unity' between 'God's saving activity and God's ineffable mystery' or *theologia* (*GfU*, 321). The Trinity does not exist only in our experience. Her point is that trinitarian theology became marginalised as a science of God's self-relatedness. The way out of the impasse, she contends, is to make the economy of salvation 'the basis, the context, and the final criterion for every statement about God' (*GfU*, 22). True, but that is not to exclude statements about the immanent Trinity. We gain some understanding of the immanent Trinity precisely on the basis of what God has revealed to us of God's self. The triune God of love exists not simply 'for us' but *in se*. We have to be able to speak, along with classical trinitarian theology, of the inner-trinitarian life, of the pre-existing, eternal communion of Father, Son, and Holy Spirit – independent of their manifestation in the economy – and into which we have been invited.[53] The difficulty is to strike the right balance in our conception of the God–world relationship. We can distinguish without separating the immanent and the economic Trinity, even while acknowledging that the latter is the starting point for theological reflection. Still, our understanding does not proceed in just one direction. Deductive and inductive, theocentric and anthropological approaches are not mutually exclusive.[54]

---

[51] See, for example, Thomas Weinandy, *The Father's Spirit of Sonship: Reconceiving the Trinity* (Edinburgh: T&T Clark, 1994), 123–36; Stanley J. Grenz, *Rediscovering the Triune God: The Trinity in Contemporary Theology* (Minneapolis: Fortress Press, 2004), 160–1; and Veli-Matti Kärkkäinen, *The Trinity: Global Perspectives* (Louisville KY: Westminster/John Knox Press, 2007), 187–93.

[52] Grenz, *Rediscovering the Triune God*, 160.

[53] J. A. DiNoia, Review of *God for Us*, *Modern Theology* 9/2 (1993): 216.

[54] Earl Muller, 'The Science of Theology. A Review of Catherine LaCugna's *God for Us*', *Gregorianum* 75/2 (1994): 311–41.

Granted LaCugna's conviction that the mystery of God is revealed in the mystery of salvation, we still come up against what we have referred to as the paradox of knowing and not knowing at the root of all discourse about God. We worship a God who has been revealed to us and at the same time acknowledge that God is ultimately beyond our rational understanding and comprehension.[55] Acknowledging the limitations of theological statements is not, however, an option for an agnosticism that excludes the possibility of saying anything meaningful about God as triune. Nor does it restrict us to simply repeating biblical terms and language in a fundamentalist fashion. Rather, our language is here strained to the limit. Theological formulations, however true, always point beyond themselves to a God who cannot be circumscribed by human speech or by images.

When we speak of a 'renewal' in current trinitarian theology, we are referring to a 'ressourcement' or return to the patristic and medieval roots of the doctrine. Such approaches (e.g., the work of Lewis Ayres, Michel Barnes, and Sarah Coakley) aim to overcome caricatures of the Western tradition, as if this was a monolith. Certainly, some of LaCugna's more sweeping comments about the Western tradition leave her open to such criticism. On a more general level, the ongoing discussion (which is beyond the scope of this introduction) raises the question of the relationship between patristic (and medieval) scholars and systematic theologians, between the past and the present, between 'historical' and 'systematic' theology, in short, the question of how theology is practised. Scholars of a more historical bent will want to stress that *all* theology must be historical, while most systematic theologians insist that theology requires a strong ethical and political commitment.

Recent trinitarian theology places a greater emphasis on the relational and dynamic character of God. The Trinity is described as being-in-relationship, and is presented as a resource and inspiration for the kind of community that should exist in the Church, a paradigm for its worship, as well as for the kinds of relationships that should characterise social and political life. Feminist and liberation theologians, for example, have highlighted the patriarchal frame-work in which much (trinitarian) theology has operated – a theology and Church which was often dominating and oppressive rather than liberating. At the pastoral level too, there have been attempts to link a theology of the Trinity with issues such as suffering, forgiveness, community, and authority. Here again political and liberation theologians have been to the fore. Jürgen Moltmann, for example, though he has been criticised for making suffering

---

[55] Joseph Cardinal Ratzinger, *Introduction to Christianity* (San Francisco: Ignatius Press, 1990, 2004), 162.

central to the nature of God, has retrieved key biblical anthropomorphic insights about the divine *pathos* and about how God is affected by human actions and suffering in history. This is developed into a trinitarian theology of the cross as an inner-trinitarian event, where the Father suffers and is involved in the cross of the Son.[56] Moltmann accepts the risk of humanising God in order not to reduce God to an impersonal concept that would be of little value to those dealing with the question of suffering in a pastoral context. Hans Urs von Balthasar has also avoided the notion of God as unmoved mover, while managing to safeguard the transcendence of a God who suffers (*TD*, 317–28). We shall return to these two theologians in Chapters 5 and 6. Given the political and social dimensions of much current theological reflection, it is not surprising that God is perceived not only as the source of our salvation, but also as the foundation and paradigm of society and liberation. If the Trinity is a symbol of interdependence and communion, this has consequences for humankind made in God's triune image and likeness. Despite the current revival of trinitarian theology, however, the impression remains that the revolution in our image of God, in our conception of Church, society, and indeed in all our relationships, implied in the doctrine of the Trinity, has yet to be fully implemented.

SUGGESTED READINGS

Bracken, Joseph A., *God: Three Who Are One*, Engaging Theology: Catholic Perspectives (Collegeville, MN: Michael Glazier Books, 2008).

Fiddes, Paul, *Participating in God* (London: Darton, Longman, and Todd, 2000).

Jenson, Robert, *Systematic Theology, vol. 1. The Triune God* (Oxford: Oxford University Press, 1997).

Kärkkäinen, Veli-Matti, *The Trinity: Global Perspectives* (Louisville, KY: Westminster/John Knox Press, 2007).

LaCugna, Catherine Mowry, *God for Us: The Trinity and Christian Life* (San Francisco: HarperCollins, 1991).

Placher, William C., *The Triune God: An Essay in Postliberal Theology* (Louisville, KY: Westminster/John Knox Press, 2007).

Staniloae, Dumitru, *Orthodox Dogmatic Theology, vol. 1. Revelation and Knowledge of the Triune God: The Experience of God*, trans. and ed. I. Ionita and R. Barringer (Brookline, MA: Holy Cross Orthodox Press, 1994).

---

[56] Jürgen Moltmann, *The Crucified God* (London: SCM Press, 1974), 206 (henceforward abbreviated to *CG*). See also his *Experiences of God* (London: SCM Press, 2000), 303–12. Paul Fiddes, *Participating in God* (London: Darton, Longman, and Todd, 2000), 152–90 also explores the question of suffering and the vulnerability of God.

CHAPTER 2

The Trinity and its scriptural roots

If the doctrine of the Trinity did not emerge until about the fourth century, in what sense can it be said that there is a doctrine of the Trinity in the Old and New Testaments? Theologians have come a long way from the old manuals of theology that tried to 'prove' that there were clear references to the Trinity in Scripture. Texts such as Gen. 1:26 ('Let *us* make man in *our* image and likeness') and Isa. 6:3 ('Holy, Holy, Holy, the Lord God of Hosts, all the earth is full of his glory') were presented as a clear allusion to the mystery of the Trinity. This kind of biblical interpretation is now regarded as fanciful and strained.[1] Instead, Scripture scholars acknowledge that the Hebrew Bible does not contain a *doctrine* of the Trinity as such. Yet, just as we cannot ignore the Jewishness of Jesus and his disciples, neither can we discount the Old Testament understanding of God. In this Testament there are what might be termed 'personifications' of God. In Word, Wisdom, and Spirit, the God of Israel was active among the chosen people revealing God's plans to them.

Another issue that emerges in this and in the next chapter is what it means to say that a doctrine is 'based' on Scripture. A fundamentalist approach tends to merely repeat biblical statements assuming there is no distance between biblical times and today. While some Protestant theological positions have traditionally espoused the principle of *Sola Scriptura* (Scripture alone), Karl Barth, one of the most influential Protestant theologians, insisted that the ongoing task of theology is to go beyond repeating what the prophets and apostles said to what we, as contemporary believers, have to say based of course on the apostles and prophets. If theology is

---

[1] This is not to claim, however, that the historical-critical method is the only way of reading Scripture. Other, more traditional, readings that are not necessarily at odds with a historical-critical approach include non-literal, allegorical, and moral readings, all of which influenced the development of traditional theologies of the Trinity, as we shall see in Chapters 4 and 5.

'thinking about how to speak the Gospel' then believers, guided by the Spirit, are tasked with an ongoing process of understanding and growth into truth.[2] Scripture cannot be the final arbiter of all disputed questions. It remains an 'open' book (not closed following the resurrection and ascension) to be interpreted by the community.

We are alluding to the development of doctrine and specifically to the affinity between Scripture and later trinitarian thought. At first sight it might appear that there is little affinity between the often vivid and concrete language of Scripture and subsequent trinitarian creeds and doctrines. Technical terms like 'substance', 'consubstantial', and so on go beyond the language of Scripture, but going beyond is not going away.[3] What Scripture says at length, creeds and doctrines distil and condense.[4] But there is always the danger that a dogma cuts loose from its biblical base and becomes a substitute for the more existential language of Scripture. Development of doctrine does not take place independently of Scripture, however, but always in close connection with it. In the case of the doctrine of the Trinity, however, this did not always happen. When the biblical link is lost, trinitarian theology is likely to go in a speculative direction and focus more on the immanent Trinity.

WORD, WISDOM, AND SPIRIT OF GOD

In the New Testament, God was present to Israel in God's *Word*, God's *Wisdom*, and God's *Spirit*. Word, Wisdom, and Spirit were personified agents of God, through whom the Israelites were enabled to experience the divine and find out what they were to do. They represent 'dynamic expressions of Yahweh's manifestation in human history'.[5] Word, Wisdom, and Spirit, while not formally recognised as divine persons, constituted a medium of revelation and communication between God and God's people. In Isaiah (55:10–11), we hear of the Word, which issues from Yahweh, accomplishes what Yahweh intends, and returns again to Yahweh:

---

[2] Robert Jenson, *Systematic Theology*, vol. 1. *The Triune God* (Oxford: Oxford University Press, 1997), 11.
[3] Alasdair Heron, 'The Biblical Basis for the Doctrine of the Trinity', in *The Forgotten Trinity*, A Selection of Papers presented to the BCC Study Commission on Trinitarian Doctrine Today (Council of Churches for Britain and Ireland, 1991), 38.
[4] See Nicholas Lash, *Believing Three Ways in One God: A Reading of the Apostles' Creed* (London: SCM Press, 1992), 4–16.
[5] Jacques Dupuis, *Toward a Christian Theology of Religious Pluralism* (New York: Orbis, 1997, 2000), 42.

For as the rain and the snow come down from heaven, and do not return there until they have watered the earth, making it bring forth and sprout, giving seed to the sower and bread to the eater, so shall my word be that goes out from my mouth; it shall not return to me empty, but it shall accomplish that which I purpose, and succeed in the thing for which I sent it.

Word here represents a dynamic entity, a way of personalising God's will and action in the world. As Walter Brueggemann puts it, 'Yahweh causes to be by utterance'.[6] In Solomon's prayer, Word (and Wisdom) are agents of divine creation:

God of my fathers and Lord of mercy, you made all things by your Word, and by your Wisdom fashioned humankind. (Wis. 9:1–2)

This is the language of metaphor, and thus the differences as well as the similarities in the analogy need to be kept in mind. While God's Word cannot be reduced to human speaking, neither is it dissimilar to human speech. Indeed, it is mediated through human words. Metaphors for the Word of God include: fire (Jer. 5:14), messenger and rescuer (Ps. 107:20), and more vividly, warrior (Wis. 18:15–16).

Israel's God is a God who speaks, who has spoken, and who is in continual dialogue with the world.[7] This is in contrast to the idols 'who have mouths but do not speak' (Ps. 115:5). The Word expresses God's will for a specific situation; to experience its closeness one has 'only to carry it out' (Deut. 30:14). The Word of God is not, however, a bald statement of the divine will; it assumes an ongoing relationship, a communication between God and people. It is a personal and invading Word spoken in a specific encounter (e.g., the call of Jeremiah and Amos). God's Word can reflect inner-divine reflections or emotions (Gen. 2:18; 8:21), while the manifestations of God's Word range from the spectacular to the unobtrusive, including visions and dreams.

Another, more striking, personification of God is *Wisdom*. Wisdom is both God's Wisdom, but is also referred to as God's firstborn – 'begotten' or 'created' long ago (Prov. 8:22–31). Not only does Wisdom exist with God before everything else, partaking of God's own character, but also shares in God's work of creation (Job 28:25–7). Wisdom dwells with God (Sir. 24:2)

[6] Walter Brueggemann, *Theology of the Old Testament: Testimony, Dispute, Advocacy* (Minneapolis: Fortress Press, 1997), 146.

[7] For what follows, see Terence T. Fretheim, 'Word of God', in *The Anchor Bible Dictionary*, ed. David Noel Freedman, vol. vi (New Haven: Yale University Press, 1992), 961–68 (henceforward abbreviated to *ABD*). See also Yves Congar, *I Believe in the Holy Spirit*, vol. i. *The Experience of the Spirit* (London: Chapman, 1983), 3–14.

and with humankind teaching the way that leads to salvation (Sir. 51:23–6). Wisdom (*Sophia*) is available to all who search, while remaining mysteriously inaccessible. This search entails a reverence and devotion, a 'fear of the Lord' (Prov. 1:7) who creates and orders. If her identity is unclear, she is nonetheless above the rest of creation. Though she does not possess divine status given the strict monotheism of the post-exilic period, she speaks as an agent of God (Prov. 8:32–5). In her is a spirit that immanently 'pervades and permeates all things', while, at the same time, *Sophia* is transcendently 'holy, unique', and 'almighty' (Wis. 7:22–4). In many respects the identity and action of Wisdom and the Spirit are the same. Wisdom 'is a breath of the power of God' who 'renews all things' (Wis. 7:25–7). She represents the mysterious order given by Yahweh to creation, beckoning and summoning human beings to seek her. God has 'poured wisdom out on all his works' (Sir. 1:9) or, as von Rad puts it, 'creation not only exists, it also discharges truth'.[8]

Wisdom is also at work in Israel's history (Wis. 10:15–18) delivering the people through the Exodus. Elsewhere, wisdom is depicted in terms of food and drink:

They who eat me will hunger for more, they who drink me will thirst for more. (Sir. 24:21)

This language will later be applied to Jesus, source of nourishment and life (John 6:5) and divine Wisdom in person (1 Cor. 1:24). The New Testament writers would see Jesus, like Wisdom, as active at the beginning of creation (1 Cor. 8:6; Col. 1:16–17).

God's activity in the world is further described in terms of God's *Spirit* – traditionally perceived as the 'breath' (*ruah*) of Yahweh that hovered over the waters at creation. 'Spirit' also refers to that vital breath of life or animating power that God imparts and which distinguishes the living human being.[9] This is beautifully expressed in Ps. 104:

When you hide your face, your creatures are dismayed; when you take away their breath, they die and return to their dust. When you send forth your Spirit, they are created; and you renew the face of the earth. (Ps. 104:29–30)

---

[8] Gerhard von Rad, *Wisdom in Israel* (London: SCM Press, 1972), 165. Apart from this classic text, see Roland E. Murphy, *The Tree of Life: An Exploration of Biblical Wisdom Literature*, 2nd edn (Grand Rapids, MI: Eerdmans, 1996), 133–49.

[9] F. W. Horn, 'Holy Spirit', *ABD*, vol. III, 262. See also George T. Montague, *The Holy Spirit: Growth of a Biblical Tradition* (New York: Paulist Press, 1976), 3–16.

The Spirit of Yahweh is not an impersonal principle that is immanent in the world, but refers to God's creative and redemptive presence that occasions life, justice, and wisdom. It is characterised by its difference from human weakness and frailty and is beyond a person's ability to penetrate and explain (Isa. 40:13). The transcendent and dynamic quality of the Spirit makes it an apt symbol for the divine. It is sudden and unpredictable; neither its origin nor destination can be clearly determined. Its power is seen in its effects. The Spirit drives and 'rests' on the prophets – those who have been specially singled out and anointed by God (Isa. 61:1) – who in turn stress the 'Word' of God that contains God's will. The Spirit equips the prophets and judges, for example, Gideon (Jdg. 6:34) for their respective tasks and responsibilities in the service of God and Israel. Or as David testifies, 'the Spirit of Yahweh speaks through me, his word is on my tongue' (2 Sam. 23:2). Belonging to the sphere of God's existence, the Spirit causes a person to act so that God's saving plan will be fulfilled. The Spirit of God is 'sent' and remains among the people (Hag. 2:5). With the prophets' denunciation of the sin of Israel (e.g., Mic. 3:8), the Spirit takes on an explicitly ethical dimension. In the final days, God promises to pour out the Spirit on the people through the prophets (Joel 3:1–2), recreating them anew.

Word, Wisdom, and Spirit, therefore, are increasingly viewed as personifications and extensions of God's activity – both identified with and distinguished from God. This development, in turn, reflects a sense of God's dynamic presence among the chosen people, leading them through the vagaries of their history. Yet in all of this we encounter the paradox of knowing and not knowing God referred to earlier. The God who reveals Godself through Word, Wisdom, and Spirit is at the same time a God who keeps something of God's self hidden. Even in revealing, God does not show God's face. Gerald O'Collins puts it well:

Wisdom, Word, and Spirit functioned, frequently synonymously, to acknowledge the transcendent God's nearness to the world and to the chosen people – a nearness that did not, however, compromise the divine transcendence, or that otherness that sets God 'beyond' all other beings.[10]

So, while Word, Wisdom and Spirit take on divine roles and at times vivid personifications mediating and accomplishing God's plan, and while the

---

[10] Gerald O'Collins, *The Tripersonal God: Understanding and Interpreting the Trinity* (London: Geoffrey Chapman, 1999), 32.

idea of plurality within unity is hinted at in Jewish theology, this is not yet a revelation of a *triune* God.

THE GOD OF ISRAEL — A LIVING GOD

Israel experienced her God as one who 'encountered' her in the saving events of her history. This encounter begins with a personal self-introduction along with a description of a saving event of Israel's history, for example, 'I am Yahweh, your God, who brought you out of the land of Egypt' (Exod. 20:2). For Israel, using the personal name 'Yahweh' implied that to 'know' God is to encounter a living personality.[11] A person is not known unless his or her name is known. To have no name is to cease to exist. To be 'nameless' is to be 'worthless' (Job 30:8). Naming bestows identity and distinguishes one individual or species from another. In the ordering of creation, God (Gen. 1) and man (Gen. 2:19) name each object of creation. Conferring a name asserts a claim or some form of ownership over what is named. While there were many names for the divinity in the Hebrew Bible – Yahweh, Elohim, Rock, and so on – ultimately the name of Israel's God was the unpronounced tetragrammaton, YHWH. In knowing the divine name, Israel could call upon and appeal to Yahweh, enter into community with Yahweh, and be under Yahweh's protection.

For Israel, as for the ancient Near Eastern world in general, the existence of divine beings was universally accepted. The question was not whether there is only one God, but whether there are any gods like Yahweh. The answer to this question for the Israelites was always negative. It is hard to overestimate the importance of the first commandment (Exod. 20:1) for Israel – a God all powerful yet concerned for the weak and needy. The unique and transcendent nature of Yahweh is further highlighted by the prohibition of representing Yahweh in images (Exod. 20:4–5). Yahweh alone is *elohim* and thus Israel can worship no god but Yahweh. Contrasted with this uncompromising monotheism is the tendency to speak of Yahweh in human terms. Scriptural language about God is 'drastically personal'.[12] Yahweh is 'the living God' with traits of personality and can enter into dialogue with humankind and respond to their needs. Yahweh has a countenance, eyes, ears, mouth, nostrils, and so on and

---

[11] John L. McKenzie, 'Aspects of Old Testament Thought', in Raymond E. Brown, Joseph A. Fitzmyer, and Roland E. Murphy, eds., *The New Jerome Biblical Commentary* (London: Geoffrey Chapman, 1990), 1285–8.

[12] Jenson, *Systematic Theology*, vol. 1. *The Triune God*, 222.

exhibits strong feelings from love and compassion (Isa. 54:7–8) to jealousy (Exod. 34:14) and rage (Isa. 47:6). There is a tension in this problematic character of Yahweh that does not admit of an easy resolution. Metaphors of sustenance also contain more ominous possibilities. As warrior will Yahweh fight for or against Israel (Jer. 21:5), as judge sentence or pardon (Ezek. 34:17–22), as potter build up or smash (Jer. 18:3–6)?[13]

In sum, as one exegete puts it, 'the God of the Old Testament does not easily conform to the expectations of Christian dogmatic theology, nor to the categories of any Hellenistic perennial philosophy'.[14] Rather, Israel's speech about its God is deeply embedded in its socio-economic, political and historical reality. The story that is the Old Testament is based on events rather than concepts. If anthropomorphisms make it difficult to appreciate God's transcendence, they do convey the personality of Yahweh as a 'living God' in a way that more abstract speech cannot. Israel's God while infinite is never without name or form, a jealous God (Exod. 34:14), who does not share his name with other gods (Isa. 42:8). Yahweh is typically the subject of verbs of action (e.g., of deliverance and redemption), indicating engagement with and on behalf of Israel. This speech is not simply descriptive, however. Israel also addresses Yahweh as 'Thou'. In a situation of Yahweh calling Israel and vice-versa, anthropomorphisms should not come as a surprise. And in prayer the anthropomorphic description of Yahweh attains an intimacy not possible via a more abstract discourse. Nevertheless, Israel acknowledges that Yahweh's inscrutable sovereignty remains undiminished. There is the contrast between Yahweh who can 'talk to Moses face to face' (Exod. 33:11) and the same Yahweh who cannot be revealed except from the back (Exod. 33:21–3). While the ineffable mystery of Yahweh cannot be comprehended, Israel believed Yahweh exercised an ethical consistency manifested at times in harsh and uncompromising ways. It struggled to come to terms with this unsettling character of Yahweh, with this tension between God the lover and God the punisher. How to juxtapose divine sovereignty and righteousness with solidarity and compassion? Yahweh must become neither too distant connoting a lack of intimacy, nor too familiar for fear of idolatry.

When Yahweh appears to Moses at the burning bush on the mountain of Horeb (Exod. 3:1–15) it is stated that Yahweh intends to 'come down' to rescue the people from their bondage in Egypt. Moses is commissioned as leader of the people to be Yahweh's emissary to Pharaoh, but protests his inadequacy and receives in turn the divine promise: 'I shall be with you'.

---

[13] Brueggemann, *Theology of the Old Testament*, 282.   [14] Ibid., 117.

Still fearful, Moses asks for the name of the mysterious voice. Then Yahweh said to Moses 'I am he who is' or variously translated as 'I will be with you' or 'I am who I am'.

The Hebrew verb *hayah* in this text is usually translated as 'to be' in the sense of 'to effect, to be effective'. This revelation then is not concerned with the abstract being of God. Rather, it is to be seen as a promise for the future and a pledge that God is with his people in an active and effective way: 'I will be your God and you shall be my people' (Jer. 11:4; 24:7).[15] In the Jewish imagination, God does not possess a nature with many characteristics; rather God acts in history as Saviour. Israel is not so much concerned with an abstract nature of God per se as with God's role in its community. Moses' question was not a speculative one, but an anxious inquiry about how God will be present with Israel in the ups and downs of its history.

Yahweh's ambiguous response 'I am who am' is a repudiation of any name that might seek to circumscribe, appropriate, and so turn Yahweh into an idol. God, even in revelation, remains a mystery and cannot be reduced to a definition. Still, this imageless God desires to become known and accessible. Moreover, this divine self-revelation is 'less predicative than appellative', best understood 'in terms of function than substance, in terms of narrative rather than syllogism', and 'in terms of relation rather than abstraction'.[16] It is 'theophanic and performative'[17] and brings with it a commission to announce liberation and redemption (Exod. 3:16–17). When it is translated into a statement about God's being, the dynamism in the original Hebrew expression gets lost. The Septuagint translates Yahweh's promise of being-there into a statement about being: 'I am'. English translations have traditionally followed the same line: 'I am who am' or 'I am the One who is'. In these translations God becomes a metaphysical statement, a being with an essence, not the personal, living God of history who has a covenant relationship with Israel. The Bible speaks 'not of God's being, but of God's being there, in the sense of being with us and for us'.[18] Yahweh is not a faceless abstraction, but a participant in the story of Israel, a God who does rather than a being who is. It is not a question of excluding ontological language in speaking about God, but of acknowledging, firstly, that being

---

[15] For what follows, see Kasper, *The God of Jesus Christ*, 148–51.

[16] Richard Kearney, *The God Who May Be: A Hermeneutics of Religion* (Bloomington and Indianapolis: Indiana University Press, 2001), 26.

[17] André LaCocque, 'The Revelation of Revelations', in André LaCocque and Paul Ricoeur, *Thinking Biblically: Exegetical and Hermeneutical Studies* (Chicago and London: Chicago University Press, 1998), 316, 321.

[18] Walter Kasper, *The God of Jesus Christ* (London: SCM, 1983), 151.

(following Aristotle) is said in many ways, is open to a plurality of inter-pretations, and secondly, the paradox and tension between affirmative and negative, ontological and apophatic discourses.

The God of Israel, then, is a living God, intimately involved in the history of the people of Israel. Yahweh's *shekinah* or presence – symbolised in the ark of the covenant – will continue to dwell in their midst and guide them (1 Chron. 28:20). The Hebrew Bible does not provide any specifically trinitarian understanding of God. This does not mean that its understand-ing of God is utterly at odds with the later trinitarian development of the Christian era. When it comes to the New Testament it is important to acknowledge continuity between the experience of Yahweh in the Hebrew Bible and the distinctive New Testament experience of God. The God to whom the whole New Testament witnesses is this same Yahweh; the New Testament speaks simply of 'God', the same God who was at work in the Old Testament: the God of Abraham, of Isaac, and of Jacob. Yet, it is only in the New Testament that we discover the original and distinguishing characteristic of the Christian understanding of God, namely, its identifi-cation of God with Jesus testified, for example, in the Prologue of John's Gospel. The New Testament announces that 'the Word' becomes 'flesh' in Jesus (John 1:14) and that he, as the resurrected and exalted Lord, sends the Spirit.

A RIGHT WAY TO SPEAK ABOUT GOD?

Many Christians, particularly those influenced by feminist theology, find the description of God in the exclusively masculine category of 'Father' unhelpful and limiting. They maintain that such traditional ways of speak-ing about God have, wittingly or unwittingly, contributed to the down-grading of women in Church and society. As Elizabeth Johnson puts it, 'Whether consciously or not, sexist God language undermines the human equality of women made in the divine image and likeness'.[19]

The issue of 'the right way to speak about God' is an ongoing subject of theological discussion. Sociological approaches to biblical studies have undermined any claim that there are 'innocent' texts or 'innocent' readers. Texts have ambiguous and sometimes unconscious ties with the realities of power and vested interest. There is no interest-free interpretation. Feminist theological scholarship has been to the fore in its work of deconstructing or

---

[19] Elisabeth A. Johnson, *She Who Is: The Mystery of God in Feminist Theological Discourse* (New York: Crossroad, 1992), 18.

uncovering oppressive dynamics in the Christian tradition, its language, texts, and symbolism. By drawing attention to the polyphonic character of biblical texts, hegemonic or totalising interpretive tendencies are increasingly called into question.[20]

In the Old Testament the fatherhood of God is not central, though the term 'Father' appears a little over twenty times in the historical and prophetic books. While it would become the favoured designation for God in the New Testament, the predominant metaphor for God in the Old Testament is not Father but 'King'. The worship of Yahweh was conducted in the temple built by the king, and so it was natural that Yahweh and king be linked. At the same time, God is known by many names, the most common of which is the personal name 'Yahweh' – addressed to God over 6,000 times in the Old Testament. However, in naming God as King of Israel, the Old Testament is acknowledging that God as king does what earthly kings and rulers frequently fail to do. God feeds the hungry, protects widows and orphans, and 'gives justice to the oppressed' (Ps. 146:7). This picture of divine kingship serves to critique the failure of Israel's kings to secure the rights of the weak and defenceless.[21] The rule of Yahweh as king of Israel and of all creation undermines the overly pretentious claims of worldly rulers by stressing that all authority derives from, and depends on, the sovereign God (Dan. 4:14).

When the term 'Father' is used, it is normally in a redemptive sense: 'you, O Lord, are our Father; our Redeemer from of old is your name' (Isa. 63:16) and connotes God's special relationship with Israel. A passage from Deuteronomy shows Moses recalling this special relationship:

Do you thus repay the Lord, O foolish and senseless people? Is he not your Father, who formed you, who made you, and established you? (Deut. 32:6)

Here Moses points to the covenant between God and God's people, a bond which is characterised by fidelity on God's side, and infidelity on the side of the people. Even if some passages warn that violation of the covenant will bring down God's wrath and punishment, the underlying message is that God's steadfast love of the chosen people will remain forever (Ps. 89:28–9). The Father metaphor intends to convey Yahweh's relationship with, and concern for, his people even if Israel's response is often a disappointing one (Jer. 3:19–20).

---

[20] See, for example, Phyllis Trible, *God and the Rhetoric of Sexuality* (Philadelphia: Fortress Press, 1978).

[21] O'Collins, *The Tripersonal God*, 187. In other words, God is the ground of the analogy, not the creature.

Does the Old Testament speak of God as mother? Firstly, it does not ascribe any gender to God – God is utterly transcendent. Yet there are many examples of maternal comparisons or similes, where God is compared to a woman who has carried Israel 'since the womb' (Isa. 46:6), who groans 'like a woman in labour' (Isa. 42:14) and as a midwife (Ps. 22:9–10). God comforts, like a mother, those who are suffering (Isa. 66:13). God's love is even 'more tender than that of a mother' (Sir. 4:10). In some cases, God's fatherhood is depicted using traditional maternal imagery: the father looks after the child, teaches it to walk, and catches it when it stumbles (Jer. 31:9). This tender side of God is beautifully expressed by the prophet Hosea:

I myself taught Ephraim to walk, I myself took them by the arm, but they did not know that I was the one caring for them, that I was leading them with human ties, with leading-strings of love, that, with them, I was like someone lifting an infant to his cheek, and that I bent down to feed him. (Hos. 11:3–4)

Although the Old Testament uses examples of both God's paternal role in begetting and the maternal role of birthing, it is still the case that metaphors for God such as king, father, judge, and the like became the ideal standard for the conduct of *men* in these roles. The hegemony of male imagery for God and a reluctance to draw on other metaphors or to expand the imagery used to speak of God has left many feeling excluded. When such imagery is drawn only from the world of ruling men, God tends to be perceived as a distant and controlling earthly monarch who rules over his subjects. As Janet Soskice has pointed out, it is not simply the predominant description of God as male in the tradition that is at stake; it is that the 'divine male' is described as one who is dominant, powerful and implacable.[22] There is, therefore, a link between images of God and the assignment and exercise of power. An uncritical acceptance of the fatherhood of God runs the risk of a false dependency: God wants us to remain children, punishes our offences, and is more like a man than a woman – we end up internalising a blasphemous image of God.[23] Other images of God such as mother, nurturer, friend, and the like do not purport to describe God per se so much as to suggest the quality of the relationship that is offered.[24] It is not a question of discarding the centuries old Father language of prayer and

[22] Janet Martin Soskice, *The Kindness of God: Metaphor, Gender, and Religious Language* (Oxford: Oxford University Press, 2007), 71.
[23] See Jane Williams, 'The Fatherhood of God', in Alasdair Heron, ed., *The Forgotten Trinity*, A Selection of Papers presented to the BCC Study Commission on Trinitarian Doctrine Today (Council of Churches for Britain and Ireland, 1991), 91–101.
[24] Sallie McFague, *Metaphorical Theology: Models of God in Religious Language* (Philadelphia: Fortress Press, 1982), 166.

worship. Indeed, in the New Testament Jesus describes God as 'Father' over 170 times and only invokes this title in his prayer. Rather, it is to acknowledge the limitations of all language about God and how an uncritically literal use of Father language can lead to a misunderstanding of how God relates to us and how we are to relate to each other.

In the first chapter we saw that no image or symbol is an adequate 'picture' of God and that all our knowledge of God is analogical. There is always the danger of literalising metaphors for God and of forgetting the dissimilarity in every analogy.[25] At issue is what content is given to the 'Father' metaphor. As we have seen, the Fatherhood of God in the Old Testament is presented primarily (though not exclusively) in personal and relational terms. Even if addressing God as 'Father' is not in every case patriarchal, exclusively male symbolism for God renders female symbols peripheral and undeveloped. Symbols of course are deeply ambiguous. It is doubtful whether only calling God 'Mother' adequately counterbalances the undoubted over-masculinisation of the God-image in traditional theological discourse. God has no gender. The difficulties involved here are well captured by Catherine LaCugna:

Feminine imagery for God in the Bible or in some mystical writers does not establish that God has 'feminine aspects' any more than masculine imagery establishes that God has 'masculine aspects'. In addition, this type of interpretation tends to incorporate sex-stereotypes (women are compassionate, men are strong) and to suggest that God is primarily masculine but with a feminine side.[26]

This feminist critique of one-sided God language rests on the theological principle that God transcends all images, words, and concepts. While we should be wary of absolutising particular images or metaphors – God is known by many names in both the Jewish and the Christian traditions – the tradition has privileged the names 'Father', 'Son', and 'Holy Spirit' to express the triune God's self-disclosure to humanity. Yet, in devising new ways of speaking about God's identity and activity, feminist theology faces a similar challenge that emerged (as we shall see) in the fourth century, namely, the legitimacy of using non-biblical terms to describe God, while at the same time keeping this language rooted in the scriptural tradition.

---

[25] Karl Rahner, 'Observations on the Doctrine of God in Catholic Dogmatics', in *Theological Investigations*, vol. IX (London: Darton, Longman and Todd, 1972), 128.

[26] Catherine Mowry LaCugna, 'The Trinitarian Mystery of God', in Francis S. Fiorenza and John P. Galvin, eds., *Systematic Theology: Roman Catholic Perspectives* (Dublin: Gill and Macmillan, 1991), 183.

THE FATHER OF JESUS AND THE *LOGOS* OF GOD

There is no doubt that Jesus claimed to have a unique relationship to his Father – a relationship that is characterised by the Aramaic word 'Abba'. In using 'Abba', Jesus is addressing the Father in personal terms in contrast to the prevailing Jewish mentality that stressed God's sovereignty and dared not pronounce God's name.[27] Whereas in the Old Testament the father-hood of God was seen more in terms of God's relation to God's people, that is, to the nation Israel, Jesus prayed to the God of Israel as 'my Father'. When referring to his disciples he distinguished between 'my Father' and 'your Father'. In claiming a special relationship vis-à-vis his Abba, Jesus did not put himself on the same level as his disciples, but invited them to participate in his own prayer experience, for example, in teaching them the 'Our Father'.[28] Moreover, Jesus' distinctive manner of prayer finds a resonance in all the Gospels. A striking example of this is Jesus' prayer in Gethsamene: 'Abba, Father, all things are possible to you; take this cup from me. Yet not my will but yours be done' (Mark 14:36; cf. Mt. 26:42). The Lucan Jesus prays on the cross: 'Father, into your hands, I commend my spirit' (Luke 23:46), while in John there is Jesus' prayer of thanksgiving to his Father at the tomb of Lazarus (John 11:41).

The Aramaic expression 'Abba' was a colloquial word used by children and adults in addressing their father. It connoted respect, familiarity and intimacy. Jesus pushed this usage further in addressing *God* as 'Abba' or Father. The expression 'Abba' is found only in Mark 14:36 and in Paul (Gal. 4:6 and Rom. 8:15–16). Yet the numerous examples of Jesus' use of the term 'Father' and of the Roman and Galatian congregations' use of 'Abba, Father' in their worship has led scholars to conclude that this must in some way echo the manner in which Jesus prayed.[29] The term formed part of early Christian worship and attempted to recapitulate Jesus' experi-ence of familiarity and intimacy with God.

The implications of Jesus' mode of address – rooted in his special relationship with God whom he addressed as 'Abba' – would later form

---

[27] Edward Schillebeeckx, *Jesus: An Experiment in Christology*, trans. H. Hoskins (London: Collins, 1979), 260.

[28] John J. O'Donnell, *The Mystery of the Triune God* (New York and Mahwah, NJ: Paulist, 1989), 46.

[29] The pioneer here was Joachim Jeremias. See his *The Central Message of the New Testament* (London: SCM Press, 1965), 9–30. For a more nuanced view that eschews an antithesis between Jesus' portrayal of discipleship in terms of childlike trust and prevailing Jewish piety, see James D. G. Dunn, *Jesus Remembered: Christianity in the Making*, Vol. 1 (Grand Rapids, MI and Cambridge: Eerdmans, 2003), 548–55.

one of the sources for the Church's understanding of him as the Son of God. Thus, Jesus came to be seen as more than a prophet of the end times; rather, he spoke and acted with authority (Luke 4:32), an authority based on his unique intimacy with the Father. We see this authority in the Sermon on the Mount where Jesus' words 'but I say unto you' (Mt. 5:21f.) set his own teaching above that of the commandments and the Decalogue. In so doing, Jesus was putting himself in God's place. He was subverting traditional and often oppressive notions of God and conveying a message of liberation. The disciples too could address God as 'Abba' and enter into a qualitatively new relationship of trust with God.

In sum, Jesus evidently addressed God colloquially as 'Abba', a term regarded by his religious contemporaries as too intimate, even irreverent. But Jesus used this term precisely because of its intimacy – an indication that he 'naturally or instinctively saw himself as God's son, sustained by that intimate knowledge which only a son close to his father can know'.[30]

At the same time Jesus stands firmly in the tradition of Jewish monotheism. When asked about the greatest commandment (Mark 12:28–34), he responds by quoting the *Shema* (Deut. 6:4–5), a clear affirmation of monotheistic faith. Yet, in adding a 'second like it', namely, love of neighbour, he draws out the ethical implications of this monotheistic faith. Further in Mark 10:17–22, the confession of 'God alone' is linked with Jesus' command to 'follow me'. Faith in the one God and following Jesus go hand in hand.[31]

But what about Jesus' own identity? In John we hear him variously described as 'Son', as 'Son of God', and 'Word' – each designation indicates a very intimate and unique union between Jesus and the Father. Indeed, in the Prologue to John's Gospel, the Word (or *Logos*) is not only called God, but existed with the Father from all eternity:

In the beginning, the Word was with God, and the Word was God. (John 1:1)

This *Logos* shares the character of God without being the Father, that is, without there being two Gods. Further, the Word or *Logos* acts as the mediator or agent of creation (a creative word) as well as being light and life, that is, salvation for humankind (a revelatory word). As agent of creation, and with God at the beginning, the *Logos* performs the same function as *Sophia* or Wisdom in the Old Testament (Prov. 8:22–31). As a real personification of the *Logos*, Jesus embodies God's wisdom. The creative Word has

---

[30] James D. G. Dunn, *The Evidence for Jesus* (London: SCM Press, 1985), 48.
[31] Jouette M. Bassler, 'God (NT)', *ABD*, vol. II, 1050.

become personal in Jesus.[32] Through him God has spoken to us definitively (Heb. 1:2).

The Christological title *Logos* will become more significant in trinitarian discussion. John's Prologue points to the eternal pre-existence of the Word who was always 'with God'. The conviction that the Son was on a par with God will be clearly asserted in subsequent centuries over and against those who claimed that the *Logos*/Son was a creature. The *Logos* doctrine, too, would provide an opening for Christianity as it attempted to adapt to the Greek philosophical and cultural world.[33] This was a world familiar with the concept of *Logos* understood as the universal coherence underlying the world of change or the divine mind or plan guiding the universe. The basic trinitarian question in the patristic age was whether to conceive of the *Logos* (and the *pneuma)* as lesser, subordinate mediators of God or whether he was really God, 'consubstantial' with the Father. What is unique to Christianity is John's assertion that the Word became flesh (John 1:14). Jesus is the incarnate *Logos*, the definitive Word of God to humankind, a subject distinct from God, and yet of and 'with' God. Universal meaning occurs in a historical figure – this constitutes the 'scandalous particularity' and realism of the Christian message: the *Logos* of the Prologue is both personal and transcendent.[34]

JESUS: BEARER OF THE SPIRIT

Thus far we have looked at Jesus' relationship with his Father but have not said much about the Spirit. In the Synoptic Gospels, however, Jesus is presented as the one filled with the Spirit, evidenced at his baptism (Mark 1:9–11; Mt. 3:16; Luke 3:21), a trinitarian theophany, where the Spirit descends upon him 'like a dove' and his identity as 'beloved Son' is given divine approval. The Synoptic Gospels see Jesus as one anointed by the Spirit – the Messiah – and portray his understanding of the Spirit in

---

[32] Roger Haight, *Jesus: Symbol of God* (Maryknoll, NY: Orbis Books, 1999), 173–8. The term 'offers the possibility of identification and distinction. On the one hand, words proceed from a speaker; being a kind of extension of the speaker, and are, in a certain sense, identical with the speaker (e.g., "the Word was God"). On the other hand, a word is distinct from the one who utters it ("the Word was with/in the presence of God").' O'Collins, *The Tripersonal God*, 79.

[33] It is clear that the author of the Prologue has adapted earlier material and sources into a Christological hymn.

[34] 'A Greek could certainly think of no greater opposition than that of "Logos" to "sarx", especially if the idea of suffering and death was associated with it … It was this pointed antithesis [that] gave occasions for far-reaching misrepresentations of the nature of Christ.' Aloys Grillmeier, *Christ in Christian Tradition*, vol. 1, 2nd rev. edn, trans. J. Bowden (London: Mowbrays, 1975), 31.

traditional prophetic terms as the dynamic power of God working in and through him. There is no reference to Jesus praying *to* the Spirit or to a relationship of intimacy between Jesus and the Spirit akin to his relationship with the Father. In Luke's Gospel each aspect of Jesus' life and ministry is animated by the Spirit. Even Jesus' conception, when the Spirit comes upon Mary (Luke 1:35), indicates that there never was a time in his history when Jesus was not imbued with the Spirit. At the beginning of his public ministry Jesus applies to himself the opening words of Isa. 61: 'The Spirit of the Lord is upon me, because he has anointed me to preach the good news to the poor.' Prior to his ministry the Spirit leads Jesus into the wilderness, the isolated dwelling-place of unclean spirits. As bearer of God's Spirit, Jesus overcomes the demonic powers that dominate and enslave people (Mt. 12:22–8).[35] Jesus, the anointed one, not only bears but gives the Spirit, as the Baptist testifies: 'I have baptised you with water, but he will baptise you with the Holy Spirit' (Mark 1:8). On the cross he offers himself to the Father in the Holy Spirit (Heb. 9:14), while at the resurrection Paul says that Jesus became a life-giving Spirit (1 Cor. 15:45).

While the New Testament interprets Jesus' identity and mission in terms of the category 'Spirit', the problem is to what extent such an interpretation goes back to Jesus himself.[36] We can distinguish between what Jesus might have said about himself from what others said about him, acknowledging that the Gospels are not straightforward historical sources for information about what Jesus said or did. The relation between Jesus and the Spirit, however, is not so much determined by Jesus' words on the subject (which are sparse) than with the early Christians' experience of the risen Christ. It is from this perspective of the encounter with the risen Christ that the earthly life of Jesus is retrospectively depicted as one moved by the Spirit. The assumption is that Jesus must have had some experience of God, specifically, an experience of the power of God as Spirit in his life and ministry.[37]

Jesus was also seen by his disciples as a prophet (Mark 8:27–28; Luke 24:19), and the scholarly consensus is that the category of prophecy is a suitable one to interpret how Jesus understood himself and his mission

---

[35] 'The power that Jesus claims for his liberating actions ... is the power of God that intervenes in earthly life relations: the Holy Spirit.' Michael Welker, *God the Spirit*, trans. J. Hoffmeyer (Minneapolis: Fortress Press, 1992), 213. Dunn, *Jesus and the Spirit*, 52 puts it more succinctly: 'His power to cast out demons was the Spirit of God.'

[36] For a survey of some of the important criteria here, see John P. Meier, *A Marginal Jew: Rethinking the Historical Jesus*, vol. 1. *The Roots of the Problem and the Person* (New York: Doubleday, 1991), 167–95.

[37] Haight, *Jesus: Symbol of God*, 449.

(Luke 13:33–4).[38] The prophet is the one related to, and the bearer of, the Spirit. Luke's description of Jesus anointed by the Spirit at his baptism (Luke 3:22) and at the beginning of his ministry (Luke 4:18–19) illustrates how the prophetic category links Jesus and the Spirit.

Jesus, then, had not only a unique sense of his relationship to his God as Abba, he also knew himself as a unique bearer of the Spirit. But as we have noted, he is more than the bearer of the Spirit in the line of the traditional prophets. In *giving* the Spirit he goes beyond the prophets and acts from the side of God. Through his ministry the bestowal of the Spirit takes on a definitive quality heralding a new people and a new creation. His intimate union with the Father meant that he alone 'knew' the Father and was able to communicate this knowledge to others:

Everything has been entrusted to me by my Father; and no one knows the Son except the Father, just as no one knows the Father except the Son and those to whom the Son chooses to reveal him. (Mt. 11:27)

Knowing here means more than a mere theoretical knowledge; it entails living in communion with the Father and thus being able to make his will known to others with authority (Luke 4:32).

This theme of knowing the Father is found above all in the writings of John and his disciples. The Son knows the Father because he has his 'being from him' (John 7:29); he knows the Father and keeps his word (8:55). Jesus proclaims the Father's word so that people may know the Father and Jesus whom the Father has sent – this is eternal life (17:3). There is a reciprocal relation of loving as well as knowing between the Father and the Son. Whoever knows the Son (i.e., who has communion with him) knows the Father because the Father is in the Son and vice-versa (10:38). The truth of this knowledge is manifested in love of Jesus and in the keeping of his words (14:23–4). Moreover, Jesus prays that this love may unite his disciples and that they may be 'in us' (17:21). The relationship to God as Father is mediated through the Son. And the role of the Spirit is significant at this point. The Father sends the Spirit at the request of Jesus (14:16) and the Spirit leads the believers into this truth, into this communion of love that exists between the Father and the Son (1 John 3:24). Although the Johannine writings do not speak explicitly of a Spirit of love, it is clear that the Spirit is incipiently present in how Father and Son work together.

---

[38] See O'Donnell, *The Mystery of the Triune God*, 48–53. Jesus also interprets his death in prophetic terms in Luke 13:33–4: '... I must go on, since it would not be right for a prophet to die outside Jerusalem. Jerusalem, Jerusalem, you that kill the prophets and stone those who are sent to you! ...'

In short, the Spirit is mediated through the person of Jesus. Both John's Gospel and the Synoptic Gospels highlight that Jesus, in contrast with John the Baptist, will baptise with the Holy Spirit. Jesus, as the way to true life, is the giver of God's Spirit. He who 'comes from above' gives the Spirit without measure (John 3:31, 34). The proof of God's indwelling the believer is the gift of the Spirit (1 John 4:13). For John the cross is the climax of Jesus' revelatory activity and from his side flows living water (John 19:34) symbolic of the Spirit. While Jesus is the Truth (14:6), the Spirit is described as another Paraclete (14:16) and as the Spirit of truth (14:17), whom Jesus promises to send to his disciples. It is the risen Lord who confers the Spirit. In effect, the Paraclete replaces the physical presence of Jesus mediating his presence to the disciples. With the term 'Paraclete' (meaning helper or advocate), there is the beginning of a personal mode of speaking about the Spirit. The function of this other Paraclete is to bear witness: just as Jesus bears witness to the Father, the Paraclete bears witness to Jesus (John 15:26), calling to mind and reminding the disciples of the things of Christ, and empowering them in turn to be bearers and givers of the Spirit.

THE ACTION AND IDENTITY OF THE SPIRIT

The Old and New Testaments focus primarily on the action of the Holy Spirit; the Spirit's being or nature as a rule is referred to only indirectly. The Spirit is never addressed as a 'You' nor is the direct recipient of worship or prayer.

We have already mentioned prophecy as one sphere of activity of the Spirit. For the people of Israel the Spirit symbolised both God's graciousness and might, embodied in the chosen one anointed for God's service: prophet, king, or charismatic leader. Spirit language is also future-oriented – when God's plan and purpose for humanity would be fulfilled. And it is in the New Testament where this fulfilment finds expression and where the Spirit is poured out 'on all humanity' (Acts 2:17).

It is Paul in particular who uses the term 'spirit of God' as a way of expressing God's outgoing activity both to human beings and to the world. At times Paul does not clearly distinguish the Spirit from Christ. In Rom. 8:9–11, for example, he uses the terms 'Spirit of God', 'the Spirit of Christ', 'Christ', and 'the Spirit of him who raised Jesus from the dead' interchangeably when describing how God dwells in the Christian. Sometimes he speaks of a sending of the 'Spirit of the Son' (Gal. 4:6), or of the 'Spirit of Jesus Christ' (Phil. 1:19), while elsewhere he will even say, 'The Lord is the Spirit' (2 Cor. 3:17). Paul is likely asserting a functional identity between Christ and the Spirit in that the risen Christ is present wherever the Spirit acts. He does not attempt a systematic under-standing of the Spirit or the Spirit's relationship to Christ stressing instead the Spirit as an active participant in building relationships among believers.[39]

For Paul the Spirit works not only externally but also internally, not only in striking or extraordinary phenomena but in ordinary Christian life. He links the action of the Spirit with the building up of community and with service to the Church. This is the Spirit of creativity at work for the benefit of all. The various gifts of the Spirit are therefore meant for mutual service:

There are many different gifts, but it is always the same Spirit; there are many different ways of serving, but it is always the same Lord. There are many different forms of activity, but in everybody it is the same God who is at work in them all. (1 Cor. 12:4–6)

Here Paul links his teaching on the charisms to the order Spirit, Lord, and God. The greatest of these gifts is love (1 Cor. 13:13). It is significant that Paul (1 Cor. 12:28) includes the ministry of office or 'apostleship' among the gifts and thus does not provide any basis for the later contrast between 'charismatic' and 'institutional' roles in the Church.

If possession of the Spirit is the hallmark of the Christian, there cannot be two classes of Christian: those who have the Spirit and those who do not.[40] Every Christian, in Paul's view, begins in the Spirit (Gal. 3:3), but some, while having the Spirit, live according to their natural inclinations (1 Cor. 3:1). Paul mentions the jealousy and rivalry among the community at Corinth as evidence of this. On the other hand, there are those who not only have the Spirit, but are guided and led by this Spirit (Gal. 5:16–25). The believer is pulled in two directions and cannot always do what he or she wants.[41] The power of the Spirit is contrasted with the power of the 'flesh'. For Paul, the spirit is that aspect of human nature that makes one open to God's Spirit, whereas 'flesh' represents everything that opposes this influ-ence. The opposition is not between the incorporeal and the corporeal, but between two ways of living. The biblical notion of spirit, therefore, ought not to be placed in opposition to the material or corporeal. It has to do not with the denial of the body, but its transformation.[42]

---

[39] Congar, *I Believe in the Holy Spirit*, vol. 1, 29–43.

[40] Kilian McDonnell, OSB, 'Theological Presuppositions in our Preaching about the Spirit', *Theological Studies* 59 (1998): 228.

[41] Elsewhere in Rom. 7:7–25, Paul describes this ongoing tension in the life of the believer in terms of the flesh, law, and sin. This tension or warfare does not end when the Spirit comes but is an ongoing facet of the believer's experience. See James D. G. Dunn, *Jesus and the Spirit* (London: SCM Press, 1975), 315.

[42] Robert Imbelli, 'Holy Spirit', in Joseph A. Komonchak, Mary Collins, and Dermot A. Lane, eds., *The New Dictionary of Theology* (Dublin: Gill and Macmillan, 1987), 476.

Paul, then, is primarily interested in the functional role played by the Spirit in human salvation. If Christ opened up to human beings the possibility of a new life, to be lived in him and for God, the process of sharing God's own life (what Athanasius and others would later call the 'divinisation' of the creature) is brought about by the Spirit. In his relationship with us the risen Lord is, as it were, represented or mediated by the Spirit, and it is by the Spirit's indwelling that Father and Son are present in the life of the believer. The Spirit is an 'energiser', a Spirit of 'convincing power' (1 Cor. 2:4) and the source of Christian love, hope, and faith.[43] It frees human beings from being 'under the law' (Gal. 5:18), from 'the cravings of the flesh' (Gal 5:16), and from immoral conduct (Gal. 5:19–24). It is the Spirit that assists Christians in prayer 'pleading along with us with inexpressible yearnings' (Rom. 8:26) and makes them aware of their relation to the Father. Because of the Spirit we possess the freedom of the children of God. The free person, for Paul, is not the one who does whatever he or she wants, but 'rather one who is free from himself and thus able to be there for God and for others'.[44] True Christian freedom is manifested in selflessness and love. This is the context for the fruits of the Spirit: love, joy, peace, patience, kindness, goodness, faithfulness, gentleness, and self-control (Gal. 5:22f.).

In sum, the Spirit is fundamentally a personal and experiential concept for Paul. It enables believers to know, recognise and experience Christ and makes faith and worship existentially real.[45] The Spirit is God's love active in us (Rom. 5:5). It is not that Paul depicts Christianity as a religion of pure inwardness or as a movement from one peak experience (of the Spirit) to the next. He was more than aware that 'Christians do not live on the heights, but mostly in the valleys and often in the desert'.[46] The silence and apparent absence of God (e.g., Mt. 26:36–46) also needs to be treated with theological seriousness. Theological reflection on the Spirit has often been restricted to the 'spiritual' life, on the one hand, or to office-holders in the Church, on the other. Although the Spirit is unpredictable, blows where it wills, and has a certain self-effacing quality, it is nonetheless more than a vague graciousness. Paul's conviction was that Christian life in the Spirit entails some form of personal encounter between the Spirit of Christ and the person. The Spirit indwells the Christian and the community making

---

[43] For the following, see Joseph Fitzmyer, 'Pauline Theology', *The New Jerome Biblical Commentary* 82: 61–5.
[44] Kasper, *The God of Jesus Christ*, 206.   [45] Dunn, *Jesus and the Spirit*, 201.
[46] McDonnell, 'Theological Presuppositions', 233.

them temples of God and holy (1 Cor. 3:16). God is present in the Spirit, as he is present in the Son, as someone who gives, since in the Spirit God gives God's self (1 Thess. 4:8).

If the redemption wrought by Christ provides the content or the 'what' of the Gospel, then the Spirit is the 'how'.[47] In the Spirit the *Christus incarnatus* becomes the *Christus praesens*. The Spirit actualises or makes real in the believer the objective redemption won by Christ. In short, the Spirit enables people to experience God. For Paul, the Spirit is not an object over and against us but breathes in us and through us. The Spirit is the enabler of faith or, changing metaphors, the light which enables the believer to see Christ.[48]

CONCLUSION: TRIADIC FORMULAE

Our brief scriptural survey has indicated that we do not find a fully worked out doctrine of the Trinity in Scripture. It would take centuries before the Christian community would develop and clarify its understanding of God as triune. After all, Christians right from the beginning were more monotheistic in orientation. Although the preaching of the early Church tended to be exclusively Christological, it carried over the doctrine of the 'one God', the Father and Creator of all things, from its Jewish predecessors and would use it to contrast Christianity with the polytheism of surrounding pagan religions.[49] What we find in Scripture are the seeds or elements of future trinitarian doctrine. There is an unsystematic, incipient, or 'elemental trinitarianism'[50] in the biblical witness that would provide the matrix and foundation for a later more explicitly trinitarian faith. Despite the paucity of

---

[47] Boris Bobrinskoy speaks of 'a *proper economy of the Son*, and a *proper economy of the Spirit*, provided one does not contrast them, and view them in some type of succession that would make them, as it were external the one to the other'. Boris Bobrinskoy, *The Mystery of the Trinity: Trinitarian Experience and Vision in the Biblical and Patristic Tradition*, trans. A. Gythiel (Crestwood, NY: St Vladimir's Seminary Press, 1999), 72. Nor is it the case that the Spirit acts independently as if the Father and Son had disappeared. The Johannine Jesus, for example, promises that with the giving of the Spirit to the disciples, the Father and Jesus will also 'make a home' with them (John 14:16–24).

[48] There is a tension running through the Acts of the Apostles and the New Testament Epistles between 'instrumentalising' the Spirit, that is, of seeing the Spirit more in terms of function and action, and speaking of the Spirit in more personal terms, that is, as a distinct *hypostasis*. It was only later at the Council of Constantinople (AD 381) that the Spirit would be explicitly declared divine: 'the Lord and Giver of Life ... who with the Father and the Son is together worshipped and glorified'.

[49] J. N. D. Kelly, *Early Christian Creeds*, 3rd edn (New York: Longman, 1972), 12.

[50] William J. Hill, *The Three-Personed God: The Trinity as a Mystery of Salvation* (Washington, DC: Catholic University of America Press, 1988), 28.

specific trinitarian references in the New Testament, there was an implicit trinitarian strain even in the earliest stages of Christianity.

Examples of such seeds include what have been described as 'triadic formulae' in the New Testament. The most striking is the threefold Matthean baptismal formula to baptise 'in the name of the Father and of the Son and of the Holy Spirit' (Mt. 28:19). This formula likely reflects the baptismal practice of the Matthean Church in contrast to an earlier tradition of baptising 'in the name of Jesus Christ' (Acts 2:38). However, the formula simply points to an equality and distinction between the divine Persons without clarifying their relationships.

Paul also has triadic formulations where he lines up God (or the Father), Christ (or the Son), and the Spirit expressing God's threefold revelation to humanity and paving the way for the development of the doctrine. One such is his closing triadic blessing to the Corinthians: 'The grace of our Lord Jesus Christ, the love of God, and the fellowship of the Holy Spirit be with you all' (2 Cor. 13:13). This is probably a formula Paul took over and expanded from his briefer benedictions (e.g., 1 Cor. 16:23) and continues to be used by Christians in the liturgy. This closing blessing summarises the message of salvation by highlighting the grace, love, and fellowship that believers share with God and with one another. Here, as elsewhere, Paul is primarily interested in the soteriological dimension, driven by the Church's and his own experience of salvation. Similarly, Paul's reference to a possible double sending of the 'Son' and the 'Spirit of his Son' (Gal. 4:4–6) is formulated in terms of God's 'economy' or plan of salvation. Finally, the call to unity in Eph. 4:3–6 links 'one Body, one Spirit' with 'one Lord, one faith' and culminates in the monotheistic 'one God and Father of all, over all, through all and within all'.

In sum, the New Testament does not develop a *theology* of the Trinity. The emphasis is on divine activity, and there is little exploration of the triune nature of God. The early Christians were primarily concerned with Christ's message of salvation, not abstract speculation. Their claim was that through the life, death, and resurrection of the Lord, and through his sending of the Spirit, Christians are drawn into and included in the life of God. The accent is on the actions of God in the world, that is, on the economic Trinity. As a contemporary commentator puts it, 'God's revealing and saving activity is the work of the whole Trinity'.[51]

---

[51] Thomas F. Torrance, *The Christian Doctrine of God: One Being Three Persons* (Edinburgh and New York: T&T Clark, 1996), 64.

At the same time there is an awareness, particularly in the Fourth Gospel, of Jesus' oneness with, and simultaneous distinctness from, his Father: 'The Father and I are one' (John 10:30) and 'anyone who has seen me has seen the Father' (John 14:9). The Fourth Gospel also distinguishes the Spirit from the Father and the Son with the word 'Paraclete' (John 14:16). It acknowledged that the Spirit 'proceeds from the Father' (John 15:26) but the question whether the Spirit is a separate *hypostasis* would only arise later. In short, the terms of the relationship between Father and Son and between Father and Son and Holy Spirit at this stage are not yet fully clarified. Nor did Paul, for his part, abandon his monotheistic roots in the Jewish faith – 'there is no God other than the One' (1 Cor. 8:4) – and there is a certain priority or ultimacy accorded to the Father (1 Cor. 14:27–8) as source and goal of all – yet he saw this oneness unfolding in God's economy through the Son and in the Spirit. The first doctrinal controversy in the post-biblical period would be whether Jesus was truly divine. At issue was the salvation of humankind: to paraphrase Paul, if Christ has not been raised and so is not truly divine, he is a creature like us and has no unique status before God. We are still in our sins (1 Cor. 15:16–17) since only God can save.

SUGGESTED READINGS

Bobrinskoy, Boris, *The Mystery of the Trinity: Trinitarian Experience and Vision in the Biblical and Patristic Tradition*, trans. A. Gythiel (Crestwood, NY: St Vladimir's Seminary Press, 1999).

Brueggemann, Walter, *Theology of the Old Testament: Testimony, Dispute, Advocacy* (Minneapolis: Fortress Press, 1997).

Congar, Yves, *I Believe in the Holy Spirit*, vol. 1. *The Experience of the Spirit* (London: Geoffrey Chapman, 1983).

O'Collins, Gerald, *The Tripersonal God: Understanding and Interpreting the Trinity* (London: Geoffrey Chapman, 1999).

Torrance, Thomas F., *The Christian Doctrine of God: One Being Three Persons* (Edinburgh and New York: T&T Clark, 1996).

Wainwright, Arthur, *The Trinity in the New Testament* (London: SPCK, 1962).

CHAPTER 3

The doctrine of the Trinity: its emergence and development in the life of the Christian community

Towards the end of the previous chapter we noted that there is an 'elemental trinitarianism' in the New Testament. In this chapter we shall see how the understanding of God as triune developed as Christianity moved from its initial Jewish surroundings into a wider Greco-Roman culture. Throughout this journey it will be apparent that it was the religious convictions and experience of Jesus and that of the early Christian community that provided the starting point and foundation for trinitarian doctrine. Some aspects of these 'original' experiences of Jesus, of his Jewish antecedents, and of his disciples have been alluded to already. These include the faith of Israel in the one God who has created all, and who is continually active in history in a wise and powerful way. Such convictions also comprise the experience of the early Christian communities at Easter, where Jesus was fully acknowledged as the Son of God and Saviour of the world. The New Testament writings bear witness to the conviction that Jesus Christ, the Saviour sent from God, is himself true God, although not identical with the Father, and is present to his people only in the Holy Spirit.[1]

SCRIPTURE, DOCTRINE, AND WORSHIP

Dogmatic manuals and treatises on the Trinity in the nineteenth and in the early part of the twentieth century adopted a proof-text approach to certain scriptural texts alluding to the Trinity.[2] Today there is a greater appreciation

---

[1] Basil Studer, *Trinity and Incarnation: The Faith of the Early Church*, trans. M. Westerhoff, ed. A. Louth (Collegeville, MN: The Liturgical Press, 1993), 5.

[2] An example of this is the assumption that the reference in Isa. 6:3 ('Holy, Holy, Holy, the Lord God of Hosts, all the earth is full of his glory') is an allusion to the mystery of the Blessed Trinity. See Joseph Pohle, *The Divine Trinity*, adapted by Arthur Preuss, 6th rev. edn (St Louis: Herder, 1911), 11.

of the *liturgical* nature of many scriptural texts used to support later trinitarian doctrine. Although the New Testament does not contain collections of hymns akin to the book of Psalms in the Old Testament, it does contain canticles and hymns incorporated into Gospels, letters and apocalyptic visions. There are the canticles of Luke, including the Magnificat (Luke 1:46–55) and the Benedictus (1:67–78), while explicitly Christological hymns are found in Paul's letter to the Philippians (2:6–11) and in the letter to the Colossians (1:15–20). Some hymns are addressed to Christ, while others are addressed to God (e.g., Eph. 1:3–14).[3]

One can probably say that people are less concerned about abstract doctrinal formulations unless these directly impact on the celebration and practice of their faith. But this is, in fact, what happened in the case of trinitarian doctrine. The liturgy soon became a forum where competing doctrinal views would find expression. Many of the early theologians were bishops, not merely participants but leaders in the liturgical life of the Church.[4] It is not surprising, therefore, that the Church's practices of worship would have a direct bearing upon their doctrinal beliefs. Many of the phrases that would later develop into doctrinal or creedal statements on the Trinity derive from liturgical settings.

An example of such a liturgical context is the Christological passage from Paul's letter to the Philippians (2:6–11). It is almost certainly an ancient hymn to Christ:

> Who, being in the form of God,
> did not count equality with God something to be grasped.
> But he emptied himself, taking the form of a slave,
> becoming as human beings are;
> and being in every way like a human being, he was humbler yet,
> even to accepting death, death on a cross.
> And for this God raised him high,
> and gave him the name which is above all other names;
> so that all beings in the heavens, on earth and in the underworld,
> should bend the knee at the name of Jesus
> and that every tongue should acknowledge Jesus Christ as Lord,
> to the glory of God the Father.

---

[3] It is not always easy to distinguish hymns from confessional formulae (e.g., 1 Cor. 15:3–8) or from doxologies (e.g., 1 Tim. 6:15–16). Hymns in the New Testament are normally only detectable by scholarly investigation given that the introduction or incorporation of a hymn into a letter is rarely announced. See also Raymond E. Brown, *An Introduction to the New Testament*, The Anchor Bible Reference Library (New York: Doubleday, 1997), 489–93.

[4] See Maurice Wiles, *The Making of Christian Doctrine* (Philadelphia: Westminster Press, 1978), 62–93.

This is a description of Christ both as a servant to be imitated and as one who enjoyed divine status – being in the form (Gk *morphē*) of God. The text is sometimes designated 'binitarian' because only God (the Father) and Jesus Christ are mentioned. Though the early Church was very much aware of the Holy Spirit, the Spirit would be the last of the three to be explicitly declared divine (by the Council of Constantinople in 381). In the opening greetings of other Pauline and Deutero-Pauline letters, God is called 'Father of our Lord Jesus Christ', indicating that praise is to be rendered to God through Christ (e.g., Eph. 5:20: Give thanks 'in the name of our Lord Jesus Christ to God the Father'). There are also 'triadic' texts, where the Father, Christ, and the Spirit appear alongside each other, for example, the baptismal command in Matthew (28:19). The Matthean Church seems to have been familiar with this baptismal formula, which replaced an earlier custom of baptising solely in the name of Jesus (Acts 2:38; 8:16; etc.). This is not a fully worked out trinitarian *doctrine*; rather, the phrase reflects the Matthean community's conviction that the salvation brought to them by Jesus in obedience to his Father could be experienced through the power of the Spirit. And this was specifically linked to incorporation into the community at baptism.[5] We have already referred to Paul's closing blessing to the Corinthians (2 Cor. 13:13). Such formulae, deriving from baptismal and liturgical contexts, indicate the important influence of the practice of worship on the early stages of thinking about God as triune. Baptismal confession, therefore, influenced the pattern of Christian prayer: Christians dared to address God as Father guided by the example of Jesus' prayer thus participating in the community between them. They prayed *to* the Father, *with* the Son, *in* the Spirit.

The doctrine of the Trinity, then, did not develop as a result of an abstract exercise cut off from daily living, but in connection with liturgical practices, which came to be recognised as 'depositories of the Church's living doctrinal inheritance'.[6] But how did the early Christians pray? They did not see themselves as a new religion, but derived their prayer from Jewish practice. This prayer was adapted to their belief that Christ is the mediator of God's work and will (*GfU*, 111–42). There was a popular practice of brief, pithy prayers in the form of a direct address to Christ, which remained the custom of the second and third centuries. The New Testament shows the early martyrs, like Stephen, calling directly upon

[5] See Jane Schaberg, *The Father, the Son, and the Holy Spirit: The Triadic Phrase in Matthew 28:19b*, Scholars Dissertation Series 61 (California: Scholars Press, 1982), 1–29.

[6] J. N. D. Kelly, *Early Christian Doctrines*, 5th edn (London: Adam & Charles Black, 1977), 44.

Jesus, while there is evidence in popular piety of Christians worshipping the Son and singing hymns to Christ. In his in-depth study of devotion to Jesus in earliest Christianity, Larry Hurtado maintains that:

this intense devotion to Jesus, which includes reverencing him as divine, was offered and articulated characteristically within a firm stance of exclusivist monotheism ... At an astonishingly early point, in at least some Christian groups, there is a clear and programmatic inclusion of Jesus in their devotional life, both in honorific *claims* and in devotional *practices*.[7]

But did Christians then worship two divinities? Those who insisted on upholding the single unique rule of God, as we noted in the first chapter, were called Monarchians. Monarchianism, in its various forms, tried to preserve the oneness or 'monarchy' of God. It claimed that expressions such as Father, Son, and Holy Spirit within history are simply *modes* of God's appearing. The problem with this emphasis on God's oneness, however, is that it failed to elucidate the real *distinctions* between the Father, Son, and Holy Spirit and so eliminated any plurality within the Godhead. It would not be long before the Arian controversy erupted in the fourth century when a choice had to be made about Christ's divinity. The debates varied from an emphasis on the *sameness* of the Father and Son to an emphasis on the *diversity* between the two.[8] Can we speak of Father and Son as both 'true God' or can we speak of degrees of divinity? Was Christ a creature, albeit the primary creature, whom God has made at the first beginning of creation, *or* was he the *consubstantial* Son of the Father, very God of very God? That the Council of Nicea (325) would eventually opt for the latter position indicates how the popular practice of worshipping the Son would influence the developing theology of the Church.

A key figure in this early development was Origen. Born in Alexandria about 185, he was a prolific writer on a wide range of topics – scripture, doctrine, and spirituality. Origen distinguished between prayers and hymns directed to God (which he considered absolute or primary) and those to Christ (which he considered secondary or relative). He had no problem on a personal level and at the level of popular piety with prayers addressed to the Son, but he felt that some Christians had, unfortunately, regarded praying to the Son as the normative pattern of prayer. The difficulty here is trying to provide a theology for the language of devotion. It was possible to identify

---

[7] Larry W. Hurtado, *Lord Jesus Christ: Devotion to Jesus in Earliest Christianity* (Grand Rapids, MI and Cambridge: Eerdmans, 2003), 3, 4.

[8] Lewis Ayres, *Nicea and its Legacy: An Approach to Fourth-Century Trinitarian Theology* (Oxford: Oxford University Press, 2004), 41.

Jesus as God while kneeling to pray, but it was another step to translate this practice into the official teaching of the Church.[9]

Yet Origen's claim that the popular piety of his day should not be regarded as doctrinally normative did not win out. In the long run 'the popular piety of devotion to the person of Jesus was not content to be taken with anything less than full theological seriousness'.[10] Christ was becoming a central figure in the Church's worship: converts were baptised 'in the name of the Lord Jesus Christ' (Acts 2:38) and they assembled 'in his name' where he was 'there among them' (Mt. 18:20). Not only did believers confess Jesus as Lord at baptism and invoke his name in the Christian assembly, they also worshipped him as Lord in anticipation of the day when every knee would bow – reflected in the hymn of Phil. 2:5–11.[11] Thomas' acknowledgement of Jesus as 'My Lord and my God' (John 20:28) reflects the New Testament's linking of the resurrection and the lordship of Christ. The death of Jesus was followed by God's exaltation of him as Lord (Acts 2:36). This practice of invoking the name of Jesus in worship indicates that he was the recipient of a doxology appropriate to God, and would influence the later doctrinal definition of the precise relationship of the human and divine natures of Christ.

The main issue, then, facing the Church in the post-biblical period – indeed right up to the Council of Nicea (325) – concerned the relationship of the Son to God the Father. The question was whether the Son was *equally* to be adored with the Father. Arius (*c*.250–*c*.336), a priest of Alexandria, and his followers denied this. For them, only the Father is God – the Son, despite his exalted status, is a creature like us and does not possess the essence of the divinity. The error of this doctrine, however, is that it turned Christians into creature-worshippers. This error of 'subordinationism' (in contrast to 'monarchianism'), while it distinguishes a threefoldness in God, assigns an inferior status to the Son and places the Holy Spirit subordinate to both.[12] For Arius, the Son is subordinate to the Father and not 'true God of true God', as the Council of Nicea would maintain. In condemning the position of Arius, the Council was affirming the full divinity of the Son. This decision would soon be accompanied by the proliferation of prayers

---

[9] Jaroslav Pelikan, *The Christian Tradition: A History of the Development of Doctrine 1: The Emergence of the Catholic Tradition (100–600)* (Chicago and London: University of Chicago Press, 1971), 178.

[10] Wiles, *The Making of Christian Doctrine*, 75.

[11] Geoffrey Wainwright, *Doxology: The Praise of God in Worship, Doctrine and Life* (London: Epworth Press, 1980), 46–9.

[12] The term 'subordinationism' is a problematic one. Many theologians prior to Nicea, including Origen, attempted to emphasise a continuity or closeness between Father and Son, while also asserting that Father, Son, and Spirit each have a distinct identity and existence.

addressed directly to the Son in the public liturgy of the Church. There was a shift in emphasis from the human Christ as mediator and High Priest in his humanity (Heb. 4:14–16) to the Son as the second Person of the Trinity and therefore himself a recipient of worship. Before Nicea we have the model where:

> Christ 'reaches up into heaven' and mediates our worship *to God*. In the post-Nicene anti-Arian era, Christ 'reaches down from heaven' and mediates God's blessings *to us*. Christ's human mediation has become divine intervention. (*GfU*, 127)[13]

We have noted how the early Christians confessed Jesus as Lord in short 'creed-like slogans' such as 'Jesus is Lord' (1 Cor. 12:3; Rom. 10:9) or 'Jesus is the Son of God' (1 John 4:15).[14] His divine significance is expressed in terms of his relationship to the one God. Such phrases were often part of a baptismal confession of faith and served to encapsulate core teaching in summary form. The baptismal command at the end of Matthew's Gospel (Mt. 28:19) reflects the liturgical practice of his community, who invoked the name and presence of God (Father, Son, and Spirit) at baptism. Knowing the *name* of the God invoked served as a guarantee that the being that lies behind the name would be present.[15] The candidate would have been asked a triple set of questions: 'Do you believe in God the Father the Almighty . . . ? Do you believe in Jesus Christ . . . ? Do you believe in the Holy Spirit . . . ?' An affirmative response to this questioning was followed by a triple immersion in water. The newly baptised was convinced that the new life that he or she was undertaking was accompanied by the blessing and protection of Father, Son, and Spirit.[16]

Despite the gradual development of a trinitarian consciousness in the Christian communities of the second century, the general pattern of prayer, however, was to God *through* Christ. Christ as high priest intercedes for us on our behalf and thus mediates our worship to God (the Father). In general, we can discern, not only in the New Testament, but also in the earliest liturgical texts, examples both of prayer *to* Christ and prayer *through*

---

[13] In the prayer of the Church, therefore, there is a shift from praise rendered to God through Christ to glorifying the Trinity. In reaction to Arianism, some Eastern Christians began in the fourth century to pray to the Father *and* the Son *and* the Holy Spirit. The form of *Gloria* used was a way of expressing a particular theological allegiance.

[14] J. N. D. Kelly, *Early Christian Creeds*, 3rd edn (New York: Longman, 1972), 13.

[15] This invoking of God is called *epiclesis*. Studer, *Trinity and Incarnation*, 26.

[16] Although baptism was the original setting of early Christian creeds, there are no creeds in the strict sense of the term in the New Testament except slogans such as 'Jesus is Lord'. Only gradually did creeds evolve into uniform and fixed summaries of doctrine designed to exclude heretical interpretations. See Kelly, *Early Christian Creeds*, 6–23.

Christ – Christ as receiver of prayer and Christ as mediator of prayer.[17] Christian worship, then, is directed to God the Father. It does not simply pass 'through' Christ; rather, Christ actively takes up our imperfect worship and mediates this to the Father, while he also acts as the mediator of divine blessings to humanity. There are 'two key components' here: '(1) a strong affirmation of exclusivist monotheism in belief and practice, along with (2) an inclusion of Christ along with God as rightful recipient of cultic devotion'.[18]

ONENESS AND DISTINCTION IN GOD

An important backdrop to this discussion is the notion of monotheism, that is, the doctrine of the 'one God', the Father and Creator of all things. The Christian conception of God, inherited from the Old Testament, was that there is one Lord, who is the living God, the Holy One, a hidden and active presence in the history of the chosen people. Alongside this affirmation is the call to exclusive devotion to Yahweh, since 'Yahweh is our God, Yahweh alone' (Deut. 6:4) – the opening words of the *Shema*, the principal Jewish confession of faith. In the New Testament it is evident that the same one God of the Old Testament is the Father of the Lord Jesus Christ. The Father is *the* God, God with the definite article (Gk *ho theos*), the one God, as Christ is the one Lord. Monotheism was a fundamental premise of the Church's faith from the very beginning and was defended over and against the gods of the Roman Empire. For example, Paul, while mentioning that he turns to Christ as *Kyrios* in private prayer, 'I thank Christ Jesus our Lord, who has given me strength. By calling me into his service he has judged me trustworthy' (1 Tim. 1:12), sees this as the exception rather than the rule. Communal prayer, on the other hand, is addressed to *God*, the Father, as the hymn of Philippians (2:9–11) concludes: 'that every tongue should acknowledge Jesus Christ as Lord, *to the glory of the Father*'. There is a measure of subordinationism here, insofar as the lordship of Christ is penultimate to the final kingdom when God will be all in all (1 Cor. 15:24–8).

---

[17] For example, in the liturgical treatise of St Hippolytus of Rome (*c.*170–*c.*236), the so-called *Apostolic Tradition*, the liturgical prayers are directed to God (though sometimes concluding with a reference to God in his three persons). Christ, however, always stands as mediator of the prayer: 'That we may praise and glorify thee through thy child Jesus Christ, *through whom glory and honour is unto thee, the Father and the Son with the Holy Spirit*, in thy holy Church, now and in eternity.' See Joseph Jungmann, *The Place of Christ in Liturgical Prayer*, 2nd rev. edn, trans. A. Peeler (London: Chapman, 1965), 5–9.

[18] Hurtado, *Lord Jesus Christ*, 50.

Thus Paul could confess: 'For us there is one God the Father, from whom all things come and for whom we exist, and one Lord Jesus Christ, through whom all things come, and through whom we exist' (1 Cor. 8:6). For Paul, the one God is Lord of the cosmic universe as its Creator, and Lord of history as its Ruler. Yet, at the same time, and as we have seen, Paul places Jesus and the Spirit alongside the Father, that is, his monotheism has Christological and pneumatological dimensions.

It is God as creator of all things who is considered to be saviour in the strict sense. We see this emphasis on the oneness of God in the Apostolic Fathers of the first century (e.g., Clement of Rome, d. 100). In urging the Christians in Corinth to end their quarrels and internal divisions, Clement declared: 'Do we not have one God and one Christ and one Spirit of Christ poured out upon us?'[19] This is also the case with St Justin Martyr, an outstanding apologist of the Christian faith (*c.*100–*c.*165), who maintained that worshipping Christ did not contradict monotheism:

> We revere and worship Him and the Son who came forth from Him and taught us these things ... and the prophetic Spirit, and we pay homage to them in reason and truth.[20]

Once again the emerging trinitarian faith is set in a liturgical context of worship and thanksgiving. Nevertheless, Justin gave primacy to the Father, whom he claimed was unbegotten, that is, without origin and assigned a certain intermediary status or role to the Son, who is the agent of creation, through whom all things were made.[21] He and his disciples further viewed the Son as the expression of the Father's thought or mind, something that had been anticipated in the imagery of the divine *Logos* or Word in the Fourth Gospel.

While there is undoubtedly a certain subordinationism evident in Justin – Jesus, though Son of the living God, is 'in the second place', while the 'prophetic Spirit' is 'in the third',[22] – the problem for early Christians was how to reconcile their monotheistic faith with their experience of Jesus, who addressed Yahweh as *Abba*, and who with the Father imparted the divine Spirit. Their experience of Jesus led to the acknowledgement of a certain threefoldness within the deity:

---

[19] *The Letter of St Clement of Rome to the Corinthians* 46 in *The Fathers of the Church 1: The Apostolic Fathers*, trans. F. X. Glimm, SJ (Washington, DC: Catholic University of America Press, 1969), 45.

[20] Justin Martyr, *The First Apology* 6, in *The Fathers of the Church 6: Writings of St. Justin Martyr*, trans. T. Falls (Washington D.C.: Catholic University of America Press, 1977), 39.

[21] Justin Martyr, *The Second Apology* 6.

[22] Justin Martyr, *The First Apology* 13. Justin is unclear how the Spirit is to be distinguished from the Father or even from the Son (or *Logos*).

From the outset, Christian thinkers had to walk a fine line between lapsing into tritheism or retreating to rigid monotheism when they sought to explicate their new experience of God made possible by Jesus and his Spirit.[23]

A similar wish to preserve the oneness of God is found in St Irenaeus of Lyons (*c.*130–*c.*200), one of the more prominent Christian thinkers of the second century. Irenaeus' rule of faith starts with belief in the one God, maker of heaven and earth and everything in them. Christians, he says, must believe 'that there is one God, who created and completed all things and made everything exist out of the non-existent, he who contains all and alone is contained by none'.[24] Reacting to the Gnostics and their multi-plication of gods, Irenaeus held to the traditional doctrine that there is one sole God, the Creator and Lord of all, who is Father, Son, and Spirit. He often speaks of the Son and Spirit as the two 'hands' of God, 'the Word and the Wisdom, the Son and the Spirit, by whom and in whom … God made all things'.[25] The distinctiveness of the three appears in the 'economy', that is, in the saving plan or dispensation of God. Irenaeus was not primarily focussing on the inner life of God but on the relationship of God to the world. Although not averse to some speculation on the inner divine life, his trinitarian theology is still rather undeveloped.

In their desire to safeguard the oneness and unity of God, theologians soon came up against those who wanted to remove any kind of distinctions within God. Extreme monotheists held that distinctions between Father, Son, and Holy Spirit are merely transient manifestations of the one God and say nothing about God's inner life. This kind of atrinitarianism was exemplified by Sabellius, a third-century Roman theologian, who main-tained that God, though remaining one, appears to humankind under different aspects. Such a view of God as the sole ruling power was popular among ordinary believers. It was the African Church Father Tertullian (*c.*160–*c.*225) who rescued a specifically trinitarian notion of God by main-taining that the distinctions in God are not simply restricted to God's work *ad extra*; rather, God is three in Godself. Commenting on his opponent, Praxeas, who held that it was God the Father, and not a distinct Son, who was born, suffered, and died, Tertullian says that he has 'driven away the

[23] Gerald O'Collins, *The Tripersonal God: Understanding and Interpreting the Trinity* (London: Geoffrey Chapman, 1999), 86.
[24] Irenaeus, *Against Heresies* Bk IV. 20.2, in A. Roberts and J. Donaldson, eds., *The Writings of Irenaeus*, trans. A. Roberts and W. H. Rambaut, Ante-Nicene Christian Library 5 (Edinburgh: T&T Clark, 1910), 439–40 (translation adapted).
[25] Irenaeus, *Against Heresies* Bk IV. 20.1. Like the other Apologists, Irenaeus sees the *Logos* or Word as God's immanent rationality expressed in the economy of creation.

Paraclete (Holy Spirit) and crucified the Father'.[26] For Tertullian, the 'monarchy' of God is arranged or distributed between the Son and the Spirit. In short, Tertullian wants to show that the plurality manifested in the economy (Father, Son, and Holy Spirit) reaches back into the immanent life of God.

Tertullian is significant because he tried to find some way of relating unity and plurality within the Trinity. He devised terms that would become common parlance in trinitarian debate: God is one substance (*substantia*) in three persons (*personae*). Substance, though an elusive term, refers to what is the common fundamental reality shared by, and uniting, the three. Augustine would later talk of a unity of essence and a trinity of persons. The term 'person' designates the distinctive element in the inner life of God. Tertullian put paradox, contrast and tension to good use. *Persona*, for example, is contrasted to, and the concrete manifestation of, the more abstract term *substantia*, which means to 'stand under' – grounding the threeness.[27] He also employed comparisons and metaphors as a way of expressing unity in diversity, distinction without separation. The relation between Father and Son is similar to that between thought and speech: the Father 'utters' the Son, who derives from the Father. An example of Tertullian's use of visual metaphors is the image of the Trinity as a plant, with the Father as the root, the Son as the shoot that derives from the Father and breaks forth into the world, and the Spirit as the fruit of the plant.[28]

Tertullian effectively inaugurated a new way of believing in the one God: by the Son and the Spirit. In other words:

The three are the object of the same faith and adoration which is directed to one, unique divinity. This Godhead is that of the father, revealed in and by the others, in so far as they are united with their first principle.[29]

Tertullian, sometimes considered the Father of Latin theology, is one of the earliest trinitarian theologians who had to come to terms with a perennial problem in both philosophy and theology, namely, the relation between the one and the many, between unity and diversity, distinction and separation. Anxious to preserve the 'monarchy' of the Father as the

---

[26] Tertullian, *Against Praxeas* 1. According to Tertullian, Praxeas only preserved the unity of God by maintaining that the Father, Son, and Holy Spirit were in fact one and the same.

[27] William J. Hill, *The Three-Personed God: The Trinity as a Mystery of Salvation* (Washington, D.C.: Catholic University of America Press, 1988), 35.

[28] The other material analogies used by Tertullian are: the sun, its ray, and the point of focus of a ray; a spring or fountain, river, and stream.

[29] Eric Osborn, *Tertullian, First Theologian of the West* (Cambridge: Cambridge University Press, 1997), 138.

sole source of the divine being, he did not see this as implying a division of the divine unity. In the Trinity the unity is not destroyed but distributed. Tertullian held these contrasting truths through a new form of theological discourse and vocabulary that was at once imaginative, paradoxical, and philosophical.[30]

THE CHALLENGE OF ARIUS AND THE RESPONSE OF NICEA

Tertullian attempted to overcome a modalist conception of God that stressed the 'monarchy' of the Godhead and the identity of the Son with the Father. He did this by introducing distinctions and the notion of relatedness into the very being of God (immanent Trinity). However, Tertullian, like some of his predecessors (e.g., Justin), is open to charges of subordinationism. By employing terms like 'derivation' and 'portion' with regard to the Son, he gives the impression that the Son (and the Spirit) do not share in the totality of the divine substance.[31] Further conceptual clarification was needed and it came not just in response to Tertullian, but also to the Alexandrian presbyter, Arius.

Arius offered a one-sided solution to the issues of Christ's oneness with, and distinction from, the one eternal God. Origen and Tertullian had used the term *Logos* as a technical term for the divine in Christ: the mediator of creation and the divine agent of revelation. The *Logos* was eternal, and yet distinct from the Father. However, in noting the distinction between the *Logos* (or Son of God) and God, Origen, and later Arius, drew on Prov. 8:22–31, where Wisdom's creation by God, almost as a distinct personality, mirrors Christ's relationship to the Father. This passage seems to make the *Logos* a creature and subordinate to God: 'Yahweh created me, first-fruits of his fashioning, before the oldest of his works' (Prov. 8:22). Arius would push Origen's notion of subordination to the extreme by claiming that 'before he was begotten or created or ordained or established, he (the Son) did not exist'.[32] Arius' overwhelming desire to preserve the transcendence of God prevented him from acknowledging the Son as eternal or as created. If this were the case, so Arius argued, the Father would become divisible, changeable, corporeal, and thus capable of suffering.

---

[30] G. L. Prestige, *God in Patristic Thought* (London: SPCK, 1964), 97–111.
[31] Christoph Schwöbel, 'Radical Monotheism and the Trinity', *Neue Zeitschrift für Systematische Theologie und Religionsphilosophie* 43 (2001): 69–70.
[32] Arius of Alexandria, *Epistle to Eusebius* 5, cited in Pelikan, *The Christian Tradition*, 193.

Arius' argument is heavily influenced by the philosophical milieu of Middle Platonism, which, in order to protect the divine 'otherness', developed the notion of intermediaries or gradations between the one, unchanging and transcendent God and the rest of creation. Unlike the God of Christian proclamation, this God of Greek philosophy was not experienced via historical encounter but was inferred as the ultimate and absolute ground or principle (*archē*) of the perishable world.[33] This God was radically different from this world: imperishable, a-temporal, immaterial, unchangeable, and impassible. For Arius the gulf between creation and the transcendent God was unbridgeable.[34]

Such stark monotheism goes hand in hand with 'an equally uncompromising view of God's transcendence'.[35] So concerned was Arius not to violate the transcendence of God that God had to be kept at a distance, aloof from the world of creatures – a world of fragility and change. He could not accept the term *homoousios* as it implied the existence of two ultimate principles. Arius further accused his opponents of making the incorporeal God both corporeal and capable of suffering. He quoted Deut. 6:4 in support of his exclusive monotheism, yet the problem lay not just in his doctrine of God, but specifically in his understanding of the nature of Christ's relation to the Father. In excluding all duality from his view of God as a monad, Arius effectively reduced the hypostases of the Son and the Spirit to the creaturely sphere. God cannot really be seen as the author of salvation since all God's relations to the world are effectively external to God's being.

Although most of our information about Arius comes from his opponents, principally Bishop Athanasius of Alexandria (328–73), it is clear that he saw the Son as the first creation of the Father and as an intermediary between creation and the Father.[36] It is through this (created) *Logos* that the universe came into being. Yet the Arians (as well as the majority of Christians) also worshipped and prayed to Christ. This inconsistency between Arius' theological principles and his liturgical practice was seized

---

[33] This Hellenistic notion of God was quite different from the Jewish understanding. The Jews could perceive stability amid historical change because God always remained faithful to his covenant promises. The Greeks, on the other hand, found stability in an unchanging reality, which underlies the world of appearances and change. See Jack Bonsor, *Athens and Jerusalem* (New York and Mahwah, NJ: Paulist Press, 1993), 22–35.

[34] Aloys Grillmeier, *Christ in Christian Tradition*, vol. I, 2nd rev. edn, trans. John Bowden (London and Oxford: Mowbrays, 1975), 228.

[35] Pelikan, *The Christian Tradition*, 194.

[36] 'There was when He was not' was a familiar Arian slogan referring to a stage prior to his generation when the Son did not exist. See Kelly, *Early Christian Doctrines*, 223–31.

on by Athanasius and others, who claimed that by so doing Arius was ascribing some kind of divinity to Christ, while at the same time maintaining he is a creature. Indeed, the Arians continued the practice of baptising not only in the name of the Father, but also of the Son and the Holy Spirit.

While Arius' precursors, such as Origen, struggled to hold the separate existence of Father, Son, and Spirit, while maintaining their equality in being, his contemporaries, including Alexander of Alexandria, grappled with whether Father and Son could both be called 'true God'. There was as yet no precise way of describing the relationship between the Word and the Father. Even if particular terminologies and scriptural texts would gradually gain prominence, what counted as right belief for most of the fourth century remained fluid.[37] Alongside 'mediator' the term 'image' was used to describe the Word. The Son as true image reflects the qualities of the Father, from whom he issues, like radiance from light – as the Council of Nicea would affirm. While concerned to preserve the constant unity of God, there is the acknowledgement that the Word, while eternally with also comes forth from the Father.

Nevertheless, the Arian doctrine claiming that Christ was a creature was on a collision course with the tradition of describing him as God. The situation was exacerbated when Arius refused to accept the initial adjudication of his bishop, Alexander. Arius and his adherents were excommunicated, but matters did not end there. Arius brought the issue to the international stage since he knew that there was no unanimous view on the nature of the Son's relationship to the Father.

A synod in Egypt around 319 comprising about 100 bishops formally disowned the position of Arius and his followers. Nevertheless, Arius' views were widely propagated, and his claim that the Son was less than the Father found much popular support. Eventually the pending schism came to the attention of the Emperor Constantine, who, wishing to restore doctrinal unity to the Church formally convoked the Council.[38] It was the first time a general, 'ecumenical' council of the whole Church had been summoned and by far the greatest number of bishops (between 250 and 300) that had ever gathered. Most of the bishops were Eastern since Arianism was primarily an Eastern theological movement.

While no official account of the proceedings of the Council has been preserved, the official doctrine was promulgated for the whole Church in the 'symbol' or creed of Nicea:

---

[37] Ayres, *Nicea and its Legacy*, 80.

[38] Scholars are unclear to what extent Constantine appreciated the theological arguments of the Council. Grillmeier, *Christ in Christian Tradition*, vol. 1, 259–64.

We believe in one God, the Father almighty, maker of all things, visible and invisible.

And in one Lord Jesus Christ, the Son of God, the only-begotten generated from the Father that is, from the being (*ousia*) of the Father, God from God, Light from Light, true God from true God, begotten, not made, one in being (*homoousios*) with the Father, through whom all things were made, those in heaven and those on earth. For us men and for our salvation He came down, and became flesh, was made man, suffered, and rose again on the third day. He ascended to the heavens and shall come again to judge the living and the dead.

And in the Holy Spirit.[39]

This creed, which forms the basis of the Nicene Creed recited during Sunday Eucharist, is a clear refutation of the fundamental tenets of Arianism. The key term from the creed is *homoousios* or consubstantial. The supporters of Arius could accept claims that the Son is like the Father because it did not collide with their emphasis on the creaturely status of the Son. But by introducing a non-biblical term, *homoousios*, to indicate clearly Christ's divinity, and by asserting that Christ was of the same *ousia* or substance as the Father, the Council was remarkably innovative and met Arius head on. It placed the Son firmly on the side of God – the Son is 'from God' ('only-begotten') in a different way than creatures can be said to be from God. This was in opposition to the Arians who liked to accent the 'creaturely commonality of Christ with those he was to redeem'.[40]

The Council wished, therefore, to assert the full divinity of the Son in the sense of sharing the same divine nature as the Father. It did not, however, provide a neat solution to a difficult theological issue; its decrees were primarily negative. It was primarily intended to decide a particular point (the nature of the Son's relationship to the Father) vis-à-vis Arius' subordination-ism rather than develop a comprehensive trinitarian theology, which was still evolving through the fourth century. The Son, for example, is not described as *eternally* begotten, while there was ambivalence towards the unscriptural term *homoousios*. For some it had materialistic overtones while others suspected modalist connotations in Nicea's strong emphasis on divine unity.[41]

There is a deliberately anti-Arian tone to the creed. Arius and his followers were branded as heretics and sent into exile. Nevertheless, the problem of how to reconcile two fundamental tenets of Christianity,

---

[39] J. Neuner and J. Dupuis, eds., *The Christian Faith* (London: Collins, 1982), 7 (hereafter abbreviated to *N/D*).
[40] Dennis E. Groh, 'Arius, Arianism', in *ABD*, vol. 1, 385.
[41] See Michel R. Barnes, 'The Fourth Century as Trinitarian Canon', in Lewis Ayres and Gareth Jones, eds., *Christian Origins: Theology, Rhetoric, and Community* (London: Routledge, 1998), 47–67 for discussion of the context within which the creeds of Nicea and Constantinople were produced.

monotheism and the worship of Jesus Christ as divine, did not end with Nicea.[42] History, so often written by the winners, is written in this case by Athanasius, the great champion of Nicea. For Athanasius, unless the Son was fully divine, existing eternally alongside the Father, he could not have imparted divine life to humankind. Father and Son share a unity of essence while also remaining distinct.[43]

Much of our access to Arius' thought comes via Athanasius, whose portrayal of his opponent is rich in polemic and caricature. It is more accurate to view the controversy, which lasted almost sixty years, less in terms of a defence of an already agreed orthodoxy, than as a *search* for an orthodox doctrine of God through a process of trial and error. Prior to Nicea there were few synodal or conciliar decisions to which one could appeal. Most of the opponents of Nicea would not have called themselves Arians, while Arius himself did not leave behind a school of disciples. In the ensuing decades, debates would continue to focus on the unity and distinction between Father and Son. Some groups such as the 'Homoians' spoke of the Son being 'like' the Father, and others, termed 'Heterousian', stressed the differences between the *ousia* of the Father and Son.[44] In sum, there was no original, unchanging Nicene theology simply to be passed on over the course of the fourth century. The Church gradually recognised that although the discussions centred on the interpretation of certain biblical passages, the problems could not be resolved by a mere repetition of biblical formulae. It moved from a theology of repetition to a more profound theology that required a hermeneutics of doctrine.[45] The evolution of creeds from their original and local baptismal contexts to their later status as universal statements of doctrinal orthodoxy had begun.[46]

ARIUS AND CONTEMPORARY THEOLOGY

The search for new and creative ways of formulating Christian faith, a process of trial and error in the development of doctrine, came to a head in

---

[42] See R. P. C. Hanson, *The Search for the Christian Doctrine of God: The Arian Controversy 318–381* (Edinburgh: T&T Clark, 1988), xvii–xxi, 824–75, and Rowan Williams, *Arius: Heresy and Tradition*, rev. edn (Grand Rapids, MI and Cambridge: Eerdmans, 2001), 82–91, 233–45.

[43] 'If the Son as offspring is other than the Father, He is identical with Him as God.' Athanasius, *Against the Arians* (NPNF), vol. III, 4, cited in Kelly, *Early Christian Doctrines*, 246.

[44] For discussion of the 'fluidity of creedal formulation in the early fourth century', see Ayres, *Nicea and its Legacy*, 131–86 (here p. 162).

[45] 'The Church was impelled reluctantly to form dogma.' Hanson, *The Search for the Christian Doctrine of God*, xxi.

[46] Kelly, *Early Christian Creeds*, 205.

the fourth century and remains a permanent challenge to believers. Theology continues to grapple with the meaning and contemporary relevance of Christian dogmas, the tension between orthodoxy and heterodoxy in the search for truth, the role of episcopal authority in determining doctrinal decisions, the place of philosophy in theology, and the relation between Scripture and doctrine. Many theologians further concede that the traditional dogmatic language of the Church can appear unintelligible to Christians today, particularly in the more secularised cultures of the West.[47] The problem becomes more acute as the Church moves from one cultural milieu to another and where new formulations of faith become necessary. The development and interpretation of doctrine, including its normative value, which bedevilled Arius, persists as a challenge to mediate the past to the present. Is it a question of ever-new interpretations and formulations of the truth, or is there within this historical process of interpretation a truth in itself, which is to be affirmed in all cultures and historical situations? There is a tension between claims to universal and permanently valid truth on the one hand and the historicity of dogmas on the other.

Within the Roman Catholic tradition successive ecclesial statements have held that, while dogmas are historical in that their meaning 'is partially dependent on the expressive power of the language used at a given time and under given circumstances', this is not tantamount to a dogmatic relativism that abandons traditional Church language.[48] However, it does imply that the relation between formulation and content in dogma always calls for further clarification. Dogmas and Church teachings are forms of discourse that serve as a reminder and an interpretation of the great deeds of God. Always related to Scripture as their starting point, they speak not only of past salvific acts 'but seek to proclaim and make salvation present here and now'.[49] Dogmas also point to the future and witness to the eschatological truth and reality of salvation. They are to inspire hope and be interpreted in view of the final destiny of humanity and the world.

In the context of the interpretation of dogma, the Church's teaching office aims to fulfil its task in a pluralistic society through persuasive argumentation. It cannot demand obedience to past formulations on the basis of formal authority. Yet the teaching task transcends the ratification of a process of interpretation and includes encouragement, guidance and

---

[47] See, for example, Juan Luis Segundo, *The Liberation of Dogma* (New York: Orbis Books, 1992), 1–15.

[48] See *Mysterium Ecclesiae*, 5, and International Theological Commission (ITC), 'On the Interpretation of Dogmas', trans. Carl Peter, *Origins* 20 (17 May 1990): 1–14. In the following sections, the term 'Church' refers to the Roman Catholic Church.

[49] 'On the Interpretation of Dogmas' B.III.2, 8–9.

direction. In our postmodern age, however, life and doctrine have become radically separate, and while ecclesial authority voices concerns about theological relativism, theologians such as Karl Rahner argue that provisional theological formulae are more appropriate in terms of furthering faith understanding than authoritative universal definitions. In the previous chapter we saw how the unsettling and polyphonic nature of certain Old Testament texts about God sits uneasily with the doctrinal systems of a Church theology. The issue is how authentic doctrinal development can take place in the context of a pluralism of theologies and competing views that cannot be adequately synthesised.

The Second Vatican Council of the Roman Catholic Church reflected this theological rather than dogmatic approach. The Council made no formal dogmatic definitions, and its teaching is to be understood positively as the expression of 'instructions' or 'appeals' rather than in the context of errors to be condemned as tended to be the case with previous councils.[50] Churches have often had difficulty coming to terms with the historical, partial, and fragile character of Christian truth. But the desire for a secure and certain foundation of knowledge overlooks the fact that all human knowing is intimately connected with such factors as historical location, political contexts, ideological allegiances, conceptual frameworks, psychological assumptions, and linguistic practices. Such factors undermine the claim that there is an unchanging meaning of dogmas that can somehow be discovered outside of history. Rather, the truth of a dogma occurs only as it is appropriated in ever-new historical contexts.[51] As Rowan Williams puts it, 'there is no absolute *locus standi* above the struggle [for orthodoxy] ... Orthodoxy continues to be *made*.'[52] This means that, although the promulgated dogmas of Nicea and Chalcedon must be adhered to, it does not tie Christians today to the worldview or to the philosophical terminology of the fourth and fifth centuries. Feminist theologies, for instance, have retrieved neglected possibilities within the tradition and highlighted the historical open-endedness of talk about God.[53]

Traditionally, this question was dealt with by distinguishing between the truth, substance, or meaning of a dogma and the way it is expressed or

---

[50] Karl Rahner, 'Basic Theological Interpretation of the Second Vatican Council', in *Theological Investigations*, vol. xx (London: Darton, Longman & Todd, 1981), 89.

[51] Bonsor, *Athens and Jerusalem*, 157–72. See also his 'Postmodernism and Theology', *Theological Studies* 55 (1994): 295–313.

[52] Williams, *Arius: Heresy and Tradition*, 24–25.

[53] See, for example, Elizabeth A. Johnson, *She Who Is: The Mystery of God in Feminist Theological Discourse* (New York: Crossroad, 1996), 3–41.

presented. The value of this distinction is that it is a reminder that the language of dogmatic statements should not be absolutised in the sense of identifying the language with the reality of which they speak. As Rahner pointed out, all faith formulations are ultimately relativised in the face of Holy Mystery that is their source and goal.[54] This should lead to a greater degree of modesty in theological discourse. At the same time, the truth of a dogma cannot be identified with a meaning that somehow transcends historical formulation. Contemporary interpretation of dogmas attempts, on the one hand, to acknowledge the abiding validity of their truth. God's self-communication has a noetic or cognitive dimension, which the Spirit-guided Church is enabled to grasp. On the other hand, although doctrinal and creedal statements have a specific cognitive status, there is the challenge to present this truth not as a dead relic from the past, but as something fruitful for the life of the Church. There can be a basic continuity between development of doctrine and the patristic and conciliar heritage. It is not a question of separating dogma from its official conciliar formulations – these are canonised moments in the transmission of Christ's truth.

Christianity is not tied to any one philosophical system, and philosophical pluralism is to be encouraged to the extent that this illumines rather than distorts the Christian message. In relation to dogmatic statements, while granting the abiding validity of the truth they contain, these are not the end point of faith; they point beyond themselves to the mystery of God.

LEARNING FROM THE EAST: THE CAPPADOCIANS

In the gradual development of the doctrine of the Trinity, a significant and decisive contribution came in the late fourth century from the province of Cappadocia in the heart of Asia Minor (Eastern Turkey). The three leading figures here were Basil of Caesarea (*c.*330–79), his brother Gregory of Nyssa (*c.*335–95), and Gregory of Nazianzus (*c.*329–89). These three bishops, bound together either by blood relationship or by close friendship, not only helped consolidate the decisions of the Council of Nicea and its creed, but also provided a foundation for a more relational understanding of God as a loving communion of equals.

Despite their spiritual and theological unity, the Cappadocians were quite different personalities. The two Gregorys acknowledged Basil 'the

---

[54] Karl Rahner, 'A Theology that we Can Live with', in *Theological Investigations*, vol. XXI (London: Darton, Longman and Todd, 1988), 99–112; and his 'Experiences of a Catholic Theologian', trans. D. Marmion and G. Thiessen, *Theological Studies* 61 (2000): 3–15.

Great' as their teacher and guide. From a wealthy, land-owning Cappadocian family, Basil was educated in rhetoric in his native Caesarea, where he met his lifelong friend Gregory of Nazianzus. After his baptism in 356 he toured the monastic sites in Syria, Mesopotamia, Palestine, and Egypt and was greatly impressed by the monks' ascetic way of life. On his return, he renounced his secular career and embarked on a similar ascetic lifestyle along with some companions, including Gregory. However, even in this period of his life, Basil was a man of action, and in a short time he had established a number of monasteries. As his administrative and other talents came to prominence, it was not surprising that he was persuaded to be ordained a priest, and then, in 370, bishop of Caesarea.

For most, if not all, of their careers Basil and the other Cappadocians were engaged in an ongoing struggle to defend what they regarded as the orthodoxy of the Council of Nicea over and against Arianism, whose supporters included the Emperor Valens. For Basil, the unity of the Church was at stake. The Council of Nicea had left many aspects of trinitarian theology unresolved and Arianism was as yet undefeated. Basil was aware of the lack of precision surrounding *homoousios* that could (and did) give rise to misunderstandings. There was a variety of theological interpretations in evidence – an indication not only of the sense of dogmatic freedom in the fourth century, but also of how provisional Christianity in its ideas and institutions still remained.[55]

In trying to restore unity and orthodoxy among the vying factions in the Eastern Church, Basil clarified trinitarian thinking and language against two groups of opponents. The first group have been termed 'Neo-Arians' (Arius was long dead) and were led by Eunomius, a bishop in Asia Minor. They held to the notion that the Son was 'unlike' the Father and excluded both the Son and the Spirit from true divinity.[56] According to Eunomius, God is supremely arelational and cannot share or communicate the divine nature. The Son is radically subordinated to the Father and a product of his will. They do not share the same essence or *ousia*; the Father is complete without the Son. Underlying Eunomius' position is what he describes as God's unbegottenness or ingenerateness (*agennesia*), the consequence of which is that:

---

[55] Philip Rousseau, *Basil of Caesarea* (Berkeley: University of California Press, 1994), xv.
[56] This theology is aptly labelled 'heterousian' emphasising the differences between the *ousia* of the Father and Son. The unlikeness is according to essence, though there are other ways in which Father and Son are alike. Ayres, *Nicea and its Legacy*, 145.

He could never come into contact with generation, so as to communicate his own nature to something generated, and he must escape all comparison or association with that which is generated.[57]

For Eunomius, the impassible God cannot be subject to the experiencing of passions (*pathe*). Eunomius found it difficult to come to terms with the incarnation, which seems to have played only a minor role in his thought. In a rationalist vein he had great confidence in the power of Greek philosophy to explain all questions about God.[58]

Basil's *Against Eunomius* (364) was his first doctrinal refutation of the Arian tendency to play down the significance of the Son as well as an attempt to return unity and orthodoxy to the Church of the East. Eunomius had identified God's essence (*ousia*) with unbegottenness, and concluded that since the Son was begotten he must be of a different essence, and could not belong to the realm of the divine or be eternal. Basil, on the other hand, maintained that 'unbegotten' is not a name indicative of the essence of God; it is only one of many negative terms applied to God, none of which completely expresses the divine essence. To say that God is ingenerate or unbegotten does not tell us *what* God is, but *how* God is, that is, the mode or modes of God's existence (*Against Eunomius* I.12). Unbegottenness is only one aspect of God's *ousia*, since God's essence can never be fully understood by human reason or language. Unlike Eunomius, Basil saw God primarily as a relational being – related to the Son and to humankind.

Basil contributed significantly to the clarification of trinitarian terms. Behind his insistence that we cannot know God's essence lies an apophatic and mystical approach to theology. All dogmatic statements are essentially negative in that they do not intend to penetrate the mystery itself. Ultimately, the mystery of Father, Son, and Spirit reveals itself in worship and the liturgy. It was by silence that one gave honour to the mysteries of the Trinity. But before ending in silent worship, Basil devised a formula that maintained both the oneness and the threeness of Father, Son, and Spirit. His doctrine of the Trinity, therefore, attempted to balance the unity of the Godhead with the distinction of the persons.

The Council of Nicea had confessed that the Son is 'from the essence (*ousia*) or substance of the Father' and is 'of one essence or substance

---

[57] Eunomius, *Apology* 9 (*PG* 30, 845).
[58] It is hard to reach a fair assessment of Eunomius given that most of his works were lost and that we mostly read him through the lens of his adversaries and their interests. The fact that both Basil and his brother Gregory of Nyssa felt obliged to attack him theologically (and the latter personally) suggests he was a figure of considerable theological competence and impact.

(*homoousios*) with the Father'. It clearly advocated Christ's divinity: Christ is Son, not creature. But Basil not only followed the Council in asserting that Father and Son are one (against the Arians), he also emphasised that Father and Son are different against a second group of opponents, the Sabellians.

Sabellianism (or modalism), as has been mentioned, was an interpretation of the Trinity that so stressed the unity of Father, Son, and Spirit that personal distinctions within God were denied. The three divine names were not considered full persons but merely refer to the *roles* or modes assumed by the one God. The consequences of such a modalistic approach,

made it impossible to understand how the Son, eternally or in the Incarnation had a relation of reciprocal dialogue with the Father, praying to Him, etc., as the Gospel stories require us to believe. It would also make it impossible for the Christian to establish a fully personal dialogue and relationship with *each* of the three persons of the Trinity. Furthermore, it would appear that God was somehow 'acting' in the Economy, pretending, as it were, to be what He appeared to be, and not revealing or giving to us His true self, His very being.[59]

Basil countered this tendency by stressing the fullness and ontological integrity of each person in the Trinity. He distinguished between one *ousia* and three *hypostases* in God. *Ousia*, the essence (or substance or nature) of God corresponds to the Latin *substantia* as that essential being which Father, Son and Spirit have in common. *Hypostasis*, on the other hand, refers to a Person of the Trinity and defines that which is circumscribed or limited (akin to the Latin *persona*). As Basil puts it, '*ousia* has the same relation to *hypostasis* as the common has to the particular'.[60] Without this clarification the danger is that 'one who fails to confess the community of the essence or substance falls into polytheism, [and] the one who refuses to grant the distinction of the *hypostases* is carried away into Judaism' (*Letter* 210.5).

It is clear that Basil is anxious to avoid the pitfalls of polytheism as well as Sabellianism. The 'Cappadocian settlement', as it came to be known, would be formulated as 'one *ousia*, three *hypostases*'. While it dissipated much confusion and pointed the way for understanding into the future, it also came at a price. The price is a certain narrowing of terminology. For most of the fourth century the terms *ousia* and *hypostasis* were frequently used as synonyms, and the Cappadocians struggled to explain the distinction.

---

[59] John D. Zizioulas, 'The Doctrine of the Holy Trinity: The Significance of the Cappadocian Contribution', in Christoph Schwöbel, ed., *Trinitarian Theology Today: Essays on Divine Being and Act* (Edinburgh: T&T Clark, 1995), 46.

[60] *Letter* 214.4 (*NPNF*, vol. VIII, 254).

Indeed Basil encountered significant resistance in his attempts to assert three *hypostases* from those who thought that any kind of plurality in the Godhead implied subordination.[61]

Basil also clearly believed in and affirmed the divinity of the Holy Spirit. However, in *On the Holy Spirit*, his most important work on the subject, he refrains from explicitly calling the Holy Spirit God and does not use the term *homoousios* in this context. Perhaps he was afraid of what his enemies might have made of such an explicit affirmation, while also conceding that Scripture did not offer sufficient support for the doctrine that the Spirit is a separate *hypostasis* within the Godhead. His refusal to go beyond the language of Nicea left his pneumatology open to the charge of minimalism.[62] He preferred to describe the status of the Spirit as sharing the same honour as the Father and the Son, so preserving the unity of the Trinity, and spoke of glorifying the Holy Spirit together with the Father and the Son.[63] As with Athanasius and others in the fourth century, he liked to stress the function of the Spirit as the agent of our salvation and sanctification. The Spirit is the working of divine grace in the believer leading to a sapiential knowledge of the Trinity, informing Christian identity, and grounding *theosis* and Christian perfection. Though the divine substance or essence (*ousia*) remains beyond our reach, we gain some knowledge of God through God's diverse operations or activities (*energeia*) (*Against Eunomius* I.8). These activities originate with the Father, are accomplished through the Son, and are completed and brought to fruition in the Spirit.

He also appealed to the Church's practice of baptism in the name of the triune God as a further indication that the Spirit is not separate from the divine nature:

As we were baptised, so we profess our belief. As we profess our belief, so also we offer praise. As then baptism has been given us by the Saviour, in the name of the Father and of the Son and of the Holy Spirit, so, in accordance with our baptism, we make the confession of the creed, and our doxology in accordance with our creed. We glorify the Holy Spirit together with the Father and the Son.[64]

---

[61] One of the most vocal opponents was Marcellus of Ancyra (born *c.*280/85). For a discussion of his 'miahypostatic theology', see Joseph T. Lienhard, '*Ousia* and *Hypostasis*: The Cappadocian Settlement and the Theology of "One *Hypostasis*"', in Stephen T. Davis, Daniel Kendall, and Gerald O'Collins, eds., *The Trinity: An Interdisciplinary Symposium on the Trinity* (Oxford: Oxford University Press, 1999), 99–121.

[62] See Anthony Meredith, 'The Pneumatology of the Cappadocian Fathers and the Creed of Constantinople', *Irish Theological Quarterly* 48 (1981): 196–211.

[63] *On the Holy Spirit*, 6.15, 13 (*NPNF*, vol. VIII, 8–9). Instead of the traditional formula, 'Glory to the Father through the Son in the Holy Spirit', Basil preferred 'Glory to the Father with the Son together with the Holy Spirit' to express equality of dignity and the unity of the Trinity.

[64] *Letter* 159.2 (*NPNF*, vol. VIII, 212).

Basil was aware of the need to differentiate the origin of the Spirit from that of the Son, though he, like the other Cappadocians, was unable to explain the precise nature of the Son's generation or the procession of the Spirit. The Father is without origin and the Spirit comes from the Father not by generation (as is the case with the Son) but as the 'breath of his mouth' in a manner that remains ineffable (*On the Holy Spirit* 18.46).

Basil's great friend Gregory of Nazianzus (*c.*329–*c.*389) consolidated Basil's work on the doctrine of the Trinity. A completely different type of personality to Basil, Gregory's inclination was to shun the limelight and to flee from controversy. He had met Basil at the school of rhetoric at Caesarea in Cappadocia, and later the two renewed their acquaintance during their studies in Athens. Having opted for a life of monastic retirement in Pontus, Gregory suddenly found himself ordained presbyter, almost against his will, mainly because of his father, who was also a bishop. For most of his life, Gregory would be torn between the onerous duties of public ecclesiastical office and a desire for monastic solitude. This tension reflects the scepticism of the time about whether a genuine Christian life was possible in the midst of worldly responsibilities.

By now Basil was regarded as the leader of orthodoxy in the Eastern Church. Nevertheless, Church affairs were in a state of confusion with ongoing tensions between those loyal to the decisions of the Council of Nicea and those who supported Arianism in its various forms. It is against this backdrop that Basil prevailed upon his friend to accept ordination to the episcopate, initially to a minor see, and then, after the death of Basil, to the capital Constantinople.

Gregory's contribution to trinitarian orthodoxy is contained in his *Five Theological Orations* delivered in 379 and in 380 while he was bishop of Constantinople. A gifted orator, Gregory's *Orations* comprise a lucid summary of what would become the accepted trinitarian orthodoxy.[65] Like Basil, his opponents were in the first place Eunomius and his supporters, and, secondly, in the *Fifth Theological Oration*, the Macedonians, who denied the full divinity of the Holy Spirit. Reacting to what he saw as the excessive rationalism of the Arians, Gregory too favoured a negative or apophatic approach to theology. The Eunomians had claimed to comprehend the incomprehensible, and so reduced God to the limits of human understanding. Such theological pride, according to Gregory, overlooks the fact that the divine nature cannot be comprehended by human reason. He preferred to

---

[65] For a translation of Gregory's *Theological Orations*, see *The Library of the Christian Classics*, vol. III. *Christology of the Later Fathers*, ed. Edward Rochie Hardy in collaboration with Cyril C. Richardson (London: SCM Press, 1954), 128–214.

compare the theologian to Moses on the mountain, who was only able to see the 'back parts' of God (*Orat.* 28.11). Though the essence (*ousia*) or nature (*physis*) of God remains unknown – we cannot know *what* God is – we can know *that* God is, through God's 'majesty' and 'glory' manifested in creation.

Like Basil, Gregory maintains a harmony of unity and distinction in God: the three differ in number but not in *ousia*. The Godhead exists 'undivided in separate Persons':

> When, then we look at the Godhead, or the first cause or the *monarchia*, that which we conceive is one; but when we look at the Persons in whom the Godhead dwells, and at those who timelessly and with equal glory have their being from the first cause, there are three whom we worship. (*Orat.* 31.14)

While the Father remains the source or sole principle (*monarchia*) of the Godhead, this is a monarchy not limited to one person, but shared. All the Cappadocians aimed to safeguard the distinctness of the three Persons in the one nature and dignity of the Godhead. Gregory also follows Basil's analogy of the generic to the particular in explaining the relation of the *ousia* to the *hypostases*. Each of the divine *hypostases* is the *ousia* or essence of the Godhead, yet each has its own appropriate particularising characteristic. Basil had described these characteristics respectively as 'paternity', 'sonship', and 'sanctifying power'. Gregory defines them more precisely as 'unbegotten', 'begotten', and 'mission' (*Orat.* 25.16).

As with Basil, Gregory refuses to take unbegottenness (or ingenerateness) as the crucial characteristic of God. The name 'Father' for Gregory is primarily a relational term: 'the name of the relation in which the Father stands to the Son, and the Son to the Father' (*Orat.* 29.16). He defends the eternal generation of the Son *pace* Eunomius who conceived the Son's generation along the lines of human generation. Though Gregory speaks of a 'spiritual generation' – the Father begets without passion and outside of time – he concludes that the manner of the Son's generation is beyond our human understanding and is best honoured by silence (*Orat.* 29.8).

Gregory's second group of opponents, the Macedonians, exacerbated a general tendency among some third- and fourth-century theologians to explicitly subordinate the Spirit to the Son. The Macedonians or 'Pneumatomachians' ('Assailants of the Spirit') as they came to be known did not have an organised body of doctrine but reflect the general state of confusion at the time about the divine status of the Spirit.[66] They agreed

---

[66] Scholars no longer regard Macedonius, Bishop of Constantinople from *c.*342, as the founder of this sect.

that the Spirit is not God, does not share in the divine nature, and is inferior to the Son. Some Macedonians appealed to the Council of Nicea in support of their position, since the Council had not explicitly declared the divinity of the Holy Spirit.

In his *Fifth Theological Oration*, however, Gregory clearly affirms the divinity and consubstantiality of the Spirit. He is aware of the wide variety of views on the subject, with some conceiving the Spirit as an activity, others a creature, others God. If the Spirit is not divine, how, asks Gregory, can the Spirit join us with the Godhead? Although the Son and Spirit receive their divinity from the Father (as sole cause or source of the Godhead), they are not inferior. The Godhead is undivided in separate Persons. The Spirit is different from the Son due to a 'difference of manifestation ... or rather of their mutual relations one to another' (*Orat.* 31.9). The fact that the Spirit is not the Son, or the Son the Father, does not suggest deficiency; rather these words express the eternal relationships of each Person to the others. Gregory preserves the unity and distinction in the Trinity concisely:

The very fact of being unbegotten or begotten, or proceeding, has given the name of Father to the first, of the Son to the second, and to the third, him of whom we are speaking, of the Holy Spirit, that the distinction of the three persons may be preserved in the one nature and dignity of the Godhead. (*Orat.* 31.9)

Just as he refused to speculate on the Father's unbegottenness or on the manner of the Son's generation, so, too, does he refrain from speculating on the procession of the Holy Spirit. Rather than 'prying into the mystery of God', Gregory simply refers to 'the Holy Spirit, who proceeds from the Father' (John 15:26). Finally, he goes beyond Basil in claiming an 'unwritten' or extra-biblical tradition that witnesses to the divinity of the Spirit. In other words, the testimony of Scripture needs to be 'supplemented by, or interpreted in the context of, the religious experience of the church and of the Christian individual'.[67] Gregory describes this gradual nature of the revelation of the Holy Spirit thus:

The Old Testament proclaimed the Father openly, and the Son more obscurely. The New manifested the Son, and suggested the deity of the Spirit. Now the Spirit himself dwells among us, and supplies us with a clearer demonstration of himself ... He gradually came to dwell in the disciples, measuring himself out to them according to their capacity to receive him. (*Orat.* 31.26)

Like other supporters of Nicea, the Cappadocians recognised that in forming an orthodox doctrine of God they had to go beyond the words of

---

[67] Hanson, *The Search for the Christian Doctrine of God*, 783.

Scripture and search for new and creative formulations of their understanding of faith.

The third member of the Cappadocians, Gregory of Nyssa (*c*.335–*c*.394), was probably the most gifted speculative theologian of the three and one of the greatest Christian philosophers in the Eastern Church. Nevertheless, he tended to look up to his elder brother Basil, whom he often called his teacher. After an early education in rhetoric, he opted for a secular career and marriage, but then, due to the influence of Gregory of Nazianzus and others, he retired to a monastery founded by Basil in Pontus. In 372 he was reluctantly consecrated bishop of Nyssa, a small town in the district of Caesarea. This was because Basil, who had been made metropolitan of Caesarea a few years previously, was anxious to surround himself with supporters of the Nicene faith. Not as shrewd an administrator as his brother, however, Gregory was accused by his opponents of mismanagement of Church funds. He was deposed in 376 and went into exile only to return triumphantly two years later. In 380 he was elected archbishop, and in 381 he, along with Gregory of Nazianzus, took a prominent part in the Second Ecumenical Council of Constantinople.

After Basil's death, Gregory wrote his own *Against Eunomius* (*c*.380/381) in defence of his brother.[68] He accuses Eunomius of novel jargon in speaking of the Father as the 'highest and most real being', the Son as 'one who comes after and derives his being from the highest being', and the Spirit as one who 'is ranked with neither and is inferior to both' (*Against Eunomius* I.13). For Eunomius, the crucial characteristic or 'definition' of God (Father) is that God is from no one, that is, unbegotten (*agennetos*). Gregory, on the other hand, regards such a description as incomplete. It is simply 'a repetition of Judaism' and needs to be corrected with a more relational definition: Father is Father-of-the-Son. Rather than denigrating the status of the Son as less than fully divine, Gregory insists that the Son must always be thought of along with the Father. Without the Son, the Father does not exist: 'the name [Father] is not understood with reference to itself alone, but also by its special signification indicates the relation to the Son' (*Against Eunomius* II.2).

Gregory attempted to maintain the unity of nature within the Trinity, while at the same time acknowledging the distinctions of the persons. The divine essence is shared by, and immanent in, each person. His rule of faith, like the other Cappadocians, is that God is one *ousia* and three *hypostases*. This conviction reveals what God is like, and how God is disclosed to us,

---

[68] For a translation of Books I and II, see *NPNF*, vol. VIII, 33–134.

but not what God is. The essence of God – God's *ousia* – remains infinite and beyond our limited comprehension. And yet this 'uncreated nature' of God is not only 'perfect and incomprehensibly excellent', it is also 'differentiated by reason of the separate and distinct character of each person' (*Against Eunomius* I.22). His argument is that the unity of the *ousia* follows from the unity of divine activity. The Father does not do anything by himself in which the Son does not cooperate, nor does the Son act independently of the Holy Spirit. Rather, every such activity 'has its origin from the Father, and proceeds through the Son and is perfected in the Holy Spirit'.[69] Gregory infers the oneness of nature of the Father, Son, and Spirit from the identity of their operation. In short, while we do not know God's *ousia*, we have some knowledge of God through God's operations (*energia* or 'energies'), God's self-manifesting actions in the world, which we experience.

In trying to preserve the distinction of the Persons and their community of nature, Gregory uses a number of analogies, none of which he regarded as satisfactory. Thus, he points to the analogy of the rainbow where the colours can be observed distinctly while also being inseparable from one another, or the analogy of three men who share the one *ousia*, humanity. In his treatise on the Holy Spirit, he compares the Father, Son, and Spirit to three torches, the first of which imparts its light to the second, and through the second it imparts its light to the third. It is not surprising that, by using such analogies, Gregory and the other Cappadocians were suspected of tritheism, despite their professed desire to maintain the divine unity.

The unity of nature, then, does not mean a confusion of the persons. Gregory distinguished the persons with respect to causality indicating a difference in their manner of existence. The characteristic of the Father is to exist without cause. This does not apply to the Son and the Spirit; for the Son went out from the Father (John 16:27), and the Spirit proceeds from the Son and from the Father (John 15:26).[70]

Gregory insists that the Spirit must be treated in the same way as are the Father and the Son. Eunomius had argued for the subordination of the Spirit partly because the Spirit is mentioned in the third place. For Gregory, the sequence of order of the persons does not affect their equality:

---

[69] Gregory of Nyssa, *That there are Not Three Gods* (*NPNF*, vol. v, 334.)
[70] 'Sermon 3 on the Lord's Prayer' in St Gregory of Nyssa, *The Lord's Prayer: The Beatitudes*, trans. Hilda C. Graef, Ancient Christian Writers 18 (New York: Newman Press, 1954), 54–5.

For as the Son is attached to the Father and the fact that he derives his being from him does not diminish his status, so the Holy Spirit holds to the Son who can be regarded as prior to the *hypostasis* of the Spirit in theory on the score of origin. (*Against Eunomius* I.690)

As was the case with Gregory of Nazianzus, Gregory of Nyssa opposed the Macedonians, who had argued (not unlike Arius had regarding the Son) that the Spirit occupied a position somewhere between creator and creature. Gregory points to the close interconnection of all three persons and to the close association of the Son and Spirit as grounds for asserting the latter's divinity. In contrast to Basil, this close association is manifest in the work of creation in which the Spirit is co-creative with the Father and the Son. Finally, Gregory held that the inseparability of all three persons in baptism and the activity of the Spirit in bringing us near to God (divinisation) were further indications of the Spirit's divine status.

TRINITARIAN MONOTHEISM AND HUMAN COMMUNITY

All three Cappadocians are clear that the Son is not subordinate to the Father. They believed that the same is true ultimately of the Spirit. Further, they maintained that God's *ousia* could not be known, whereas it was possible to derive some knowledge of God through God's activities in history. In effect, the Cappadocians devised a new trinitarian vocabulary: Father is the name of a relation; the three *hypostases* manifest the unknowable *ousia* of God. As LaCugna puts it, '*what* Father, Son, and Spirit are is the same; *who* each is, is unique' (*GfU*, 69).[71] The three divine persons are coordinate realities denoting relationships – both within the immanent Trinity and *ad extra* in creation and salvation. At the same time, each of the Cappadocians was aware of the limitations of analogies and of human language, and insisted on the apophatic foundation of all true theology. Neither were they afraid to use the philosophical language and categories of their age to expound a doctrine of God, while at the same time they attempted to overcome those elements of the Platonist tradition that were incompatible with

---

[71] See also Hanson, *The Search for the Christian Doctrine of God*, 730–7. Ayres, *Nicea and its Legacy*, 202 puts it well: 'The language of relationship serves to emphasize that Father–Son terminology has important consequences for how we understand the nature of God even while telling us nothing about the *ousia* of God.'

Christianity.[72] Following Plato, Gregory of Nyssa believed in the goodness and beauty of being and of God. This beauty of the Absolute can only be attained by a life of self-control and ascesis. Gregory's vision of the spiritual journey is an ascent into the infinity of God, where salvation consists not so much in an eternal rest as in eternal movement.

While the Father is the 'sole cause' of the Godhead, God is never without God's Word and Spirit. This is the intractable problem with which the Cappadocians had to deal. They saw the doctrine of the Trinity as midway between Greek polytheism and Hebrew monotheism. The one God of faith is in the first instance the Father almighty, but in Christianity (unlike Plato) the absolute is not simply an undifferentiated monad, but triune. The one God who is love is not alone in his/her divinity. This insight of the Cappadocians dovetails with the Greek view that the Good must be in some sense self-sharing. In effect, the Cappadocians provided a new understanding of the *monarchia* or 'one rule or principle' of God, a *monarchia* not limited to one Person, but shared. God's monarchy is always viewed in trinitarian terms. There is no subordination between Father and Son. The triune God is constituted by a 'shared rule of equal persons in communion, not domination by some persons over other persons' (*GfU*, 394).

Contemporary theologians have, not uncontroversially, explored the political implications of this Christian trinitarian monotheism.[73] For Jürgen Moltmann, the Cappadocian reconception of the triune God as a communion among equals rather than the primacy of one over another undermines any attempt by earthly rulers to seek a religious legitimisation for the rule of the one over the many:

It is only when the doctrine of the Trinity vanquishes the monotheistic notion of the great universal monarch in heaven, and his divine patriarchs in the world, that earthly rulers, dictators and tyrants cease to find any justifying religious archetypes any more. (*TKG*, 197)

Moltmann and LaCugna maintain that the Trinity forms the social paradigm or exemplar of true human community, in the Church and also in

---

[72] Anthony Meredith, *Gregory of Nyssa* (London and New York: Routledge, 1999), 6–20 and 129–39. See also Thomas Hopko, 'The Trinity in the Cappadocians', in Bernard McGinn and John Meyendorff, eds., *Christian Spirituality: Origins to the Twelfth Century* [vol. XVI of *World Spirituality: An Encyclopedia of the Religious Quest*] (London: Routledge & Kegan Paul, 1985), 260–75.

[73] Jürgen Moltmann, *The Trinity and the Kingdom of God* (London: SCM Press, 1991), 191–202 (hereafter abbreviated to *TKG*). The classic study is by Erik Peterson, *Der Monotheismus als politisches Problem* (Leipzig: Jakob Hegner, 1935). See also LaCugna, *GfU*, 390–400, and Leonardo Boff, *Trinity and Society*, trans. P. Burns, Liberation and Theology Series 2 (London: Burns and Oates, 1988), 148–54.

society. It also serves as a critique of a false idea of God. Traditional conceptions of the Christian God, they maintain, were too monotheistic and overlooked the fact that the triune God is reflected only 'in a united and uniting community of Christians without domination and subjection and a united and uniting humanity without class rule and without dictatorial oppression'. This is a vision where people are defined 'by their social relationships and not by their power or their property', a world in which human beings 'share everything with one another except their personal qualities'.[74]

The Cappadocians' insight that God's Fatherhood must be thought of relationally, one person in reference to another, would be eclipsed, however, as Christianity gradually adapted itself to prevailing Greco-Roman patriarchal structures. A political accommodation between Christianity and state was brought about by the conversion of the emperor Constantine (325) and provided for greater freedom for the Church. LaCugna traces the development of a 'political' theology where the emperor or earthly political monarch was viewed as the image of, and vested with authority by, the divine monarch. 'The rule of the earthly king was the rule of the one over the many, the rule of the superordinate over the inferior subject' (*GfU*, 393).

Moltmann and LaCugna bring out, therefore, how the doctrine of the Trinity emerged from a patriarchal and imperialist culture. In Moltmann's view, the idea of a divine monarchy, projected out of the earthly monarchy, can be used to justify various forms of earthly domination – religious, moral, sexual, and political. Yet, for LaCugna, the Cappadocian doctrine of the Trinity dared to rethink God's fatherhood 'not as self-sufficiency or isolation or the inability to share self with another ... but as relation-to-another-who-is-equal' (*GfU*, 393). Against Arius and others, the Cappadocians argued that God was not the absolute monad unable to engage with the creature, but one whose very nature is to become human, like us. Their teaching, she believes, contained the nucleus of a relational trinitarian monotheism and a resource that continues to inspire political and feminist theologies.

In addition to its critical function, there are also anthropological implications arising from Cappadocian trinitarian theology. The Cappadocians clearly distinguished between *ousia* and person in God. When God is called Father or 'unbegotten', this refers to God's personhood, not to God's *ousia*,

---

[74] Jürgen Moltmann, 'The Reconciling Powers of the Trinity in the Life of the Church and the World', in *The Reconciling Power of the Trinity: Geneva Conference of European Churches*, CEC Occasional Paper No. 15 (Geneva: CEC, 1983), 56, 57.

which is beyond human comprehension. The mode of existence of God's *ousia* is as a person, and any personal characteristics of God such as unbegottenness or Fatherhood for the Father, begottenness or Sonship for the Son, and spiration for the Spirit apply to God's personhood, not to God's *ousia*. These personal or hypostatic properties are both unique and incommunicable, whereas *ousia* is communicated among the three Persons. Prior to the Cappadocians, the terms *ousia* and *hypostasis* had been used rather fluidly and interchangeably. The Cappadocians, however, gave the notion of person greater prominence: God as person – as the *hypostasis* of the Father – freely out of love begets the Son and brings forth the Spirit.[75] In describing this 'ecstatic' or outgoing character of God, the Cappadocians settled on the language of personhood and relation. It is not that they understood the divine persons as autonomous individuals. The notion of person is intimately connected with a relationship; no person is conceivable without reference to the other two.[76]

The Cappadocians, then, gave greater prominence to the divine persons (e.g., the Person of the Father) than to the concept of nature or substance. If Greek Neoplatonic philosophy emphasised the 'one' over the 'many', the Cappadocians insisted that God exists simultaneously as the 'One' and the 'Many'. The ontological monism of Greek philosophy, despite its wonderful vision of a unified world of harmony and reason, ultimately issued in a fatalistic anthropology. The partial exists for the sake of the total, the person for the 'cosmos'. The person is a 'mask' (*prosopon*), – something that is added to one's being or substance (*hypostasis*).[77] By attributing ontological primacy to person rather than to substance, however, the Cappadocians were claiming that in God nature does not precede person, the 'one' does not precede the 'many' but requires the 'many' from the very start.[78] The implication, according to Eastern Orthodox theologian John Zizioulas, is

---

[75] See Zizioulas, 'The Doctrine of the Holy Trinity: The Significance of the Cappadocian Contribution', 44–60.

[76] It is important not to read into the Cappadocians later personalist anthropological concerns (e.g. Feuerbach and Buber). They were not aware of the dangers of individualism but 'were more concerned with distinguishing between person or individual, on the one hand, and nature or substance, on the other hand, in connection with the Christian God'. Lucian Turcescu, '"Person" versus "Individual", Modern Misreadings of Gregory of Nyssa', in Sarah Coakley, ed., *Rethinking Gregory of Nyssa* (Oxford: Blackwell, 2003), 106–7.

[77] For a development of this ontology of personhood, see John D. Zizioulas, *Being as Communion: Studies in Personhood and the Church* (London: Darton, Longman and Todd, 1985), 27–49.

[78] In other words, there has been a paradigm shift in the relation between the One and the many. No longer is the One seen as the higher-order entity (as was the case in pre-Christian Greek thinking) and plurality something secondary and fragmentary, but the triune God is simultaneously *monas* and *trias*, transcending the categories of the singular and the plural. See Joseph Cardinal Ratzinger, *Introduction to Christianity*, trans. J. R. Foster (San Francisco: Ignatius Press, 1990), 178–9.

that since the human person is the 'image of God', he or she is called to exist in the way God exists, that is, as persons in community. The image of God in us relates not to nature – there can never be an image of the nature of God – but to personhood. If 'nature' tends to point to the general, 'person' connotes uniqueness and particular identity. This shift, in turn, highlights the sacredness of human personhood, since personhood constitutes the 'way of being' of God. And finally, just as God does not exist alone, the person cannot exist in isolation but only in communion with others. This is the existential significance of the Cappadocian contribution to trinitarian theology: it invites us to a way of being that reflects the way that God exists.

THE TRINITY IN THE WEST: AUGUSTINE OF HIPPO

Augustine's treatise on the Trinity, *De Trinitate*, represents the last of the great trinitarian writings of the patristic period. Though not as well known as his classic *Confessions* and *City of God*, it would have a similar enduring influence on the development of trinitarian doctrine. Augustine began the work probably as early as 400 and was continually interrupted in the writing of it over a period of fifteen years by other pastoral matters, including his struggle with the Donatists, and a period of ill health. Though scholars initially thought that the long period of composition suggested Augustine was not writing out of an urgent need or controversy, or directing himself against any individual antagonist, but presenting a mature reflection on what he termed his quest for God, it is now recognised that the polemical context is never far from the surface.[79] The *De Trinitate* comprises fifteen books in all, though the theme recurs in other writings, including his *On Christian Doctrine* and *Tractates on the Gospel of John*.

Augustine was a philosopher and an orator before he became a baptised Christian. He was acquainted with the Neoplatonism of Plotinus and his disciple Porphyry both at first hand and through various friends and mentors. Marius Victorinus, an African professor of rhetoric based in Milan, was one such influence. He had joined the Christian church and translated Plotinus and other Neoplatonic writings into Latin. Victorinus,

---

[79] While in other dogmatic writings, the polemical focus was directed against the Donatists, the Pelagians, and the Manichaeans, here it is against the Anti-Nicenes or 'Arians' (here more accurately termed 'Homoians', who asserted the Son was 'like' or 'similar' but not consubstantial with the Father). Augustine continued these disputations right up to his death. See Rowan Williams, '*Trinitate, De*', in Allan D. Fitzgerald, ed., *Augustine through the Ages: An Encylopedia* (Grand Rapids, MI and Cambridge: Eerdmans, 1999), 845; and Michel René Barnes, 'Rereading Augustine on the Trinity', in Davis et al. eds., *The Trinity: An Interdisciplinary Symposium*, 165–6.

in turn, had known a Milanese priest, Simplicianus, the spiritual mentor of the bishop Ambrose. It was Ambrose's preaching and its attempt to combine elements of Platonism and Christianity that would so fascinate Augustine. Ambrose read Greek fluently and provided his congregation with some of the most up-to-date and learned sermons in the Latin world.[80] Through such influences Augustine concluded that Platonism and Christianity had much in common. He would reject the 'ready-made' wisdom of the Manichaeans and their radical dualism for the ideal of 'Wisdom' as a lifelong search, though not a purely rational one.

It was around 386 when Augustine and Victorinus were being drawn into this other-worldly Christian Platonic culture, all the while trying to reconcile a novel metaphysical system with traditional Christian beliefs. Plotinus would be a constant backdrop to Augustine's thought, providing him with a model and a vocabulary for the mystical quest directed to the union of the soul with God. Like Plotinus, Augustine analysed human experience in terms of the intellect and senses. Similarly, he understood philosophy not as a detached intellectual technique or display of cleverness, but as a transformative way of life. From the 'books of the Platonists' Augustine found the way of 'returning into himself' and looking for God 'within'. We see this attention to the self, or, more particularly, to the mind, a method of introspection, in the second half of his *De Trinitate* (Books VIII–XV), where Augustine explores the nature of the human soul for a pointer towards an understanding of the Trinity. A further parallel is Augustine's awareness of the limitations of human writing, especially when it comes to talk about God. He was probably also familiar with the writings on the Trinity by Tertullian, Hilary of Poitiers, and the *De Spiritu Sancto* of Ambrose. Late in life, he may even have become acquainted with the work of two of the Cappadocians – Basil and Gregory of Nazianzus.

At the beginning of the fourth century Christianity was no longer a persecuted religion but the religion of the Empire. The Church needed a clearly defined and universally accepted system of belief. It therefore needed to think out and formulate a doctrine of God in a rationally coherent fashion. This was especially the case, as we have seen, in the face of heresies of various kinds (e.g., Arianism). The purpose of Augustine's *De Trinitate* was to demonstrate that the claims of the Nicene Creed (and the later additions at the Council of Constantinople in 381) about the divinity and co-equality of Father, Son, and Spirit are rooted in Scripture. Further, he wanted to convince his readers that salvation and spiritual growth are

---

[80] Peter Brown, *Augustine of Hippo: A Biography* (London: Faber & Faber, 1967), 84.

connected with knowing themselves as images of the triune God, albeit an image distorted by sin. The task of the Christian vocation is to reintegrate this image in oneself – a task in which all the divine Persons are actively involved.

Significantly, nowhere does Augustine try to 'prove' the doctrine. He accepts it as a datum of revelation which, in his view, Scripture proclaims on almost every page. His concern is not with proof, but to show the intelligibility of what the Church teaches – which is consistent with his fundamental notion of theology as belief seeking understanding (*Credo ut intelligam*).[81] In Augustine's theological method, understanding presupposes faith, not vice versa. It is not an anti-intellectual stance. Rather, first one must believe, and on this basis one seeks understanding. He was convinced – partly from personal experience – that the human intellect has its limits and needs to be enlightened by God's grace before it can perceive the things of God, and that its pride, its cardinal sin, needs to be humbled before it can begin to understand God's truth.

The underlying motif here is the search for God.[82] All his life Augustine was a powerful seeker, always asking more questions than he answered. He had an extraordinary intellectual appetite that incorporated the whole range of his sensual, emotional, and rational experience. At key points of his work he quotes Ps. 105:3–4: 'Let their hearts rejoice who seek the Lord; seek the Lord and be strengthened; seek his face always.' The goal of this search is participation in the divine trinitarian life.

Augustine's starting point is to take the Catholic doctrine of God for granted (i.e., the decision of the Council of Nicea):

[T]he Father, the Son, and the Holy Spirit constitute a divine unity of one and the same substance in an indivisible equality. Therefore, they are not three gods but one God; although the Father has begotten the Son, and, therefore, He who is the Father is not the Son; and the Son was begotten by the Father and, therefore, He who is the Son is not the Father; and the Holy Spirit is neither the Father nor the Son, but only the Spirit of the Father and the Son, and He Himself is also co-equal with the Father and the Son and belongs to the unity of the Trinity.[83]

The first half of the *De Trinitate* explores what is meant by the fact that God is one, and that the whole Trinity is active in all divine operations. The first

---

[81] For a discussion on Augustine's distinction between *credere* and *intelligere*, see Basil Studer, 'History and Faith in Augustine's *De Trinitate*', *Augustinian Studies* 28/1 (1997): 7–50, esp. 19–32.

[82] Edmund Hill, 'Introduction', in J. E. Rotelle, ed., *The Trinity*, The Works of Saint Augustine, A Translation for the 21st Century (New York: New City Press, 1991), 21.

[83] Saint Augustine, *The Trinity*, trans. S. McKenna, The Fathers of the Church (Washington, DC: The Catholic University of America Press, 1963), Bk 1.4.7 (hereafter abbreviated to *De Trin.*).

four books focus on Scripture and on the assumption of the co-equality of the divine Persons. Scripture was always Augustine's principal authority in doctrinal matters. This will be particularly the case, he claims, with the doctrine of the Trinity, a doctrine that cannot be discovered by human reason. From the outset he asserts a basic axiom of trinitarian theology, namely, that the three Persons of the Trinity work inseparably – even if it was only the Son who became incarnate, only the Spirit who was given at Pentecost, and only the Father who spoke from heaven.[84] Augustine points to the equality of the Father and the Son: 'whatever the Father does, the Son does too' (John 5:19) against the Arians, for whom only the Father was true God. Since there is no composition in God, what is said of the divine attributes like wisdom, goodness, and so on is also said of the divine activities such as creation, redemption, revelation, and mission. Augustine followed the traditional exegetical rule of his time: scriptural texts referring to the Son as less than the Father, in the form of a servant (e.g., Phil. 2:6–7), refer to the Son's humanity; texts referring to the Son as equal to the Father are referring to the Son's divinity.[85] At the same time, he adopted what became known as the practice of appropriation, that is, of assigning an attribute (e.g., wisdom) or an activity (e.g., creation) to one of the divine Persons without denying that the attribute or activity applies to all three. This is an important aspect of trinitarian discourse reflecting the way Scripture itself speaks of the activity of the divine Persons. Thus, with respect to activities such as creating, redeeming, and divinising, Augustine will hold that the Trinity creates, the Trinity redeems, the Trinity divinises, while also claiming it correct to 'appropriate' creation to the Father, redemption to the Son, and divinisation to the Spirit.[86]

The Holy Spirit too is divine, according to Augustine, through his 'abiding' in the Christian (John 14:17), an indwelling in which the Father and Son also participate (John 14:23). The purpose of the canonical rule referred to above is to underline the unity and equality of Father, Son, and Spirit. To say that the Son is from the Father, for example, is not to imply

---

[84] Elsewhere Augustine is careful not to give a 'Patripassian' reading of the doctrine of inseparable operation: 'The Father indeed suffered not, but the Son, yet the suffering of the Son was the work of the Father and the Son.' *Sermon* 52.8, composed around AD 410.

[85] Though Augustine is aware that an unnuanced application of this principle would mean the suffering of the Son is confined to his humanity with the divinity impervious to it. Hence his claim that 'it was the Lord of Glory who was crucified', *The Trinity* Bk I. 4. 28.

[86] The doctrine has been criticised by some contemporary theologians, including Rahner and LaCugna, 'because the attributions often are arbitrary and sometimes contradict biblical ways of speaking about God's activity, and second because the separateness and individuality of each divine person is more pronounced than interrelatedness and codependence' (La Cugna, *GfU*, 98).

inequality, but means from the Father as principle of origin, God from God, light from light (*De Trin.* Bk IV.20.27).[87] Augustine applies this axiom to the missions or sending of the Son and the Spirit into the world. Anti-Nicene theologians had argued that the one who is sent is inferior to the sender, and that therefore only the Father is God. For Augustine, however, the missions of the Son and Spirit in history reflect the eternal divine processions within God. They represent the high point or climax of the triune God's eternal plan of salvation. Both the 'sending' and the 'proceeding' were *ex Patre Filioque*. The purpose of the sending or the 'missions' of the Son and Spirit is to lead humanity back to the Father. Participation in the divine trinitarian life represents the ultimate fulfilment for which we are created.[88]

When it comes to trinitarian language Augustine is first of all conscious of the distance between him and his subject matter, before whom no language suffices. Though he calls God a substance, he considers *essentia* a preferable term equivalent to the Greek *ousia*. From initially able only to conceive being as material, he gradually discovered the possibility of a more spiritual, immaterial understanding. Concomitant with an understanding of God as an immaterial and unchangeable being is Augustine's metaphysics of participation: created beings are drawn into Being; to 'be' is to participate in Being itself, a participation made possible because of God's self-gift to creation.

Augustine also followed the Greek approach in basing the diversity of Persons on relations. There are no accidents in God 'for there is nothing changeable in Him, nor does everything that is said of Him refer to His substance' (*De Trin.* Bk V.5.6).[89] Here Augustine introduced a middle way, the category of relation or reference:

[B]ecause the Father is only called the Father because He has a Son, the Son must, therefore, be only called the Son because He has a Father, and so these terms are not said according to the substance. For each of them is not so called in relation to Himself, but the terms are used mutually and in relation of one to the other; nor do they refer to anything accidental, because that which is called the Father and that which is called the Son is eternal and unchangeable in them. (*De Trin.* Bk V.5.6)[90]

[87] See also Mary T. Clark, '*De Trinitate*', in Eleonore Stump and Norman Kretzmann, eds., *The Cambridge Companion to St Augustine* (Cambridge: Cambridge University Press, 2001), 94.

[88] Mary Marrocco, 'Participation in Divine Life in the *De Trinitate* of St. Augustine', *Augustinianum* 42 (2002): 148–85. See also Edmund Hill, *The Mystery of the Trinity* (London: Chapman, 1985), 84–91.

[89] The Arians had concluded that since the substance of the Father is 'Unbegotten' and that of the Son 'Begotten', the Son could not be of the same substance as the Father.

[90] Rowan Williams puts it well: '"The Father is God" or "God is Father" is a statement about definitions: all that is true of the divine nature applies to the one called *pater*. But "the Father is

In other words, the divine names signify relationships, and it is only as terms of mutual references or relationships that Father, Son, and Holy Spirit are really distinct from one another. Or, as it would come to be formulated, it is only as mutually subsistent relationships that they are distinct. Augustine is aware that the divine essence expresses itself in the Persons and so terms for the former can be used for the latter.[91] Augustine scholar, Eugene TeSelle notes:

> The divine essence is wisdom, but the Son may be called Wisdom (or 'Wisdom from Wisdom') when the term is used 'relatively' (*The Trinity*, Bk. VII. 3. 4); similarly God is spirit or love, but when the terms are used 'relatively' they refer to the Holy Spirit. (*The Trinity*, Bk. V.11.12; Bk. XV.17. 29)[92]

Augustine reacts against a human tendency 'to separate persons from essence, to treat the essence as something "behind" the persons'.[93] Rather, the essence (or divinity) is 'nothing else than the Trinity itself', and we should not conceive of the substance or essence of the Trinity as different from the Father, the Son, and the Spirit (*Letter* 120.3.17).

While Father and Son are obviously correlative terms, that is, terms which indicate relationships that are 'essential' to being God, Augustine acknowledges a problem when it comes to speaking of the Spirit. We can speak of the Spirit of the Father and the Spirit of the Son but not vice versa. To bring out the relationship character of the Spirit, Augustine, following Hilary, uses the term *donum* or 'gift'. The Spirit is related to the other two Persons as gift to giver. The Spirit is what Father and Son, as one principle, *give*; the Spirit is *datus* just as the Son is *natus* and God's gift, Augustine argues, cannot be inferior to God (*De Trin.* Bk XV.19.36).

---

the Father of the Son" is said *relative*, in reference to relation; and this has to do not with the definition of "God", but with the connection between the diverse grammatical subjects for whom divine nature is claimed (Father, Son and Holy Spirit).' Williams, '*Trinitate, De*', 847.

[91] Augustine is careful to say 'three persons of the same essence, or three persons one essence' not 'three persons from the same essence' to avoid the impression that 'essence were one thing and person another'. *De Trin.* Bk VII.6.11.

[92] Eugene TeSelle, 'Holy Spirit', in Fitzgerald, ed., *Augustine through the Ages*, 438. Augustine had difficulty with the term 'person' in connection with the Trinity as this tended to be understood as an individual human being – so undermining the inseparability of the divine persons.

[93] Lewis Ayres, 'The Fundamental Grammar of Augustine's Trinitarian Theology', in Robert Dodaro and George Lawless, eds., *Augustine and his Critics: Essays in Honour of Gerald Bonner* (London and New York: Routledge, 2000), 62. In reflecting on the grammar of divine simplicity (or immateriality) and its implications for Augustine's trinitarian theology, Ayres maintains that 'in God there are no relationships that are not eternal and essential' (p. 58), and 'that we should beware of speaking about a substance in which the three persons are "contained": there is *nothing but* the three co-eternal and consubstantial persons' (p. 68).

Augustine, as we noted, grounds the missions of the Son and the Spirit in time in the eternal processions in God. From the beginning of his priestly ministry Augustine had been interested in the manner of the procession of the Spirit. Can the Spirit be called 'gift' from all eternity even prior to creation? His reply is that the missions reveal the eternal origin of the divine persons. In relation to the Spirit he writes: 'As for the Holy Spirit to be the gift of God is to proceed from the Father, so to be sent is to know that He proceeds from Him' (*De Trin.* Bk IV.20.29). The Spirit represents as it were the eternal generosity of God. The Spirit's eternity is not compromised for a gift exists before it is given. As the Spirit is the Spirit of both Father and Son, Augustine insinuated that the Spirit is the ineffable communion or mutual love of Father and Son, the *vinculum Trinitatis*, or bond of communion between Father and Son.[94] While the Son is called the Word of God and the Spirit the Gift of God, the Spirit can also, and especially, be called love, since it is sent or given by God (*De Trin.* Bk XV.17.31). The Spirit may be called love because the spirit enables us to abide in God and God in us. The Holy Spirit's proper name, therefore, is a relational one of Gift of Father and Son. This is one of Augustine's most significant contributions to trinitarian theology. The Father has endowed the Son with the capacity to produce the Spirit, that is, the Spirit proceeds from the Father through the Son. Finally, Augustine stressed that although the Spirit is Spirit of both the Father and the Son – they share the Spirit's proceeding from them – the Spirit proceeds 'principally' or 'originally' from the Father, so preserving the monarchy or principality of the Father as the *primus inter pares* of the divine Persons.

In the second half of his work, Augustine moves from an interpretation of Scripture towards presenting the content of trinitarian faith 'in a more inward way'. This 'more inward way', the way of returning into oneself and looking for God within, represents Augustine's psychological approach to the Trinity. There is a triad within our own selves – being, knowing, and willing – which are truly distinct and yet exist within the oneness of our being. They provide us with an analogy for the unfathomable life and unity of the triune God. Associated primarily with Augustine but later developed by Thomas Aquinas, the 'psychological' analogy is based on the *imago Dei* – the human person is made in the triune God's image and likeness (Gen. 1:26–7). Hence Augustine will claim it is not unreasonable to expect

---

[94] *De Trin.* Bk VI.5.7, where Augustine uses the triad: lover, loved, and the love which unites them. Augustine also refers to the Spirit as the love between Father and Son and thus the 'love of God' in his short *On Faith and the Creed* of AD 393 (*On Faith and the Creed*, 9.19).

to find some reflection of the Trinity in the human person. He locates the image in the human person, or more specifically, in the human mind (*mens*) since the triune God cannot be seen directly.[95]

The search for an image of God by identifying triadic activities within the human person that were distinct yet one represents an indirect approach to the mystery of the Trinity. Augustine begins his introspective search for a trinity within the mind by looking at a variety of intellectual activities which are 'consubstantial'. Towards the end of Book VIII he had begun to discern a threefold structure in human loving leading to an image of the Trinity as the lover, the beloved, and love itself (*De Trin.* Bk VIII.10.14).[96] But when one looks at the love of self, it appears only two acts are involved: the lover and love. Yet, he maintains, we cannot love what we do not know – and so he restores the triadic pattern of the self or mind (*mens*), its knowing (*notitia*) and loving (*amor*). This trinity of the mind knowing and loving itself is inspired by the Prologue to St John's Gospel where the Word of God is uttered by the Father. In a similar way Augustine will say that in the act of knowledge the mind produces or begets a mental word (*verbum*) that is self-expressive, moved and sustained by love or desire, and culminates in a judgement of value or truth. Or as Étienne Gilson has put it, 'the very act of conceiving truth is but an image within us of the Word's conception by the Father in the bosom of the Trinity'.[97] In Book X he further explores the nature of mind and locates this in a seeking, dynamic self-presence: the mind knows itself even when it is looking for itself, and yet it knows itself as always in movement and always incomplete. To bring out the dynamic and interactive dimensions of the self's activities, Augustine refines the terminology of *mens*, *notitia*, and *amor* to that of memory (*memoria*), understanding (*intelligentia*), and will (*voluntas*). Memory, understanding, and will are three in that they are mutually referred to each other and contain each other, but they are 'not three lives but one life, not three minds but one mind … [T]hese three are one in that they are one life, one mind, and one essence' (*De Trin.* Bk X.11.18).[98] This final triad, Augustine concedes, is an imperfect image of the Trinity but nonetheless an image: it can be located within, but not identified with, the self.

---

[95] A key scriptural text for Augustine here is 1 Cor. 13:12, 'For now we see in a mirror dimly, but then face to face'. *Mens* or mind distinguishes us from the lower animals, but it is more than the power of reasoning; it includes the subject as self-aware: feeling, desiring, willing as well as thinking.

[96] He develops this analogy in Bk IX.

[97] Étienne Gilson, *The Christian Philosophy of Saint Augustine*, trans. L. E. M. Lynch (New York: Octagon Books, 1983), 222.

[98] Bk XI treats of lesser trinitarian analogies that originate 'from without', in particular, the act of seeing. Thus we have the visible thing itself (sense memory), its image impressed on the beholder (internal vision), and the will which combines the two.

In Books XII and XIII Augustine explores the history of the image of God in us, a history of humankind's fall and redemption, of defacement and restoration of the divine image. For Augustine, it is not just a matter of discovering a trinitarian image of God in the human mind or self. He saw the Christian vocation as a seeking for God, and the only way to find God is to become truly like the Father, Son, and Spirit. All reflection on the Trinity is inseparably connected with our spiritual growth and sanctification. In this context he distinguishes between superior and inferior reason, between *sapientia* and *scientia*. The latter refers to more practical, functional knowledge – the cognisance of things temporal and changeable – while the former is a contemplative wisdom directed towards eternal reality. As far as his search for an understanding of the Trinity is concerned, this means that it is only with divine grace that any insight into the divine mystery is possible. Concluding with a profound prayer to the triune God represents, therefore, not a pious appendix to the work but a recapitulation of the motivation of Augustine's theological life: 'May I remember You, understand You, and love You. Increase these gifts in me, until you have reformed me completely' (*De Trin.* Bk XV.28.51).[99]

Despite the originality of Augustine's approach, the psychological analogy does not feature prominently in contemporary trinitarian theology. Augustine's analogy of the individual remembering, understanding, and loving itself has been criticised as an excessively individualistic and introspective view of the human person and ultimately of God.[100] It seems we need only to look within ourselves to discover God. Contemplating that image in ourselves we are moved like the Prodigal Son to return to ourselves, to arise and make our way back to God from whom our sins had drawn us away. In fairness to Augustine, however, he sees the highest human trinity not in the human mind remembering, understanding, and loving *itself*, but in remembering, understanding, and loving *God* (*De Trin.* Bk XIV.12.15).[101] He stressed that Father, Son, and Spirit are words indicating *relationship* – a

---

[99] 'The mind of St. Augustine was always centred on God; he sought Him everywhere, and when he came across something that would help to make God better known and loved, he did not hesitate to write about it.' Stephen McKenna, 'Introduction', in *Saint Augustine: The Trinity*, The Fathers of the Church Series (Washington, DC: Catholic University of America Press, 1963), xii–xiii.

[100] Colin E. Gunton, 'Augustine, the Trinity and the Theological Crisis of the West', in his *The Promise of Trinitarian Theology* (Edinburgh: T&T Clark, 1991), 31–57. For a critical response to Gunton, see Neil Ormerod, 'Augustine and the Trinity: Whose Crisis?', *Pacifica* 16 (2003): 17–32. See also Anne Hunt, 'Psychological Analogy and Paschal Mystery in Trinitarian Theology', *Theological Studies* 59 (1998): 197–218.

[101] Bk XIV shows how it is *sapientia*, true wisdom culminating in worship, that perfects the image (of the triune God) within the person. It is in loving God, not in self-preoccupation, that the *mens* comes to truly know and love itself.

term he saw not merely as a theological tool to speak about the Trinity but as the central theme in the Christian journey.[102] His *De Trinitate* is a fusion of meditation and speculation aware that no image can ever adequately represent the triune God.[103] Finally, by integrating the concept of love into his theology, particularly his theology of the Spirit, he laid the foundations for a spirituality based on a trinitarian rhythm of giving and receiving love.[104]

CONCLUSION: THE TRIUNE GOD BETWEEN AFFIRMATION AND NEGATION

Augustine maintained that everything that exists bears the stamp of the source whence it has received its being. Thus he saw traces of the one and triune God in nature and in the human mind with its self-related trinitarian structure. While his philosophical background included influences from the Neoplatonic Victorinus and Plotinus, and though he believed Platonism and Christianity had much in common, it was his discovery of Christ as the only Way that moved Augustine beyond the 'books of the Platonists'.[105] His way to God by way of the intellect or mind is one whereby the latter is illuminated by the divine light from above. Real knowledge of God requires divine assistance and calls for a right relation to God. God is to be found not simply by turning inward to the centre of the soul but, further, by turning upward. The mind is perfected in love, and real knowing is proportionate to the love of what is known. Indeed, the dignity of the mind or soul is manifest in its *capax Dei*, that is, in its ability to possess and worship God, by whom and in whose image it is (*De Trin.* Bk XIV.4.6).

At the same time we have seen that Augustine's way of thinking about God clearly has a negative or apophatic character. Always conscious of the distance between himself and the triune God, Augustine suggests that we:

think of God, if we are able, and insofar as we are able, in the following way: as good without quality, as great without quantity, as creator without need, as presiding without posture, as containing all things without possession, as whole everywhere

---

[102] Mary T. Clark, 'The Trinity in Latin Christianity', in McGinn and Meyendorff, eds., *Christian Spirituality: Origins to the Twelfth Century*, 285.

[103] While memory as a source of understanding can serve as a pointer to the Father, understanding a pointer to the Son (as self-communication of the Father), and will to the Spirit, who is love, the analogy is inadequate in that it could give the impression that each Person of the Trinity lacked what the other possessed.

[104] Clark, '*De Trinitate*', 99.   [105] For what follows see *Confessions* 7.9.13ff. See also 7.18.24.

without place, as eternal without time, as making mutable things without any change of Himself and undergoing nothing.

And he concludes:

Whoever so thinks of God, even though he does not yet discover fully what God is, nevertheless, by his pious attitude of mind avoids, as far as is possible, thinking about Him what He is not. (*De Trin.* Bk V.i.2)

Augustine's distinction between speaking about God, thinking about God, and the being of God (*dicere–cogitare–esse*) form three levels by which we attempt to formulate our relationship with God.[106] Though recognising God as a spiritual substance, he can still describe God as great, good, wise, just, and so on, but he is careful to insist that goodness, truth, wisdom, and love cannot be considered accidents in God for God *is* goodness, truth, wisdom, love, and so on. These properties of God, however, are subordinated to the mysterious name that God revealed to Moses, 'Ego sum qui sum' (Exod. 3:14), 'I am who am' or 'I am He who is'. For Augustine, 'Being', or better 'To Be', is God's proper name:

He is without doubt a substance or essence, which the Greeks know as *ousia*, for as wisdom derives from being wise and knowledge from the act of knowing, so what we know as essence comes from being ... And so he who is God is the only unchangeable substance or essence, to whom being itself, from which the name essence derives, most truly belongs. (*De Trin.* Bk V.2.3)

Ultimately, for Augustine, God's Being is an object of faith. We are unable to understand fully God's name as revealed to Moses. We can only touch it with our mind but not attain to it. We have made a good start, he states, in our task of knowing God if we understand what God is *not* – leading to a kind of 'learned ignorance' (*docta ignorantia*).[107] While we will see God after this life, even then we will not comprehend God fully; we will rather participate in God's divinity. Augustine's desire 'to speak things unspeakable', however, was not only to avoid false representations of God or to assist those who had gone astray, but also to proclaim, honour, and praise God's ineffable greatness and goodness.[108]

---

[106] 'For what is thought of God is truer than what is said, and His being is truer than what is thought.' *De Trin.* Bk. VII.4.7. See T. J. van Bavel, 'God in between Affirmation and Negation According to Augustine', in Joseph T. Lienhard, Earl C. Muller, and Roland J. Teske, eds., *Collectanea Augustiniana: Augustine: Presbyter Factus Sum* (New York: Peter Lang, 1990), 73–97 (esp. pp. 80–5).

[107] 'If you cannot now comprehend what God is, at least comprehend what He is not. You will have made much progress if you do not think of God something other than He is.' *Tractates on the Gospel of John* XXIII.9. See also *Sermon* CXVII.iii.5. This theme of noetic darkness is also to be found in the Cappadocians. See Gregory of Nyssa, *The Life of Moses*, trans. A. J. Malherbe and E. Ferguson (New York: Paulist Press, 1978), 95.

[108] *De Trin.* Bk VII.1.2. See also *On Christian Doctrine* I.6.6.

In drawing attention to the apophatic character of Augustine's methodology – he affirmed by negating – it is also important to recall Augustine's so-called hermeneutical circle: we understand in order to believe and believe in order to understand. And in this process *both* faith and reason have a part to play. Knowledge and grace go hand in hand: knowledge is also a divine gift. A person would never seek something if it were not already known, desired, or given in some way or other.[109]

By seeking to make statements which, while not claiming to apprehend or grasp God, at least point in the right direction, Augustine's approach is not dissimilar to the Cappadocians', and in particular that of Gregory of Nyssa. Eastern theology, be it the Cappadocians, John Damascene, or Pseudo-Dionysius, evinces a negative or apophatic theology that entails not merely an intellectual quest, but an inward purification (*catharsis*): to know God one must draw near to God. The way of knowledge of God is necessarily the way of deification. Speculation gradually gives way to contemplation.[110] Until recently, however, the tendency among systematic theologians has been to oppose Latin and Greek versions of trinitarian theology. Augustine, as the representative figure of the West, is said to begin with the reality of the unity of the divine nature, while the East (e.g., the Cappadocians) begins with the reality of the divine persons. The picture is, of course, subtler than this. It is easy to present a caricature of Augustine as the father of modern individualism, that is, to view his trinitarian theology and its development of the psychological analogy as a precursor to the later Cartesian pre-occupation with the self-constituting, autonomous subject. Similarly, the Cappadocians are sometimes viewed as representing a unified theology, grounding a more relational or social trinitarian doctrine that contrasts sharply with Augustine. That there is a strongly apophatic strand in both the Cappadocians and Augustine, that Augustine also treats of the trinitarian economy and the relational implications of trinitarian doctrine is overlooked.[111] Patristic scholars sound a timely warning about drawing up categories of polar opposition (whether for pedagogical or ideological reasons) or false disjunctions between East and West.

---

[109] For the desire latent in seeking, see *De Trin.* Bk IX.12.18.

[110] Vladimir Lossky, *The Mystical Theology of the Eastern Church* (Cambridge and London: James Clarke & Co., 1957, 1973), 37–42.

[111] In *De Trin.* Bk IX.12.17, Augustine identifies the Holy Spirit with love, and elsewhere (Bk VI.5.7) spells out its implications: 'For whether he [the Holy Spirit] is the unity between both of them [Father and Son] or their holiness, or their love, or whether the unity is because he is the holiness, it is obvious that he is not one of the two. Through him both are joined together; through him the begotten is loved by the begetter, and in turn loves him who begot him ... And we are commanded by grace to imitate this unity, both in our relations with God as well as among ourselves.'

Michel Barnes, for example, speaks of a 'polarizing hermeneutic of doctrine' in current theology where 'details matter less than perspective'. Systematicians, he contends, prefer an architectonic and idealistic style of writing, whereas his claim is 'that the more tightly controlled a reading is by an ideological end the more damaged is the historical sensitivity'.[112] In relation to the Cappadocians, specifically to Gregory of Nyssa, Sarah Coakley has cautioned against anachronistically importing 'modern' conceptions of human personhood into patristic texts.[113] That said, however, the impression is that patristic scholars (e.g., of Augustine) can be overly defensive of, and reluctant to reproach, their theological heralds. The challenge is to explore how some of the major theological figures discussed here can provide seeds for a renewal of current trinitarian theology and practice, on the one hand, while not projecting contemporary concerns and biases – epistemological, theological, or political – eisegetically back into fourth-century theological culture and texts, on the other. Most systematic theologians currently writing on the Trinity generally take their cue from its legacy of marginalisation and functional irrelevance for a large part of the twentieth century. If greater dialogue between patristic scholars and systematic theologians can help overcome this unfortunate legacy, then it is only to be welcomed.

SUGGESTED READINGS

Ayres, Lewis, *Nicea and its Legacy: An Approach to Fourth-Century Trinitarian Theology* (Oxford: Oxford University Press, 2004).

Davis, Stephen T., Daniel Kendall and Gerald O'Collins, eds., *The Trinity: An Interdisciplinary Symposium on the Trinity* (Oxford: Oxford University Press, 1999).

Grillmeier, Aloys, *Christ in Christian Tradition*, vol. 1, 2nd rev. edn, trans. John Bowden (London and Oxford: Mowbrays, 1975).

Hanson, R. P. C., *The Search for the Christian Doctrine of God: The Arian Controversy 318–381* (Edinburgh: T&T Clark, 1988).

Hill, William J., *The Three-Personed God: The Trinity as a Mystery of Salvation* (Washington, DC: Catholic University of America Press, 1988).

Kelly, J. N. D., *Early Christian Doctrines*, 5th edn (London: Adam & Charles Black, 1977).

Studer, Basil, *Trinity and Incarnation: The Faith of the Early Church*, trans. M. Westerhoff, ed. A. Louth (Collegeville, MN: The Liturgical Press, 1993).

---

[112] Michel René Barnes, 'Augustine in Contemporary Trinitarian Theology', *Theological Studies* 56 (1995): 241, 242 (n. 23).

[113] Sarah Coakley, '"Persons" in the "Social" Doctrine of the Trinity: A Critique of Current Analytic Discussion', in Davis et al., eds., *The Trinity: An Interdisciplinary Symposium*, 123–44, at 129.

CHAPTER 4

Theology of the Trinity from Richard of St Victor to the Reformation

In the next two chapters we will give a historical overview of the developments of the theology of the Trinity from the medieval period until today. Most textbooks claim that in the medieval period two distinct models of trinitarian theology were developed. The first model is usually called the intrapersonal model (or the psychological model). This model draws its inspiration from the analysis of the mental processes of intellect and will. The other is usually called the interpersonal model: this model generally attempts to portray the Trinity in terms of the loving encounter of three 'Persons'.

We will first discuss the theology of the Trinity of Richard of St Victor, who sees the Trinity in terms of a community of love. St Bonaventure (who was both an academic theologian and a mystic) adopted some of the key ideas of Richard, but he also drew on St Augustine's theology of the Trinity. This observation is not without significance, for it illustrates that the two models should not necessarily be regarded as mutually exclusive. The Augustinian approach was further developed by Aquinas, the greatest of the scholastic theologians. We will also examine the thought of Jan van Ruusbroec, who presents us with a beautiful and dynamic theology of the Trinity, which is of immediate relevance to Christian spirituality.

All these medieval authors, in their diversity, share a number of key presuppositions in relation to the way faith and reason, and tradition and faith, should relate to one another. From the late-medieval period onwards, however, we witness a number of important intellectual developments that would undermine this shared worldview: a growing separation of faith and reason (from the end of the thirteenth century onwards); the gradual disappearance of the sacramental worldview (in which creation is seen as somehow reflecting the glory and beauty of God); a declining emphasis from the beginning of the sixteenth century upon the authority of the *tradition* of faith as a legitimate perspective from which to interpret the Scriptures, combined with an increasing awareness of the historicity of the Scriptures after the Reformation; and, finally, a growing scepticism of allegorical readings of those Scriptures. All these elements had major implications for the interpretation of traditional approaches to the mystery of the Trinity. Although some of these issues date from the late medieval period, *all* these tensions begin to surface at the time of the Reformation, and come to a climax during the Enlightenment period, when the harmonious relations between faith and reason, scriptural interpretation and tradition were severed, with serious implications for the theology of the Trinity. It is our aim to sketch some of these developments in the following two chapters.

This is of more than merely historical interest. Without any knowledge of this late-medieval and early-modern context a proper engagement with the issues of theology today is not possible. As we will see in Chapter 6, the two most popular models of the Trinity – the social and the psychological – still dominate discussion in the twenty-first century. The innovations of Luther and Hegel continue to influence the theological agenda. Moreover, as medieval theologians such as Richard of St Victor, Bonaventure, and Thomas Aquinas operated from within a hermeneutical perspective which differs significantly from the modern one, we may perhaps find in their works rich resources to construct a theology of the Trinity for a 'postmodern' era.

RICHARD OF ST VICTOR (D. 1173) AND THE TRINITY AS INTERPERSONAL LOVE

We will first examine the trinitarian theology of Richard of St Victor, a canon regular who resided at St Victor near Paris. Scholars regard his major work *The Trinity* (*De Trinitate*) as an alternative to the Augustinian-Thomistic intrapersonal model, which, according to its critics, fails to do full justice to the tri-personal nature of the Trinity.[1] It is argued that by developing an understanding of the Trinity in terms of interpersonal love, rather than in terms of an intrapersonal psychological analogy, Richard is more faithful to the Christian understanding of God as love (1 John 4:8). However, it has long been noted that Richard actually draws his inspiration from Augustine's *De Trinitate* (see Augustine, *De Trinitate* VIII.12, 14;

---

[1] For the text of Richard's *De Trinitate* we used Richard de Saint-Victor, *La Trinité*, ed. Gaston Salet, Sources Chrétiennes 63 (Paris: Cerf, 1998). Book III has been translated by Grover A. Zinn in Richard of St Victor, *The Twelve Patriarchs. The Mystical Ark. Book Three of* The Trinity, Classics of Western Spirituality (New York: Paulist Press, 1979).

IX.2). Also, when he discusses personal names of the Word and the Holy Spirit, Richard remains indebted to Augustine.

A more profound engagement with Richard's thought on its own terms may challenge the way his thought has been adopted and championed by some twentieth-century theologians, such as Jürgen Moltmann. A key issue is the different ways of understanding the notion of 'personhood'. For us moderns, the word 'persons' conjures up associations of 'spiritual centres of activity, of several subjectivities'.[2] For Richard, such an understanding of personhood is in danger of resulting in gross tritheism.

Another indication that some of the popular presentations of Richard's thought as a social trinitarian thinker *avant la lettre* need to be qualified is that Richard devotes as much intellectual energy to discussing the divine substance or unity as to examining the divine threeness. The discussion of the divine unity (*unitas divinitatis*, I.25), which exists by itself and is its own origin (*substantia a semetipsa*, I.11), and which is the ground of all beings (I.12), precedes a discussion of the divine Persons. This illustrates that a thinker who starts with a discussion of the divine unity or substance before a discussion of the divine Persons does not therefore *de facto* compromise his trinitarian credentials (a point often raised against Aquinas' treatment).

We will first discuss how Richard argues that we can harmonise belief in God's unity with belief in the threeness of the Persons. In doing so, we will also pay attention to the contemplative disposition Richard, and many medieval theologians after him, believe we should cultivate to approach the mystery of the Trinity. Given his presuppositions on the nature of love we will examine how Richard argues for a plurality of persons within the divinity, while paying specific attention to the notion of personhood. This will pave the way for an engagement with his theology of the Trinity and his discussion of the divine names.

a. Divine unity and the contemplative disposition

From the contingency and finitude of creation Richard argues that there must be a being which is its own origin. For if there were no being which is its own origin, there would be no principle which would be capable of bringing into existence those beings which are not their own existence (I.8). The counterargument that perhaps the whole world has always existed simply clashes with our experience of contingency.

[2] Karl Rahner, *The Trinity*, rev. edn, trans. J. Donceel, intro. Catherine Mowry LaCugna (New York: Crossroad, 1998), 106.

Rather than examining the merits of Richard's argument in its own right, we would like to pause and examine the way this argument reveals something of how Richard sees the relation between faith and reason (and which differs rather considerably from the way it is seen in modern philosophy). For Richard's argument is, of course, not a philosophical proof in the strict sense: when he states that our reasoning (*ratiocinando*) leads us 'from the visible to the invisible', 'from the transient to the eternal, from the worldly to the supra-worldly, from the human to the divine' (I.8) he stands squarely in the Anselmic tradition of faith seeking understanding:

> To understand these truths of which it has been rightly said 'If you do not believe, you will not understand,' you must enter by faith. But we must not immediately halt here; rather we should constantly reach out towards a more intimate and profound understanding, and with a complete studiousness and highest diligence penetrate deeper from day to day, through newly acquired insights into an understanding of our faith. (I.3)

Richard's theology of the Trinity both arises from, and results in, a contemplative disposition. He describes it as a ladder by which we climb from a reflection (*speculatio*) of the visible to a contemplation (*contemplatio*) of the invisible mystery of God (I.10), which nevertheless will always remain beyond our grasp (I.19). In short, Richard, writing long before the modern divide between faith and 'autonomous' reason, requires from his readers an almost aesthetic receptivity towards the world, in order to be able to see the world as a pointer to the mystery that grounds it. As we will see, Bonaventure too adopts this stance and develops it further. One of our arguments throughout this chapter will be that when this sacramental worldview (and the religious-aesthetic disposition it entails) is displaced in the modern period by a mechanistic worldview that leaves no room for God, it becomes more difficult to appreciate, let alone construct, a theology of the Trinity.

Having discussed in the second book of *De Trinitate* the divine attributes, such as uncreatedness, immutability, eternity, infinity, incommunicability, indivisibility, and simplicity, Richard, in Book III, examines the divine plurality. How can we square the unity of the divine substance with a plurality of Persons?

b. *Plurality of Persons and the order of love*

Given that within God there is plenitude of goodness, and goodness implies true love (*caritas*), Richard states that love demands a plurality of Persons, for love by its nature entails an orientation towards another. Not only does it belong to the nature of love to be shared, but it is only when love is reciprocated that it is the source of supreme happiness. Richard then takes his analysis of love one step further: if love is to be genuinely perfect it must have a triadic structure:

> Certainly in mutual and very fervent love nothing is rarer or more magnificent than to wish that another be loved equally by the one whom you love supremely and by whom you are supremely loved. And so the proof of perfected charity is a willing sharing of the love that has been shown to you. So a person proves that he is not perfect in charity if he cannot yet take pleasure in sharing his excellent joy ... Therefore it is necessary that each of those loved supremely and loving supremely should search with equal desire for someone who would be mutually loved (*condilectus*) and with equal concord and willingly possess them. Thus you see how the perfection of charity requires a Trinity of Persons ... (III.11, trans. 384–5)

This analysis of love is at the heart of Richard's theology of the Trinity. Love between only two divine Persons would not be perfect; it would be somewhat self-enclosed and exclusivist, at odds with the harmonious (*concordialis*) and shared or communal (*consocialis*) nature of love (III.20). The key term is *condilectus*, a term coined by Richard himself. It can be translated as 'co-beloved', the one who is loved by two lovers as the perfect expression and union of their love.[3] It is with the co-beloved (*condilectus*) that the others share the delights of the love they harbour for each other (VI.6; III.14 and 15).

c. Divine plurality and the intricacies of personhood

In order to illuminate the mystery of the Three in One, Richard considers the meaning of the word 'Person' at length. This issue, which is rather technical, is nevertheless of immediate relevance to present-day debates on the theology of the Trinity. For instance, whether or not some social trinitarian thinkers are in danger of flirting with tritheism hinges on their understanding of personhood. Similarly, whether or not theologians (such as Karl Rahner or Karl Barth) who espouse a 'mono-personal trinitarian model' are insufficiently trinitarian will, again, largely depend on how they interpret the traditional notion of personhood – for instance as 'modes of

---

[3] As Richard puts it: 'Shared love (*condilectio*) is properly said to exist when a third Person is loved by two Persons harmoniously (*concorditer*) and in community (*socialiter*), and the affection of the two Persons is fused into one affection by the flame of love for the third' (III.19).

being (*drei Seinsweisen*) of the one personal God'[4] or as 'distinct manners of subsisting' (*distinkte Subsistenzweise*).[5]

Richard defines 'Person' as 'an incommunicable existence (*incommunicabilis exsistentia*) of the divine nature' (IV.18 and 22). In this way he distances himself from Boethian substantialist views on personhood.[6] Two elements are important here: existence and incommunicability.

In relation to the first point, Richard provides an analysis of the word 'existence' (*exsistentia*) which reinforces his relational understanding and which, incidentally, foreshadows some of the twentieth-century existentialist analyses. He points out that the word 'existence' is derived from the word 'exist' (*exsistere*). This word consists of two parts: 'ex' (= from, out of) and 'ist' (*sistere*), which means 'to be'. While the word 'sistere' seems to denote something which is, the word 'ex-ist' (*exsistere*) does not simply denote being, but it also seems to contain a reference to a kind of origin. Something 'ex-ists' when it has its being from elsewhere or from somebody else: 'what does to exist (*exsistere*) mean but to be (*sistere*) from (*ex*) somebody, to receive one's substantial being from somebody?' (IV.12; also IV.23)

Thus, Richard's analysis of divine ex-istence already points to his understanding of Persons in terms of origin, which is the only way in which the Persons can be distinguished from one another without compromising the divine unity (IV.15). He is aware of the importance of this discovery: 'Thus we have found what we had been looking for: how there can be distinction (*alteritas*) of Persons without any distinction (*alteritas*) of substances' (IV.15).

This brings us to the issue of incommunicability (or distinctiveness): although the three divine Persons share the divine nature (*exsistentia communis*), the Persons themselves are constituted by their own unique way of being: their *exsistentia incommunicabilis* (IV.16–17), that is, those personal characteristics that cannot be shared. The personal characteristic or property (*proprietas personalis*) is that which makes each of the Persons distinct. To claim that a personal property could be shared would amount to saying that an individual person could be two persons (IV.17). Thus, the divine Persons share the one divine substance in their distinct manner (IV.19). In this way there can be a plurality of existences or *hypostases* within the unity of the divine substance (IV.20). In short, for Richard, the divine being itself – understood as love – yields an inner plurality of Persons who differ in their

---

[4] Barth, *CD* IV/ 2, 44.   [5] Rahner, *The Trinity*, 109ff.
[6] Boethius had defined person as 'an individual substance of a rational nature'. Richard prefers 'existence' over 'substance'.

origin. It is through the origin of the divine Persons that we can discern their distinguishing properties (V.1). Let us examine in more detail how the Persons differ through their origin.

In the first part of his book Richard had argued for the existence of God as *causa sui* on the basis that to deny this would lead to an infinite regress. He now applies a similar reasoning to the Trinity: there must be a Person in the divinity who is his own cause and does not derive his being from another. Otherwise there would be an infinity of Persons in the Godhead (V.3). Richard will identify this Person with the Father, who alone is his own origin (*innascibilis*), and it is this characteristic that constitutes him as a unique (*incommunicabilis*) existence (V.5).

Recalling his arguments from Book III about the nature of love and the need for a co-beloved (*condilectus*), Richard distinguishes in Book V between love that is freely bestowed (*gratuitus*), freely received (*debitus*), or a combination of both (i.e., freely given and received, *ex utroque permixtus*) (V.16):

> Love is freely given (*amor gratuitus*) when one freely bestows one's love on somebody from whom one has not received anything. Love is received (*amor debitus*) when one returns (*rependit*) to the one who freely bestowed his love nothing but love. Love is a combination of both (*ex utroque permixtus*) when one freely receives and freely bestows love. (V.16)

The Person who freely bestows (*communicare*) the plenitude of his love is, of course, the Father (V.17). The Son both receives and bestows love (*permixtus*): he receives love from the Father and bestows it on the Spirit (*filioque*) (V.19). Richard usually describes the Spirit as the one who receives love without bestowing it on another divine Person. However, in the above quotation Richard states that the Spirit 'returns' (*rependit*) love. We will come back to this ambiguity. What is clear is that Richard sees the Trinity as a community of love, with the Father as the origin, the Spirit as the one who receives love, and the Son as the one who receives love and co-bestows it (with the Father) on the Spirit.

d. Divine names

For Richard each of the divine Persons shares the divine love in his own distinctive manner (V.20). In Book VI he discusses the distinctiveness of the divine Persons by way of origin in more detail by examining the personal names (Father, Son, Holy Spirit, Word, Image, Gift) and appropriations (power, wisdom, goodness). A personal name is a name that strictly applies to one of the three Persons only. When a name can be applied to the Trinity as such but is especially associated with one of the three Persons, it can be appropriated. For instance, 'Wisdom' is usually appropriated to the 'Word' (a personal name), although strictly speaking the whole Trinity is 'wise'.

'Father' is the personal name of the first Person of the Trinity as he is the origin of the Trinity, while 'Son' is the name of the second, as he is generated by the Father (VI.4). The third Person is called 'Holy Spirit' as he is the common love of Father and Son, which is then breathed – in-spired – into the hearts of the saints by the Father and the Son. As air is necessary for the life of the body, so too the divine Spirit is necessary for a saintly life (VI.10): here an interesting connection is made between Richard's theology of the Trinity and Christian spirituality.

The Son is also called 'Word' as this name points to the fact that the Son reveals or expresses the glory and truth of the Father – in the same way as a word originates from the heart of a person (VI.13). Richard combines here an 'intrapersonal' explanation, at least partly derived from Augustine (*De Trin.* XV.20, 23, 24), with an 'interpersonal' analysis of love. This illustrates that for him at least the psychological and social models are not mutually exclusive.

Richard's discussion of the personal name 'Gift' for the Holy Spirit offers rich insights for those, like John Milbank (see Chapter 6), who would like to develop a trinitarian ontology of gift. As the Holy Spirit is the expression of the love between Father and Son (as Love received), it is this love which is given to us; it is Love received which we receive and which 'in-spires' us (VI.14). As creaturely beings we receive everything from God, and in our sanctification we become 'configurated' to the Spirit, that is, we learn to love God with a love that is utterly owed or received. The Holy Spirit in which we share is the 'outcome' of the Love between Father and Son. This too is traditional Augustinian teaching (*De Trin.* V.15, 16). In this instance Richard's approach allows him to convincingly argue how the mission of the Holy Spirit reveals the procession of the Spirit (whereas in the case of the mission of the Word the link with Love both received and given remains unclear).

e. Evaluation

For Richard the Trinity is a mystery of interpersonal Love. Developing a sophisticated analysis of the 'ecstatic' nature of Love, he develops an original model in which the Father is the origin of the Trinity, the Son is the one who receives this Love from the Father and bestows it, with the Father, unto the Holy Spirit who receives it without bestowing it unto another divine Person. The immediate appeal of Richard's model is that it seems to do full justice to the New Testament understanding of God as love. Another strength – although Richard does not explicitly develop this – is that in principle it allows us to establish a close link between the intra-trinitarian generation of the Son from the Father as an act of love and the Father's loving surrender of the Son on the cross – a link which the intrapersonal model cannot make particularly clear. There is, however, a certain ambiguity in relation to the Person of the Holy Spirit. In some places Richard seems to suggest that the Holy Spirit merely receives love and does not actively love another (divine) Person: the property of the Holy Spirit is to possess love without giving it to another Person (*Proprium autem Spiritui sancto habere nec alicui dare*) (VI.11). Especially in those passages where Richard is at pains to distinguish the Spirit from the second Person (the Son, the image of the Father) he emphasises that the Spirit, unlike the Son, does not share in the spirative plentitude of the Father: 'No person whatsoever receives from the Holy Spirit the plenitude of the divinity. For this reason he does not express in himself the image of the Father' (VI.11). This seems to lead to a somewhat passive pneumatology: the Holy Spirit is merely given but does not love us actively, reflecting his 'passive' or receptive status within the immanent Trinity. In other places Richard does seem to suggest that the Spirit loves (*rependit*) the other Persons, albeit with a love that is utterly 'received'. This, however, raises the question whether he can still maintain the personal distinction between Son and Spirit within the Trinity.

We have expressed some reservations about interpretations (such as Moltmann's) that appeal to Richard as a precursor to the social model of the Trinity (to be discussed later). Richard's reservations about a substantialist understanding of personhood, inspired by his desire to steer well away from tritheism, illustrates that he would be uncomfortable with some versions of social trinitarianism. It is, however, fair to say that Richard offers an alternative to the psychological model. The latter model implies a close link between our 'psychology' and the intra-trinitarian processions, and it therefore offers resources to link the theology of the Trinity with spirituality, that is, how to participate in the life of the Trinity. In Richard's interpersonal model this link is not so easy to establish.

Richard's ideas were highly influential. St Thomas Aquinas initially commented on them with some apparent approval (in *De Pot.* 9.9), but he later criticises the key presupposition (the necessity of love to be shared), which, he suggests, only holds 'in the case of not having perfect goodness'

(*ST* I.32.2 *ad* 2). It was St Bonaventure who was to fully espouse and further develop some of Richard's key insights.

ST BONAVENTURE (D. 1274) AND A SAPIENTIAL THEOLOGY OF THE TRINITY

In the Franciscan theology of St Bonaventure we find a harmonious synthesis of Augustinian, Pseudo-Dionysian and Richardian elements. Few theologians in the West have been imbued with such a strong sense of the splendour of the trinitarian God. Bonaventure developed his theology of the Trinity in all his major works. His works are usually divided into two categories: his more theoretical works (such as his *Commentary on the Sentences* (*Sent.*), the *Breviloquium* (a wonderful summary of the Christian faith) or the *Disputed Questions on the Mystery of the Trinity*, and his more devotional works such as *The Soul's Journey into God* (*Itinerarium mentis in Deum*). Another work in which Bonaventure attempts to disclose the significance of the theology of the Trinity for our understanding of our world is the *Collations on the Hexameron* (*Hex.*).

We have seen that Richard of St Victor starts with a discussion of the divine unity. Bonaventure is often hailed as an author who takes a different approach. It is true that in the *Breviloquium* he first briefly discusses the doctrine of the Trinity. In his equally profound *Disputed Questions on the Mystery of the Trinity* (*Myst. Trin.*), however, he first deals with the question of God's existence as such, before embarking on a consideration of the Trinity. Clearly we should not read too much into the sequence of the treatises of the oneness and threeness of the Christian God.

a. Sapiential theology

For Bonaventure, as for Richard, it is essential to approach the mystery of the Trinity with a proper disposition or receptivity, deeply shaped by faith and devotion. In Bonaventure's view 'autonomous' reason is nothing but a self-inflicted tutelage. Philosophy has to subject itself to theology if it is to flourish. An independent philosophy will ultimately result in errors (*Hex.* IV.1). Only faith can separate light from darkness (cf. Gen. 1:4) while a presumptuous, supposedly autonomous philosophy will only lead to error.[7] Theology as wisdom (*sapientia*) is both knowledge (*cognitio*) and love

---

[7] *Hex.* VII.13: 'only faith "separates the light from the darkness" (cf. Gn. 1:4) [. . .] Faith, with hope and love and its works, heals the soul and, thus healed, purifies it and renders it deiform.'

(*affectum*) (I *Sent* Prooem q. 3 concl.).[8] This sapiential understanding of theology implies a close link between theology and spirituality: 'There is no sure passage from science to wisdom; a medium must be provided, namely holiness'. (*Hex.* XIX.3)

This devout and loving disposition, which is a central aspect of theology as Bonaventure sees it, is crucial to make sense of the theology of the Trinity. It will prove essential, for instance, to see how he deduces the threeness of God from the divine unity. A quotation from the *Breviloquium* I.2.3 makes Bonaventure's stance clear:

> Since faith is the source of our worship of God and the foundation of that doctrine which is according to piety (cf. 1 Tim. 6:3), it dictates that we should conceive of God in the most elevated and most loving manner. Now our thought would not be the most elevated if we did not believe that God could communicate himself in the most complete way, and it would not be the most loving if, believing him so able, we thought him unwilling to do so. Hence, if we are to think of God most loftily and most lovingly, faith tells us that God totally communicates himself by eternally having a beloved and another who is loved by both (*condilectum*). In this way God is both one and three.[9]

This passage – and especially the use of the word *condilectus* – echoes the theology of Richard of St Victor. We will discuss this later. For the moment we would like to focus a little more on Bonaventure's hermeneutical stance – that is, the presuppositions that govern his approach to the doctrine of the Trinity.

Our present illumination in the divine light is seen as an imperfect participation in the fullness of divine light which the blessed enjoy in heaven. Now, crucially, it is this participation that assists us in developing the proper receptivity and sensitivity to be drawn into the mystery of the Trinity. Bonaventure's views invite us to fundamentally rethink our own disposition when we even begin to consider the dogma of the Trinity. The question whether the doctrine can be found in the Scriptures is, for instance, only secondary (although Bonaventure answers it with a resounding yes, at least insofar as the New Testament is concerned). More important is the hermeneutical starting point, which is one obviously informed by faith. Bonaventure's approach, writing before the modern separation of faith and 'autonomous' reason, or tradition and history, is very different from most theological stances taken today:

---

[8] See Charles Carpenter, *Theology as the Road to Holiness in St. Bonaventure* (New York: Paulist Press, 1997), 24–7.
[9] *Works of St Bonaventure*, vol. IX. *Breviloquium*, trans. D. Monti, Bonaventure Texts in Translation Series (New York: The Franciscan Institute, 2005), 30–1 (hereafter abbreviated to *Brevil.*).

If it is asked what it is that moves us to believe this – is it Scripture, or miracles, or grace, i.e., the eternal truth itself – the answer should be that that which moves us principally is the illumination which begins in the natural light and finds its consummation in the infused light, for this leads us to think of God not only in a lofty manner but also in a reverent manner, because this illumination proceeds from the eternal light itself which takes our intellect into obedient captivity (cf. 2 Cor. 10:5); in capturing the mind, it subjects it to God in worship and veneration and renders it ready to believe whatever pertains to the divine honor and veneration, even though such things be beyond our reason. (*Myst. Trin* I, 2 concl.)[10]

This quotation illustrates that, according to Bonaventure, one needs a certain mindset, informed by grace, to approach the mystery of the triune God. Today we would say that one needs a kind of religious receptivity, an openness – not unlike the openness needed to appreciate great works of art. The fact that we revert to aesthetic categories is no coincidence: for Bonaventure the created world is like a piece of art, which reflects and reveals the splendour of its triune Creator. When Bonaventure claims that it is necessary to cultivate a certain mindset in order to interpret reality properly, he does so because reality itself is trinitarian. This is why reason needs to be supplemented by faith in order to perceive reality properly (III *Sent.* d. 24 a. 2 q.2, vol. III, 520–1).[11]

b. Divine oneness and threeness, simplicity and primacy

We need to keep in mind this hermeneutical stance when evaluating Bonaventure's arguments, for instance, when he makes a case for the existence of God by appealing to Anselm's argument: If God is 'that than which nothing greater or better can be conceived' it follows that God exists:

No one can be ignorant of the truth that 'the best is the best,' and no one can think this is false. But that which is best is the most complete being, and every being that is complete to the highest degree by that very fact exists in actuality. Therefore, if the best is the best, the best exists. It can be argued in a similar way: If God is God, then God exists (*Si Deus est Deus, Deus est*). (*Myst. Trin.* I, q.1 a.1, 29, p. 113)

The same reasoning is used to argue for the oneness of the divine nature: if the word *God* signifies the first and highest principle, it follows that the divine nature is one (*Myst. Trin.* q. 2 a. 1). But how does Bonaventure deal with the question whether unity of nature can exist with a Trinity of

---

[10] *Works of St Bonaventure*, vol. III. *Disputed Questions on the Mystery of the Trinity*, trans. Z. Hayes, Bonaventure Texts in Translation Series (New York: The Franciscan Institute, 2000), 132 (hereafter abbreviated to *Myst. Trin.*).

[11] See 'Introduction' by Hayes to *Myst. Trin.*, 79.

persons? There are a number of steps to be discerned in Bonaventure's reasoning.

First he argues that the divine nature is love and therefore shares itself, drawing both on biblical witness (1 John 4:8, 16) and on the Pseudo-Dionysian view that goodness is self-diffusive (*Bonum diffusivum sui*): goodness wants to share itself. Following Aristotle who had distinguished between three types of emanation (fortuitous, natural, and voluntary in *Meta.* 6.22, 1032a12–13), and excluding fortuity in God, Bonaventure concludes that there must be two modes of emanation in God: by nature (*per modum naturae*) and by will (*per modum voluntatis*):

> Since the perfect production, emanation and germination is realized only through two intrinsic modes, namely by way of nature and by way of will, that is, by way of the word and of love, therefore, the highest perfection, fontality, and fecundity necessarily demands two kinds of emanation with respect to the two hypostases which are produced and emanate from the first person as from the first producing principle. Therefore, it is necessary to affirm three persons. (*Myst. Trin.* VIII, concl., p. 263)

Bonaventure argues that the divine nature of the Father is fruitful goodness which has to share itself, and it does so in two ways: by way of nature and by way of love. Before discussing these two processions in the next section, we would like to draw attention to another aspect of Bonaventure's thought, namely, how he harmonises belief in the divine oneness with belief in the threeness of the Persons, by emphasising the notions of divine simplicity and primacy: 'by reason of *simplicity*, the Essence is communicable and able to be in more. By reason of the *primacy*, the (first) Person is naturally bound to produce Another from himself' (I *Sent.* d.2 a. un., q.2 concl.).

The emphasis upon the divine *simplicity* allows Bonaventure to develop the theological notion of divine *perichoresis*, thereby avoiding the charge of tritheism. Oneness and threeness co-exist in God because of the simplicity of the one divine nature which is shared by the three Persons: 'since the divine nature is entirely indivisible and without any matter, therefore it is not multiplied or numbered by division or partition. Therefore it is entirely one in the produced and in the producer. But because no one can produce himself, it is necessary that there be a plurality at the level of person' (*Myst. Trin.* I, 2 concl., p. 152). For Bonaventure, therefore, the issue is not a choice between emphasis upon the oneness of the divine nature on the one hand, and the threeness of the divine Persons, on the other hand. In his understanding, the one divine love is shared amongst the three Persons, and oneness and threeness do not exclude but rather strengthen one another. It is only *in* the divine Persons that we find the unity. There is nothing but the

Persons and each of these Persons is of one essence, which is utterly simple. Bonaventure proves himself an heir to what Lewis Ayres has called the Augustinian 'grammar of simplicity': 'in using the grammar of simplicity to articulate a concept of Father, Son, and Spirit as each God, and as the one God, we find that the more we grasp the full reality of each person, the full depth of being that they have from the Father, the more we are also forced to recognise the unity of their being'.[12]

Similarly, Bonaventure argues that because God is the *primary* principle of everything, he must be the most fruitful – hence primacy and oneness can imply plurality. (In Latin this reasoning makes more immediate sense than in English: in Latin *primitas* is derived from *primus*, meaning first; and if there is firstness it stands to reason that there is more than one.) The very fact that Bonaventure links the fruitfulness of the divine nature with the notion of primacy makes clear that we should not interpret his talk of 'divine nature' in terms of quaternity, that is, a fourth entity 'behind' the three Persons. On the contrary, Bonaventure's views are always personalist: the fruitfulness of the divine nature is always the *Father's* nature, and not an entity behind the Father. It is the primacy and fecund plenitude of the *paternal* nature that is the source of the Son and Spirit – not an abstract divine nature behind the Father. Indeed, the Fourth Lateran Council (AD 1215) had already condemned the view that the divine substance generates the Trinity. It is important to stress this point as some twentieth-century theologians (especially Orthodox theologians such as John Zizioulas) have claimed that the Western tradition is not sufficiently 'personalist' and too 'substantivist'.

In sum, Bonaventure claims that the Father, as the First Principle, by the very fact that he is First (i.e., most perfect, most actual, most fruitful) is the origin of the Trinity. Because of the divine simplicity we can hold the belief that there are three Persons in one shared nature. We now examine in more detail the two processions.

c. The generation of the Son and the procession of the Spirit

Sacred Scripture declares that God the Father has an offspring whom he supremely loves: a Word co-equal with himself whom he has begotten from

---

[12] Lewis Ayres, *Nicea and its Legacy: An Approach to Fourth-Century Trinitarian Theology* (Oxford: Oxford University Press, 2004), 379–80. This is an important book, dispelling some of the ideological readings that have bedevilled scholarship of the Trinity during the last decades, exposing the roots of these readings, and offering an alternative, more accurate interpretation of the Western theological tradition.

all eternity and by whom he produces all things (*Brevil.* I.2.4). Out of the fruitfulness of the paternal nature the Son is generated as a second Person. Like Richard before him, Bonaventure distinguishes the divine Persons through their origin: while the Father is without origin, the Son is from the Father.

The Father, in the fruitfulness of his nature, produces the Son, and from their mutual loving contemplation the Holy Spirit proceeds as their bond of Love:

> the Love, who is the Holy Spirit, does not proceed from the Father, inasmuch as He loves Himself, nor from the Son, inasmuch as He loves Himself, but inasmuch as the One loves the Other, because it is a nexus: therefore the Holy Spirit is the Love, by which One loving tends unto the Other: therefore there is a Love both from Another and unto Another. (I *Sent.* d. 13, a .1, q. 1 fund. 4)

The Father and the Son tend to one another in a mutual love which is freely bestowed by them on a third Person. Thus, while the Son is generated through the fecundity of the divine nature, the Holy Spirit proceeds by way of will or love: *per modum voluntatis* rather than *per modum naturae*.

Itin. VI.2 offers a good summary: 'good is said to be self-diffusive; therefore the highest good must be most self-diffusive'. Now, unless 'a beloved and a co-beloved were present, i.e., the generated Son and the spirated Holy Spirit, God could not be considered the highest good'.[13] He concludes:

> If, therefore, you can behold with your mind's eye the purity of goodness, which is the pure act of a principle loving in charity with a love that is both free and due, and a mixture of both, which is the fullest diffusion by way of nature and will, which is a diffusion by way of the Word, in which all things are said, and by way of the Gift, in which other gifts are given, then you can see that through the highest communicability of the good there must be a Trinity of the Father and the Son and the Holy Spirit. (*Itin.* VI.2)

This quotation resounds with Richardian elements: the Father as the Origin of the Trinity freely bestows his Love out of the fecundity of the divine nature (by way of nature); the Son receives this Love and in turn freely co-bestows it with the Father on the Spirit who is Love received or due (by way of love, or will). As this quotation suggests, a discussion of the generation of the Son and the procession of the Spirit brings us to the topic of personal names (Word, Gift, etc.).

---

[13] St Bonaventure, *The Soul's Journey into God. The Tree of Life. The Life of St Francis*, trans. E. Cousins, Classics of Western Spirituality (New York: Paulist Press, 1978), 103.

d. The personal names

We recall that by personal names scholastic theologians mean names that apply to one Person of the Trinity only. Only the second Person, for instance, can be called 'Son', 'Word', or 'Image'; only the third Person can be called 'Holy Spirit' or 'Gift'. Other names are called appropriations. For instance, although the whole Trinity is Creator, we especially associate the term 'Creator' with the Father as the origin of the Trinity and the world. Creator is not a personal name of the Father but it assists us in better understanding the Person of the Father (cf. *Brevil.* I.6.1). This is a case of appropriation.

As we noted, Bonaventure, like Richard, distinguishes the Persons from each other through their origin. The first Person is called 'Father' because he is the unbegotten one, the Principle who proceeds from no other (*principium non de principio*). His 'unbegottenness' is not so much a negative characteristic, but rather suggests an affirmation of the plenitude of divine fruitfulness (*Brevil.* I.3.7).

The main personal names of the second Person are Son, Image, and Word. 'Word' is even richer in meaning than 'Son' for while 'Son' only expresses the relationship of the second Person with the first, from whom he proceeds, 'Word' also expresses a link with creatures (exemplarism), incarnation (the utterance of the divine mystery as Word), and the teaching that he communicated in revelation (*Comm. on John* I.6). In expressing his Word, the Father has expressed his full nature, and all things that he wished to create have an eternal existence in his Word (*Hex.* I.13). Since the Father brings forth the Son, and through the Son and together with the Son brings forth the Holy Spirit, God the Father through the Son and with the Holy Spirit is the principle of everything created. For if the Father did not produce (*producere*) the Son and the Spirit from all eternity, he could not, through them, produce creatures in time (*Myst. Trin.* VIII, reply 7, p. 266).

The Son takes a central role in the theology of the Trinity. He is the *Middle Person* (*persona media*), not just between Father and Spirit within the Trinity, but also between the Father and the created world, both in its creation and its redemption through his incarnation.[14] The Son is at the middle of the Trinity because he is between Father (who communicates his being to the Son) and the Spirit (who only receives); the Son is first receptive and then responsive or communicative (see *Hex.* I.14). All creation, which bears the stamp of sonship in the core of its being, is pure reception of

---

[14] See Gilles Emery, *La trinité créatrice* (Paris: Librairie J. Vrin, 1995), 199; III *Sent.* d.1 a.2 q.3 ad 1.

being.[15] The central role that the Son occupies in the Trinity is reflected in Bonaventure's theology of creation, epistemology (theory of illumination), Christology, soteriology, and eschatology (*Hex.* I.11–39). This is one of the major attractions of the scholastic theology of the Trinity: it posits an intimate link between the intra-trinitarian processions of Son and Spirit, and the creation and sanctification of the world: 'as the Word is the inner self-expression of God, the created order is the external expression of the inner Word'.[16] The fecundity at the heart of the Trinity finds further expression in the creation and sanctification of the world.

As we have seen, the Son is generated from the fruitfulness of the divine nature of the Father (*fecunditas naturalis*), while the Spirit proceeds *per modum voluntatis* (I *Sent.* d. 6 a. un. q. 2 resp.). Adopting Richard's model, Bonaventure argues that the Spirit proceeds as the *Love* between the Father and the Son (I *Sent.* d. 10 a. 1 q. 1 fund. 1). However, the whole Trinity can also be called Love ('God is Love'). Therefore, in order to make clear the meaning of 'Love' as a *personal* name for the Holy Spirit, Bonaventure draws an original comparison between the love of husband and wife (I *Sent* d.10 a.2 q.1 resp., p. 201). The term 'Love' can thus be used in three ways: it can refer to the whole Trinity (God is Love); it can refer to the love between Father and Son (this is a notional use in the sense that it is this love by which the third Person becomes known); and, finally, it can be used as a personal name for the Holy Spirit, who proceeds as Love from the Father and the Son. The love between husband and wife is compared to the notional love between Father and Son, while their love for their child is compared to the Love which constitutes the Spirit as a Person.[17]

Another personal name for the Holy Spirit is 'Gift'– the *Gift* in whom all gifts are given. Again we need to make a number of distinctions. After all, the whole Trinity could be called a Gift (this is an 'essential' understanding, i.e., it refers to the self-giving nature of God as such); or both Son and Spirit could be said to be given in the incarnation and at Pentecost respectively; but as a personal name it specifically applies to the Holy Spirit only as the one who has been bestowed by the Father and the Son, and it is this bestowal which constitutes the Spirit as a distinct Person. As all things are contained and virtually produced in the Word, so too all the gifts of grace are contained in the Gift that is the Holy Spirit: 'In the beginning was the Gift', Bonaventure writes, adapting the opening of John's Prologue: 'before the production of things at the beginning there was the Word; therefore

---

[15] Hayes, 'Introduction', 49.   [16] Hayes, 'Introduction', 47.
[17] See Hayes, 'Introduction', 55–6; Emery, *La trinité créatrice*, 203–4.

before the conferral of graces at the beginning was the Gift' (I *Sent.* d.18 a. un. q. 2 contra 5 fund. 5).[18] As the Son is the exemplar of the production of creatures in that he himself emanates as Exemplar or Image, so too the Holy Spirit is the archetype of created gifts in that he himself is Gift in a personal manner. Just as every emanation of creatures is contained in the Son as their first principle, every gift given to creatures is contained in the Spirit who proceeds as Gift.[19] As suggested earlier, this is part of the attraction of Bonaventure's theology of the Trinity (and of that of the Schoolmen in general): it establishes a close connection between the intra-trinitarian processions of Son and Spirit on the one hand, and creation and their missions in the economy of salvation, on the other.

e. Theology of the Trinity and spirituality

This brings us to the relevance of Bonaventure's theology of the Trinity for spirituality. As the previous section made clear, according to Bonaventure our creation and our sanctification cannot be understood without reference to the processions of Son and Spirit. The Holy Spirit, for instance, as the uncreated Gift in which all gifts are bestowed, is the archetypal principle of all gifts, including the economy of grace which results in our sanctification. But Bonaventure also develops a trinitarian anthropology, and this too brings out the significance of his theology of the Trinity for Christian spirituality.

Bonaventure draws on Augustine's intrapersonal model when considering the soul as made in the image of the Trinity. In marked contrast to modern scholarship, Bonaventure does not seem to oppose it with the Richardian interpersonal model. We have already quoted a passage from *Itin.* VI.2, which illustrated the interpersonal approach. The following quotation, also from *Itin.*, is characteristic of the intrapersonal approach:

From memory, intelligence comes forth as its offspring, since we understand when a likeness which is in the memory leaps into the eye of the intellect in the form of a word. From memory and intelligence love is breathed forth as their mutual bond. These three – the generating mind, the word, and love – are in the soul as memory, understanding and will, which are consubstantial, coequal, and coeval, and interpenetrate each other. If, then, God is a perfect spirit, he has memory, understanding and will; and he has the Word generated and Love breathed forth ... When, therefore, the soul considers itself, it rises through itself as through a mirror to behold the blessed Trinity of the Father, the Word, and Love: three persons, coeternal, coequal and consubstantial. (*Itin.* III.5, trans. p. 84)

---

[18] Emery, *La trinité créatrice*, 207–8.   [19] Ibid., 211.

This may at first seem a somewhat static understanding of our image-character, positing merely a parallel between memory, intellect, and will, on the one hand, and the three Persons, on the other. However, Bonaventure's view of the relation between the Trinity and its image (the human soul) is more dynamic than an initial reading might suggest. As we saw with Augustine, the human soul only becomes image of God in the full sense when memory, intelligence, and will turn towards God and conform to him (I *Sent* d.3 p. 2 a.1 q.2, concl.). If the soul only takes itself as object, it remains only a potential image. Through knowledge and love we mirror the processions of Son and Spirit.

While Bonaventure attempted to harmonise his Richardian (interpersonal model) and Augustinian (intrapersonal model) sources, Thomas Aquinas will abandon the interpersonal model in his mature writings. In his influential thought we find a re-engagement with key insights from Augustinian trinitarian theology.

ST THOMAS AQUINAS (D. 1274) AND THE 'PSYCHOLOGICAL' ANALOGY

a. Introduction

The theology of the Trinity of Thomas Aquinas has come in for severe criticism in the last decades. It is argued that it is unscriptural; that Aquinas dissociates the theology of the Trinity from the rest of theology; that Aquinas' decision to deal with the immanent Trinity before dealing with the economic Trinity is ill-considered; that Aquinas puts too much emphasis upon the divine unity and fails to do justice to the tri-personal nature of God, for instance by first treating of God as one, before dealing with God as Trinity, or by adopting the Augustinian mono-personal model; and so forth. In our view these often-repeated claims need in turn to be critically examined – the reader will by the end of this section hopefully be in a position to make up his or her own mind whether they are accurate or in need of revision.

It is often alleged that the fact that Aquinas first treats of the one God before he deals with the doctrine of the Trinity reveals a lack of trinitarianism. Now it is true that in his unfinished masterpiece, the *Summa Theologiae* (*ST*) Aquinas first discusses God's unity – in line with the Old Testament revelation of God as one, and as the One who is (cf. Exod. 3:13; *ST* I.13.11). He then goes on to discuss in *ST* I.27–43 the doctrine of the Trinity. In each case, however, Aquinas is discussing the Christian understanding of God: as one and three. It is not the case that his discussion of the oneness of God is a philosophical preparation to a theological discussion of the Trinity: in *both* cases we are dealing with a theological discourse.[20] Again, the fact that Aquinas discusses the divine unity before the Persons does *not* mean that he believes that first there is a divine nature which is then actualised by Persons: the divine Persons and divine essence are identical.[21] Moreover, the fact that God acts as one does not mean that the Christian faith does not allow for specific roles within this one divine activity. For instance, although the whole Trinity was involved in the incarnation only the Son assumed a human nature.

Modern-day readers may also be wondering why a discussion of God's inner life precedes a discussion of the economy of salvation. There are a number of reasons for this. First, it should be remembered that the discussion in question 43 of the divine missions into the world – the last question of the treatise on the triune God – is also the climax of Aquinas' discussion, and the vantage point from which to understand the rest of the *Summa*. For medieval authors final causality is more important than efficient causality, and question 43 on the mission of the divine Persons constitutes the goal of Aquinas' discussion of the Trinity. In other words, the fact that a discussion of the economy (in the missions of the Persons) comes towards the end should not be seen as an indication of its lesser significance – on the contrary.

Furthermore, Gilles Emery has argued that the speculative reflection on the Trinity is guided by a double motive: the defence of faith against errors (i.e., Aquinas tries to demonstrate that objections against the doctrine can be shown to be not necessary) and the contemplation of revealed truth (i.e., a foretaste of what believers may hope to enjoy in the beatific vision of God).[22] The first aspect accounts for the distinction Aquinas makes between immanent actions (accomplished in the agent himself, e.g., to think) and transitive actions (those that are exerted on an exterior object, e.g., to make something).[23] The main purpose of this distinction is to refute Arianism: Aquinas will argue that the processions are immanent actions within the Godhead, and not transitive ones. Therefore they do not lead to tritheism. In other words, in order to refute Arianism a discussion of the

---

[20] It is true, however, that only those who have faith can approach the mystery of the triune God while by natural reason we can know 'what concerns the unity of essence, not what concerns the distinction of the Persons' (*ST* I.32.1).

[21] See Joseph Wawrykow, 'Trinity', in *The SCM Press A–Z of Thomas Aquinas* (London: SCM Press, 2005), 164.

[22] Gilles Emery, *Trinity in Aquinas* (Ave Maria, FL: Sapientia Press, 2006), 127–8.   [23] Ibid., 131.

immanent Trinity should precede that of the economy of salvation.[24] Moreover, although Aquinas would agree that we come to know the revelation of the triune God through the cross of Christ and the sending of the Spirit, that is, the economy of salvation,[25] he would also insist that creation and salvation in reality find their origin in, and are an extension of, the intradivine processions of Son and Spirit: 'the processions of the divine Persons are the reasons of the production of creatures, inasmuch as they include the essential attributes of knowing and willing' (*ST* I.45.6).[26] For this reason, the option to start with a discussion of the immanent processions is a perfectly defensible one, for the immanent processions are the cause of creation and sanctification. This is entirely coherent with Aquinas' theocentric understanding of theology.

b. Processions

Let us start with a text which captures Aquinas' mature teaching on the Trinity well. Having reiterated his point that there are immanent processions in God (cf. John 8:42; 15:26) Aquinas continues:

> Such action in an intellectual nature is that of the intellect, and of the will. The procession of the Word is by way of an intelligible operation. The operation of the will within ourselves involves also another procession, that of love, whereby the object loved is in the lover; as by the conception of the word, the object spoken of or understood is in the intelligent agent. Hence, besides the procession of the Word in God, there exists in Him another procession called the procession of love. (*ST* I.27.3)

A number of comments should be made. Firstly, the passage is deeply indebted to Augustine's theology of the Trinity, and more specifically Augustine's so-called psychological model. Secondly, it is important to remember that this is a case of analogy. Aquinas does not consider the psychological analogy a proof, nor is it univocal use of language (*ST* I.32.1 *ad* 2). Analogy, as we have seen in previous chapters, means that our creaturely language when applied to God changes in meaning without, however, becoming utterly equivocal. Hence, analogy holds the middle between univocal and equivocal use of language. If the language we use

---

[24] Ibid., 131.

[25] See Matthew Levering, *Scripture and Metaphysics: Aquinas and the Renewal of Trinitarian Theology* (Oxford: Blackwell, 2004), 110–43.

[26] See also I *Sent.* d.2; *ScG* II.1.2; *ST* I.34.3; and Gilles Emery 'Trinity and Creation', in Rik Van Nieuwenhove and Joseph Wawrykow, eds., *The Theology of Thomas Aquinas* (Notre Dame, IN: University of Notre Dame Press, 2005), 58–76.

were predicated univocally we would fall into the trap of anthropomorphism. If it were merely a case of equivocal predication we would not be saying anything meaningful at all (our words would acquire a totally different meaning, totally unrelated to their 'creaturely' sense; cf. *ST* I.13.5). So the psychological analogy is just that: it is a mere analogy. When we think of something, there is a kind of inner movement in our mind, and the divine procession of the Word is somewhat like this (but with the difference that there is never a 'moment' that the Father is without his Word while we can abstain from thinking about something). Thirdly, as Matthew Levering has emphasised, 'Aquinas's account of the psychological analogy flows from his effort to illumine biblical revelation, as interpreted in the Church's Tradition'.[27] It has been argued that his views are 'unbiblical' and more akin to 'philosophico-religious speculation' than to a 'biblically inspired theology'.[28] Aquinas' interpretation, it is alleged, is too ontological, not sufficiently dynamic or functional. It focusses too much on the being of God rather than on his activity in Christ. Against this critique it can be argued that it is unhelpful to artificially separate activity from being: what you do reflects the kind of person you are. Moreover, Aquinas' exegesis relies on a whole array of biblical texts, mainly from John and Paul, but also from the Old Testament. It must be admitted that in the *Summa contra Gentiles* there is a much more profound engagement with the Scriptures in the development of this trinitarian doctrine than in the *Summa Theologiae*, where this material appears to be simply presupposed. Finally, what Aquinas says about the use of the word 'Person' – itself an extra-biblical term – applies to his exegetical activity in general:

Although the word person is not found applied to God in Scriptures, either in the Old or New Testament, nevertheless what the word signifies is found to be affirmed of God in many places of Scriptures ... If we could speak of God only in the very terms of Scripture, it would follow that no one could speak about God in any but the original language of the Old or New Testament. The urgency of confuting heretics made it necessary to find new words to express the ancient faith about God. (*ST* I.29.3 *ad* 1)

As we will see, Luther will later echo these sentiments in almost the same words. For the time being it suffices to state that Aquinas views the psychological model as the expression and outcome of exegetical activity

---

[27] Levering, *Scripture and Metaphysics*, 155.

[28] See David Coffey, *Deus Trinitas: The Doctrine of the Triune God* (Oxford: Oxford University Press, 1999), 30, quoted by Levering, *Scripture and Metaphysics*, 144.

which is aimed at trying to make sense of the faith as handed down, and at dispelling views that are at odds with this faith.

Readers often miss the point that Aquinas' concern is soteriological: we can only come to a personal relation with God if the Son and the Holy Spirit are truly divine (quoting 1 John 5:20 and 1 Cor. 6:19). But if the Son and the Holy Spirit are truly divine, this raises questions about the nature of the one God – questions that are answered by arguing that there are inner or immanent processions in God, one of knowledge and one of love. In other words, biblical exegesis invites metaphysical considerations.[29] When Jesus says, 'From God I proceeded' (John 8:42), the first biblical passage Aquinas quotes in the treatise on the Trinity (*ST* I.27.1), we are invited to consider the meaning of this 'procession'. Does it mean that the Word is a creature? Does it mean that the Word is divine? Thus, by using the psychological analogy Aquinas attempts to show how there can be inner differentiation within the Godhead without having to concede the heretical view that there are three gods.

It is not just the desire to make sense of the biblical words about God that led Aquinas to develop his theology of the Trinity. There is a more spiritual dimension to it as well. As we have been made in the image of God (Gen. 1:26), we actualise our image character most supremely when we know and love God. As D. J. Merriell has shown, Aquinas' presentation is much more dynamic than the standard medieval reading of Augustine, which effectively sees the analogy of the human soul with the Trinity in terms of how the three faculties (memory or mind, intellect, and will) mirror the divine triad. Aquinas prefers a much more dynamic understanding which focusses more on the two processions (of Word and Spirit or Love) than on the three Persons.[30] When we truly know God and love him rightly we share in, and most resemble, the intratrinitarian processions of Word and Love (*ST* I.38.1). As he puts it:

As the uncreated Trinity is distinguished by the procession of the Word from the Speaker, and of Love from both of these [cf. *ST* I.28.3]; so we may say that in rational creatures wherein we find a procession of the word in the intellect, and a procession of the love in the will, there exists an image of the uncreated Trinity. (*ST* I. 93.6)

---

[29] Levering, *Scripture and Metaphysics*, 154.

[30] See D. Juvenal Merriell, 'Trinitarian Anthropology', in Van Nieuwenhove and Wawrykow, eds., *The Theology of Thomas Aquinas*, 123–42. See also Rik Van Nieuwenhove, 'In the Image of God: The Trinitarian Anthropology of St Bonaventure, St Thomas Aquinas and the Blessed Jan van Ruusbroec', *Irish Theological Quarterly* 66 (2001): 109–23 and 227–37.

Aquinas, of course, allows for a gradation of the image character in the human being. As created beings, each of us has a natural aptitude or potential for understanding and loving God; when we actually know and love God in this life in response to grace, we actualise this potential, albeit only imperfectly. It is only in the afterlife that our image-character will be fully realised (*ST* I.93.4). It is here that the significance of the 'psychological' analogy becomes fully clear. Unlike Richard's model (and present-day social trinitarian thinkers), the psychological model allows for a very fruitful connection between the theology of the Trinity and theological anthropology and spirituality. Put in a slightly different manner, there is an intimate link between the intradivine life and the understanding of the human being as made in the image of God. The implications for Christian spirituality are far-reaching: all aspects of human life can be seen in the context of 'knowing and loving God'.

To sum up, Aquinas argues that in order to do justice to biblical revelation, we need to allow for processions within God, and this without compromising monotheism. There has to be a real difference between Father, Son, and Spirit without implying that Son and Spirit are created. Aquinas has identified two processions: a procession of the Word from the Father, and the procession of the Spirit in Love from the Father and the Son. The latter is a more outgoing, or ecstatic, aspect of the Trinity: the procession of the Spirit is 'by way of impulse and movement' towards an object (*ST* I.27.4). Aquinas recaptures something of the biblical connotation of *pneuma* (or breath) when he writes that the word 'spirit' expresses 'a certain vital movement and impulse' (*vitalis motio et impulsio*).

c. Relations

Having established that there are two immanent processions (allowing Aquinas to maintain the divinity of the Persons against Arius, and their distinct subsistence against Sabellianism), Aquinas then treats of the relations. This is a crucial discussion because it makes even clearer that the Persons do not compromise the divine unity. The relations imply a 'relative opposition' according to origin (*ST* I.28.3). Aquinas distinguishes four relations:

- paternity (the relation of the Father to the Son)
- filiation (the relation of the Son to the Father)
- active spiration (the relation of the Father and Son to the Spirit)
- passive spiration (the relation of the Spirit to the Father and Son)

These four relations constitute three Persons (see Fig. 2)

Thus, the two processions lead to four ways of relating to one another (the arrows) (cf. *ST* I.28.4). But these four ways of relating result in only

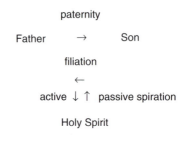

Figure 2. Four relations and three Persons

three Persons (not four) because Father and Son are not constituted as distinct Persons in the active spiration of the Spirit but only through paternity and filiation. (Because active spiration is common to Father and Son it does not constitute them as distinct Persons.) The Holy Spirit is constituted as a distinct Person by passive spiration (*ScG* IV.24.8).

For Aquinas relations are identical to the divine essence. However, because of the relative opposition they imply, relations allow us to distinguish the three Persons from one another. Hence, in *ST* I.28.2 Aquinas can write that 'relation really existing in God is really the same as his essence'. And he can also state (in *ST* I.28.3): 'as in God there is a real relation there must also be a real opposition', and this implies distinction. All of this may sound rather abstract. But it boils down to this: the Father is God, the Son is God, the Holy Spirit is God, and yet Father, Son, and Spirit are distinct (through their 'relative opposition'). As he puts it, 'although paternity, just as filiation, is really the same as the divine essence, nevertheless these two in their own proper idea and definitions import opposite respects. Hence they are distinguished from each other' (*ST* I.28.4 *ad* 1).

For Aquinas it is 'relation' that allows us to develop the doctrine of the three Persons in the one God. The being (*esse*) of the divine relation is the same being as the divine subsistence; but as relation as such (*ratio*) it implies 'opposition' or distinction (*ST* I.28.2). These two aspects of relation (as identical to the essence, and as implying distinction) are crucial in his understanding of personhood.

d. Personhood

By defining personhood in terms of 'subsisting relation' Aquinas manages to harmonise the relational and essential understanding of personhood that was bequeathed to him by the tradition.

Let us examine this in more detail. In *ST* I.29.4 Aquinas recalls Augustine's puzzlement, namely that the concept 'Person' does not in itself refer to another, as do words which express relation (such as 'Father', or 'Son'). In order to solve the difficulty, Aquinas makes the point that in God distinction is through relation of origin, and relation is subsistent in the divine essence. (The Father is not the Son, and yet Father and Son are the divine essence.) The reason why relations are subsistent in God is the simplicity of the divine nature. There is no composition or anything accidental in God. If you are a father of a child, your fatherhood is not subsistent. It remains, in scholastic terms, an accident (i.e., it does not belong to your ontological essence to be a father). Not so with God: whereas fatherhood has only accidental existence in creatures, it has substantial existence in God. The relation of fatherhood can therefore be identified with the divine essence ('the Father is God'). The same applies to filiation and procession. But, of course, 'relation' always implies a reference to another, and this implies distinction ('the Father is distinct from the Son'). It is therefore crucial to recall the difference between the two aspects of relation: the existential one (the relation is the same as the divine essence) and the formal aspect (in which relation implies distinction). Anselm Min summarises it well:

Relations that remain accidental and distinct from the essence in creatures are identified with the essence and become subsisting relations in God. Regarding its formal aspect, however, relation signifies a reference (*habitudo*) to something else, to its opposite term, not to the essence.[31]

This is why Aquinas can say that relation is the same as divine essence and, also, that relations in God are really distinct from one another. In summary: 'there must be real distinction in God, not indeed, according to that which is absolute – namely essence, wherein there is supreme unity and simplicity – but according to that which is relative' (*ST* I.28.4). In this way, by defining a divine Person in terms of a relation as subsisting (*Persona divina significat relationem ut subsistentem*) Aquinas harmonises the essentialist and relational understandings of personhood.

It is clear that Aquinas uses the word 'Person' when applied to God and humans in an analogical sense (*ST* I.29.4 *ad* 4). Aquinas, unlike Richard, is happy to adopt the Boethian definition of person as 'the individual substance of a rational nature'. But the word 'person' changes in meaning from

---

[31] Anselm Min, *Paths to the Triune God: An Encounter between Aquinas and Recent Theologies* (Notre Dame, IN: University of Notre Dame Press, 2005), 183; Emery, *Trinity in Aquinas*, 139–42.

when applied to a human (such as Jack, i.e., an individual human being) to when applied to God. In the latter case the word 'substance' in the definition refers to the *hypostasis* and not to the essence (*ST* I.30.1 *ad* 1). In other words, it acquires a relational dimension (more specifically, a subsisting relation) that creaturely substances do not have. It is important to see how radically Aquinas' use of the word 'person' differs from the modern use (in terms of 'individual or separate centres of consciousness').[32] Having dealt with Aquinas' understanding of divine personhood in terms of subsistent relations we now turn to his discussion of personal names.

e. Personal names

The main personal name of the first Person is 'Father'. The Father is the principle of the whole Godhead (*ST* I.39.5 *ad* 6). But indirectly he is, of course, also the Father of all created beings. Again we encounter the close link between the intradivine processions and the extradivine activity (creation and sanctification): just as an architect first conceives of the plan of a house in his mind before he builds it, so too the Son of God first proceeds from the Father before the world is created (cf. *ST* I.33.3 *ad* 1).

When discussing the personal names of the Son, Aquinas examines 'Word' and 'Image'. The personal name 'Word' (understood here as the inner word or concept formed by the intellect, not a vocalised word) goes to the heart of Aquinas' theology of the Trinity as it is intimately linked with his understanding of the generation of the Son in terms of an intellectual emanation (*ST* I.34.2). Again the link between the generation of the Word and the creation of the world is explicitly drawn out by Aquinas: 'because God by one act understands himself and all things, his one only Word is expressive not only of the Father, but of all creatures' (*ST* I.34.3). Because God's knowledge is creative, there is an intimate connection between the generation of the Word from the Father and the creation and redemption of the world.[33]

The main personal names Aquinas examines when dealing with the Holy Spirit are Love and Gift. Like Bonaventure he distinguishes between an essential understanding of love (the whole Trinity loves) and a notional or personal understanding: the Holy Spirit proceeds as the fruit of the act of love of Father and Son. The connection between the intradivine processions

---

[32] The word 'individual' in the Boethian definition refers to the fact that each of the three Persons subsists distinctly from the others in the divine nature (cf. *ST* I.30.4).

[33] Emery, *Trinity in Aquinas*, 152–3.

Economy of salvation as testified in Scriptures

↓

Theology of the Trinity of the Fathers and the theology of immanent Trinity of Aquinas

↓

Hermeneutical starting point from which to interpret economy of salvation as witnessed in the Scriptures and the life of the Church

Figure 3. Aquinas' hermeneutical approach to the Trinity

and the economy of salvation is alluded to in a passage which offers a good summary of some of the main elements we have discussed:

> as the Father speaks himself and every creature by his begotten Word, inasmuch as the Word begotten adequately represents the Father and every creature; so he loves himself and every creature by the Holy Spirit, inasmuch as the Holy Spirit proceeds as the love of the primal goodness whereby the Father loves himself and every creature. Thus it is evident that relation to creature is implied both in the Word and in the proceeding Love ... (*ST* I.37.2 *ad* 3)

In light of these texts Gilles Emery is surely right to challenge the widespread view that Aquinas' doctrine presents an 'abstract' approach to the Trinity, a Trinity 'locked within itself'. In fact, there is a most intimate link between the doctrine of the Word and Love, and the economy of salvation.[34] Indeed, it would be correct to describe Aquinas' theology of the Trinity as performing a hermeneutic spiral: building on a profound engagement with the legacy of the theology of the Trinity by Augustine and others, which, in turn, is based on an in-depth engagement with the economy of salvation as testified in the Scriptures, Aquinas develops a theology of the Trinity which allows us, in turn, to see both the whole creation and the economy of salvation and sanctification in light of the intratrinitarian life of Word and Spirit. In schematic form (where the arrow denotes 'leads to'), see Fig. 3.

Moreover, as we have already suggested, Aquinas' 'psychological' model also allows for a fruitful spirituality. As we have been made in the image of the Trinity, whenever we know and love God we share, albeit in an imperfect manner, in the divine processions of Word and Spirit.

Perhaps some will still want to claim that Aquinas' theology of the Trinity is abstract and philosophical. Even in his own time the influence of 'secular' Aristotelian philosophy in the faculties of theology was

---

[34] Emery, *Trinity in Aquinas*, 156.

considered deeply problematic by some authorities, and was condemned in 1277 in the Universities of Paris and Oxford. The Condemnations of 1277 both expressed, and contributed to, a different theological climate, in which there is a growing awareness of the limitations of philosophy in its dialogue with theology, thereby reinforcing a growing separation of faith and reason, theology and philosophy. For instance, whereas the immortality of the soul was considered a demonstrable truth for most theologians up to Aquinas, it will cease to be considered a philosophically demonstrable conclusion by Duns Scotus, Ockham, and others.[35] In general, theologians will rely on revelation and faith more than upon philosophical reasoning to ascertain the truth of theological conclusions.[36] Although Aquinas had achieved a delicate balance between the reason and faith, the Condemnations of 1277 were to result in a growing separation of theology and philosophy, to the impoverishment of both. Even so, scholastic theology continued to ponder the mystery of the Trinity throughout the fourteenth and fifteenth centuries. Henry of Ghent, Duns Scotus, Peter Auriol, William of Ockham, Gregory of Rimini, and others made important contributions, which, unfortunately, are beyond the confines of this book.[37]

Any theology of the Trinity will use non-biblical terms and adopt philosophical language of some kind. The problem is that contemporary students of the theology of the Trinity may no longer be familiar with the traditional philosophical vocabulary (or with any philosophical vocabulary at all). As Anselm Min reminds us, our philosophical diet is often more phenomenological, personalist, or empiricist than ontological. Aquinas' ontological language is quite appropriate to a sapiential theology which seeks to contemplate God and all created things from a theocentric perspective: 'his sapiential theology was cosmological, not anthropocentric, and universalist, not intentionally confined to the needs of a particular time'.[38] It is precisely this contrast with the activist, historicist bias of present-day theology which makes Aquinas' contemplative and theocentric theology so subversive and appealing for readers today.

Apart from a growing divide between theology and philosophy, there also occurred around the same time a deepening chasm between theology

---

[35] Étienne Gilson, *History of Christian Philosophy in the Middle Ages* (London: Sheed & Ward, 1980), 409. Gilson (p. 408) called the condemnation of 1277 'a landmark in the history of medieval philosophy and theology'.

[36] Gilson, *History of Christian Philosophy in the Middle Ages*, 465.

[37] See the important book by Russell Friedman, *Medieval Trinitarian Thought from Aquinas to Ockham* (Cambridge: Cambridge University Press, 2010).

[38] Min, *Paths to the Triune God*, 240–1.

and spirituality, as we mentioned in Chapter 1. While an author like St Bonaventure can legitimately be called a mystic and an academic theologian, after 1300 it becomes increasingly difficult to name great theologians who are also great mystical writers.[39] Thus, while creative theological thinking on the Trinity did not cease in scholastic circles after Aquinas, as Russell Friedman has shown, it must be admitted that scholastic speculations about the Trinity became increasingly severed from spirituality.

One of the last representatives of the traditional synthesis of theology and spirituality is Jan van Ruusbroec, who presents us with one of the most beautiful trinitarian spiritualities in the West. To his mystical theology of the Trinity we now turn.

JAN VAN RUUSBROEC (1293–1381): THE EBBING AND FLOWING OF THE TRINITY

a. Ruusbroec's trinitarian theology: activity and enjoyable rest

Ruusbroec first became a priest in Brussels, but he later retired to a new monastery in the Zonien Forest, where the members of his community adopted the rule of St Augustine (Augustinian canons). He wrote all his works in Middle Dutch (Flemish), although a number of letters survive only in Latin translation. His most important work is *The Spiritual Espousals* (*Die Geestelike Brulocht*).[40]

Ruusbroec describes the inner Trinity as a vibrant and pulsating source of life. In the following quotation he outlines the processions of Son and Spirit from the fruitfulness of the paternal nature – a perspective which clearly echoes that of Bonaventure's Christian Neoplatonism – but he also suggests that the divine Persons then return in their shared unity. Thus the Persons flow back into the divine essence or being (*wesen*) in a never-ending dynamic of ebbing and flowing:

For this noble nature that is the principal cause of all creatures is fruitful. Therefore it cannot rest in the unity of the Fatherhood, because of the stirrings (*ghedueren*) of fruitfulness; but it must without cease give birth to the eternal Wisdom, that is, the

---

[39] See Denys Turner, *The Darkness of God: Negativity in Christian Mysticism* (Cambridge: Cambridge University Press, 1995).

[40] Jan van Ruusbroec's own works (*Opera Omnia*, as edited by Guido De Baere) are available in a trilingual edition (Middle Dutch, Latin, English translation) in *CCCM* 100–10, published by Brepols in Turnhout (1988–2005). An overview of Ruusbroec's theology and mysticism can be found in Rik Van Nieuwenhove, *Jan van Ruusbroec: Mystical Theologian of the Trinity* (Notre Dame, IN: University of Notre Dame Press, 2003).

Son of the Father. Always, without cease, the Son of God was born, and is born, and will remain unborn: nevertheless it is all one Son. Where the Father beholds his Son, the eternal Wisdom, and all things in the same Wisdom: there he has been born and is a Person other than the Father ... Neither out of the fruitful nature, that is, Fatherhood, nor out of the Father's giving birth to his Son does Love, that is, the Holy Spirit, flow; but out of the fact that the Son is born a Person other than the Father, where the Father beholds him as born, and everything one with him as the life of everything, and the Son, in turn, beholds the Father giving birth and fruitful, and himself, and all things, in the Father – this is seeing and seeing-back in a fruitful nature – from this comes Love, that is, the Holy Spirit, a bond from the Father to the Son and from the Son to the Father. By this Love, the Persons are embraced and permeated and have flowed back (*wedervloeit*) into that unity out of which the Father without cease is giving birth. Now, even though they have flowed back into unity, there is no abiding, on account of nature's fruitfulness. This birth-giving and this flowing back into unity is the work of the Trinity. Thus, there is threeness of Persons and oneness of nature.[41]

There are a number of points to be noted in order to unpack this quotation. First, Ruusbroec, like Bonaventure before him, sees the divine nature of the Father as 'bubbling over', of necessity having to share itself with the other divine Persons. This is why Ruusbroec calls the divine nature 'fruitful'. Second, the Son is being begotten from the Father as his Word, and from their mutual contemplation the Spirit proceeds as their bond of Love – this is standard medieval Augustinian trinitarian doctrine. Third, the most original and astonishing idea is the view that the divine Persons flow back into the divine essence. This view (called *regiratio* in scholastic Latin or *wederboeghen* in Middle Dutch) makes Ruusbroec's theology of the Trinity so wonderfully dynamic. Ruusbroec describes the Trinity as 'an ebbing, flowing sea', with the Son and the Spirit *going out* from the Father and then *flowing back* into the divine unity, where they *rest* in enjoyment. The Holy Spirit is the principle of this return because the Spirit, as the mutual bond of Love between Father and Son, is the unifying principle who initiates the loving return into the divine unity. After all, it belongs to the nature of Love to return what it receives, not because it feels indebted and wants to settle the balance, but rather out of sheer gratuity, in order to allow the other to give once more, in a never-ending dynamic of giving and receiving love.[42] This never-ending dynamic of divine going-out, flowing back in, and resting in enjoyment determines every aspect of Ruusbroec's thought.

---

[41] *Opera Omnia*, vol. IV. *Dat Rijcke der Ghelieven*, lines 1597–1624 (translation partly modified. All references to the *Opera Omnia* will include references to the lines in the Middle Dutch text).
[42] *Opera Omnia*, vol. VII A. *Vanden XII Beghinen*, 2b 674; see Van Nieuwenhove, *Jan van Ruusbroec*, 136–8.

The notion of love as bestowed and returned moulds, for instance, his understanding of the economy of grace. God bestows his grace but we need to 'return' (or respond to) his gift through our charitable works. Similarly, the gift of the God-man can be seen in the same way: God bestows his Son, but in the humanity of the God-man we are allowed to participate in the return of this gift – a perspective which allows us to interpret the cross and the Eucharist in terms of the trinitarian dynamic of Love bestowed and returned.[43]

Ruusbroec's theological anthropology is also patterned by the same dynamic. Because the human soul is made in the image of God (Gen. 1:26) the soul will reflect the Trinity in its three aspects, that is, (a) an outgoing moment (the procession of Son and Spirit); (b) an ingoing moment of return into their shared unity; and (c) a moment of rest or enjoyment.

The faculties of the soul (memory, intellect, will) are usually engaged in outgoing activities, such as when we are engaged with the things of this world, for instance, when we think about something, or when we want something. However, there is also a tendency of the faculties to draw inwards and to rest in stillness, inactivity, or quietude. This is a tendency that can be cultivated, and although there is nothing wrong with this cultivation as such, it can become a source of fixation and escapism. Ruusbroec attributed this practice of quietist meditation to the so-called 'Brethren of the Free Spirit' who supposedly engaged in techniques of passive stillness, without any reference to Christian charity, or the life of the Church. When 'mysticism' is turned into a psychological 'experience' of stillness it is no longer recognisably Christian but degenerates into a self-seeking technique:

These are the people who do not practice virtue and whose understanding is exempt from images. They find their essential being in themselves and possess it in the naked idleness of their spirit and nature. For they lapse into an idle blind emptiness of their essential being and they no longer pay attention to any good works, outer or inner. For they spurn all inner works, such as wanting, knowing, loving, desiring and all the works that join them with God ... They pass away and sink away from themselves in essential natural rest ... These people's way is a quiet sitting down of the body without work, with idle, unimaged sensuality turned inward into themselves.[44]

Throughout his writings Ruusbroec is at pains to distinguish his 'mystical theology' from this experiential understanding. So now we turn to how

---

[43] Van Nieuwenhove, *Jan van Ruusbroec*, 138–56.
[44] *Opera Omnia*, vol. x. *Vanden Vier Becoringhen*, 183–206; translation partly modified.

exactly Ruusbroec sees our participation in the life of the Trinity, and how his own ideal differs from 'quietist' practices.

b. The common life

In Ruusbroec's ideal of 'the common life' (*ghemeyne leven*) – perhaps better translated as 'universal or catholic life' – virtuous activity and enjoyment of God are fully integrated, and in harmony with one another. This ideal reflects the trinitarian life of activity and 'rest' or 'enjoyment'.

Ruusbroec distinguishes three aspects (he calls them 'lives' too):

- the active life: a life of virtue, which mirrors the 'outgoing' aspect of the Trinity (the generation of the Son and the procession of the Spirit);
- the inner or God-yearning life, which mirrors the 'ingoing' aspect of the divine Persons (*regiratio*);
- the contemplative life where we possess God in utter emptiness of self, detached and totally focussed on God, mirroring the 'fruition' or enjoyable 'rest' of the divine Persons in their perichoretic unity.

The common life is then a combination of these aspects, that is, the true mystic will engage in virtuous activity (thereby mirroring the 'activity' of the divine Persons in the bosom of the Trinity) and also 'rest' in God (just like the divine Persons 'rest' in the shared essence). We will clarify below what this 'resting in God' means for Ruusbroec. Let us first look at how he describes this integration of activity and rest:

> God's Spirit breathes us out to love and perform virtuous works, and he draws us back into him to rest and enjoy: this is an eternal life, just like in our bodily life we breathe air in and out … to go in, in idle enjoyment, and to go out with works, and always remaining united with God's Spirit: that is what I mean. Just like we open and close our bodily eyes, so quick that we do not feel it, likewise we die in God and live from God, and constantly remain one with God. Thus we will go out into our ordinary life and go in with love and cleave to God, and always remain united with God in stillness.[45]

Ruusbroec's ideal of the common life echoes and radicalises Gregory the Great's ideal of the *vita mixta* (the mixed life) in which charitable activity and contemplation are in perfect harmony with one another. But how exactly are we to understand this? How can we both enjoy and rest in God, and be active? What does it mean to rest in God or to enjoy God?

In order to answer this question we need to examine the crucial notion of the single intention (*meyninghe*) or theocentric focus. To know and to love

---

[45] *Opera Omnia*, vol. IX. *Van Seven Trappen*, 1120–32.

God in whatever we do, however opaquely, means to be intent solely upon God. This active love/knowledge is what distinguishes Ruusbroec's project from that of the 'heretics' who understand it in more psychologising terms of quietist experience.

Resting in God means that our love and knowledge have to be solely focussed on God: 'Whoever is not intent on God and does not love him above himself and all things will always be reckless and not heed the honour of God and all true virtue and God himself.'[46] Thus, when Ruusbroec writes that to become deified we have to 'turn within and deliver our naked unimaged intelligence to God's incomprehensible truth', he is not promoting an experiential state of vacant idleness in which the faculties are not preoccupied, but rather he wants to stress the importance of an intention (*meyninghe*) or disposition which focusses solely on God and which does not allow for disordered creaturely distractions or attachments. This is entirely in line with the Augustinian understanding of solely 'enjoying' God (*frui* and *uti*).

The common person, then, actualises this ideal of a perfect integration of action and contemplation. As Ruusbroec puts it succinctly: 'therefore he has a common life, for contemplation and action come just as readily to him and he is perfect in both'. Ruusbroec's originality lies not so much in the actual ideal of contemplation in action (although he gives a fairly radical version of this) but in the trinitarian foundation of this key idea: the common life is a life of enjoyment or fruition, and activity – just as the Trinity itself is both activity in the Persons and enjoyment in their mutual interpenetration (*perichoresis*). In a celebrated passage Ruusbroec describes how the common person participates in the trinitarian pulse of divine love. This person should

behold the rich, generous flowing-forth of God, with glory and with himself, and with incomprehensible bliss into all the saints, according to the appetite of all spirits. And how they are flowing back with themselves and with all that they have received and can do, into the same rich unity from which all bliss comes forth. This flowing of God always demands a flowing-back, for God is a flowing, ebbing sea, which flows without cease into all his beloved, according to each one's needs and dignity. And he is ebbing back in again, drawing all those whom he has endowed on heaven and earth, together with all that they have and can do.[47]

Ruusbroec's ideal of the common life is one in which we actively love and yet rest enjoyably in God through dispossession of self, that is, we exhibit a radically theocentric focus.

---

[46] *Vanden Vier Becoringhen*, 51–4.   [47] *Opera Omnia*, vol. III. *Die Geestelike Brulocht*, b 1142–51.

Few authors in the Latin tradition have combined such a daringly speculative theology of the Trinity with a spirituality that expresses and lives this theology in such a down-to-earth manner in everyday Christian life. His ideas proved influential in his immediate circle and in the *Devotio Moderna*. Through the writings of Harphius (Hendrik Herp), who is deeply indebted to Ruusbroec, and the Latin translation of Ruusbroec's works by Surius, his ideas exerted an influence, albeit hard to trace, throughout Europe, especially on the French mystics.[48]

As mentioned earlier, after the death of Ruusbroec, theological innovation did not cease. However, given the parameters of this book we will not discuss these developments as they had little impact on contemporary trinitarian thought. We will rather turn to the theology of the Reformers, Luther and Calvin. The thought of Martin Luther, in particular, continues to exert a major influence upon the trinitarian thinking of all Christian denominations.

MARTIN LUTHER (1483–1546): NEW AVENUES FOR THE THEOLOGY OF THE TRINITY

When a young Augustinian monk called Martin Luther voiced his critique of some of the abuses of the Church in 1517, he could scarcely have guessed that he would inaugurate a new era in Western history and a radically new chapter in the history of Christian doctrine, including in the theology of the Trinity. Initially, however, the theology of the Trinity did not occupy Luther because it did not constitute a matter of dispute with the Church of Rome.[49] Gradually, however, from about 1533 onwards, Luther devoted more space to the traditional doctrine, especially in light of the anti-trinitarian stance adopted by a number of the more radical Reformation theologians.

---

[48] For a good overview of the influence of Ruusbroec's theology, see Bernard McGinn, 'The Significance of Ruusbroec's Mystical Theology', *Louvain Studies* 31 (2006): 19–41, especially 33–41.

[49] Luther states: 'this article of faith remained pure in the papacy and among the scholastic theologians, and we have no quarrel with them on that score'. 'Treatise on the Last Words of David, 2 Samuel 23:1–7', in Jaroslav Pelikan and Helmut T. Lehmann, eds., *Luther's Works*, 55 vols. (St Louis: Concordia and Philadelphia: Fortress Press, 1955–1986), 15,310 (hereafter abbreviated to *LW*), quoted in David Lumpp, 'Returning to Wittenberg: What Martin Luther Teaches Today's Theologians on the Holy Trinity', *Concordia Theological Quarterly* 3/4(2003): 228. The major primary texts are: *Die Drei Symbola* (1538) [The Three Symbols] in *LW* 34, 199ff. (*WA* 50, 262–83), and *Von den letzten Worten Davids* (1543) [On the Last Words of David], to be found in *WA* 54, 28–100. *WA* refers to *D. Martin Luthers Werke kritische Gesamtausgabe* (Weimar, 1884 vv). Also important is *Von den Konziliis und Kirchen* [On the Councils and the Churches], *LW* 41, 3ff. and the *Large Catechism*.

A discussion of Luther's theology of the Trinity is important for at least two reasons: first, because the *Sola Scriptura* principle will raise very important issues in relation to the scriptural basis of the Christian understanding of God as Trinity.[50] Second, because the understanding of the Trinity in light of the paschal mystery – a major theme in some of the most influential twentieth-century theologians – finds its remote origins in Luther's theology.

Although Luther accepted that belief in the Trinity had a scriptural foundation, he held that the theological terminology devised by the Councils (such as *homoousios*, person, *hypostasis*, etc.) could be dispensed with because 'the integrity (*sinceritas*) of Scripture must be guarded, and a man ought not to presume that he speaks more safely and clearly with his mouth than God spoke with his mouth'.[51] Elsewhere, however, Luther endorses the strategy of introducing non-scriptural words in order to refute heretical views – something we also saw with Aquinas. As Luther puts it in 1539, speaking of *homoousios*:

It is certainly true that one should teach nothing outside of Scripture pertaining to divine matters, as St Hilary writes in *On the Trinity*, Book I [ch. 18], which means only that one should teach nothing that is at variance with Scripture. But that one should not use more or other words than those contained in Scripture – that cannot be adhered to, especially in a controversy and when heretics want to falsify things with trickery and distort the words of Scripture.[52]

He is now happy to use the word *homoousios* which he considers a true rendering of the meaning of the Scriptures.

Given the strong Christocentric perspective with which he approaches the Scriptures, Luther could maintain that the doctrine of the Trinity enjoys a scriptural basis. For instance, Luther interprets the words of Ps. 2:7 'Thou art my Son. Today I have begotten Thee' as a reference to the eternal generation of the Son by the Father, and not just as a reference to the human birth of Christ.[53] Similarly, he interprets the plural in Gen. 1:26 and 11:7 as a reference to the Trinity;[54] while the reference to the 'three men' (Gen. 18) who visit Abraham is also interpreted from a trinitarian perspective.[55]

---

[50] The *Sola Scriptura* (by Scripture alone) principle refers to the practice of using the Scriptures only (and not tradition) to develop theological thought.

[51] *Against Latomus*, *LW* 32, 244; see also Arie Baars, *Om Gods verhevenheid en Zijn nabijheid: De Drie-eenheid bij Calvijn* (Kampen: Uitgeverij Kok, 2004), 570–1. We have benefited from Baars' outline in this section.

[52] *On the Councils and the Church*, *LW* 41, 83.

[53] *Comm. on Psalm 2:7* in *LW* 12, 47 and 52; *Lecture on Hebrews* 1:5 in *LW* 29, 113.

[54] *Lectures on Genesis* 1:26, *LW* 1, 57 and *LW* 2, 227; *Three Symbols or Creeds of the Christian Faith*, *LW* 34, 224.

[55] *Three Symbols*, *LW* 34, 225; see also *Lectures on Genesis*, *LW* 3, 191.

Although Luther's allegiance to the dogma of the Trinity is explicit, and while he maintains the doctrine has a scriptural foundation, the *Sola Scriptura* principle was, nevertheless, to prove a challenge to the theology of the Trinity in the long run. As Samuel Powell states:

Something had entered into the stream of Protestant trinitarian thought that would prove difficult to control and unpredictable in its consequences ... Luther and Melanchthon had unwittingly driven a wedge between creeds and Bible by insisting that the creeds are subject to inspection and criticism according to their agreement with the Bible. Although honest in their conviction that the ancient trinitarian creeds merely restated the teachings of the Bible in technical and defensive language and that the subordination of the creeds to Scripture did not entail their rejection, they did open up the possibility of later theologians finding tension and even contradiction between creed and Bible.[56]

Radical anti-trinitarian reformers in the sixteenth century, such as Servetus, found it increasingly difficult to square the traditional theology of the Trinity with their interpretation of Scripture. The school of liberal theology in the nineteenth century (Ritschl, von Harnack, Hermann, and Troeltsch) was the true heir to these radical anti-trinitarian thinkers. Their work culminated in the total indifference with which Rudolf Bultmann treated the doctrine in the twentieth century.

In many ways Luther's doctrine of the Trinity is traditional. He continues the understanding of 'Person' in terms of relation,[57] though in some places he expresses reservations about the psychological analogies,[58] while elsewhere he accepts them as an illustration of the Trinity. Although Luther was mainly interested in the economic Trinity and more specifically how God is present and reveals himself in the salvific work of Christ, he occasionally treats of the immanent Trinity, distinguishing the divine Persons in terms of their mutual relationships and origin:

[T]he Father is a different and distinct nature from the Son in the one indivisible and eternal Godhead. The difference is that He is the Father and does not derive His Godhead from the Son or anyone else. The Son is a Person distinct from the Father in the same, one paternal Godhead. The difference is that He is the Son and that He does not have the Godhead from Himself, nor from anyone else but the Father, since He was born of the Father from eternity. The Holy Spirit is a Person distinct from the Father and the Son in the same, one Godhead. The difference is that He is the Holy Spirit, who eternally proceeds both from the Father and the

---

[56] Samuel Powell, *The Trinity in German Thought* (Cambridge: Cambridge University Press, 2001), 21–2.
[57] See his 13th Thesis from *The Disputation with Hegemon*, WA 39-II, 340.
[58] *Kirchenpostille* (John 1:1–14), WA 10-I-1, 188.

Son, and who does not have the Godhead from Himself nor from anyone else but from both the Father and the Son, and all of this from eternity to eternity.[59]

This quotation also illustrates that Luther accepted the *filioque*, which he attempted to justify by appealing to John 15:26: because Jesus sent the Spirit, the Spirit must proceed from the Father and the Son from all eternity.[60] This reasoning suggests that for Luther, as for Augustine (in *De Trin.* IV.29), the missions reveal the inner-trinitarian mystery: 'The Son shows his eternal birth through his physical birth, and the Holy Spirit shows his eternal proceeding through his physical proceeding [cf. Mt. 3:16 and Acts 2:1–13]. Each of them has an external likeness or image of his internal essence.'[61] Finally, although there is distinction of Persons within the Trinity, the divine Persons act as one *ad extra* – another Augustinian theme (cf. *De Trin.* II.9).[62] Nevertheless, this stance is counterbalanced by a firm use of appropriation in which Creator, Redeemer, and Sanctifier are attributed to the Father, Son and Holy Spirit respectively, allowing Luther to summarise the whole creed in three articles:

the Creed has three articles, the first concerning the Father, the second concerning the Son, the third concerning the Holy Spirit. What do you believe about the Father? Answer: He is the creator. About the Son? He is the redeemer. About the Holy Spirit? He is the sanctifier.[63]

Of course, in these appropriations we do not 'divide God subjectively, for the Father is not known except in the Son and through the Spirit'.[64]

In short, Luther's theology of the Trinity contains many traditional elements. However, as we mentioned, his principle of *Sola Scriptura* – the notion that we should rely solely on the Scriptures as a source for the Christian faith, excluding tradition – was to lead to a growing chasm between Christian doctrine and the traditional theology of the Trinity. Given his traditional, if not conservative, theological outlook it may very well be that Luther would have disapproved of this growing divide between scriptural readings and the traditional doctrine of the Trinity. Luther had no interest in reinventing the doctrine; he merely defended it against some anti-trinitarian thinkers. His main interest lay in salvation through Christ. However, his soteriological views and especially his interpretation of the

---

[59] *Last Words of David*, *LW* 15, 303, quoted by Dennis Ngien, 'Trinity and Divine Passibility in Martin Luther's "*Theologia Crucis*"', *Scottish Bulletin of Evangelical Theology* 19 (2001): 34.

[60] *Three Symbols*, *LW* 34, 217.   [61] *Three Symbols*, *LW* 34, 218.   [62] *LW* 15, 302 and 311.

[63] *Ten Sermons on the Catechism* (1528), *LW* 51, 162; see the contribution by C. Arand, 'Luther on the Creed', *Lutheran Quarterly* 20 (2006): 2–3.

[64] *Lecture on Genesis 1:26* in *LW* 1, 58.

communicatio idiomatum would also lead to innovations in the theology of the Trinity in the subsequent history of doctrine. We will now examine these soteriological views in more detail.

According to Luther we encounter the triune God only through Christ. In Christ God has fully revealed himself, albeit in a paradoxical manner: God reveals himself by hiding himself in the incarnation and in the suffering of his Son. God reveals himself as hidden in that which seems his very opposite (*absconditus sub contrario specie*).[65] The whole majesty of God is hidden in the man Jesus. This explains why Luther had such a strong understanding of the *communicatio idiomatum*. By the *communicatio idiomatum* (lit. 'the sharing of properties') theologians attempt to account for the fact that human features are predicated of God, and vice versa, because of the incarnation. For instance, we can say that 'God is born' or 'God is crucified', although strictly speaking it is the human nature of Christ, united with the divine Person in the incarnation, that is born or that dies. As Luther sees it, in Christ the human and the divine are united so intimately that the human nature shares in the divine properties, and vice versa. The reason Luther interpreted the doctrine of the *communicatio idiomatum* in this way, that is, safeguarding the unity of Christ, was because of the Eucharistic controversy – Luther wanted to uphold the real presence of Christ in the bread and the wine, and it is for this reason that he adopted a fairly radical interpretation of the *communicatio idiomatum*. This has implications for his soteriology and, by implication, for his trinitarian theology. For Luther, when Christ died, this was the whole Christ, human and divine. Although Luther admits that God cannot suffer and die in his divinity, he does state that God suffers and dies in the Person of Christ. There is therefore a strong theopaschite thrust in Luther's thinking:

> We Christians should know that if God is not in the scale to give it weight, we, on our side, sink to the ground. I mean it in this way: if it cannot be said that God died for us, but only a man, we are lost; but if God's death and a dead God lie in the balance, his side goes down and ours goes up like a light and empty scale … he could not sit on the scale unless he had become a man like us, so that it could be called God's dying, God's martyrdom, God's blood, and God's death. For God in his own nature cannot die; but now that God and man are united in one person, it is called God's death when the man dies who is one substance or one person with God.[66]

As Dennis Ngien comments: 'In order to redeem human beings from the power of death, God has to co-suffer and co-die in Christ'.[67]

---

[65] Baars, *Om Gods Verhevenheid*, 563–4. [66] *On the Councils and the Church*, *LW* 41, 104.
[67] Ngien, 'Trinity and Divine Passibility', 48.

For Luther the *communicatio idiomatum* is much more than a linguistic device that allows us to attribute human categories of Christ to his divine nature, and divine categories to his human nature. Rather, in places Luther appears to suggest that because of the incarnation (and the union of the two natures in one Person it involved) the divine nature in Christ begins to become passible: 'Since his incarnation the two natures are united; and the divine nature confers its properties on the human, and vice versa, the human on the divine.'[68] Writing against the ancient views of Nestorius that God cannot be crucified or suffer, Luther states that this only applies as long as God has not yet been made man.[69] This effectively introduces an element of historicity or temporality in God: God becomes passible through the incarnation.

Another innovation of Luther was his notion that Christ identifies in a most radical fashion with *sinful* humanity. Consider the following passage in which he comments on Gal. 3:13:

And all the prophets saw this, that Christ was to become the greatest thief, murderer, adulterer, robber, desecrator, blasphemer, etc., there has ever been anywhere in the world. He is not acting in his own Person now. Now he is not the Son of God, born of the Virgin. But he is a sinner, who has and bears the sin of Paul, the former blasphemer, persecutor, and assaulter; of Peter, who denied Christ; of David, who was an adulterer and a murderer, and who caused the Gentiles to blaspheme the name of the Lord (Rom. 2:24). In short, he has and bears all the sins of all men in his body – not in the sense that he has committed them but in the sense that he took those sins, committed by us, upon his own body, in order to make satisfaction for them with his own blood. Therefore this general Law of Moses included him, although he was innocent so far as his own Person was concerned; for it found him among sinners and thieves. Thus a magistrate regards someone as a criminal and punishes him if he catches him among thieves, even though the man has never committed anything evil or worthy of death. Christ was not only found among sinners; but of his own free will and by the will of the Father he wanted to be an associate of sinners, having assumed the flesh and blood of those who were sinners and thieves and who were immersed in all sorts of sin. Therefore when the Law found him among thieves, it condemned and executed him as a thief.[70]

---

[68] *Sermons on the Gospel of St John*, LW 22, 493.

[69] WA 39, 101, quoted by Ngien, 'Trinity and Divine Passibility', 48–9: 'From eternity He has not suffered, but since He became man, He is passible.'

[70] Martin Luther, *Lectures on Galatians 1535*, ed. Jaroslav Pelikan (Saint Louis, MO: Concordia Publishing House, 1963), 277. The reference to making satisfaction should not be taken as an indication that Luther accepts the Anselmic understanding of satisfaction. In the same passage (p. 279) we find: 'Is. 53:6 speaks the same way about Christ [i.e., that our sin must be Christ's sin]. It says: "God has laid on Him the iniquity of us all." These words must not be diluted but must be left in their precise and serious sense. For God is not joking in the words of the prophet; He is speaking

Luther criticises those who 'segregate Christ from sins and sinners', claiming that Christ thereby becomes 'useless' to us. Only when Christ 'bears the sins of the world' and 'his innocence is pressed down with the sins and the guilt of the entire world', and 'our sins are as much Christ's own as if he himself had committed them', only then can Christ be subject to the divine judgement on our behalf: 'And this is our highest comfort, to clothe and wrap Christ this way in my sins, your sins, and the sins of the entire world, and in this way to behold him bearing all our sins.'[71]

Luther's radically new insight is that in a sense Christ becomes the universal sinner. This was to pave the way in Reformed circles for an understanding of salvation in penal terms (as punishment) rather than in terms of penance or 'making satisfaction', which had been the traditional Catholic view. In Anselm of Canterbury and Thomas Aquinas the *sinlessness* of Christ had been stressed as this was considered to be of central importance for his role as the holy representative of humanity, who freely restores the relationship between God and humanity.[72] Given the close connection theologians in the twentieth century established between the paschal mystery and the theology of the Trinity, the adoption of Luther's soteriological views will have important consequences for trinitarian theology.[73] As Luther's interest was in the economic Trinity and not in the immanent Trinity he did not develop this line of thinking. Others (in different ways, Hegel and Moltmann) would not be as hesitant. For Moltmann, for instance, the Lutheran notion of a radical identification of the Son of God with the godless and godforsaken will provide an important impetus to develop a theology of a suffering God. Through the writings of Hans Urs von Balthasar these views, albeit in a somewhat different way, have also entered Catholic theology.

---

seriously and out of great love, namely that this Lamb of God, Christ, should bear the iniquity of us all. But what does it mean to "bear"? The sophists reply: "To be punished." Good. But why is Christ punished? Is it not because He has sins and bears sins? That Christ has sin is the testimony of the Holy Spirit in the Psalms. Thus in Ps. 40:12 we read: "My iniquities have overtaken me"; in Ps. 41:4: "I said: 'O Lord, be gracious to Me; heal Me, for I have sinned against Thee!'"; and in Ps. 69:5: "O God, Thou knowest My folly; the wrongs I have done are not hidden from Thee." In these psalms the Holy Spirit is speaking in the Person of Christ and testifying in clear words that He has sinned or has sins.'

[71] Ibid., 279.

[72] For a more in-depth discussion of these issues, and the contrast between Lutheran and Catholic views on salvation, see Rik Van Nieuwenhove, 'St Anselm and St Thomas Aquinas on "Satisfaction": Or how Catholic and Protestant Understandings of the Cross Differ', *Angelicum* 80 (2003): 159–76.

[73] This interconnection between the paschal and trinitarian mysteries has been described by Anne Hunt as 'an extraordinary development in Christian theology'. See Anne Hunt, *The Trinity and the Paschal Mystery: A Development in Recent Catholic Theology* (Collegeville, MN: The Liturgical Press, 1997), 6.

JOHN CALVIN (1509–1564): BETWEEN TRADITION AND RENEWAL

A number of issues that preoccupied Luther will return in the work of John Calvin, such as the scriptural foundation of the doctrine of the Trinity and the legitimacy of using non-biblical terms to describe the mystery of the Three in One. Calvin discusses the doctrine of the Trinity in a number of works: while in the second chapter of his *Institutes of the Christian Religion* of 1536 it only receives relatively minor attention, he paid more attention to it in subsequent editions (1539, 1543; final edition in 1559) in response to the growth of anti-trinitarian opposition.[74] In his sermons, however, he hardly discusses the doctrine.[75]

Calvin's theology of the Trinity, and the way it evolved, was deeply shaped by anti-trinitarian thinkers, such as Michael Servetus and others. Servetus was one of the most eloquent anti-trinitarian thinkers of the era. The details of his doctrine need not detain us. On the one hand, it freely draws upon Neoplatonic themes, especially in his later works; on the other hand, Servetus alleges that the traditional doctrine of the Trinity had become corrupted since the time of the Council of Nicea by drawing on Greek sources. Servetus therefore calls for a return to the biblical sources, and to ante-Nicene theology (Irenaeus, Tertullian) so as to purge trinitarian doctrine of extra-biblical additions. The result is a modalist and subordinationist theology which, at least according to Calvin, abolishes the difference between the Son and the Spirit. Other anti-trinitarian thinkers include Giorgio Biandrata (1516–88) who had to leave the church in Geneva because of his unorthodox trinitarian views. He went to Poland where he contributed to the unitarian cause propagated by Socinus (Fausto Paolo Sozzini, d.1604). Gentile (1520–66), another Italian exile, arrived in Geneva in 1556, but he too met with opposition from Calvin, and (like Servetus in Geneva) would be executed by the Reformers (Bern, 1566) for his heretical views.

In these anti-trinitarian debates the *Sola Scriptura* principle played a major role – for the traditional doctrine of the Trinity is certainly not the

---

[74] Other important discussions can be found in Calvin's *Defense of the Orthodox Faith concerning the Holy Trinity against the Errors of Michael Servetus*, also known as *Refutation of the Errors of Michael Servetus (Refutatio Errorum Michaelis Serveti, CO* VIII, 453–644), dating from 1554, and a number of other writings against anti-trinitarian authors, such as Biandrata (1516–88) and Gentile (1520–66). For a helpful and comprehensive study of Calvin's theology of the Trinity and his opponents, see Baars, *Om Gods Verhevenheid.*

[75] See Richard Stauffer, *Dieu, la création et la Providence dans la predication de Calvin* (Bern: Peter Lang, 1978), 151–76.

only possible interpretation of the scriptural witness. The issue of extra-biblical terminology looms large in these debates as well.

Calvin's major discussion of the theology of the Trinity is in the last edition (1559) of the *Institutes of Christian Religion*, especially Book I, chapter 13. It is a matter for debate whether or not the *Institutes* is ordered in a trinitarian way. Calvin divides the work into four books, dealing with the structure of the creed as he sees it (Father, Son, Spirit, and Church). For this reason Arie Baars contends that the structure of the *Institutes* cannot therefore be called trinitarian without qualification, but should rather be called trinitarian-soteriological.[76]

As with Luther there are a number of traditional elements in Calvin's trinitarian theology. Drawing on Heb. 1:3, Calvin argues that the *hypostasis* of the Son differs from the Father. In this context he observes that the Church is perfectly justified – even compelled – to use extra-biblical terminology (such as 'Person', 'Trinity',) to explain what the Scriptures declare (*Instit.* I.13.3). Calvin then defines the word 'Person':

By Person, then, I mean a subsistence in the Divine essence (*subsistentia in Dei essentia*), – a subsistence which, while related to the other two, is distinguished from them by incommunicable properties (*proprietate incommunicabili distinguitur*) ... Each of the three subsistences while related to the others, is distinguished by its own properties. (*Instit.* I.13.6)[77]

By subsistence Calvin seems to mean *hypostasis*.[78] Father, Son, and Spirit dwell in the divine essence and are distinguished by their incommunicable properties: 'whatever is proper to each I affirm to be incommunicable, because nothing can apply or be transferred to the Son which is attributed to the Father as a mark of distinction' (*Instit.* I.13.6). By emphasising that the three divine Persons are three subsistences in the essence of God, distinguished from one another through an incommunicable property, Calvin refutes the modalism of Servetus and the subordinationism of the Italian anti-trinitarian thinkers.

A number of observations can be made. First, Calvin retains the Augustinian insight that we can distinguish the three Persons from one another on the basis of their mutual relations.[79] Second, his reference to the

---

[76] Baars, *Om Gods Verhevenheid*, 446.

[77] John Calvin, *Institutes of the Christian Religion*, trans. H. Beveridge (Grand Rapids, MI: Eerdmans, 1998), 114.

[78] In *Instit.* I.13.2 Calvin had already noted: 'The Latins having used the word *Persona* to express the same thing as the Greek *hypostasis*, it betrays excessive fastidiousness and even perverseness to quarrel with the term. The most literal translation would be subsistence' (p. 111).

[79] Augustine, *De Trin.* VIII, prooem-1; VII.6–12.

incommunicability of the Persons may seem reminiscent of Richard of St Victor. However, we should refrain from seeing Calvin as a predecessor of social models of the Trinity.[80] After all, Calvin is not interested in speculations about the nature of the immanent Trinity. Nor does he ever consider an analysis of love to explore the mystery of the Three in One as Richard does.

Calvin is equally sceptical of developing psychological analogies (cf. *Instit.* I.13.18). He merely draws upon Scripture, but his reading of the Scriptures is undoubtedly informed by the Church teachings of the first centuries.[81] This hermeneutical perspective explains why he accepts the Father as 'the beginning and the source' of the Trinity (*Instit.* I.13.20), why he speaks of 'the begottenness' of the Son (*Instit.* I.13.4, 7, 23, 24), and even accepts the *filioque* (*Instit.* I.13.17 and 18: 'the Son is said to be of the Father only; the Spirit of both the Father and the Son'). Similarly, although Calvin had refused to endorse the Nicean and Athanasian Creeds in his dispute with Caroli in 1537,[82] he emphasises in the last edition of the *Institutes* the need to use the extra-biblical terminology of the early Councils (*Instit.* I.13.5).

Calvin's interest in the so-called immanent Trinity is very limited. For him, as for Luther, the doctrine of the Trinity has a soteriological significance.[83] This can be illustrated by the beautiful quotation on the effects of baptism:

> He who baptizes into Christ cannot but at the same time invoke the name of the Father and the Spirit. For we are cleansed by his blood, just because our gracious Father, of his incomparable mercy, willing to receive us into favour, appointed him Mediator to effect our reconciliation with himself. Regeneration we obtain from his death and resurrection only, when sanctified by his Spirit we are imbued with a new and spiritual nature. Wherefore we obtain, and in a manner distinctly perceive, in the Father the cause, in the Son the matter, and in the Spirit the effect of our purification and regeneration. (*Instit.* IV.15.6)

Through baptism in the name of the Father, the Son, and the Spirit, we begin to know, and participate in, the trinitarian God, as the following quotation from his *Commentary on Matthew* makes clear:

---

[80] See John R. Loeschen, *The Divine Community: Trinity, Church and Ethics in Reformation Theologies* (Missouri: The Sixteenth Century Journal Publishers, 1981).

[81] Paul Helm, *John Calvin's Ideas* (Oxford: Oxford University Press, 2006), 36.

[82] For an extensive discussion of the dispute, see Baars, *Om Gods Verhevenheid*, 104–21.

[83] See Philip W. Butin, *Revelation, Redemption and Response: Calvin's Trinitarian Understanding of the Divine–Human Relationship* (Oxford: Oxford University Press, 1995), 39ff.

Furthermore, there is a profound reason why the Father, the Son, and the Spirit are mentioned here explicitly. For we cannot obtain the power of baptism unless we first receive the freely given mercy of the Father who has reconciled us with ourselves through his only-begotten Son. Then, secondly, the Son must join with the sacrifice of his death; finally, the Holy Spirit must come forward by whom he cleanses and renews us, and by whom he makes us partakers in every goodness. Thus we see that we cannot know God properly unless our faith envisages three distinct Persons in one essence, and that the effect and the fruit of baptism thus leads to God the Father adopting us as his children in his Son, and restores us into righteousness, after we have been purified by the Spirit from the iniquities of our flesh.[84]

We have seen that Luther had a particularly strong understanding of the *communicatio idiomatum*, at times understanding it in terms of an inter-penetration of the human and divine properties in Christ. Luther's stance had been inspired by Zwingli's denial of the real presence of Christ in the Eucharist: Christ's body is not really present in the Eucharist, according to Zwingli, because the humanity of Christ sits at the right hand of the Father. Luther rejected this view, safeguarding the real presence, by affirming the unity of the humanity and divinity of Christ.

Calvin was worried that Luther was in danger of mixing the divine and the human, thereby compromising the majesty and transcendence of the divinity. In fact, according to Calvin the divinity of Christ exists also outside the humanity of Christ:

although the boundless essence of the Word was united with human nature in one person, we have no idea of any enclosing. The Son of God descended miraculously from heaven, yet without abandoning heaven; was pleased to be conceived miracu-lously in the Virgin's womb, to live on earth, and hang upon the cross, and yet always filled the world as from the beginning. (*Instit.* II.13.4)

This notion that the divine nature of Christ also exists outside (*extra*) his human nature, is called the *extra calvinisticum*.[85]

Given Calvin's reluctance to press the *communicatio idiomatum* and given his concern that we must not 'destroy the two natures' in emphasising the unity of the Person, Calvin avoids the theopaschite tendencies we encountered in Luther's theology. For Calvin, the human and divine natures are clearly distinct, and Christ suffers only in his humanity, not in his divinity.[86] Commenting on John 1:14 he writes:

---

[84] *Comm. in Matth. 28:19* (1555) – *CO* XLV, 824, quoted (in Latin and Dutch) by Baars, *Om Gods Verhevenheid*, 430–1 (our trans.).
[85] Baars, *Om Gods Verhevenheid*, 586.   [86] *Instit.* II.12.3.

Here there are two chief articles of belief: First, in Christ two natures were united in one person in such a way that one and the same Christ is true God and man. Secondly, the unity of his person does not prevent his two natures from remaining distinct, so that the divinity retains whatever is proper to it and the humanity likewise has separately what belongs to it ... [87]

Referring to this passage, Paul Helm captures Calvin's spirit well when he writes:

if the incarnation is truly the incarnation of the Son of God, then it must preserve the divinity of the Son of God unaltered and unimpaired. For otherwise it would not be a true incarnation of the Son ... since the Son of God is essentially God and thus impassible, immense and omnipresent, he must remain in his incarnation impassible, immense, and omnipresent. [88]

Followers of Luther could of course raise the question whether Calvin's understanding of God as impassible can be maintained in the light of the divine revelation of his Son on Calvary. They would argue that an understanding of God in terms of impassibility is foreign to the biblical understanding of God. An example of this line of critique can be found in the works of Moltmann. At any rate, our discussion of both Luther and Calvin has made clear the diversity between the two main Protestant thinkers and, also, the tension involved in presenting a theology of the Trinity when adhering to the principle of *Sola Scriptura*. In different ways their theologies further witness to the growing divisions between faith and reason, and between Scripture and tradition. These growing divisions would have a major impact on the theology of the Trinity in the centuries to come.

SUGGESTED READINGS

Emery, Gilles, *Trinity in Aquinas* (Ave Maria, FL: Sapientia Press, 2006).

Friedman, Russell, *Medieval Trinitarian Thought from Aquinas to Ockham* (Cambridge: Cambridge University Press, 2010).

Hayes, Zachary, *Saint Bonaventure's Disputed Questions on the Mystery of the Trinity* (New York: The Franciscan Institute, 2000).

Helm, Paul, *John Calvin's Ideas* (Oxford: Oxford University Press, 2006).

Van Nieuwenhove, Rik, *Jan van Ruusbroec: Mystical Theologian of the Trinity* (Notre Dame, IN: University of Notre Dame Press, 2003).

---

[87] *Comm. John 1:14* from David Torrance and Thomas Torrance, eds., *Calvin's Commentaries: The Gospel according to St John 1–10* (Grand Rapids, MI: Eerdmans, 1995), 20.

[88] Helm, *John Calvin's Ideas*, 62.

CHAPTER 5

The Trinity from Schleiermacher to the end of the twentieth century

THE ENLIGHTENMENT AND THE DETRADITIONALISATION OF THE THEOLOGY OF THE TRINITY

Between the time of the Reformation and the beginning of the nineteenth century a number of intellectual developments took place which impacted on the theology of the Trinity. First, the separation of faith and reason, already begun in the late medieval period (Condemnation of 1277) became even more pronounced during the Reformation and its aftermath. In the light of the religious conflicts within Western Christendom, an appeal to mere reason without any reference to the tradition proved popular. Descartes' *Meditations* (1641) is a clear example of this approach. This modern understanding of reason as 'autonomous', separate from faith, led in our view to the impoverishment of both reason and faith, for it led to the decline of the contemplative disposition, which had been central to the approach to the mystery of the Trinity amongst medieval schoolmen. A merely rationalistic or a merely fideistic approach was alien to them. A second major development was the rise of empirical sciences which ultimately led to the concept of a mechanistic universe which was explicable in its own terms, without reference to God. In philosophical terms, British empiricism, by acknowledging only sense data as a source of true knowledge, led to the marginalisation of traditional religion, to deism, and even to scepticism. The titles of some of the main works of this time speak for themselves. John Locke (1632–1704), one of the fathers of empiricism, wrote a book entitled *The Reasonableness of Christianity* in which he attempted to show that the core of Christian beliefs – when interpreted properly – are not at odds with reason. His contemporary, the Irishman John Toland went even further in his work *Christianity Not Mysterious* by rejecting any kind of supernaturalism as superstitious or corrupt. But it is Matthew Tindal (1657–1733) who is considered to be the father of deism. In his book *Christianity as Old as the Creation* he states that revelation cannot go against reason (if it does it is wrong); morality is grounded on reason (not on God); and the Bible should be read like any other book. These presuppositions result in a 'clockmaker God' who differs rather dramatically from the trinitarian God of Christianity.

However, it was soon realised that merely relying on sense data cannot provide us with secure knowledge of the world and how it operates. For instance, the Scottish philosopher David Hume (1711–76) argued that we cannot observe causality – it is a mere habit of the mind. In the area of religious thought he is remembered for his attack on traditional religion in *Dialogues Concerning Natural Religion*. Immanuel Kant (1724–1804), the greatest of the Enlightenment thinkers, rejected Hume's epistemological scepticism by arguing that the human mind structures its environment by subjecting it to a priori conditions of knowledge (causality, time, space). Because one cannot use these categories outside the phenomenal world classical metaphysics is doomed to failure – including the proofs for the existence of God. However, since practical reason demands a necessary connection between virtue and happiness, Kant postulates the existence of God and the immortality of the soul. We cannot prove the existence of God, but if we recognise any moral obligation at all we are implicitly asserting a moral order which in turn implies the immortality of the soul and the existence of God. Kant was obviously a deist: he accepts the existence of God but he does not accept the claims of revelation. Kant was to reduce key religious beliefs in the existence of God or the immortality of the soul to mere postulates of practical reason. Given this reductionist orientation, that is, his understanding of religion in terms of morality, it is not surprising that Kant had no interest in a theology of the Trinity.[1]

Another important development in the intellectual scene of the eighteenth century, closely associated with the philosophical movements already discussed, was the emergence of the historical-critical approach as developed by Hermann Reimarus (1694–1768) and others. For Reimarus, the New Testament is a historical document to be interpreted against the background of first-century Judaism. He likewise argued that in our readings of the New Testament we should disregard all supernatural elements (resurrection, miracles, divinity of Christ). By denying the inspired nature of the New Testament and by pursuing a 'historical' reading deeply

---

[1] In *Der Streit der Fakultäten* Kant dismisses the doctrine in the following words: 'From the doctrine of the Trinity, taken literally, nothing whatsoever can be gained for practical purposes, even if one believed that one comprehended it – and less still if one is conscious that it surpasses all our concepts.' Quoted by Jürgen Moltmann, *The Trinity and the Kingdom of God* (London: SCM Press, 1991), 6 (henceforward abbreviated as *TKG*).

coloured by Enlightenment presuppositions, Reimarus drove a deep wedge between the tradition of faith (including the doctrine of the Trinity) and the New Testament as he interpreted it. Given this intellectual context Reimarus too can only find a moral purpose for religion: in his reading Jesus becomes a noble moral figure whose legacy, however, was distorted by his followers. The rise of the historical-critical method banished allegorical readings of the Scriptures to the margins of theological practice, and it is only in the second half of the twentieth century that scholars have begun to re-engage with allegorical readings, exposing merely historical-critical readings as one-sided at best.[2]

Authors who accepted the conclusions of Kant's *Critique of Pure Reason* but who were uncomfortable with his reductionist approach to the Christian faith had to find a different vantage point from which to develop their theological thought. One of the authors who attempted to do this was Friedrich Schleiermacher (1768–1834). It is in light of these two challenges – the Kantian and the historical-critical one – that we must situate the work of Schleiermacher, often called the father of modern Protestant theology.

In short, between the time of the Reformation and the beginning of the nineteenth century a number of intellectual developments originated which impacted on the theology of the Trinity. This is not to say that traditional approaches to the theology of the Trinity simply vanished (as is often alleged); but it is to acknowledge that very influential rivalling intellectual approaches originated in the Western tradition which proved hostile to these more traditional approaches. Having mentioned some of the key issues in the preceding pages, we will now continue to discuss two authors who should be considered as exponents of these rival discourses: Schleiermacher and Hegel.

FRIEDRICH SCHLEIERMACHER (1768–1834) AND THE TURN TO THE SUBJECT

Schleiermacher accepted that one could no longer read the Bible in a non-historical manner. Although the Old Testament has a limited value because of the historical links with Christianity, we should 'utterly discard Old Testament proofs for specifically Christian doctrines'.[3] He also accepted

---

[2] See the pioneering work of Henri de Lubac, *Medieval Exegesis* 4 vols. (Grand Rapids, MI: Eerdmans, 1998ff.).

[3] Friedrich Schleiermacher, *The Christian Faith* (Edinburgh: T&T Clark, 1994), abbreviated as *CF*, followed by number of section and paragraph: *CF* 132.2.

that Kant had convincingly shown that a metaphysical approach to the God-question only led to antinomies. Schleiermacher therefore turned to the subjective experience of absolute dependence. Schleiermacher's key notion – *Abhängigkeitsgefühl* – is often translated as 'the feeling of absolute dependence', but this does not quite capture Schleiermacher's meaning. He is not interested in feelings but rather in the receptivity that characterises our self-consciousness, a consciousness of self as essentially dependent on infinite being. This 'absolute dependence which characterizes not only man but all temporal existence' (*CF* 4.4) does not need proofs for the existence of God. Such proofs are entirely redundant (*CF* 33.3).

Contrary to what some scholars (such as Karl Barth and Jürgen Moltmann) have claimed, the anthropological turn that Schleiermacher effected in theology does not necessarily exclude a theocentric focus. Some of Schleiermacher's expressions may at first appear problematic, such as his famous statement that 'doctrines are only expressions of inward experiences' (*CF* 100.3).[4] Nevertheless, the whole system of Schleiermacher hinges on the affirmation that God was present in Christ in a unique, because perfect, manner:

[T]o ascribe to Christ an absolutely powerful God-consciousness, and to attribute to him an existence of God in him, are exactly the same thing ... He is the only 'other' in which there is an existence of God in the proper sense, so far, that is, as we posit the God-consciousness in his self-consciousness as continually and exclusively determining every moment, and consequently also this perfect indwelling of the Supreme Being as his peculiar being and his inmost self. (*CF* 94.2)

This theocentric stance does not, however, imply a trinitarian stance, and claims that Schleiermacher has to be seen as one of the major innovators in the theology of the Trinity, or responsible for its revival, are difficult to sustain. Given his methodological and hermeneutical presuppositions, Schleiermacher rejects the traditional doctrine of the Trinity, especially the doctrine of the immanent Trinity: 'the assumption of an eternal distinction in the Supreme Being is not an utterance concerning the religious consciousness, for there it could never emerge' (*CF* 170.2). And because it is not an utterance concerning religious consciousness, it ultimately has no doctrinal value for Schleiermacher. He is happy to concede that God was present in Christ and in the Church, but he rejects any

---

[4] This appears hermeneutically naïve, for it can be argued that doctrines shape experience rather than the other way around. See George Lindbeck's study *The Nature of Doctrine: Religion and Theology in a Postliberal Age* (Philadelphia: The Westminster Press, 1984).

suggestion that there is therefore, from all eternity, a distinction between Father, Son, and Spirit.[5]

Another critique he levels at the traditional doctrine of the Trinity is that it never managed to successfully harmonise the belief in the oneness of God and the belief in the threeness of Persons. According to official doctrine, the three are co-equal and, in turn, equal with the divine essence. This, so Schleiermacher reasons, implies that each of the divine Persons is less than the divine essence.[6]

Again, he raises the charge of subordinationism against traditional doctrine: the fact that the Son is 'begotten' from the Father must imply, 'if the term means anything at all', a relationship of dependence; hence the power of the Father is greater than that of the Son. Pursuing the same line of critique: if we accept that the relationship between the three Persons and the divine nature should be conceived in terms of members of a species and the species itself, then one will end up with either subordinationism if one adopts a realistic stance (what is really real is the essence), or tritheism if one adopts a nominalist stance (only the three Persons – as instances of the divine – exist) (*CF* 171.3). If we refuse to conceive the relationship between the three and the oneness in terms of species and members, then 'we really are not in a position to form any definite ideas on the subject, and hence can have no interest in it' (*CF* 171.3). This last remark, and the criticisms Schleiermacher put forward, appear to reveal an impoverished theological imagination when dealing with the traditional doctrine of the Trinity.[7]

Most of the critique we have discussed so far was raised by Schleiermacher in the 'Conclusion' (not an 'Appendix', as is so often alleged) to his major work *The Christian Faith*.[8] Given his presuppositions,

---

[5] Appealing to the Prologue of St John's Gospel is futile, he informs us, for this text can be read with equal plausibility in an Arian manner; besides, the Spirit is not mentioned in the Prologue. All John hoped to make clear, Schleiermacher claims, is the presence of God in Christ (*CF* 170.2, 3).

[6] Schleiermacher's rationalistic spirit transpires in the application of this 'impeccable' calculation: if $a + b + c = D$, then a and b and c are each less than D.

[7] There is no need to refute Schleiermacher's critique in detail: theologians have traditionally refrained from applying numerical terms to God (see *ST* I.30.3); besides, when dealing with infinity it may very well be argued that the Three can be One without being any less than the perichoretic Oneness. They also warned against understanding it in terms of species and members of species. Schleiermacher's criticism seems to presuppose quaternity, a stance to be rejected on the basis of *perichoresis*.

[8] Another criticism, not often noted by scholars, is raised much earlier (*CF* 96.1). Criticising the language of Chalcedon, and wondering how it could possibly be squared with the language of trinitarian theology, Schleiermacher alleges that traditional doctrine effectively implies tritheism: in the Trinity we supposedly have 'three Persons in one Essence'; in Christ we supposedly have 'one Person out of two natures'. If the word 'Person' retains the same meaning as in Christology – that is, as an individuation of a nature – we end up with three divine individuals. We will come back to this critique when dealing with the trinitarian theology of Hans Urs von Balthasar.

it is clear that Schleiermacher cannot accommodate traditional understandings of the Trinity: 'We have only to do with the God-consciousness given in our self-consciousness along with our consciousness of the world; hence we have no formula for the being of God in himself as distinct from the being of God in the world' (*CF* 172.1). Schleiermacher sees his own work as a first, preliminary step towards a revision of the doctrine, a revision which the Protestant churches had failed to pursue (*CF* 172.3). He considers the traditional doctrine of the Trinity as nothing but an expression of the insight that God is present in both Christ and the Holy Spirit (*CF* 172.1). Pre-existence of both the Son and the Spirit is excluded.[9]

How then does Schleiermacher conceive of the Trinity? The following quotation captures his intentions well:

Unless the being of God in Christ is assumed, the idea of redemption could not be thus concentrated in his Person. And unless there were such a union also in the common Spirit of the Church the Church could not be the Bearer and Perpetuator of the redemption through Christ. Now these exactly are the essential elements in the doctrine of the Trinity. (*CF* 170.1)

Let us first deal with the presence of God in Christ. This is 'the innermost fundamental power within him, from which every activity proceeds and which holds every element together' (*CF* 96.3). As this quotation suggests, Schleiermacher attempts to move beyond static language of human and divine *natures* and instead prefers to speak of divine *activity* in Christ. Given this more dynamic understanding of the union between the divine and the human, Schleiermacher can also dispense with the *communicatio idiomatum*: since divine attributes are simply activities, there is no need to speak of a sharing of these with human activities (*CF* 97.5). Nothing but his essential sinlessness distinguishes Christ from other people. Schleiermacher's rejection of the *communicatio idiomatum* also implies that he refuses to attribute suffering to the divine nature – a view that is, in his opinion, both untraditional and based on misconceived ideas of redemption (*CF* 97.5). Schleiermacher understands our redemption in terms of receiving blessedness from Christ 'in the consciousness that Christ in us is the centre of our life' (*CF* 101.2). Here Schleiermacher's pietist background makes itself felt, and he is quite happy to call this element of his thought 'mystical' (*CF* 101.3).

[9] See *CF* 123.1: 'In Christ's promises of the Holy Spirit of truth there is nowhere the slightest whisper that this Something had been present earlier and had vanished only temporarily, or indeed that he is anything at all except as he is for the disciples of Christ.' The Holy Spirit is the union of the divine essence with the community of Christian believers. The pre-existence of the Son is also explicitly ruled out (*CF* 96.1): 'the New Testament knows nothing of this usage; even the expression "Son of God" it uses . . . only of the subject of this union, and not of the divine element in it before the union.'

This brings us to Schleiermacher's pneumatology. It is the work of the Holy Spirit to bring Christ into memory, and glorify him in us (*CF* 124.2). The Spirit is the unifying force derived from Christ, residing in the believers, which builds up the Christian community to constitute 'a moral personality' (*CF* 121.2). The Spirit is an effective spiritual power which animates the life of believers from within (*CF* 123.3).

To attribute the work of redemption to the Son and sanctification to the Spirit is fairly traditional doctrine. Commentators have noted, however, that Schleiermacher does not discuss the role of the person of the Father in *The Christian Faith*.[10] The most surprising element from a traditional point of view is his outright denial of the pre-existence of Son and Spirit. In this sense we can state that Schleiermacher undoubtedly develops an interesting soteriology and pneumatology; but he is not interested in trinitarian theology as such. However, his views (including his rejection of the pre-existence of Christ and Spirit) have an important implication: they introduce an element of historicity in God's being. God appears to become trinitarian in the course of history.[11] This train of thought is merely suggested in *The Christian Faith* and is not developed given Schleiermacher's methodological presuppositions. It was Hegel who would develop this line of thinking.

For Schleiermacher, the definitions of scholasticism had long since become a dead letter (*CF* 96.2) and he therefore attempted to reinvent the Christian faith for the modern period. We may not share his presuppositions, methodology or conclusions, but his status as a 'classic' author is beyond dispute. One author who did not share Schleiermacher's approach (and explicitly criticises it) is Hegel, the greatest idealist philosopher of the nineteenth century.

G. W. F. HEGEL (1770–1831): A PHILOSOPHICAL REINTERPRETATION OF THE TRINITY

Hegel offers one of the most sweeping and profound philosophical systems in the history of the West. He took issue with the Romantic reduction of religion to mere feelings of devotion, such as in pietism or even in Schleiermacher's emphasis upon 'feelings of dependence', stating rather sarcastically that if this were the correct approach 'a dog would be the best Christian'.[12] But he also disagrees with the Kantian Enlightenment

---

[10] See Samuel Powell, *The Trinity in German Thought* (Cambridge: Cambridge University Press, 2001), 101.
[11] Ibid., 100.
[12] *Hegel's Berliner Schriften*, ed. J. Hoffmeister, 1944, p. 346, quoted by Bernard M. G. Reardon, *Hegel's Philosophy of Religion* (London: Macmillan Press, 1977), 85.

approach, rejecting it as fundamentally sceptical. More specifically, he takes issue with the narrow emphasis upon *Verstand* (usually translated as 'understanding') as distinct from the more profound *Vernunft* (usually translated as 'reason' although 'intelligence' might be a better alternative). Whereas *Verstand* only detects contradictions, working with static concepts, *Vernunft* comes to a more profound understanding which grasps identity in difference. Hegel is therefore very much the philosopher of reconciliation, that is, his system of thought wants to bring competing views together in a higher synthesis, for instance, the Enlightenment concern with truth and reason, and the Romantic or pietist concerns with religion in terms of devotion and subjective feelings of the heart.

Methodologically the so-called dialectical approach is one of his key features. In textbooks this is usually presented in terms of thesis-antithesis-higher synthesis. Hegel however prefers to speak of reconciliation of opposites rather than synthesis. In reconciliation the opposition, division, or separation between two competing elements is overcome. As we will see, the incarnation is an important example of the way in which opposition between God and his estranged world is overcome, for it is in the unity of the divine and human natures of the God-man that reconciliation between God and world is achieved (*PR* II, 348).[13]

As Hegel's thought deals with almost every aspect of life and culture it defies summary. For our purposes we will focus mainly on his views on religion, philosophy, and the Trinity as expounded in his *Lectures on the Philosophy of Religion* (*PR*). In it, Hegel describes the whole movement of 'God' and world from a trinitarian perspective. We put the word 'God' in quotation marks as Hegel's God is not to be identified with the God of traditional Christian theism. For Hegel, God as *Geist* (Spirit, or Mind) not only manifests himself in the world, but the world, its history, and its human institutions (including state, art, religion, morality) embody and actualise God. As Charles Taylor puts it:

Like finite subjects, the absolute subject [= 'God'] must go through a cycle, a drama, in which it suffers division in order to return to unity ... And the drama is not another parallel story to the drama of opposition and reconciliation in man. It is the same one seen from a different and wider perspective.[14]

In other words, humanity and its cultural (religious, artistic, moral, legal) institutions and expressions are the vehicle of the spiritual life of *Geist*.

---

[13] We use the translation *Lectures on the Philosophy of Religion* from the second German edition (1840) in three volumes by Ebenezer B. Speirs (London: Routledge, 1974).

[14] Charles Taylor, *Hegel and Modern Society* (Cambridge: Cambridge University Press, 1992), 41.

The whole of reality is the self-unfolding of Spirit in its movement towards greater actualization. Nature is self-alienated Spirit, God in his otherness. Hegel also distinguishes between subjective Spirit (the emergence of subjectivity in the human being), objective Spirit (the social objectification of *Geist* in cultural and ethical institutions of society, including the State), and absolute Spirit (in which Spirit knows and actualises itself in art, religion, and philosophy). This is certainly a vision full of majesty – but whether it is compatible with the Christian worldview is debatable.

Religion is of particular interest to Hegel as it is 'the self-consciousness of God' (*PR* II, 327). Hegel discusses a number of different religions in which the absolute Spirit ('God') finds expression. Greek religion, for instance, expresses the divine in human form (e.g., statue of Apollo): the divine is not seen as something utterly other. However, Greek religion remains parochial, intrinsically linked with the city-state. Jewish religion, on the other hand, is more universalistic, but here God remains too distant, too transcendent, and this separation of divine and human leads to unhappy consciousness. It is in Christianity that we encounter true universality without having to espouse an utterly transcendent God. Here the universal, infinite Spirit and the particular, finite Spirit are inseparably connected (*PR* II, 330).

Thus, more than in other religions it is in Christianity that God reveals himself supremely. Indeed, it is in Christianity that the absolute Being (Hegel's 'God') attains self-consciousness. Hegel understands God very much in terms of consciousness or mind, and it is characteristic of mind or Spirit (*Geist)* to differentiate itself, to manifest itself:

God posits or lays down the Other, and takes it up again into his eternal movement. Spirit just is what appears to itself or manifests itself; this constitutes its act, or form of action, and its life; this is its only act, and it is itself only its act. What does God reveal, in fact, but just that he is this revelation of himself? What he reveals is the infinite form. Absolute subjectivity is determination, and this is the positing or bringing into actual existence of distinctions or difference ... It is his Being to make these distinctions eternally, to take them back and at the same time to remain within himself, not to go out of himself. What is revealed, is, that he is for an Other. (*PR* II, 335)

As this quotation suggests, an analysis of *Geist* (mind, spirit) makes clear that it necessarily implies self-differentiation. Self-consciousness implies that I can relate to myself as other. This self-differentiation at the heart of *Geist* explains why Hegel is drawn towards the doctrine of the Trinity, as we find this kind of self-differentiation in the trinitarian God. And it is a self-differentiation which involves the whole universe. First, God is to be understood as he is in himself, as the absolute and eternal Idea, and Hegel calls this the realm of the Father. Here God is 'outside of or before the creation of the world' as eternal Idea, abstract and not yet posited in its reality (*PR* III, 7). The second movement considers how the Idea 'passes out of its condition of universality and infinity into the determination or specific form of finitude' (*PR* III, 33). It is in this context that Hegel discusses the realm of the Son, and also the created world. The third movement is the realm of the Holy Spirit. It belongs to God's essential nature to reconcile to himself the otherness of the second realm, and to make it return to himself. This is associated with the Christian notion of the Holy Spirit.

Hegel thus adopts the language of trinitarian theology to describe how it belongs to God's nature, as Spirit or mind, to differentiate itself (*PR* III, 10). In his description of this process of differentiation and self-manifestation in otherness, and subsequent reconciliation, two things are noteworthy: first, it introduces movement or process into God's self; and, secondly, the created universe is an intrinsic part of this intradivine process. Both views are profoundly at odds with the traditional view, which does not allow for development or progression in God and which also refuses to make God dependent on creation, or to allow creation to be swallowed up in the intradivine life of the Trinity.

When discussing the realm of the Son, Hegel pays particular attention to the created world, and its inherent evil. The created world itself is an estrangement from God, and in need of return to God, which is its reconciliation. What appears problematic from a more traditional point of view is that Hegel appears to associate evil with finitude itself, thereby effectively downplaying the traditional view that the created world is good. Evil is necessitated by the self-differentiation and self-determination of God. Evil is essentially connected with otherness, and otherness can only be seen in light of the self-differentiation of the divinity.[15] The reconciliation that overcomes the contradiction of evil rests on the conscious recognition of the unity of divine and human natures (*PR* III, 71). This unity of the divine and human natures occurs in Christ, the God-Man (*PR* III, 72–3; 76–7). Thus, in the Hegelian scheme Christ's activity is interpreted as an instrument of the divine unfolding into otherness which will allow the fulfilment of a higher consciousness (*PR* III, 78). As a consequence Hegel pays fairly little attention to the historical life of Christ (*PR* III, 84). More

---

[15] See William Desmond, *Hegel's God: A Counterfeit Double?* (Aldershot: Ashgate, 2003), 152.

important is the death of Christ, in which 'the conversion of consciousness' begins (*PR* III, 84). The death of Christ is 'the central point round which all else turns' (*PR* III, 86). The significance of the Passion of Christ lies in the fact that it does away with the human side of Christ's nature (*PR* III, 87) and reveals that Christ was the God-Man, the God who had at the same time a human nature, even unto death (*PR* III, 89): the reconciliation of the infinite and the finite.

The natural will, the finite, the Other-Being or otherness is yielded up and transfigured in the death of Christ (*PR* III, 89), and we are called to accomplish this same transformation within ourselves, yielding up our natural will (*PR* III, 95). But Hegel does not see atonement of the spiritual and the world merely in terms of a moral example we should follow. Rather, he sees the cross as a trinitarian event: 'God has died, God is dead – this is the most frightful of all thoughts, that all that is eternal, all that is true is not, that negation itself is found in God . . .' Predictably, this death itself is only another moment in the divine unfolding, and the death of God is only 'the death of death. God comes to life again, and thus things are reversed' (*PR* III, 91).

In short, Hegel sees the life and death of the incarnate Son as a moment within a divine unfolding: from universality to particularity, which is done away with and absorbed in his death (*PR* III, 92). The death of Christ is 'the negation of the negation', meaning: the negation of the otherness that the finite, created world is. This finite world is, in turn, a negation of the universal nature of God the Father: 'This death is thus at once finitude in its most extreme form, and at the same time the abolition and absorption of natural finitude, of immediate existence and estrangement, the cancelling of limits' (*PR* III, 93). Hegel leaves us in no doubt that the death of Christ is 'a moment in the nature of God; it has taken place in God himself' (*PR* III, 95) – and this will prove an extremely influential idea throughout trinitarian theology in the twentieth century. It is revealing that Hegel quotes a Lutheran hymn in this context, which states that 'God himself is dead.' He comments: 'the consciousness of this fact expresses the truth that the human, the finite, frailty, weakness, the negative, is itself a divine moment, is in God himself' (*PR* III, 98). Finitude as divine self-differentiation is 'a moment in God himself, though, to be sure, it is a vanishing moment' (*PR* III, 99). As suggested earlier, it is debatable whether this view can be reconciled with the Scriptures in which we encounter a God who is not dependent on the world and its history.

The negation that is the death of Christ is overcome in the resurrection, which makes space for the outpouring of the Spirit and the establishment of the spiritual community, which is the Church. It is only after the immediateness and the sensuousness of the incarnate Son had disappeared that the Spirit is poured out (*PR* III, 110). This is the third moment within the Hegelian Trinity.

To recapitulate, in the first moment, 'God' is conceived as the undifferentiated universal, an infinite and abstract reality. In the second moment, God becomes particular in the incarnate Son. The third moment is that of individuality, of the return of the finite to the infinite, in which separation and alienation are transcended. Hegel speaks of 'universal individuality' (*PR* III, 100). To make clear what he means Hegel draws a comparison with ordinary love. In ordinary love we abstract from all worldly things, and the loving person centres all his satisfaction on one particular individual. But this is still the realm of particularity. In the realm of the Spirit, individuality becomes universal; the sensuous passes over into the spiritual without abolishing the sensuous (*PR* III, 102–3). It is here that the Church or the spiritual community is established: it represents 'the transition from what is outward, from outward manifestation to what is inward. It occupies itself with the certainty felt by the subject of its own infinite non-sensuous substantiality, and of the fact that it knows itself to be infinite and eternal, knows itself to be immortal' (*PR* III, 104). To pursue the analogy with love: distinction of authority, power, position, or race does not matter any more in Christian love ('Before God all are equal'). The love that reigns in the spiritual community is universal and non-preferential (*PR* III, 105–6).

It is by appropriating the divine drama, by passing through this divine history and process in our own selves that we become members of the spiritual community (*PR* III, 109). This presupposes faith, the belief that reconciliation has been accomplished (*PR* III, 109–10). Through faith we acquire a totally different perspective on the outward history of the life of Christ. From being a material, empirically existing element, it has become a divine moment, an essentially supreme moment in God himself. This is the reason why it cannot be verified in a purely positivistic, historicist manner (*PR* III, 116). It is the Church or the spiritual community which produces this faith, not the words of the Bible, nor a historical reconstruction of the life of Jesus (*PR* III, 121–2). It is through the spiritual community, or the Church, that people can reach the truth (preserved in the creeds) and appropriate it for themselves (*PR* III, 124–6). We are born in the Church, destined to become partakers of the truth, and this is expressed in the sacrament of baptism (*PR* III, 127). In the Eucharist we attain unity with God, the abiding and dwelling of the Spirit within us (*PR* III, 132).

Although Hegel values the Church and its doctrines ('dogma') he claims that it is only the philosopher who grasps religious truths in their full clarity and meaning (*PR* II, 345). For Hegel, art and religion contain truths which can only be properly conceptualised by the (Hegelian) philosopher. Art presents us with truth in a sensuous form, embodying it, so to speak (*Darstellung*). Religion is the domain of *Vorstellung* or pictorial representation, which relies on images and metaphors (e.g., the story of Adam and Eve in the Garden of Eden). This also applies to the doctrine of the Trinity: speech about Father, Son, and Spirit is a somewhat 'childlike' presentation of a truth which the religious imagination fails to fully grasp (*PR* III, 25). It is only philosophy, which relies on thought (*Denken*), that succeeds in disclosing and capturing the truth. The philosopher is thus the new priest whose task it is to protect the possession of truth (*PR* III, 151).

Hegel has exerted a very considerable influence on what we called rivalling or competing trinitarian discourses which came to full fruition in the twentieth century, as we shall see. In particular, his view that God is subject to history and process has proved extremely influential, from process thinkers to Jürgen Moltmann. Given this influence it may be useful to voice a number of concerns.[16]

First, there is a strong monist tendency in Hegel. Hegel does not allow for the real otherness of either God or the world. He does not develop a theory of analogy which would allow him to remain sensitive to the distinction between God and creation. Divine consciousness and human consciousness converge: God's self-knowledge is his self-consciousness in us: 'God is God only so far as he knows himself: this self-knowledge is, further, a self-consciousness in man and man's knowledge of God, which proceeds to man's self-knowledge in God'.[17] Similarly, what we could call, in traditional language, the distinction between the generation of the Son from the Father on the one hand and the creative act on the other is not always clearly maintained. This illustrates a wider problem: Hegel failed to maintain a proper distinction between the immanent and the economic Trinity – an issue which will recur throughout twentieth-century trinitarian debates too.

As suggested earlier, Hegel's view of creation and evil is problematic. He seems to identify finite creation (as the external manifestation or even alienation of the divine) and evil. Again, creation is seen as nothing but a necessary stage in the evolving life of the Spirit. The view that sin

---

[16] For a challenging critique of Hegel's *Philosophy of Religion*, see Desmond, *Hegel's God*.

[17] See *Encyclopaedia of the Philosophical Sciences* (1830), no. 564, trans. William Wallace as *Hegel's Philosophy of Mind* (Oxford: Clarendon Press, 1978), 298.

is a necessary stage in our spiritual emancipation raises the question: if the transgression is necessary, does this not alter its character *qua* transgression?[18]

Again, some have argued that Hegel's philosophical reinterpretation of the dogma of the Trinity in terms of subjectivity and self-consciousness results in a mono-personal account of the Trinity, which is deeply alien to the triune nature of the Christian God. In Jürgen Moltmann's opinion this Hegelian understanding of God in mono-personal terms has infected the trinitarian doctrine of both Karl Barth and Karl Rahner.

Finally, there is the reductionism present in Hegel's account. It is clear that for Hegel only philosophy really captures the truth that lies embedded in religious *Vorstellung* (pictorial representation). Hegel seems unaware that there is a surplus in meaning in religious discourse which is lost in his philosophical account. His philosophical reinterpretation of Christian doctrines is like a prosaic rephrasing of a beautiful poem – so much suggestive meaning is lost in translation. Charles Taylor quite rightly claimed that 'Hegel's philosophy is an extraordinary transposition which "saves the phenomena" (that is, the dogmas) of Christianity, while abandoning its essence'.[19] Therefore, rather than portraying Hegel as the major nineteenth-century hero of the renewal of trinitarian theology,[20] we should interpret Hegel (and Schleiermacher) in terms of inaugurating an *alternative* discourse on the theology of the Trinity – one which came to full fruition in the twentieth century.

KARL BARTH (1886–1968): REVELATION AND THEOLOGY OF THE TRINITY

a. Barth and the nature of theology

The work of Karl Barth, the greatest theologian of the twentieth century, offers a sustained critique of some of the key presuppositions of modern theology (which find their roots in Schleiermacher) and the historical-critical method. Barth very much emphasises the otherness of God, his utter transcendence, thereby questioning those theological approaches that elevate historical research above revelation; or that prefer to 'turn to the

---

[18] Desmond makes this point. He continues (*Hegel's God*, 153): 'If the transgression *had to be* if humanity were to become the spirit it implicitly is, is this not a rational justification of evil's necessity?'

[19] Charles Taylor, *Hegel* (Cambridge: Cambridge University Press, 1989), 494.

[20] This is the line taken by Stanley Grenz and others. See Stanley Grenz, *Rediscovering the Triune God: The Trinity in Contemporary Theology* (Minneapolis: Fortress Press, 2004), 24ff.

subject' rather than to be receptive to God's Word. In his early commentary on *The Epistle to the Romans*, Barth rejected historical-critical ways of reading the Scriptures as reductionist. These so-called scientific methods treat the Scriptures as mere text – without being sensitive to revelation as an act or event in which *God* makes himself known and addresses and challenges us (*CD* I/1, 305).[21] Similarly, when lecturing on Schleiermacher, Barth expressed reservations about the subjectivism that characterises Schleiermacher's theology. Rather than allowing God in his objectivity and sovereignty to address us, Schleiermacher appears more interested in the human subject and his or her receptivity towards this divine address. In short, Schleiermacher's approach is anthropological, and in this regard he is a typical exponent of modern approaches, effectively negating the Word of God (*CD* I/1, 193).

Barth's theology stands squarely in the Reformed tradition. It attempts to be a faithful interpretation of the act of God's self-revelation in the Scriptures. While it also draws on a number of traditional theologians (mainly Luther, Calvin, other Protestant theologians of the sixteenth and seventeenth centuries, but also Augustine and Aquinas), it refrains from appealing to extra-theological sources, such as historical-critical or philosophical ones. It is no coincidence that Barth's major work (extending to over 8,000 pages) is called *Church Dogmatics*. For theology is the self-examination of the Church in light of the self-disclosure of God. Insofar as dogmatics conforms to Jesus Christ, it has true content. This implies that 'it does not have to begin by finding or inventing the standard by which it measures. It sees and recognizes that this is given with the Church' (*CD* I/1, 12). Any attempt to occupy a non-theological starting point when beginning to engage in theology is therefore misguided and effectively masks a modernist (i.e., non-Christian) bias (*CD* I/1, 38). Anyone who wants to engage in dogmatics needs to have faith, and without obedience to Christ dogmatics is 'quite impossible' (*CD* I/1, 17, 189). Barth thus pleads for a prayerful way of doing theology, displaying a distinct impatience with non-theological approaches which bracket out the key presuppositions of the Christian faith in order to kick-start a dialogue with a secular world. Instead of denying their own presuppositions for the sake of 'dialogue' or 'openness' towards the secular world, Christian theologians should simply put forward 'the witness of faith against unbelief (*CD* I/1, 30).

This is not to say that Barth reduces theology to proclamation of the faith (in preaching and sacraments), although it is true to say that theology and

---

[21] *CD* refers to Karl Barth, *Church Dogmatics* (Edinburgh: T&T Clark, 1956–75).

proclamation are closely linked. Theology critically reflects upon proclamation (*CD* I/1, 51, 84) and serves it by examining it in terms of its orthodoxy (*CD* I/1, 82). The orthodoxy of proclamation depends on whether or not it remains faithful to the Scriptures, which should not be regarded as a 'historical monument' but rather as a Church document which bears witness to God's revelation (*CD* I/1, 102). For Barth the Bible is the supreme authority which, when being interpreted, should not be subjected to dogmatic or historical criteria lest we undermine its supremacy (*CD* I/1, 259). On the other hand, by pointing out that the Bible 'bears witness' to revelation, Barth avoids falling into the trap of fundamentalist readings of the Scriptures: the Bible is not revelation itself (*CD* I/1, 112) but provides an account of it (just like an account of an event is not the same as the event itself).

What is of crucial importance to Barth is his claim that we are not in a position to understand the Bible ourselves. The Bible gives itself to be understood by us, so that we can come to hear the Bible as God's Word. We have already mentioned the need for faith, which allows us to hear the human words of the Bible as bearers of the eternal Word. Ultimately it is Jesus Christ, the Son of God, who is God's revelation (*CD* I/1, 137). The Bible and proclamation are God's Word only indirectly (*CD* I/1, 116–17).

There are thus three distinct forms in which the Word of God is given to us: as revelation (the event of God's unveiling himself), in the Bible, and in proclamation. Revelation underlies and finds expression in the other two. We never meet revelation directly, in abstract form – we know it only indirectly, through Scripture and proclamation.

b. Trinity and revelation

Barth's radical theological stance, rejecting all non-theological approaches, had a massive impact on the theological scene of the twentieth century. But this is not why we have outlined his views so far. Barth is also an important and original trinitarian thinker. And what is original about his theology of the Trinity is precisely its link with how he understands revelation.

Theologians have traditionally emphasised the link between the dogma of the Trinity and revelation, insofar as the dogma of the Trinity had always been considered the revealed doctrine par excellence (*CD* I/1, 303). But Barth proposes something much more radical and original: for him the biblical concept of revelation itself is the root of the doctrine of the Trinity (*CD* I/1, 334). For Barth argues that just as we never encounter revelation as such but only insofar as it is expressed in Scriptures and proclamation, so too we do not encounter God the Father directly but only through the Son and the Holy Spirit (*CD* I/1, 121). The reason that Barth can draw such a close parallel between the doctrine of revelation and the doctrine of the Trinity is that God, the Revealer, is identical with his act in revelation, and with its effect (*CD* I/1, 296). More simply, the question: 'Who is God?' also implies the questions 'What is he doing?' and 'What does he effect (in us)?' (*CD* I/1, 297). Barth usually puts this in terms of the Revealer (who), revelation (what is he doing), and revealedness (effect). Just as there is a source of revelation, which is distinct from his revelation, so too is there an inner differentiation within God, as Father and as Son. The Holy Spirit then is the self-impartation of God, just as revealedness refers to the effect of the act of revelation upon us. This is the manner in which Barth links his analysis of revelation with the traditional biblical names of Father, Son, and Holy Spirit. The Father is, as it were, the Speaker, the Son is the Word of the Speaker, and the Holy Spirit is the meaning (*CD* I/1, 363–4).

That Barth construes his doctrine of the Trinity on the basis of his analysis of the concept of revelation should not be taken to imply that he is reducing the Trinity to revelation (as if God were the triune God only in his revelation). Although it is certainly the case that we 'arrive at the doctrine of the Trinity by no other way than by an analysis of the concept of revelation' (*CD* I/1, 312), this does not mean that the triune God is only found in his act of revelation (the 'economic Trinity'). Barth affirms that God is also triune in his inner nature (the 'immanent Trinity') (*CD* I/1, 333). Nor is he implying that in unveiling himself God loses anything of his mysteriousness or freedom (*CD* I/1, 324).

c. The divine 'Persons'

Before he discusses Father, Son, and Holy Spirit, Barth deals with the unity of God. He is at pains to emphasise that the so-called 'Persons' in God are in no sense three gods (*CD* I/1, 349, 205). The problem is that the word 'Person' as used in the Church doctrine of the Trinity has nothing to do with our modern-day understandings of person as self-conscious personality (*CD* I/1, 351, 357). If we speak of a divine Person (in the modern sense of the word) we should reserve this concept for the triune God as such (*CD* I/1, 351). Although Barth appears to be sympathetic towards Aquinas' strong relational understanding of the trinitarian Persons (*CD* I/1, 357, 365), he prefers to drop the notion of 'Person' altogether and instead chooses to speak of divine 'modes of being' (*Seinsweisen*) (*CD* I/1, 359). This has led, almost predictably, to accusations of modalism, despite Barth's explicit refutation of these claims (*CD* I/1, 382). That Barth adopts the notion of *perichoresis* or mutual indwelling of the three Persons ('modes of being' in Barthian parlance) in one another without dissolution of their distinctiveness should take the sting out of these charges (*CD* I/1, 396).

We saw earlier that Barth developed a trinitarian doctrine on the basis of an analysis of revelation, that is, in terms of a revealer (the Father), revelation (his Son, the Word), and revealedness (the Holy Spirit). This effectively means that Barth distinguishes the three 'Persons' in terms of their distinctive relations of origin – a theme which we encountered already in Richard of St Victor (*CD* I/1, 363): there is a source, the revelation from this source (i.e., the Son), and the Holy Spirit who proceeds as meaning from the revealer and his revelation. In this light it will come as no surprise that Barth defends the traditional Western doctrine of the *filioque*, the notion that the Holy Spirit proceeds from the Father and the Son. Barth backs up this argument by pointing to the 'economy' of revelation: throughout the Scriptures we find the Spirit characterised as 'the Spirit of Christ' (*CD* I/1, 479ff.).

Other traditional doctrines Barth adopts are the Augustinian view that the external operations of the triune God are one (*opera trinitatis ad extra sunt indivisa*) or the theory of appropriations as we find it in Aquinas (*CD* I/1, 373).

Barth then discusses the three 'Persons'. He first discusses God the Father, the Lord of our existence, or our Creator. It is perhaps somewhat odd that Barth expounds the nature of the first Person first as 'Creator' which is, by his own admission (*CD* I/1, 373, 394), an appropriation. In a second section Barth does refer to the relation of Fatherhood to describe the first Person: because he manifests himself as a Father in his relation to the One through whom he is manifested (i.e., his Son), we may deduce that he is Father in himself (*CD* I/1, 391–2).

God the Son is discussed as the Reconciler, the Word that has been spoken to us, the revelation of the Father (*CD* I/1, 412). In this section Barth makes the case for the divinity of the Son. He acknowledges that the affirmation of the divinity of the Son is dogma, that is, an interpretation, and is not to be found as such in the biblical texts – but it is 'a good and relevant interpretation of these texts' (*CD* I/1, 415).

The Holy Spirit is discussed under the heading of the Redeemer. How can we acknowledge Jesus as Lord? In order for the revelation of the Father in the Son to become manifest, a 'subjective side in the event of revelation' is necessary, and this presence of God in the human subject is the Holy Spirit

(*CD* I/1, 448–50). When revelation becomes an event in us, the Holy Spirit is at work in us. Through the Holy Spirit we become receptive to the revelation of God in Christ. It is the Holy Spirit who creates the Christian community, and in it the faith, hope, and love of Christians (*CD* IV/2, 126).

Thus far we have mainly focussed on the first part of the *Church Dogmatics*, entitled *The Doctrine of the Word of God*. But it can be argued that the rest of the *Church Dogmatics* is structured in a trinitarian way, with the doctrine of creation being dealt with in Part III, and the doctrine of reconciliation in Part IV (dealing with the saving activity of the Son), while Part V would have consisted of the work of the Holy Spirit (as the Redeemer). However, Barth did not live to finish the fourth part, and never started working on the fifth, and the *Church Dogmatics* is therefore unfinished. Given the inexhaustibility of the divine mystery this is perhaps as it should be.[22]

In what follows we will take a brief look at the connection between the soteriology as developed in Part IV of the *Church Dogmatics* (the doctrine of reconciliation) and the theology of the Trinity. Within the limits of this chapter, however, we cannot provide a comprehensive outline of Barth's views on the saving activity of Christ.

d. The cross and the Trinity

In a valuable monograph Anne Hunt celebrates the connection she discerns in recent Catholic theology between the paschal mystery and the doctrine of the Trinity.[23] We have argued in the previous chapter (where we examined Luther's interpretation of the *communicatio idiomatum*, and its implications for the theology of the Trinity) that this theme finds its roots in Lutheran theology.

There is, however, another element to the connection between Christology (and soteriology) and the theology of the Trinity in Luther's thought. The implicit connection between Luther's emphasis upon Jesus' radical solidarity with sinners and his theology of the Trinity was brought into the open in twentieth-century theology. Luther's emphasis upon Jesus as the universal sinner differs radically from pre-Reformation theology.[24]

---

[22] Barth remarks in *CD* I/2, 878 that the doctrine of the Trinity is not the primary structuring principle of his *Church Dogmatics* but rather revelation to which the doctrine of the Trinity attests. This should not be taken as a denial of the way the doctrine of the Trinity functions indirectly as the structuring motif in his *Church Dogmatics*. For a different view, see Grenz, *Rediscovering the Triune God*, 54.

[23] See Chapter 4, n. 73.

[24] For relevant texts from Luther and others, see Rik Van Nieuwenhove, 'St Anselm and St Thomas Aquinas on "Satisfaction" – or How Catholic and Protestant Understandings of the Cross Differ', *Angelicum* 80 (2003): 159–76. A key text is Luther's Commentary on Gal. 3:13, duly quoted by Barth in *CD* IV/1, 238; see also *CD* IV/1, 215–16.

Whereas Anselm of Canterbury's theory of satisfaction, adopted by Aquinas and other scholastic theologians, emphasizes the sinlessness of the man Jesus Christ, the representative of humanity, who restores the broken relationship with God, Luther saw Jesus in radical solidarity with *sinful* humanity, thereby shifting Protestant soteriology in a direction which understands salvation through Christ in more penal terms. Thus, whereas medieval Catholic theology interpreted Christ's cross as an act of penance, Calvin, following Luther's view that Christ is the universal sinner, was to understand it in terms of punishment.

Barth too understands Christ's cross in terms of punishment rather than in terms of penance (*CD* IV/1, 253). In order to avoid the offensive view that a wrathful God punishes an innocent man, it then becomes necessary to say that, in a sense, God himself suffers and atones for us. Now that is a traditional enough position – but it is expressed with an emphasis that is rather more radical than patristic or medieval theologians would have allowed. The penal understanding of soteriology leads to a position which attributes genuine suffering to the Trinity (and not just simply through the human nature of the incarnate Son). As Barth puts it, Jesus' 'human action and suffering has to be represented and understood as the action and, therefore, the passion of God himself' (*CD* IV/1, 245, 250, 254).

Barth has certainly not given the most radical expression to these views, but he is undoubtedly one of the earliest exponents of this position in German theology in the twentieth century. Talking about the self-humiliation of God in his Son, Barth, referring to Jesus' cry of dereliction (Mark 15:34), writes that God's solidarity with us means that he has not abandoned the world but that he willed 'to bear this need as his own, that he took it upon himself, that he cries with man in this need' (*CD* IV/1, 215). Or again, God humiliates himself in his Son, and this humiliation is not contrary to his divinity but reveals the true divinity of the Christian God as distinct from all other gods. In Christ God becomes a servant of us all, thereby challenging any preconceived notions we might have had about divine sovereignty and power (*CD* IV/1, 134).

The traditional theory of *communicatio idiomatum* would have allowed patristic and medieval theologians to make similar statements. But they would not have said that the Trinity itself suffers for us as this would have been at odds with the divine bliss God is said to enjoy. Now Barth attempts to do justice to this traditional view while at the same time allowing for a certain theopaschite theology.

A passage which illustrates this tension in his views is *CD* IV/1, 185ff. It shows Barth's dialectical way of thinking, attempting to harmonise the notion that God enjoys blissful perfection with the view that God gets radically involved (through the life and death of his Son) with our sinful, suffering world. How can we say, on the one hand, that God is impassible and genuinely transcendent, and yet in radical solidarity with sinful, struggling humanity?

Barth's Lutheran debt comes to the fore when he states that the incarnation is more than God becoming human: it also means

> his giving himself up to the contradiction of man against him, his placing himself under the judgment under which man has fallen in this contradiction, under the curse of death which rests upon him. The meaning of the incarnation is plainly revealed in the question of Jesus on the cross: 'My God, my God, why hast thou forsaken me?' (Mark 15:34). The more seriously we take this, the stronger becomes the temptation to approximate to the view of a contradiction and conflict in himself. (*CD* IV/1, 185)

The reasoning is clear: the emphasis upon God's radical solidarity with sinful humanity seems to lead to the Hegelian view that there is conflict and contradiction within God himself. But then, having wondered whether this is indeed the view that we must adopt in order to do justice to the depth and mercy of God, Barth recoils: 'But at this point what is meant to be supreme praise of God can in fact become supreme blasphemy. God gives himself, but he does not give himself away ... He does not cease to be God. He does not come into conflict with himself.' He then goes on to argue that if in reconciling the world God set himself in contradiction with himself, God could not possibly reconcile the world with himself. Instead, God himself would be in need of salvation. He asks: 'Of what value would his deity be to us if – instead of crossing in that deity the very real gulf between himself and us – he left that deity behind him in his coming to us, if it came to be outside of him as he became ours?' So he concludes with a warning that is as relevant today as it was when written in 1953: 'A God who found himself in this contradiction can obviously only be the image of our own unreconciled humanity projected into deity' (*CD* IV/1, 186). The view that God is somehow in conflict with himself therefore needs to be flatly rejected. But how then does Barth avoid the accusation of portraying God as an indifferent God?

Barth first states that God's immutability does not stand in the way of a radical solidarity with his creation. On the contrary, God's solidarity and compassion is grounded in his divine nature of gratuitous love. God is not his own prisoner (*CD* IV/1, 187). Only an abstract, non-Christian understanding of power sees omnipotence and compassionate involvement in opposition to one another (*CD* IV/1, 187). Ultimately, however, Barth refers to a trinitarian solution to harmonise divine transcendence and radical solidarity. He argues that there is not just humility in God's nature (*CD* IV/1, 193), but there is obedience within God himself, namely in the relationship between the Son and his Father. The prayer of Christ in Gethsemane is merely a reflection of this inner-trinitarian obedience (*CD* IV/1, 193–5, 201).

This solution raises, of course, the issue of subordination, as Barth acknowledges (*CD* IV/1, 200–1). One way in which Barth tackles this accusation is by arguing in *CD* IV/2 that the Father himself is subject to a kind of kenosis. Here Barth maintains that the Father assumes suffering in the humiliation of his Son, by giving and sending his Son for our salvation, and this 'fatherly fellow-suffering of God is the mystery, the basis, of the humiliation of his Son' (*CD* IV/2, 357).

In summary, Barth tries to avoid the view that there is conflict or contradiction in God, not by arguing that God ceases to be divine or immutable (see *CD* IV/1, 187), but rather by claiming that God has, in fact, abased himself. This we must say if we want to remain faithful to the New Testament witness, which reveals that God is 'more great and rich and sovereign than we had ever imagined' (*CD* IV/1, 186). We should not be guided by our own notions of omnipotence and immutability but rather by those of God. As the cross reveals, in God the deepest mercy and the loftiest majesty coincide (*CD* IV/2, 358). It is in light of the cross that we can say that there has to be an obedience at the heart of the Trinity, in the relationship between the Father and the Son. It is in the work of Moltmann and von Balthasar that we find this theme developed in greater detail.

e. Critique of Barth

Barth's theology of the Trinity is based on an analysis of revelation itself. The organic and intrinsic connection between the doctrine of the Trinity and the Scriptures which is thereby established in his theology allows him to circumvent one of the key difficulties of modern theologies of the Trinity: how to legitimate the doctrine of the Trinity in light of historical-critical approaches to the Bible. For Barth, the doctrine of the Trinity is in fact exegesis of the biblical text:

It is not [. . .] an arbitrarily contrived speculation whose object lies elsewhere than in the Bible [. . .]. On the contrary, its statements may be regarded as indirectly, though not directly, identical with those of the biblical witness to revelation. It is Church exegesis ... (*CD* I/1, 333)

As Church exegesis it can only be approached by those who have faith. Historical-critical methods are Promethean ways of attempting to domesticate and subject the primacy of God's address to us in the revelation of his Word. For Barth, on the other hand, revelation is a trinitarian event: God speaks his creative Word, which is heard and returns to him in the achievement among humans of faith and obedience in the power of the Holy Spirit.[25] Some have argued that this sweeping trinitarian movement of revelation from the Father, in the Son, to the Holy Spirit in us uncannily echoes the Hegelian dynamic of Absolute Spirit in its differentiations as universal (Father), particular (Son), and individuality (the Spirit).[26] However, these resemblances are merely superficial: the monism that characterizes Hegel's thought is utterly alien to Barth.

In recent years scholars have debated the status of Barth's work. Should it be considered a pre-modern project? After all, Barth rejects 'the turn to the subject'; he adopts a radical theocentric theological stance; and he discards historical-critical readings of the Scriptures as an inadequate approach to revelation because they put too much weight on method, thereby ignoring the normative subject-matter of theology. And if it is pre-modern in outlook, could Barth's work be fruitfully brought into dialogue with today's postmodern concerns? Or does Barth remain a modern thinker insofar as he, as a reformed theologian, effectively agrees with Kant's view that faith and reason, philosophy and theology are separate?[27]

The discussion is ongoing and in this context some brief remarks must suffice. It is true that Barth agrees with Kant that philosophical approaches to God are illegitimate. On the other hand, Christoph Schwöbel has persuasively argued that Barth relocates issues of epistemology – the typical primary concern of modern philosophy – to a secondary place.[28] For Barth, how we know God is effectively determined by the being of God as revealed in his Word. In other words, whereas Kant exemplifies and furthers the modern preoccupation with the subject (and how we know), Barth's

---

[25] Trevor Hart, 'Revelation', in John Webster, ed., *The Cambridge Companion to Karl Barth* (Cambridge: Cambridge University Press, 2000), 49.

[26] See the classic article by Rowan Williams, 'Barth on the Triune God', in Stephen Sykes, ed., *Karl Barth: Studies of his Theological Methods* (Oxford: Clarendon Press, 1979), 147–93.

[27] For a more in-depth discussion, see Graham Ward, 'Barth, Modernity and Postmodernity', in Webster, ed., *The Cambridge Companion to Karl Barth*, 274–95.

[28] Christoph Schwöbel, 'Theology', in Webster, ed., *The Cambridge Companion to Karl Barth*, 29ff.

theology is 'a theological turn from the subject'.[29] Barth deals with questions of epistemology in the light of his doctrine of God, rather than the other way around. And he does so by arguing that it is effectively the triune God as revealed in the Word who is the condition of possibility of us knowing God.[30] Revelation is God's doing; it breaks into our world and challenges it. We can only relate to it through faith, which is not a human capacity or an anthropological given (as in Schleiermacher and his modern followers) but rather a gift from God, a 'loan' (*CD* I/1, 238), and part of the dynamic of revelation (the acting of the Holy Spirit in us as 'revealedness'). Undoubtedly, in this regard Barth recaptures something of that aesthetic receptivity within theology which we encountered in patristic and medieval theologians.

We now turn to a Catholic theologian who has been credited, like Barth, for assisting in the re-engagement of theologians with the doctrine of the Trinity.

KARL RAHNER (1904–84): THE SELF-COMMUNICATION OF THE TRINITARIAN GOD IN US

Scholars have rightly argued that Karl Rahner, although he never wrote an extensive treatise on the subject, has exercised a major influence on the field of trinitarian theology.[31] This Jesuit theologian did, however, write a small treatise, translated in English as *The Trinity*, as well as a number of shorter articles.[32] Particularly influential is his so-called axiom or rule, while his own specific contribution to the theology of the Trinity from a transcendental perspective remains largely undiscussed in the literature.

Rahner begins his classic treatise *The Trinity* (*Trin.*) with a strong criticism of the textbooks of his day, which, he argues, treat the theology of the Trinity as unrelated to the rest of theology, and severed from all existential knowledge about ourselves (*Trin.*, 15). Indeed, as he famously wrote, 'should the doctrine of the Trinity have to be dropped as false, the major part of religious literature could well remain virtually unchanged' (*Trin.*, 11). Rahner, like Barth before him, expresses his reservations about

---

[29] Hart, 'Revelation', 38. [30] Schwöbel, 'Theology', 32.

[31] David Coffey, 'Trinity', in Declan Marmion and Mary Hines, eds., *The Cambridge Companion to Karl Rahner* (Cambridge: Cambridge University Press, 2005), 98.

[32] Other articles available in English include his entry 'Trinity, Divine', in Karl Rahner, ed., *Encyclopedia of Theology: A Concise Sacramentum Mundi* (London: Burns & Oates, 2004); and 'Remarks on the Dogmatic Treatise "De Trinitate"', in *Theological Investigations*, vol. IV (London: Darton, Longman and Todd, 1966), 77–102.

the concept 'Person', arguing that it evokes incorrect associations in today's parlance, suggesting 'several spiritual centres of activity of several subjectivities and liberties'. Instead, he proposes (again not unlike Barth) 'three distinct manners of subsisting' (*Trin.*, 109).

Rahner singles out Thomas Aquinas as the author who first took the momentous step to treat first of the divine essence, and only subsequently of the three divine Persons. This led, so he argues, in the Latin West (in contrast to the Greek approach) to a philosophical and abstract approach, which separates the theology of the Trinity from the salvation history as witnessed in the Scriptures (*Trin.*, 16–18). From our previous chapter we know that this often-repeated critique does not stand up to critical scrutiny: medieval Western theologians, including Aquinas, were profoundly trinitarian thinkers; some of the authors that Rahner singles out as genuinely trinitarian thinkers (including Richard of St Victor and Bonaventure in *Myst. Trin.*) began their theology of the Trinity like Aquinas with a discussion of the divine oneness. If recent scholarly work on the Latin tradition has allowed us to better appreciate the continuing vibrancy of the theology of the Trinity in the West, despite competing constructions (such as the Hegelian one), the facile contrast (with which Rahner concurs) between the Latin West and the supposedly more trinitarian East must also be discarded.[33] Rahner also expresses reservations about the psychological analogy, arguing that it led to a theology of God in which the Trinity is 'absolutely locked within itself', severed from salvation history. As he puts it elsewhere: 'The psychological theory of the Trinity neglects the experience of the Trinity in the economy of salvation in favour of a seemingly almost Gnostic speculation about what goes on in the inner life of God'.[34] We have questioned the validity of this criticism in the previous chapter.

The distinction between 'the inner life of God' and 'the experience of the Trinity in the economy of salvation' brings us to one of Rahner's most celebrated contributions to trinitarian scholarship. In order to make clear the connection between the doctrine of the Trinity and salvation history (as expressed in the biblical witness), Rahner puts forward his famous axiom that 'the "economic" Trinity is the "immanent" Trinity and the "immanent" Trinity is the "economic" Trinity' (*Trin.*, 22). As was mentioned in the first chapter, the "immanent" Trinity refers to the way God is in his

---

[33] See for instance *Trin.*, 83–4. Rahner appears indebted to Theodore de Regnon's narrative, which has come in for recent severe criticism by Lewis Ayres and Michel Barnes (see our conclusion in Chapter 3).

[34] Karl Rahner, *Foundations of Christian Faith: An Introduction to the Idea of Christianity* (New York: Crossroad, 1997), 135 (henceforward abbreviated as *FCF*).

inner nature, from all eternity; the "economic" Trinity refers to the way this God reveals himself in the world and in salvation history (from the Greek word *oikonomia*). There are different ways of interpreting Rahner's rule or axiom. We can take it to mean (in a minimalist but correct sense) that everything we know or say about the inner nature of God ('immanent' Trinity) must be based on the way God reveals himself in salvation history as witnessed in the Scriptures, and on our experience of this. This is a traditional enough approach, and one Augustine also used: the missions reveal something of the intradivine processions. In this case the axiom is interpreted primarily as a hermeneutical principle which assists us in constructing a theology of the Trinity that remains faithful to revelation. Thus, Rahner is simply stating that there is an intrinsic connection between the missions of the divine Persons in salvation history (incarnation, Pentecost) and the intradivine life (*Trin.*, 30). However, a broader interpretation is also possible, and in this case the axiom can be interpreted as saying something about the nature of God, namely that the way God is in himself – the 'immanent' Trinity – is nothing else but the way God is present in world and history. In this interpretation the axiom becomes disturbingly Hegelian, reducing the ever-transcendent mystery of God to how it can be known by us in our world. In our view the very emphasis Rahner puts upon the mysteriousness of God precludes this broader interpretation (see *Trin.*, 50–1 and 88, note 10). Nor can we see how any theologian could make this kind of claim, as it would presuppose a point of view external to God and world (i.e., a kind of bird's-eye point of view from which one could scan the relation between God and world).

But how do we know how God reveals himself? After all, theologians had traditionally argued that the operations of the Trinity *ad extra* (outside the Trinity) are indivisible, so as to keep the charge of tritheism at bay. If any one of the three Persons does 'his own thing' so to speak, we end up with three gods, not the Christian Trinity. Rahner accepts that the triune God acts as one (*opera ad extra sunt indivisa*), but he argues that the one God acts in a threefold way. The incarnation illustrates this. Here we have an instance of a mission that is proper to the Son and which cannot be merely appropriated to him. Each of the three Persons contributes to this one relation to the world (*Trin.*, 28, 76). When discussing the incarnation Rahner makes the point that the humanity of Christ is not something extraneous but it is 'the constitutive, real symbol of the Logos himself' (*Trin.*, 33). This implies that human nature is already predisposed towards the incarnation, and is not alien to it. We will come back to the significance of Rahner's theological anthropology for his theology of the Trinity. For now we observe that this anthropological stance – so different from Karl Barth's approach – will also allow Rahner to take seriously the patristic claim that even before Christ there were anticipations of belief in the Trinity (*Trin.*, 20, 40–1).

How does the triune God relate to us in a threefold manner? Rahner, like Barth, argues that God's self-communication is truly a *self-* communication, genuinely bestowing himself (*Trin.*, 36). But whereas Barth mainly examined the self-communication of God in revelation, Rahner considers the self-communication of God in us (the indwelling of the trinitarian God through grace). While Barth's approach is more historical-salvific, Rahner examines more the way the triune God is 'the transcendental ground' of our salvation. This is how Rahner describes in general terms the threefold self-communication of God to us:

This self-communication of God has a three-fold aspect. It is the self-communication in which that which is given remains sovereign, incomprehensible, continuing, ever as received, to dwell in its uncontrollable, incomprehensible originality. [This is the self-communication of God as Father.] It is a self-communication in which the God who manifests himself 'is there' as self-uttered truth and as freely, historically disposing sovereignty. [This is the self-communication of God as Son.] It is a self-communication, in which the God who communicates himself causes in the one who receives him the act of loving welcome … [This is the self-communication of God as Holy Spirit]. (*Trin.*, 37)

The revelation of God in this threefold manner occurs historically (both in Jesus Christ, and in the bestowal of the Holy Spirit) but it also occurs at a transcendental level. According to Rahner, our everyday engagements with the world (our knowing and willing) are always accompanied by an unthematic horizon, which is God. Just as we can only see objects of this world in light but not light as such, so too we have a transcendental experience of God in the midst of the world. 'Transcendental' is a Kantian term which refers to 'the conditions of possibility' of our knowledge and will (or love). The divine mystery can never be grasped but it grounds our existence, and it is its necessary condition:

This transcendental experience of human transcendence is not the experience of some definite, particular objective thing which is experienced alongside of other objects. It is rather a basic mode of being which is prior to and permeates every objective experience … It is … the a priori openness of the subject to being as such, which is present precisely when a person experiences himself as involved in the multiplicity of cares and concerns and fears and hopes of his everyday world. (*FCF*, 34–5)

Now Rahner argues that God's self-communication at the heart of our being can be understood in two different modalities: as an offer or call to our freedom on the one hand, and as response to this offer (be it acceptance or rejection) on the other (*FCF*, 118). Our acceptance of God's self-communication is only possible because of this very self-communication at the heart of our existence.

In light of this brief account of Rahner's rich theological anthropology we can now flesh out in some more detail how God communicates himself to us in the Son and the Holy Spirit, both historically and transcendentally. According to Rahner this self-communication contains four basic aspects, namely (a) Origin-future, (b) History-transcendence, (c) Invitation-acceptance, and (d) Knowledge-love. The first aspect of each of these four pairs refers to God's self-communication in the Son, the second to the Holy Spirit. As addressee of God's self-communication, the human person has an origin and a future; we are embedded in history but our history is situated in a wider horizon which always transcends us. Constituted as beings who are history in transcendence, and a duality of origin and future, we are essentially free beings, free to accept the invitation of God's self-communication. Finally, we are knowing and loving beings. A self-communication of God to us must present itself as a self-communication of absolute truth and absolute love (*Trin.*, 93–4).

Rahner then attempts to show the unity of the first element of each of the four pairs. The unity of *origin-history-offer* becomes clear in light of the offer of God's self in our history through the incarnation of his Son. To see the connection with *truth* we need to remember that in its most profound sense truth refers not primarily to a correspondence between idea and reality but must rather be understood in terms of revelation (or unveiling) of a person's true nature. Truth is 'the deed in which we firmly posit ourself for ourself and for others, the deed which waits to see how it will be received' (*Trin.*, 96). Or again, truth in the full sense is the lived truth in which someone freely deploys his being for himself and others, manifesting himself as faithful and reliable.[35] Understood in such existential terms, we can begin to see how the offer of divine self-communication in the Son can be truth for us.

The unity of the other four moments (future-transcendence-acceptance-love) can best be understood by starting with the last one, love. God's love creates its own acceptance. In it we encounter the transcendence of God, who gives himself as the future (*Trin.*, 96–8). Rahner then summarises: 'the

---

[35] Rahner, 'Trinity, Divine', 1761.

divine self-communication possesses two basic modalities: self-communication as truth and as love' (*Trin.*, 98). The first modality refers to God's self-communication in his Son, the truth in history, a divine invitation; the second refers to God's self-communication in the Holy Spirit, which assumes the form 'of love in transcendence towards the freely accepted absolute future' (*Trin.*, 98).

We have indicated that Rahner's account must be understood at both the historical and transcendental-anthropological levels. Thus, the Word of God, as Truth embodied, has entered history, inviting us to share in his life. The Holy Spirit transforms the Christian community (at Pentecost and through the ensuing life of grace in the Church) and, bestowing charity upon us, assists us in accepting the invitation of the Son, making us receptive to the future of the transcendent God. But at the core of our being (at the transcendental level) we are also receptive to the truth and love of God, even if only in an implicit manner. A critical reader may well ask: What is the connection between history and anthropology? In reply it must be remembered that the creation of human nature took place for the sake of the divine self-communication. Human nature is already attuned towards receiving the divine self-communication (*Trin.*, 89–90). All human experience therefore offers the possibility of an encounter with God – but it is in its encounter with the Word who became incarnate in the midst of our history that the riddle at the heart of our existence finds its ultimate answer.

This original but somewhat elusive parallel between historical missions of Son and Spirit, on the one hand, and theological anthropology, on the other hand, is one of the most fascinating (and least noticed) aspects of Rahner's theology.[36] It allows him to show how 'the doctrine of the Trinity is not a subtle theological and speculative game' but rather:

> It is only through this doctrine that we can take with radical seriousness and maintain without qualifications the simple statement which is at once so very incomprehensible and so very self-evident, namely, that God himself as the abiding and holy mystery, as the incomprehensible ground of man's transcendent existence is not only the God of infinite distance, but also wants to be the God of absolute closeness in a true self-communication, and he is present in this way in the spiritual depths of our existence as well as in the concreteness of our corporeal history. Here lies the real meaning of the doctrine of the Trinity. (*FCF*, 137)

Although Rahner encourages theologians to focus on salvation history when constructing a theology of the Trinity, his primary concern is with the

---

[36] It is this parallel which explains why Rahner, after having dealt with his transcendental anthropology in *FCF* then goes on to deal with the doctrine of the Trinity (see *FCF*, 133–7).

trinitarian missions (incarnation, and grace of the Holy Spirit) rather than with the paschal mystery.

The trinitarian theology of both Karl Rahner and Karl Barth has been criticised by Jürgen Moltmann. In his view, Barth and Rahner operate with a Hegelian understanding of the subject, which sees the triune God as one subject and three modes of being. There is one, identical divine subject that relates to itself: the Father is assigned to the 'I', the Son to the 'self', and the Spirit to the identity of the divine 'I-self'.[37] In Moltmann's view, the unity of the absolute subject is stressed to such a degree that the trinitarian Persons disintegrate and become mere aspects of the one subject or substance.[38] Rahner and Barth, by effectively adopting the secular meaning of the word 'person' (only to discard it as inadequate) are effectively fighting a straw man. For this secular meaning of the word 'person' implies extreme individualism, in which each individual is seen as 'a self-possessing, self-disposing centre of action which sets itself apart from other persons'. By refusing to apply this (distorted) understanding of person to Father, Son, and Spirit, and by adopting instead the concept of 'three distinct modes of subsistence', reserving the concept of personhood for God as such, Rahner and Barth have, in Moltmann's view, transformed the classical doctrine of the Trinity into a reflection of the absolute subject.[39] It is to Moltmann's trinitarian theology that we now turn.

JÜRGEN MOLTMANN (1926–): A TRINITARIAN THEOLOGY OF A SUFFERING GOD

Rahner and Barth put a strong emphasis upon the mono-personal nature of God: only God as such is 'person' in the modern sense of the word; Father, Son, and Holy Spirit are not three 'persons' in the modern meaning of the term.[40] Rahner even goes as far as saying that there is no *mutual* love between Father and Son (*Trin.*, 106). As we noted above, his views (and those of Barth) have been criticised by Jürgen Moltmann, who has become in recent years an influential spokesperson for the so-called 'social doctrine of the Trinity', conceiving of God as three divine subjects in a fellowship of love, a communion open to the world and humanity.[41] This aspect will be discussed in the following chapter. Here we will examine his influential theology of the suffering God.

---

[37] See *TKG*, 139–48.   [38] Ibid., 18.   [39] Ibid., 144–8.
[40] For Augustine (and medieval theology after him), it was the inverse: only the three are Persons, but God should not be called a Person.
[41] *TKG*, 19.

Moltmann's theology is very much written in the shadow of Auschwitz, and boldly addresses the issue of theodicy. (Theodicy explores how we can speak of a good God in the face of so much suffering in the world.) According to Moltmann, it is only by developing a trinitarian theology of the cross that we can begin to construct a credible theodicy (*CG*, 227).

Moltmann's first major work was *Theology of Hope* (1964). In this work he emphasised the importance of eschatology for Christian theology. More specifically, the resurrection of Christ, as the radical contradiction of the cross, generates the Christian hope that a transformed world, no longer subject to suffering and sin, is possible, and challenges us to pursue it here and now. A second work, *The Crucified God* (1972), focussed on the cross of Christ, and will be discussed in some detail here. The final part of this trilogy, *The Church in the Power of the Spirit* (1975) developed Moltmann's pneumatological and ecclesiological thought. In the 1980s and 1990s Moltmann published a number of other works, starting with *The Trinity and the Kingdom of God* (1981), a work that reiterates much of the material of *The Crucified God*. *God in Creation* (1985), *The Way of Jesus Christ* (1989), and *The Spirit of Life* (1991) followed in quick succession.

As suggested, Moltmann's theology of a suffering God is deliberately developed as a theodicy (*TKG*, 47–50; *CG*, 207–27). He argues, echoing Dostoyevsky, that 'the suffering of a single innocent child is an irrefutable rebuttal of the notion of the almighty and kindly God in heaven. For a God who lets the innocent suffer and who permits senseless death is not worthy to be called God at all' (*TKG*, 47; also *CG*, 220).

What Moltmann suggests is that the traditional God of classical theism (omnipotent and all-good) who enjoys heavenly bliss in his impassibility and immutability – 'the Unmoved Mover' of Aristotle – is utterly alien to the God revealed in the cross of Christ (*CG*, 222). One of the key passages in *CG* is a quotation from Elie Wiesel's book *Night*, in which Wiesel, a Holocaust survivor, describes how the prisoners were forced to witness the hanging of some fellow-prisoners:

The SS hanged two Jewish men and a youth in front of the whole camp. The men died quickly, but the death throes of the youth lasted for half an hour. 'Where is God? Where is he?' someone asked behind me ... And I heard a voice in myself answer: 'Where is he? He is there. He is hanging there on the gallows ...'[42]

As Richard Bauckham has made clear in an excellent contribution, this story can be interpreted in at least two very different ways. One way is to interpret

---

[42] Elie Wiesel, *Night* (New York: Avon Books, 1969), 75 as quoted in *CG*, 273–4.

it in terms of loss of faith: confronted with bottomless evil Wiesel loses his faith in God.[43] But that is not how Moltmann interprets the story. He tries to understand it in light of the cross, in which God has revealed himself in his self-emptying in the crucified Christ (*CG*, 275). The only convincing answer Christians have against the atheist critique is to point to the radical solidarity of the Christian God who suffers with us: 'The only way past protest atheism is through a theology of the cross which understands God as the suffering God in the suffering of Christ and which cries out with the godforsaken God, "My God, why have you forsaken me?"' (*CG*, 227). Contemplating the cross, we come to realise that 'God and suffering are no longer contradictions as in theism and atheism, but God's being is in suffering and the suffering is in God's being itself, because God is love' (*CG*, 227).

Love, for Moltmann, implies vulnerability and involvement: 'one who cannot suffer cannot love either' (*CG*, 222, 230). If the cross is a genuine revelation of God, it follows that we must speak of a suffering God (*TKG*, 21). Christian theology that refuses to attribute suffering to God has failed to develop an authentically Christian understanding of God, and remains indebted to Greek ways of thinking, in which divine perfection and blessedness imply impassibility (immunity to suffering) (*TKG*, 22; *CG*, 227). For this reason Moltmann rejects the Chalcedonian teaching of the two natures in the one person of Christ, as it allowed traditional Christology to state that only the man Jesus suffered (in his human nature) and not the divinity (*CG*, 227–35). We will return to the question whether Moltmann gives a fair interpretation of the traditional doctrine. For now, we examine how Moltmann portrays this intradivine suffering as a trinitarian event.

Taking his lead from the cry of dereliction (Mark 15:34; see *CG*, 225–7; *TKG*, 77–83), Moltmann writes:

To understand what happened between Jesus and his God and Father in the cross, it is necessary to talk in trinitarian terms. The Son suffers dying, the Father suffers the death of the Son. The grief of the Father here is just as important as the death of the Son. The Fatherlessness of the Son is matched by the Sonlessness of the Father, and if God has constituted himself as the Father of Jesus Christ, then he also suffers the death of his Fatherhood in the death of his Son. (*CG*, 243)

But the cross is not just the moment in which Father and Son are most deeply separated from one another in their forsakenness. At that very moment they are also 'most inwardly one in their surrender' and shared

---

[43] Richard Bauckham, *The Theology of Jürgen Moltmann* (Edinburgh: T&T Clark, 1996), 77–80.

love for the world (*CG*, 244). This union of 'boundless love which proceeds from the grief of the Father and the dying of the Son' (*CG*, 245) is the Holy Spirit, as the bond of love of Father and Son. In short, according to Moltmann, God so radically identifies himself with 'the godless and the godforsaken' (*CG*, 276) that his own Son shares in this abandonment, having been given up by his own Father and freely accepting this offer. The Holy Spirit represents the bond of love of Father and Son (a distinct Augustinian echo) in their utmost separation (*TKG*, 82–3). In contrast to apathetic conceptions of God, the cross reveals that self-sacrifice is at the heart of God's being. The suffering of Christ is the suffering of the passionate God, the suffering of passionate love.

Following Luther, Moltmann wants to show 'that the historical passion of Christ reveals the eternal passion of God' (*TKG*, 32) since 'a God who cannot suffer cannot love either' (*TKG*, 38). Questions about God and suffering go hand in hand, so theology must go further than its traditional association of suffering with sin. Moltmann speaks of a 'patricompassionism'.[44] The Father is 'the one who suffers with', the one who is in solidarity with the victims of injustice and violence. Describing how God is affected by human actions and history constitutes a 'pathetic' theology: 'God is interested in the world to the point of suffering' (*CG*, 270–1).[45] The Father is drawn into the destiny of his Son; they are distinct yet one in the 'bond of love', to use Augustine's phrase. The Spirit completes the work of Father and Son by taking believers into the trinitarian history of the Father, Son, and Spirit, a history of relationships in community.

By placing suffering at the heart of God, Moltmann has, in turn, been accused by Rahner and others of ending up with a 'pauper' God who is as helpless as we are in the face of suffering and evil. God in a sense becomes tied to the world and incapable of providing consolation. God's freedom and transcendence are compromised.[46] Critics have further noted how Moltmann 'weakens the ontological unity of the Trinity by seeking a

---

[44] Jürgen Moltmann, 'Cross, Theology of the', in Alan Richardson, ed., *Dictionary of Christian Theology* (London: SCM Press, 1983), 136.

[45] Moltmann notes how some medieval depictions of 'mercy seats' (*Gnadenstuhl*) illustrate this point in that the pain of the Son's death is reflected on the Father's face. At times though, Moltmann's trinitarian theology of the cross is more binitarian than trinitarian, and it was only later that he developed an explicit pneumatology. See his *History and the Triune God: Contributions to Trinitarian Theology* (London: SCM Press, 1991), 174.

[46] This is not too dissimilar to Barth's 'anthropomorphic' critique: 'A God who found himself in this contradiction can obviously only be the image of our own unreconciled humanity projected into deity' (*CD* IV/1, p. 186).

solution in terms of history'.[47] Though his emphasis is on the history of Jesus and on how the New Testament narrates this history in a trinitarian way, the question remains – in positing the world as the arena of God's self-realisation – whether he has compromised God's independence and onto-logical distinction from the world. In other words, Moltmann's theology is in danger of dissolving the Trinity in history and presenting a Hegelian God dependent on the world for self-actualisation. Moltmann accepts the Hegelian claim (and explicitly acknowledges his indebtedness to him) that the trinitarian God is affected by history, and incorporates this history within his own life, including its alien and sinful aspects: 'If one describes the life of God within the Trinity as the "history of God" (Hegel), this history of God contains within itself the whole abyss of godforsakenness, absolute death and the non-God' (*CG*, 246). Moreover, this intra-trinitarian life is itself shaped by the Hegelian dialectic of opposition (between Father and Son), and reconciliation (through the Spirit) in the bridging of this separation. Moltmann's debt to Hegel is evident.[48]

Moltmann's assertion that traditional theology did not allow for the notion that 'one of the Trinity suffered in the flesh', is incorrect (*CG*, 228). As Bauckham states, this was endorsed by the Council of Constantinople of AD 553, although it is true to say that traditionally theology was reluctant to attribute suffering to the divine nature. According to the Chalcedonian view, the Son suffered in his human nature by undergoing the human experience of Jesus as his own.[49] Therefore, traditional theology allows one to say that in the incarnation God suffers as man. But it emphasised the need to distinguish between what can be said of Christ as a human and as divine, because failing to do so would jeopardise the genuineness of the human nature of Christ. As Bauckham puts it, 'Precisely in order to preserve the reality of the incarnation, we must not abolish the difference between what is possible for God in incarnation and what is otherwise possible for God.'[50] Also, as Weinandy makes clear, 'strange as it may seem, but not paradoxically, one must maintain the unchangeable impassibility of the Son of God as God in order to guarantee that it is actually the divine Son of God, one in being with the Father, who

---

[47] John O'Donnell, 'The Trinity as Divine Community. A Critical Reflection upon Recent Theological Developments', *Gregorianum* 69/1 (1988): 21. For a similar, more recent, critical assessment, see Veil-Matti Kärkkäinen, *The Trinity: Global Perspectives* (Louisville, KY: Westminster/John Knox Press, 2007), 115–22.

[48] Bauckham, *The Theology of Jürgen Moltmann*, 154.

[49] Bauckham, *The Theology of Jürgen Moltmann*, 60–3. See also the classic study by Thomas Weinandy, *Does God Suffer?* (Edinburgh: T&T Clark, 2000) for a robust rebuttal of a theology of a suffering God.

[50] Bauckham, *The Theology of Jürgen Moltmann*, 64.

truly suffers as man'.[51] Readers will recall that this echoes Calvin's critique of Luther.

Moltmann applies human categories to God (such as 'suffering') without developing a proper theory of analogy which sets out the boundaries and limitations of human concepts when applied to God. In short, because Moltmann does not adopt a proper theory of analogy[52] his talk of 'a suffering God' is in danger of anthropomorphism.[53]

Moltmann also eschews the distinction between the immanent and the economic Trinity because he wants to place the cross and the reality of suffering at the heart of the Trinity and to show that the economic Trinity not only reveals the immanent Trinity but also has a retroactive effect on it (*TKG*, 160). Commentators sympathetic to his project would argue that Moltmann does not intend God's radical dependence on the world but points to a real interaction between the two. We might say that there is a dialectical or dipolar dimension to his *theologia crucis*. Thinking of God in abstraction from the experience of revelation, prayer, and liturgy gives rise to the classical divine attributes of immutability, impassibility, and so on, whereas thinking of God temporally and historically leads to the attributes of faithfulness, compassion, and love. Moltmann's trinitarian theology of the cross wants to show how the second group of attributes belong just as much to divine personhood as the more classical ones.[54]

HANS URS VON BALTHASAR (1905–88): A TRINITARIAN THEOLOGY OF THE PASCHAL MYSTERY

In this section we discuss another significant contemporary theologian who puts the paschal mystery at the heart of his theology of the Trinity,

---

[51] Weinandy, *Does God Suffer?*, 205. He continues (p. 206): 'This is what humankind is crying out to hear, not that God experiences, in a divine manner, our anguish and suffering in the midst of a sinful and depraved world, but that he actually experienced and knew first hand, as one of us – as a man – human anguish and suffering within a sinful and depraved world. This is what a proper understanding of the Incarnation requires and affirms ... The eternal, almighty, all-perfect, unchangeable, and impassible divine Son, he who is equal to the Father in all ways, actually experienced, as a weak human being, the full reality of human suffering and death.'

[52] Analogy is a theory about speech about God, which holds a middle position between univocal and equivocal use of language. Univocal use leads to anthropomorphism; equivocal to utter agnosticism. See Aquinas' *ST* I.13, and Brian Davies, *The Thought of Thomas Aquinas* (Oxford: Clarendon Press, 1992), 58–79 for a brief discussion.

[53] Bauckham, *The Theology of Jürgen Moltmann*, 65–9.

[54] 'God is free in himself and at the same time interested in his covenant relationship and affected by human history.' *TKG*, 272. See also Bruno R. Brinkmann, 'The Cross in Question. I', *The Clergy Review* 60 (1975): 286.

namely, Hans Urs von Balthasar. This Swiss theologian ranks as one of the most important Catholic theologians of the twentieth century. His theological output is only rivalled by that of Karl Barth, whose works left a deep imprint on Balthasar. Like Barth, Balthasar is not particularly interested in the latest findings of historical-critical research. What is more important, in his view, is the receptivity and openness of the believing person towards the mystery of the triune God as revealed in Christ. This receptivity has an aesthetic quality: just as we can be captivated by a profound piece of art, and cannot appreciate it if we approach it with a merely objective, scientific mindset, so too the believer needs to be captivated by the Christian story. This implies that Balthasar is profoundly unhappy with the manner in which theology and spirituality have become separated since the late-medieval period.

Given the emphasis on the need to be captured by the beauty of the triune God, it will come as no surprise that Balthasar's first major work, *The Glory of the Lord – A Theological Aesthetics* (comprising seven volumes) deals with the transcendental of beauty. In this project, he attempts to make the reader aware of the beauty of Christian revelation. A second major project focusses on the transcendental of goodness, and in this work, called *Theo-Drama – Theological Dramatic Theory* (comprising five volumes) Balthasar tries to do justice to the dramatic aspects of God's redemptive activity in the light of human sinfulness. Finally, he looks at the transcendental of truth in *Theo-Logic* (three volumes).[55] The three projects are deeply intertwined: *beauty* is the way in which God's *goodness* gives itself to us, and is understood by us as *truth* (*GL* I, 11).

Balthasar develops his theology of the Trinity throughout his works. Apart from different volumes in his major trilogy, we will also refer to his *Mysterium Paschale* (*MP*), a profound treatise in which he explores in a highly original manner the theological meaning of the descent of Christ into hell. We will first deal with the problem of human sin. In a second section we will discuss how sin was overcome by the obedience of Christ in the paschal mystery. Then we will show that the obedience and self-surrender of Christ is grounded in the kenotic or self-emptying love at the heart of the Trinity.

---

[55] Hans Urs von Balthasar, *The Glory of the Lord: A Theological Aesthetics*, 7 vols. (San Francisco: Ignatius Press, 1982–9); *Theo-Drama: Theological Dramatic Theory*, 5 vols. (San Francisco: Ignatius Press, 1988–98); *Theo-Logic*, 3 vols. (San Francisco: Ignatius Press, 2000–5). These works will be abbreviated as *GL*, *TD*, and *TL*, followed by the number of the volume, and page number in the English translation.

a. Sin and pride

For Balthasar, at the heart of sin is the inordinate desire to be like God and the refusal to accept our creaturely limitations. Balthasar develops this idea by examining the nature of human freedom. He argues that finite, human freedom only comes to fulfilment when it becomes receptive to infinite freedom, the freedom of God. He distinguishes freedom as 'autonomous motion', the freedom of choice, and freedom as 'consent', that is, freedom towards God (*TD* II, 207–42). In a powerful analysis of evil in *TD* IV, 137–201, he shows that the primal sin is to inflate the first dimension of freedom (freedom as autonomy) while refusing to acknowledge the second (indebtedness to God). We genuinely do *have* autonomous freedom of choice, but it is a freedom which has been *given* to us. We should acknowledge this gift-character in order to be true to our nature: finite freedom 'cannot see itself as purely autonomous but must also realise that ... [it] is a gift, owing its existence to some other source' (*TD* IV, 150). When we refuse to acknowledge that we ourselves are a gift from the Creator at the core of our being, when we regard the autonomous dimension of our freedom as something absolute, then our orientation towards God is being dissolved. Our freedom turns in on itself, and the dynamism towards God (the second dimension) is attributed to the first dimension of freedom. That is: in seeking to arrogate freedom to itself, we attempt to set ourselves up as absolute good, as the norm of the good. But this is a contradiction: it is the contradiction of 'the will to power', which attempts to determine what is good and evil without, however, wanting to acknowledge the Source of all Goodness (i.e., God):

Autonomous freedom, once it has been set forth as absolute, can only understand *itself* as the norm of the good. In other words, it has the good in its power, which is an internal contradiction, since, in the absolute, the good is identical with power ... This contradiction ... not only deprives finite freedom of its harmonious relationship with absolute freedom: it also deprives it of such a relationship with itself. Its undeniable finitude has usurped an element of the infinite; this renders its finitude unintelligible ... (*TD* IV, 163)

The more we try to liberate ourselves without wanting to acknowledge our relationship with God, the more we get entangled in the blind and meaningless pursuit of power and self-assertion, thereby becoming a riddle to ourselves, and eliciting antagonistic relationships with our fellow human beings. In short, setting ourselves up as the standard of the good, and thus trying to subordinate goodness to our own exercise of power, is the primal temptation, the attempt to be 'like God, knowing good and evil' (cf. Gen.

3:5). It is original sin (*TD* IV, 151). We try to determine what is good and evil, without acknowledging Goodness itself, that is, God, as our origin and goal. This leads to a profound self-alienation: when we exclusively opt for our own autonomy, and cut it loose from freedom as consent (which implies an acknowledgement that we are not our own origin), the freedom of autonomy acquires a purposeless dynamic of its own. We become our own origin and goal, and we become unintelligible to ourselves. The history of modernity (and its attempt to master the whole earth aided by instrumental rationality) is the most disturbing illustration of this dynamic.[56]

The Christian response is different. We can only attain fulfilment when we acknowledge our created status, the fact that we are a gift (*TD* II, 284ff.). This acknowledgement leads to gratitude for the gift of ourselves, transforming our whole existence in a word of thanksgiving.

It is not only a theology of creation (and its implication that we are a gift from God) which grounds this spirituality of surrender. Even more important for Balthasar is God's revelation in the self-emptying, obedient love of Christ. Finite freedom must be *summoned* by divine freedom, calling to open itself to the divine self-disclosure. This brings us to Balthasar's soteriology.

b. Christology and soteriology

It is in the paschal mystery that Christ's obedience and self-surrender finds its utmost expression. By assuming what is so radically contrary to the divine (i.e., sinfulness), the Son reveals the true nature of the divinity in what is utterly opposed to him (*sub contrario*) (*MP*, 52). This is the great paradox of Balthasar's theology, Lutheran in inspiration: God's love shows itself in the desolation of Christ; his power reveals itself in weakness; the silence on the cross is God's most eloquent revelation. Because of his solidarity with sinful humanity, Jesus experiences the godforsakenness and guilt of sinners, and their separation from God.

This notion of radical solidarity of Christ with sinful humanity is a recurring theme in twentieth-century theology. We also encounter it in the thought of Moltmann. However, drawing on insights from his friend, Adrienne von Speyr, Balthasar develops a highly original theology of Holy Saturday – the time that the dead Christ lies in the tomb in passive silence.

---

[56] Balthasar, following Heidegger, sees Descartes as the source of the modern project (because of his emphasis upon self-reliance) which culminates in the thought of Nietzsche, who 'does not know the happiness of those who receive'. This 'inability to receive' is the hallmark of the modern age – an age which believes it can produce everything. Against this Balthasar argues that we must cultivate 'a receptivity for the wealth and poverty of being' (*TD* IV, 159).

Taking centre stage, between the cross and the resurrection, is Holy Saturday, the time Christ lay in the tomb, and 'descended into hell', as an article of the creed of Nicea has it. It is here that Balthasar makes his most original – and most controversial – contribution.

The biblical sources for the descent of Christ into hell are slim (1 Pet. 3:19; 1 Pet. 4:6; Mt. 16:18; Rom. 14:9; Rev. 1:18). Whereas traditionally this had been portrayed as a triumphant opening of the gates of hell, Balthasar portrays it in much starker colours. Resisting all mythological interpretations (*MP*, 152), he argues that hell is not a place. It is 'no-where', chaos, a state of sin and total separation from God, who is the source of life. It is absence of faith, hope, and love, and all communication. Hell is an existence of total alienation from God, 'the condition of the self-enclosed "I", the "I" unliberated by God' (*MP*, 76–7). Experiencing hell means experiencing the full weight of abandonment and rejection by the Father, and it is this abandonment that Christ experienced, both on the cross (Mark 15:33) and in the tomb: 'Since the sin of the world is "laid" upon him, Jesus no longer distinguishes himself and his fate from those of sinners . . . and thus in that way he experiences the anxiety and horror which they by rights should have known for themselves' (*MP*, 104). The death of Christ and his sojourn in hell reveals the utter obedience of the Son. It is 'the obedience of a corpse' (St Francis of Assisi) (*MP*, 174), in total abandonment, without enjoyment of the beatific vision, or anticipation of future resurrection (*MP*, 106).

c. Trinitarian kenosis

Although Balthasar's theology of Holy Saturday is undoubtedly highly original, we can only grasp its full significance in light of his trinitarian views. Drawing on the work of Sergei Bulgakov, Balthasar claims that the kenosis or self-emptying (cf. Phil. 2:7) of the incarnation and death of Christ is, in turn, based upon a kenotic love within the Trinity. Christ's 'existence rests on a kenotic act of obedience that moved him to let go of the "form of God" and embrace the "form of slave"' (*TD* IV, 498). He describes this kenotic love in terms of 'infinite distance' at the heart of the Trinity. The following major quotation captures his key ideas:

[T]he Father's self-utterance in the generation of the Son is an initial 'kenosis' within the Godhead that underpins all subsequent kenosis. For the Father strips himself, without remainder, of his Godhead and hands it over to the Son; he 'imparts' to the Son all that is his . . . This divine act that brings forth the Son . . . involves the positing of an absolute, infinite 'distance' that can contain and embrace all the other distances that are possible within the world of finitude,

including the distance of sin. Inherent in the Father's love is an absolute renunci-
ation: he will not be God for himself alone … The Son's answer to the gift of the
Godhead … can only be eternal thanksgiving (eucharistia) to the Father, the
Source – a thanksgiving as selfless and unreserved as the Father's original self-
surrender. Proceeding from both, as their subsequent 'We', there breathes the
'Spirit' who is common to both: as the essence of love, he maintains the infinite
difference between them, seals it and, since he is the one Spirit of them both,
bridges it. (*TD* IV, 323–4)

Undoubtedly, as with Moltmann, this quotation resonates with Hegelian
echoes, especially in its portrayal of the Holy Spirit as the One who 'bridges'
the infinite distance between Father and Son. We will examine shortly how
Balthasar transforms this Hegelian influence.

The three Persons have to make space for one another, allowing the
Others to be. Letting-be, surrender, is at the heart of the Trinity, and this is
the ultimate reason why finite freedom is not threatened by infinite freedom
but rather finds its fulfilment in it:

If *letting-be* belongs to the nature of infinite freedom – the Father lets the Son be
consubstantial God, and so forth – there is no danger of finite freedom … becoming
alienated from itself in the realm of the Infinite. It can only be what it is, that is, an
image of infinite freedom, imbued with a freedom of its own, by harmonising with
the (trinitarian) 'law' of absolute freedom (of self-surrender) … (*TD* II, 259)

Of course, the possibility of finite freedom, which is grounded in the
trinitarian letting-be, also allows for the possibility of evil, which is why
Balthasar states that 'the distance of sin' is also made possible by the infinite
distances within the Trinity.

Thus, this letting-be at the heart of the Trinity finds expression in
creation: the trinitarian God has to make room for the created world 'to
be'.[57] But this self-surrender at the heart of the Trinity finds its supreme
expression in the obedience of the incarnate Son. As Mark McIntosh has
convincingly shown, this obedience and self-emptying at the heart of the
Trinity allows Balthasar to combine a high Christology (which strongly
emphasises the divine identity of Jesus Christ) with a low Christology
(which safeguards the genuineness of the humanity of Jesus). If self-
emptying (kenosis) is at the heart of the Trinity, then the humanity of
Jesus, in all its frailty, reveals the divine precisely by being so human.[58]

---

[57] In this context (*TD* II, 271ff.) Balthasar adopts the Jewish idea of *tsimtsum*: God withdraws to a certain
extent from creation, respecting the freedom of his creatures, and becomes somewhat hidden,
without, however, abandoning creation.

[58] Mark McIntosh, *Christology from within: Spirituality and the Incarnation in Hans Urs von Balthasar*
(Notre Dame, IN: University of Notre Dame Press, 2000), 41.

Everything that Jesus does reflects his divine mission and filial obedience within the Trinity. These insights have important implications for Christian spirituality, and we shall now unpack some of these.

The reader may recall the objections that Schleiermacher had raised against using the same terminology of 'Personhood' and 'nature' in the theology of the Trinity and in Christology.[59] Balthasar's approach allows us to counter this critique. Because Balthasar understands personhood in terms of mission, he can establish a close link between Christology and theology of the Trinity. Mission (a trinitarian concept referring to the Persons 'being sent') constitutes the Son as a Person.[60] This, in a sense, applies to all of us: we only come to know ourselves – who we are – through the acceptance and fulfilment of commitments, goals, and acts of love. We speak of 'finding one's mission in life', suggesting that it is only when we identify ourselves with certain ideals, when we are captivated by them, that we find our true sense of self. It is like an artist 'who is so possessed by his vocation that he only feels free, only feels totally himself, when he is able to pursue this task that is so much his own' (*TD* III, 225). This analogy may assist us in understanding how Christ's mission (his being sent by the Father) constitutes who Christ is. Christ's earthly mission reflects his eternal receptivity and obedience to his Father, and it is this which constitutes him as a Person:

It is when God addresses a conscious subject, tells him who he is and what he means to the eternal God of truth and shows him the purpose of his existence – that is, imparts a distinctive and divinely authorised mission – that we can say of a conscious subject that he is a 'person'. This is what happened, archetypically, in the case of Jesus Christ, when he was given his eternal 'definition' – 'You are my beloved Son.' (*TD* III, 207)

As Mark McIntosh puts it:

What makes Jesus unique is that in him mission and person coincide perfectly, indeed are one; for his mission is *to be* the Son. He is definitively 'person', and since all humanity is oriented towards fulfilment in him, each human being achieves his or her own personhood and stability of identity, expressly by sharing in Christ's mission.[61]

Indeed, it is only when we respond in obedience to God's calling, by surrendering ourselves, that we find ourselves and attain true selfhood. In

---

[59] The gist of Schleiermacher's critique is that in Christology, 'personhood' is understood as that which particularises the human and divine natures of Christ. If personhood is understood in the same way in the theology of the Trinity, then we end up with tritheism.

[60] McIntosh, *Christology from within*, 51.　[61] Ibid., 52.

Christ there is an identity of personhood and mission, and both can only be properly understood in terms of receptivity and obedience. By reinterpreting personhood in dynamic terms (as a filial mission), rather than in a static, reified manner, Balthasar can link theology of the Trinity and Christology (including the notion of personhood) in a way that is quite innovative and fruitful for Christian spirituality: we can only attain true selfhood when we surrender ourselves as the Son surrendered himself, within the bosom of the Trinity, and in his life and death on earth.

We have seen that the ultimate presupposition of kenosis is the self-lessness of the Persons in the inner-trinitarian life (*MP*, 35). Because the kenotic existence of the Son on earth reflects the kenotic obedience within the Trinity, neither creation nor incarnation necessitates a change in God (*TD* V, 513). This is an important difference between Moltmann's thought and that of Balthasar: whereas Moltmann's God is in danger of succumbing to the Hegelian influence of bringing change into God, and making God open to suffering, Balthasar's views, based on a kenotic trinitarian love, do not have to imply this: the life and death of Christ does not import passibility and change into God; it is the inverse: because the Trinity is a community of kenotic love, we can begin to understand why creation, the incarnation, and the death of Christ take place: the kenotic selflessness is the basis of the kenosis that occurs in the creative act, as well as in the incarnation and death of the Son (*GL* VII, 214).

The Spirit is the 'excess' or ecstatic dimension of the kenotic love between Father and Son (*TL* III, 159). In developing his pneumatology, Balthasar explicitly draws on Richard of St Victor's idea that 'shared love is not perfected without an inner fruit' (*TL* III, 164). The Holy Spirit is both the bond of love between Father and Son, and the fruit and witness of this love (*TL* III, 160, 243, 296). One way of clarifying the role of the Holy Spirit within the Trinity is by adopting the analogy of love between man and woman, and the fruit of this love, the child, as a genuine *imago Trinitatis* (*TL* III, 140–1, 160). As we saw in an earlier quotation, Balthasar describes the Holy Spirit as the 'We' of Father and Son, which partly explains the somewhat elusive character of the Holy Spirit.[62] The Holy Spirit's freedom to blow whither he wills, to distribute gifts as he wills, reflects the kenotic nature of the love of Father and Son which the Holy Spirit is (*TL* III, 241). The Holy Spirit is poured out after the resurrection (*MP*, 203, 210) and is the interpreter of God's self-proclamation in Jesus Christ, leading believers

---

[62] See Hans Urs von Balthasar, 'The Holy Spirit as Love' from *Explorations in Theology*, vol. III. *Creator Spirit* (San Francisco: Ignatius Press, 1993), 128.

into the divine revelation (*TL* III, 107, 141). He is the gift of Father and Son, the liberator who bestows freedom (*TL* III, 236), the one who eternally arouses the divine love and witnesses to it (*TL* III, 242–9).

It is through the operation of the Holy Spirit that the resurrected Christ becomes a eucharistically fruitful body for the world (*TD* V, 477). The Holy Spirit 'universalises' the existence of Christ, so that it can become 'the immediate norm of every individual existence' in a number of ways: first, through the ascension (closely associated with Pentecost); then through the sacraments, especially the Eucharist in which the Lord, in another instance of kenosis and surrender, is distributed in bread and wine throughout the world (*GL* VII, 151, 226); and, finally, in the life of the Christian who lives by Christ's commandments and the example of his love.[63]

d. Evaluation

Balthasar's approach may at first seem similar to that of Moltmann. Moltmann, following Hegel, is, however, in danger of making the intra-trinitarian life dependent on, and conditioned by, the history of the world, thereby attributing suffering to God himself. Balthasar's emphasis upon the eternal self-emptying love within the Trinity allows him to argue that the cross is the revelation of the self-emptying love of God, without meaning to imply that the cross changes God, or effects pathos within the Trinity, turning God into 'a tragic, mythological God' (*TD* IV, 322). The key difference between Moltmann and Balthasar is that while Moltmann is inclined to abolish the distinction between the immanent and the economic Trinity, thereby attributing historicity and temporality into God, Balthasar, by maintaining this distinction, can see the cross as the manifestation and result of the intra-trinitarian kenosis, rather than its cause.[64] Moreover, Balthasar is very much aware that all God-talk is analogous, while Moltmann does not develop a proper theory of analogy.

Undoubtedly, Balthasar's theology of Holy Saturday is the most original aspect of his theology. But it is controversial, and Alyssa L. Pitstick has raised a number of probing questions in relation to this key aspect of Balthasar's theology.[65]

---

[63] See Hans Urs von Balthasar, *A Theology of History* (San Francisco: Ignatius Press, 1994), 81–111.

[64] See Thomas G. Dalzell, *The Dramatic Encounter of Divine and Human Freedom in the Theology of Hans Urs von Balthasar*, Studies in the Intercultural History of Christianity 105 (Bern: Peter Lang, 1997), 161–93.

[65] Alyssa L. Pitstick, *Light in Darkness: Hans Urs von Balthasar and the Catholic Doctrine of Christ's Descent into Hell* (Grand Rapids, MI: Eerdmans, 2007).

It will have become clear that Balthasar's emphasis upon the kenotic love within the Trinity allows him to establish an intimate link between the theology of the Trinity, Christology, and spirituality. But the question can be raised: Why exactly is self-surrender on behalf of another to be identified with love? Pitstick points out that this is a deficient understanding of love. For instance, if love is nothing but self-surrender, can we still be said to love ourselves? And if not (for how can we surrender ourselves to ourselves?), how then do we love our neighbour as ourselves?[66]

Moreover, and more fundamentally, Balthasar's theology of the descent is profoundly untraditional. Balthasar sees the descent as an extension of the cross in which Christ suffers the consequences of his radical solidarity with the sinfulness of humanity, while in the tradition it was seen as the victorious entry of Christ into the underworld, opening the gates of hell.[67]

Although Balthasar has acquired the status of a modern Church Father in some (conservative) Catholic circles, we note that Balthasar's soteriology actually has a close affinity with some Protestant perspectives. While Balthasar distances himself from the excesses of some Reformed views (*GL* VII, 205, 232; *TD* III, 241), and although he states that the divine wrath must be understood in the light of divine love (*GL* VII, 205, 232; *MP*, 139), his notion that Jesus identifies himself radically with *sinful* humanity (Christ's 'real assumption of universal guilt' *MP*, 101) seems more reminiscent of Luther's thought, and shares similar ambiguities. It leads to a soteriology in which the Father actively withdraws from his Son and loads the punishment for sin upon him (*GL* VII, 209; *MP*, 108–12, 136). Balthasar makes it clear, however, that the aggression comes from us, and that the cross does not turn an angry God into a loving one. Admittedly, Balthasar argues that his view is different from the Protestant view in that the Son freely accepts this abandonment (*TD* III, 242). Still, this is a very different approach to soteriology from that of Anselm or Aquinas, who, rather than seeing Christ's salvific work in terms of *punishment*, see it in terms of a freely undertaken *penance* for the sake of humanity. Again, Balthasar's more radical ideas on the descent and eschatology are indebted not to the Scriptures or the Church Fathers, but to the mythological ideas of his friend Adrienne von Speyr whose work is, by his own admission, inseparable from his own.[68]

---

[66] Ibid., 214.   [67] Ibid., 100.
[68] Hans Urs von Balthasar, *My Work in Retrospect* (San Francisco: Ignatius Press, 1993), 89.

JOHN ZIZIOULAS (1931–): TRINITY, PERSONHOOD,
AND CHURCH

We have seen that Rahner and Barth criticised the use of the word 'person' in theology of the Trinity, arguing that it effectively leads to modern misunderstandings of God as tritheist. The Greek Orthodox theologian and Metropolitan of Pergamon John Zizioulas puts forward a different view in two influential works, both a collection of essays, namely *Being as Communion: Studies in Personhood and the Church* (*BC*) and *Communion and Otherness: Further Studies in Personhood and the Church* (*CO*).

According to Zizioulas, the concept of 'person' is the 'most dear and precious good ... which the world owes to Greek patristic theology' (*BC*, 65; *CO*, 166). More specifically, he claims that the Cappadocian Fathers (St Basil the Great, St Gregory of Nazianzus, and St Gregory of Nyssa) redefined personhood in relational terms, giving it ontological priority over universal being. This shift had a fundamental impact on Christian thought and culture, according to Zizioulas. His key idea is that relationship is introduced into substance itself, and this results in a relational understanding of being (*BC*, 84–9). This is supremely the case within the Trinity; but it is only through participation in Christ that the human drive to personhood can be fulfilled (*CO*, 108–9). In what follows we will explicate Zizioulas' thinking.

As we saw in Chapter 3, the Cappadocian Fathers argued for the ontological priority of personhood over substance. In order to fully appreciate the Cappadocian revolution (as Zizioulas sees it), we need to say a few words about Greek philosophy. For Greek philosophy the universal nature always had priority over the particular manifestations of this universal nature. Human nature, for instance, is ontologically prior to and more important than any of its particular manifestations (such as Rose or Henry) (*CO*, 102). The particular person exists only for the sake of the whole (human species, society, ...) (*CO*, 164). Similarly, classic Greek tragedy invites humans to succumb to the order and justice that held the universe together. It is here that the trinitarian theology of the Cappadocians introduced a major change, as we saw in Chapter 3: for them the particular is not secondary to being or nature. This implies that the concept of personhood acquires ontological priority (*CO*, 166).

Of course, divine and human personhood are different from one another. Each human person is an individual, that is, an entity ontologically independent from other human beings. Also, in human existence nature precedes the person: when Rose and Henry are born, the one human nature precedes them – they embody only part of the human nature (*CO*, 158–9). In God, however, the three persons of the Trinity do not share a pre-existing divine nature, but they coincide with it. The three persons of the Trinity are united in an unbreakable communion of love, and therefore none of the three can be conceived apart from the other two (*CO*, 159).

The important reversal that Zizioulas has documented – in God persons have priority over divine nature or being – had, in his view, significant implications for the Christian heritage and our culture in general. First, nothing is 'more sacred than the person since it constitutes the "way of being" of God himself. The person cannot be sacrificed or subjected to any ideal' (*CO*, 166). Second, personhood must be understood in terms of communion and relationship: 'It is the other and our relationship with him that gives us our identity, our otherness, making us "who we are", that is, persons' (*CO*, 166). The meaning of our existence is to be found in being a person, not in our nature: 'As a person you exist as long as you love and are loved. When you are treated as nature, as a thing, you die as a particular entity … Nature always points to the general; it is the person that safeguards uniqueness and absolute particularity' (*CO*, 167). Thirdly, while nature and species are perpetuated and replaceable, the person is something unique and unrepeatable. It is our personhood, constituted by our relation with others (including and especially God), which gives us our identity and value.

The uniqueness of each person also has implications for a theology of love and death. Death strikes us as tragic only when we regard human beings as persons, in their unique identity. After all, through procreation and child-bearing the survival of the species is guaranteed. But the survival of the uniqueness of a person cannot be guaranteed through the substance, that is, human nature. Christians can only begin to conceive of the immortality of each person through love, which endows something 'with uniqueness, with absolute identity and name' (*BC*, 49, note 44). This love is always trinitarian at heart:

The life of God is eternal because it is personal, that is to say, it is realised as an expression of free communion, as love. Life and love are identified in the person: the person does not die only because it is loved and loves; outside the communion of love the person loses its uniqueness and becomes a being like other human beings, a 'thing' without absolute 'identity' and 'name', without a face. (*BC*, 49)

Being loved by God and loving him in return opens the door to eternal life. It is this which the Fathers call 'divinisation' (*BC*, 49). It is a mirroring of the personal life in God by realising personhood in ourselves.

This can only occur through a new mode of existence, which Zizioulas calls the 'hypostasis of ecclesial existence'. This new mode of existence, or regeneration, is inaugurated by baptism (*BC*, 53). Here our personhood or *hypostasis* becomes rooted in an ontological reality which does not suffer from createdness (the way our biological reality does) (*BC*, 54–6). This happens through Christ:

> Thanks to Christ man can henceforth himself 'subsist', can affirm his existence as personal not on the basis of the immutable laws of his nature but on the basis of a relationship with God which is identified with what Christ in freedom and love possesses as Son of God with the Father. This adoption of man by God, the identification of his hypostasis with the hypostasis of the Son of God, is the essence of baptism. (*BC*, 56)

In baptism we are born as an ecclesial person, able to 'transcend' the biological laws, allowing us to love unconstrained by the natural laws (*BC*, 57). Baptism, a new birth, is 'nothing but the acquisition of an identity not dependent on the qualities of nature but freely raising nature to a hypostatic existence identical with that which emerges from the Father–Son relationship' (*CO*, 109). Now we can love without exclusivism, as Christ did.

Some readers may want to object that this ecclesial way of being does not do away with our biological way of being, and with it, death. Zizioulas grants this point and qualifies his argument by arguing that our ecclesial identity refers not to that which we are but to that which we will be: the ecclesial identity is linked with eschatology, the final outcome of our existence (*BC*, 59). Our present identity has its roots in the future but its branches in the present (*BC*, 59). It is a sacramental or Eucharistic identity or *hypostasis*.

Thus, the emphasis upon communion, which is at the heart of the Trinity, also finds expression in the Eucharistic community. The Eucharist is first and foremost an assembly, a community, in which we 'subsist' in a manner different from a biological way of existing. In the Eucharist we transcend every exclusiveness of a biological or social kind. The Eucharist manifests the principle that the *hypostasis* expresses the whole: the whole Christ is present, and every communicant is the whole Christ and the whole Church. But the Eucharist is not solely an assembly. It is also a movement towards our eschatological existence (*BC*, 59–61). It makes us realise that our authentic, true personhood is not in the pursuit of goods and values of this world (*BC*, 62).

Zizioulas' insights into the Eucharist have a strong pneumatological dimension. It is the Holy Spirit who brings history to fulfilment, who 'eschatologises' it. In the Eucharistic event the presence of the *eschaton* in history is manifested, and this is nothing less than communion with the triune God.[69] If the Son's role is to become history, then the role of the Holy Spirit is the exact opposite: it is the fulfilment of history, bringing the triune presence into history.[70] The Holy Spirit transforms everything he touches into a relational being: 'The Spirit de-individualises and person-alises beings wherever he operates' (*CO*, 6). It is the Spirit who supports us in loving the other as person, as a unique and irreplaceable other with whom we enter into relationship, rather than somebody who can be pigeonholed in general categories (i.e., in social, racial, and moral terms) (*CO*, 111–12).

While developing his pneumatology Zizioulas returns to the contribu-tion made by the Cappadocian Fathers. His interpretation of their contri-bution to the Second Ecumenical Council of Constantinople (AD 381) is especially significant in relation to the issue of the *filioque*, the belief that the Holy Spirit proceeds from the Father *and the Son*. It is fair to say that until recently the *filioque* was a defining issue in the identity of Western Catholicism and Eastern Orthodox theology. Given its historical and theological importance, we will conclude this section with a brief discussion of this issue.

The historical background to this topic is well known. The original Creed of Constantinople (325) does not contain the *filioque*. In response to the Arian threat, and influenced by the theology of Augustine, it made its way into the confession of the Creed in Spain during the sixth century. The addition of this phrase was a gradual process. From Spain it spread to Gaul and Germany. At the beginning of the ninth century Charlemagne requested Pope Leo III to officially include it into the Creed, but he refused. In the East, Patriarch Photius rejected the *filioque* in an encyclical of 866, mainly on the grounds that it undermines the monarchy of the Father. The cultural and political separation of East and West deepened in subsequent centuries, leading to a *de facto* religious division in the middle of the eleventh century (with mutual excommunications in 1054). It was, however, only in 1014 that Pope Benedict VIII admitted the *filioque* into the Latin version of the Creed. Attempts at reconciliation were made during the Councils of Lyons (1274) and again, for political reasons (the need for support from the West against the threat of the Turks, which resulted in the fall of Byzantium), at the Council of Ferrara-Florence (1438–9).

---

[69] Aristotle Papanikolaou, *Being with God: Trinity, Apophaticism, and Divine–Human Communion* (Notre Dame, IN: University of Notre Dame Press, 2006), 32.
[70] Papanikolaou, *Being with God*, 36.

In the twentieth century, in a climate of renewed ecumenism, there appeared to be, if not a convergence of views and greater tolerance, at least a better understanding of the historical origins of the diverse views on this matter. A more profound engagement with the historical and theological background has also dispelled some of the deep linguistic mis-understandings that had bedevilled the discussions in earlier centuries.

Orthodox theologians have traditionally claimed that (a) the unilateral insertion by the Latin Church of the *filioque* into the Creed of an Ecumenical Council is unacceptable. (b) They have argued that attributing spirative power to the Son as such obfuscates the distinction between Father and Son, which inevitably results in a kind of modalism. For Orthodox theologians, only the Father is the cause of the procession of the Holy Spirit. There are not two causes within the Trinity. (c) It tends to give primacy to the divine substance or essence over the personal nature of the Trinity. Orthodox theologians claim that the West (by regarding not the Father but the Father and the Son as the source of the Holy Spirit) is in danger of considering the impersonal essence the principle of unity in the Trinity. In their view the Person of the Father is the origin of the Trinity; it is the Person of the Father who guarantees the unity of the three Persons, and not an impersonal divine substance or essence. Also, (d) Orthodox theologians point out that that the Western position leads to a subordination of the Holy Spirit, which results in extreme Christocentrism in the West at the expense of pneumatological thinking – a charge not entirely without justification.

A text from the Pontifical Council for Promoting Christian Unity, entitled 'The Greek and Latin traditions about the procession of the Holy Spirit'[71] tackles a number of these issues. It explicitly states (a) that the Catholic Church acknowledges the 'normative and irrevocable value' of the Creed of Constantinople, and goes on to say: 'No profession of faith peculiar to a particular liturgical tradition can contradict this expression of faith.' In response, Zizioulas has welcomed this statement 'with deep satisfaction' and considers it 'a very good basis for discussion'.[72] It means that the Catholic Church does not consider the *filioque* a creedal innovation but rather a clarification, or interpretation. This is in line with the view

---

[71] The text was published by *Osservatore Romano* (13 September 1995) and in *Catholic International* 7/1 (January 1996), 36–43. It is also widely available online, such as in: www.catholicculture.org/culture/library/view.cfm?recnum=1176 or www.ewtn.com/library/CURIA/PCCUFILQ.HTM

[72] The text 'One Single Source' is available online at www.agrino.org/cyberdesert/%20zizioulas.htm

expressed in *The Decree for the Greeks* from 1439 during the Council of Florence.[73]

Against (b) and (c) Western theologians could, of course, argue, in turn, that a denial of the *filioque* makes it very difficult to distinguish the Son from the Holy Spirit. Even so, it is important to dispel a number of misunderstandings. First, we need, once more, to reiterate that the popular view, shared by Zizioulas (see *CO*, 198), that the Latin West puts more emphasis upon the impersonal divine essence, at the expense of a personal understanding of the Trinity, is incorrect. Zizioulas' presentation of the Western tradition is in danger of becoming a caricature. He describes it as shaped by 'the Boethian individualistic tradition' (*CO* 208–12). From previous chapters the reader will know that the Western tradition too understood personhood in terms of relation. Similarly, Zizioulas follows Rahner uncritically (who, in turn, bases his views on those of De Régnon) in his claim that the Western tradition gave priority to the divine substance, while the existence of God as triune was treated as secondary (*BC*, 40, note 34, and *CO*, 106: 'Substance is something common to all three Persons of the Trinity, but it is not ontologically primary until Augustine makes it so'). In fact, the Fourth Lateran Council (1215) explicitly stated that it is not the divine substance that is the cause of the Son's generation and the Spirit's procession, but it is the Father, who generates.[74]

Moreover, while the Father, and not the divine substance, is the origin of the other divine Persons, Western theology does not claim that there are two causes of the Spirit. Indeed, the Second Council of Lyons (1274) confessed that 'the Holy Spirit proceeds eternally from Father and Son, not as from two principles but from one (*ex uno principio*), not by two spirations but by only one'.[75] According to the Western view, the Spirit does not proceed from the Father and the Son as if from two separate causes. In that sense it is clearly misleading to speak of a 'double procession' (as some Orthodox theologians have done when discussing the Latin view). This point is reiterated in the document from the Pontifical Council for

---

[73] See *The Decree for the Greeks* (1439), *DS* 691, which states that 'the explanatory words' (*explicationem verborum illorum*) have been added to the creed legitimately and with good reason 'for the sake of clarifying the truth'.

[74] The Latin view is not uniform either. As we saw in the previous chapter, for St Bonaventure innascibility, for instance, has positive connotations, as it implies the fontal plenitude of the Father. Aquinas rejects this point of view (*ST* I.33.4 *ad* 1). The Franciscan approach is more amenable to the Greek view, which distinguishes the Holy Spirit from the Word by different modes of procession rather than by their relationships. See Yves Congar, *I Believe in the Holy Spirit*, 3 vols. (New York: Crossroad, 1997), vol. III, 180–1.

[75] *DS* 460.

Promoting Christian Unity, which explicitly acknowledges the monarchy of the Father, stating that the Father is the sole trinitarian Cause (*Aitia*) or Principle (*Principium*) of the Son and of the Holy Spirit. Thus, the *filioque* does not undermine the notion of the sole monarchy of the Father, the one origin of the Son and of the Spirit.[76] In short, the *filioque* does not imply that the Holy Spirit finds his origin in two distinct causes (Father and Son); rather, it refers to the communication of the consubstantial communion of Father and Son, to the Spirit.

Orthodox theologians themselves, including Zizioulas (*CO*, 193), admit that the Son has a mediating role in the procession of the Holy Spirit: the Spirit proceeds from the Father through the Son. Because the Son has the faculty of being the co-principle of the Spirit entirely from the Father, the *filioque* does not necessarily imply the rejection of the thesis that the Father is the sole cause of divine existence (*CO*, 197).[77] Clearly, a rapprochement between the East and the West is possible on this issue.

Nevertheless, an important issue remains outstanding. It seems to us that the crucial element in the debate over the *filioque* is how our understanding of the economic Trinity shapes our theology of the immanent Trinity. A crucial text, which illustrates the different approaches of the East and the West, is John 15:26, in which Christ says: 'When the Paraclete comes, whom I will send to you from the Father, the Spirit of truth, who proceeds from the Father, he shall give testimony of me.' Latin theologians will argue that the revelation of the sending of the Spirit into the world by the Son (the economy) mirrors the immanent Trinity. In other words, the economy reveals something of the immanent processions within the Trinity (in this case: the fact that the Son is involved in the procession of the Holy Spirit). Orthodox theologians, on the other hand, will argue that the scriptural text says nothing about an immanent procession of the Holy Spirit from the Son. They accept that the Son sends the Holy Spirit in the economy but they refuse to deduce from this that there is a similar sending (or 'procession') within the Trinity. At first sight the view of Western theologians seems to have an important advantage: if the economy does not reveal the immanent Trinity, and if our statements about the immanent Trinity are not founded on the economy (as witnessed by the Scriptures), then these theological statements about the immanent life of the Trinity risk becoming

---

[76] Nevertheless, it must be admitted that there is a certain ambiguity in the Western position. *The Decree for the Greeks* (1439), for instance, does state that the Son is a 'cause' of the subsistence of the Spirit (cf. DS 691).

[77] Zizioulas is indebted for this view to Yves Congar, whose work *I Believe in the Holy Spirit* (vol. III, 86) he quotes in *CO*, 197.

mythology. However, in the history of salvation (the economy) as witnessed by the Scriptures, we notice that the Holy Spirit has an important role to play in the annunciation, the conception, the baptism, and the ministry of our Lord. Hence Zizioulas is correct in arguing that 'if one looks at the Economy in order to arrive at *Theologia*, one begins with the Holy Spirit, then passes through the Son, and finally reaches the Father' (*CO*, 188) – the reverse order to that which Latin theology ascribes to the immanent Trinity.[78] In other words, the economic Trinity seems to sit uneasily with the immanent Trinity (as construed in Latin theology), at least if one insists, as Western theologians do, that our portrayal of the immanent Trinity must be based on our understanding of the economic Trinity.

It is clear that this debate needs to be continued, and no consensus has as yet been reached. Western theologians will argue that the *filioque* can be retained as a valid theological opinion (or *theologoumenon*), although most Westerners will now concede that its unilateral inclusion in the Creed of Constantinople was canonically and ecumenically dubious.

SUMMARY AND CONCLUSION

When we examine the trajectory covered in the last two chapters, a number of issues strike us. First, there is a rich diversity in the understanding of the theology of the Trinity. Although a number of authors may share a certain approach (such as those who espouse the intrapersonal model of the Trinity), almost every author we discussed has made a distinct contribution to the doctrine of the Trinity.

Second, we dispelled a number of untenable scholarly views. The notion that the West puts more emphasis upon the divine substance than the divine Persons proved difficult to sustain in light of the rich theologies of the Trinity we encountered from the medieval period to the present day. Nor did we find any traces of a 'decline' and 'reinventing' of the theology of the Trinity. What we did notice, however, was the gradual appearance of theologies of the Trinity which 'rival' traditional patristic and medieval theologies of the Trinity. These 'rival' theologies of the Trinity are usually Hegelian in inspiration. The indebtedness to Hegel becomes evident in a number of ways: process and change are attributed to the inner life of God, which can also be affected by, and become dependent upon, events on

---

[78] It should be noted that Ruusbroec's theology, with its circular view of the trinitarian life, contains resources to solve this theological problem.

earth. Indeed, the reduction of the immanent Trinity to the economic Trinity is one of the distinctive features of the Hegelian influence.

The 'rival' theology which Hegel developed must, in turn, be seen in light of intellectual developments that characterise modernity, and which find their origins in the late-medieval period and Reformation thought (especially Lutheran theology). We will recall the major focal points and indicate how we believe recent developments in theology may redress some of the imbalances that have grown over the centuries.

First, there was the collapse of the scholastic *synthesis of faith and reason*. Although authors such as Richard of St Victor, Bonaventure, or Thomas Aquinas held different views on how faith and reason should relate to one another, they all shared the view that some engagement of faith and reason, and theology and philosophy, was desirable. By the time Descartes, the father of modernity, wrote his *Meditations*, this kind of rapprochement between faith and reason is no longer considered viable or even desirable. The resulting chasm, separating faith and reason, and theology and philosophy, led to an impoverished view of human understanding, which became increasingly 'rationalistic' rather than sapiential. The religious-aesthetic mindset, which most pre-modern authors shared (and which found its most eloquent expression in St Bonaventure's work), faded away in the modern paradigm. Its decline was accompanied by the gradual displacement of a sacramental by a mechanistic worldview. Creation (even the human being herself) was now increasingly understood in mechanistic terms, and no longer as a reflection of the trinitarian glory. In short, what we called the aesthetic receptivity (which we encountered in Richard, Aquinas, and Bonaventure) appears to dissipate in the late-medieval period. As we indicated, the Reformation was to widen this gap between faith and reason even further.

In order to approach the mystery of the Trinity, a rationalistic approach will be insufficient, or even a hindrance. A broader view of human understanding, which pre-modern authors shared, is a necessary condition for traditional approaches to the Trinity to flourish. It is hardly surprising that unitarianism and deism are modern phenomena.

Schleiermacher attempted to reconstruct theology after the Kantian challenge, which further cemented the separation of faith and reason. His emphasis upon human subjectivity certainly proved very influential and has deeply shaped modern theology. It could not, however, do justice to traditional approaches to the mystery of the Trinity, and it comes as no surprise that Schleiermacher duly rejects them, with arguments that prove particularly rationalistic. Hegel promisingly argued for a broader understanding of human rationality, but in his preference for philosophy over religious 'imagination' he succumbs to a key prejudice of modernity. Karl Rahner's original transcendental analysis attempts to reveal how the mystery of the trinitarian God grounds our being and everyday existence. In this Rahner proves a sophisticated heir to Schleiermacher's fundamental stance: the turn to the subject.

As we noted, it is difficult to place Karl Barth in the modern landscape. On the one hand, he accepts the separation of faith and reason, theology and philosophy. But he also vehemently reacts against the Schleiermacherian turn to the subject. His unapologetic theocentric stance leads to an original theology of the Trinity, based upon the revelatory act itself. The relevance of this approach for Christian spirituality is that our faith and obedience is part of the trinitarian event that is the revelatory act. Only those who have already been transformed in faith by the Holy Spirit will heed the Word of God. His theocentrism, which is alien to most modern theology, goes a long way in qualifying his Kantian epistemological position (and the separation of faith and reason it implies). Thus, in different ways the authors we discussed have grappled with the challenges of modernity.

In the postmodern era, however, we have become much more aware of the fiduciary nature of human rationality. The Cartesian 'autonomous reason' has been discredited. Michael Polanyi has shown that even scientific knowledge and practices presuppose procedures and beliefs which are simply assumed and never questioned. Hans-Georg Gadamer, working in the field of hermeneutics, has shown the significance of pre-understandings in the interpretative process. Alasdair MacIntyre has emphasised the importance of specific traditions for human rationality and morality.[79] All these authors allow us to challenge the notion of 'autonomous reason'. In doing so, they open up opportunities for theologians to recapture a broader understanding of human rationality, closer to the sapiential understanding that proved so central in the pre-modern development of trinitarian theology. In our view the work of Balthasar attempts to reintroduce something of this religious-aesthetic disposition, which is fully aware of the fiduciary nature of human rationality, and which can be called a sapiential theology that offers important resources for our present era.

---

[79] For a readable and very useful introduction to these issues, see Trevor Hart, *Faith Thinking: The Dynamics of Christian Theology* (London: SPCK, 1995).

A second key issue we identified is the rise of *different readings of the Scriptures*. We argued that Luther and Calvin adopted fairly traditional trinitarian views. Luther's *Sola Scriptura* principle, however, led to a growing divide between traditional theologies of the Trinity and the interpretation of the Scriptures. Indeed, some of Luther's more innovative principles led to a 'detraditionalisation' of the theology of the Trinity. It is no coincidence that both the historical-critical method and radical anti-trinitarianism find their origin in Protestant theology. Catholics would argue that without the prism of tradition it becomes increasingly difficult to interpret the Scriptures in such a way that they support the traditional doctrine of the Trinity. In fact, St Irenaeus had already made this important hermeneutical point against the Gnostics: without the Rule of Faith (i.e., the Creed) it becomes difficult, if not impossible, to interpret the Scriptures faithfully. In order that this argument does not become circular, Irenaeus also introduced the notion of apostolic succession, supposedly safeguarding the validity of the Rule of Faith.[80] Thus, Irenaeus emphasises the hermeneutical significance of a perspective shaped by faith, but he also underscores a more historical dimension: the Rule of Faith has been handed down from the time of the apostles onwards, and this is (allegedly) historically verifiable.

Irenaeus' contribution offers us resources to tackle a complex theological issue: how, if at all, should historical-critical readings of the Scriptures shape our understanding of Christian faith, including a theology of the Trinity? While the historical-critical method initially flourished in Protestant circles only (given their general anti-traditionalist stance), Catholic theology became more open to the contribution it could make during the first half of the twentieth century (cf. *Divino Afflante Spiritu* by Pope Pius XII). It is fair to say that modern biblical scholarship both illustrates and perhaps, at times, has furthered the decline of non-literal, allegorical readings of Scripture. Modern biblical scholarship has often exposed traditional ways of reading the Scriptures as untenable. These allegorical ways, however, proved rather important in nurturing the religious-aesthetic dimension of pre-modern theology; they were also a major resource for developing traditional theologies of the Trinity.

---

[80] The circularity is as follows: a 'faithful' interpretation of the Scriptures is one which is in accordance with the Rule of Faith; and: the Rule of Faith, accepted as a faithful summary of the history of salvation narrated in the Scriptures, determines which interpretations of the Scriptures are faithful or proper. The notion of the apostolic succession introduces a historical dimension into this, that is, the Rule of Faith has been accurately handed down from the apostles to the present bishops.

In the twentieth century a number of authors, inspired by Henri de Lubac's magisterial *Medieval Exegesis*, have argued that we need to retrieve the riches of pre-modern readings of the Scriptures. Now, in pre-modern readings of the Scriptures the literal (or historical) sense is only one of four possible readings. There are also the allegorical, moral, and anagogical senses (cf. *ST* I.1.10). In short, pre-modern readings are quite inclusivist, and allow for literal or historical-critical interpretations as acceptable readings. Similarly, we are pleading for an inclusivist position, which is willing to include the findings of balanced historical-critical scholarship, but which is also open to alternative, more traditional readings that are not at odds with historical-critical findings. The retrieval of inclusivist, pre-modern interpretative strategies may assist us in bridging the gap between modern biblical exegesis and systematic theology (including the theology of the Trinity). Few theologians have attempted such a synthesis. Authors such as Balthasar, Barth, or Zizioulas have not fully engaged with modern biblical scholarship, while scholars who have done so, such as Edward Schillebeeckx, show little interest in a theology of the Trinity.

Another important element we identified is the connection between *soteriology* (especially the paschal mystery) and the development of trinitarian theology. Again, Luther's emphasis upon the radical identification of Christ with sinful humanity, and his tendency towards radically emphasising the unity of the divine and human natures in Christ, opened the door for a theopaschite theology, of which Hegel is the philosophical heir. Through Luther and Hegel it became a key theme in Moltmann's theology of the suffering God, Balthasar, and others. Especially in Moltmann's theology the Hegelian influence is in danger of undermining the divine transcendence.

In conclusion, a future theology of the Trinity should, in our view, recapture the sapiential, religious-aesthetic stance of pre-modern authors in a postmodern context. Aware of the fiduciary nature of all human rationality, it will be critically aware that human understanding is broader than mere reason (*raison, ratio*). It will also engage with the findings of biblical scholarship without excluding other, more spiritual or allegorical ways of reading the Scriptures. And it will continue to focus on the paschal mystery as a key revelatory event, without succumbing to the temptations of a Hegelian God who is in need of salvation himself. Thus, we need to construe a theology of God who is in radical solidarity with humanity, without, however, becoming guilty of anthropomorphism.

Another issue we identified is the tension between interpersonal and intrapersonal *models of the Trinity*. Balthasar has identified the weaknesses of each model: 'The interpersonal model cannot attain the substantial unity of God, whereas the intrapersonal model cannot give an adequate picture of the real and abiding face-to-face encounter of the hypostases' (*TL* II, 38). He states that these models can, at best, converge but they cannot be fully integrated with one another 'within the horizon of this world'. Still, it seems to us that a number of authors have attempted this kind of convergence, especially St Bonaventure. A future theology of the Trinity should, in our view, attempt to harmonise both models as much as possible. While the interpersonal model appears to be the one that finds most favour with scholars at present, the intrapersonal model has the distinct advantage of allowing us to establish a closer link between theology of the Trinity and spirituality, although the social model is not without its practical and spiritual implications, as we will make clear in the next chapter. This brings us to our final observations in this chapter: the importance of the *link between theology and spirituality*.

Richard's analysis of the Trinity in terms of a community of shared love continues to inspire theologians to this day, especially those who favour social trinitarianism (such as Moltmann). Also, Richard's view that the Father generates the Son out of gratuitous love can be beautifully linked with the paschal mystery in which the Father surrenders his Son for our salvation. Similarly, the economy of grace must be interpreted in terms of the gift of the Holy Spirit, love freely received (*amor debitus*) from the Father and the Son. It is this love which is breathed into the hearts of the Christian faithful by the Father and the Son.

Bonaventure's sapiential theology allows us to contemplate the whole of creation in light of the Trinity, and where the human soul in particular bears this trinitarian imprint in a supreme manner. When memory (or mind), intellect, and will turn to God we become fully deiform and actualise our trinitarian calling. Bonaventure's theology of the Holy Spirit as Gift offers major resources for theology today, as John Milbank's contribution (see Chapter 6) will suggest.

Aquinas' so-called psychological model, although often maligned in recent scholarship, proves particularly fruitful for Christian spirituality. Following Augustine, Aquinas develops a rich analogy between the generation of the Word and the procession of the Spirit as Love, on the one hand, and the movements of the inner word and love within the mind, on the other hand, that allow for a dynamic understanding of the soul as the image of the Trinity. When we know and love God, we share in the intra-trinitarian processions of Word and Spirit.

While Aquinas' rehabilitation as an important spiritual writer of trinitarian doctrine is overdue, Ruusbroec's status in this regard has never been disputed by anyone familiar with his writings. Ruusbroec's original theology of the Trinity finds a rich application in his spiritual ideal of the common life. This ideal combines charitable activity, desire and devotion for God, and fruition of God in a harmonious synthesis. The common life reflects, and participates in, the intra-trinitarian dimensions (outgoing, ingoing, and fruition or rest in the shared unity).

In the twentieth century both Balthasar and Rahner have called for a re-engagement between theology and spirituality. Especially Balthasar's innovative theology of Holy Saturday offers interesting trinitarian perspectives (as does Moltmann's theology of the suffering God). According to Balthasar, the paschal mystery can only be understood in terms of a kenosis within the Trinity. We also discussed the importance of his understanding of mission for finding one's own identity – again a theme of direct relevance for Christian spirituality.

Finally, John Zizioulas' analysis of personhood and communion provides the foundation for an attractive theology which asserts the unique value of every person, which death (from a Christian perspective) can never abnegate. As we saw, Zizioulas' rich trinitarian thought branches out into ecclesiology, sacramentology (especially baptism and Eucharist), pneumatology, and eschatology. In Zizioulas' work we encounter a theologian who attempts to remain faithful to the legacy of the Church Fathers but who is also willing to engage with contemporary understandings of human existence, personhood, and Church. As such his work witnesses to the continuing vibrancy of more traditional, non-Hegelian approaches to the Trinity.

In our final chapter we discuss a number of other contemporary issues that will impact on a future theology of the Trinity, such as the ongoing influence of the interpersonal model of the Trinity, the postmodern and interreligious contexts.

SUGGESTED READINGS

Bauckham, Richard, *The Theology of Jürgen Moltmann* (Edinburgh: T&T Clark, 1996).

Grenz, Stanley, *Rediscovering the Triune God: The Trinity in Contemporary Theology* (Minneapolis: Fortress Press, 2004).

Hunt, Anne, *Trinity: Nexus of the Mysteries of Christian Faith* (New York: Orbis, 2005).

Pitstick, Alyssa Lyra, *Light in Darkness: Hans Urs von Balthasar and the Catholic Doctrine of Christ's Descent into Hell* (Grand Rapids, MI: Eerdmans, 2007).

Powell, Samuel, *The Trinity in German Thought* (Cambridge: Cambridge University Press, 2001).

CHAPTER 6

Contemporary trinitarian theology: problems and perspectives

TRINITARIAN ANTHROPOLOGY AND THE SOCIAL IMAGE OF GOD

In the previous chapter we dealt with Jürgen Moltmann's innovative theology of a suffering God. In this discussion it became clear how Lutheran and Hegelian elements led to a critique of traditional under-standings of God, especially the traditional view on divine impassibility, and the way the created world relates to God.

Within contemporary theology Moltmann has probably done most to develop a social and political trinitarian theology, and it is this important contribution we take up at the outset of this chapter. The reader will recall that trinitarian tradition has, in effect, left us two models or analogies for the Trinity, namely, the social and the psychological model. By social we mean a focus on the Trinity as a community of persons and the anthropological and political ramifications of the doctrine – a trinitarian *orthopraxis*. The 'psychological analogy', on the other hand, associated initially with Augustine and later developed by Aquinas, is based on the doctrine of the *imago Dei* – the human person made in the triune God's image and likeness (Gen. 1:26–7). Augustine, as we have seen, found a reflection of the Trinity in the individual human person, specifically in the human mind and heart.

Many contemporary theologians see in this psychological model a shift away from the biblical narrative to a focus on relations 'internal' to the Godhead rather than on God in relation to creation. The doctrine of the Trinity, they fear, could become reduced to the doctrine of the immanent Trinity alone. 'Social' trinitarians criticise Augustine's analogy of the indi-vidual remembering, understanding, and loving as an overly introspective view of the human person and ultimately of God.[1] Thus it is not surprising that more social approaches find greater resonance today since they

[1] See the section on Augustine in Chapter 3.

underscore the relationality of the triune God, a relationality not self-contained but overflowing into the economy of creation and redemption. Such emphases want to overcome the limitations of the psychological analogy which is perceived as too speculative and cut off from the historical story of redemption. They explore how the doctrine of the Trinity has practical as well as spiritual consequences by developing a trinitarian vision of humanity and society, and showing how knowing the triune God has a participative and doxological character. The notion of participation in the dynamic of the divine life is of course typically Augustinian, but it is only comparatively recently that the political, social, and ecclesial implications have been more fully worked out.

In this process a frequently mined resource is the theology of love developed by the medieval canon Richard of St Victor (d.1173). For Richard, as was discussed more fully in Chapter 4, the nature of true charity or love entails not only a giving and a receiving, but a sharing in community. Exclusively personal love of self does not constitute charity because it is not directed towards another and there is an absence of a plurality of persons. Though love is essentially 'other-directed', Richard extended the lover–beloved or giver–receiver dynamic: the beloved wishes to share the delights of charity with a third, for which he coined the term *condilectus* or equal co-beloved. 'Shared love is properly said to exist when a third person is loved by two persons harmoniously and in community, and the affection of the two persons is fused into one affection by the flame of love for the third.'[2] Richard's view of the Trinity as a community of love based on the inter-personal dynamics of charity and friendship continues to provoke discussion on how the human person as *imago Dei* can reflect the divine life in community with others.

As we mentioned, Jürgen Moltmann has developed this line of thought and has become in recent years an influential spokesperson for the so-called 'social doctrine of the Trinity', conceiving of God as three divine subjects in a fellowship of love, a communion open to the world and humanity.[3] He criticises traditional and classical presentations of the Trinity, from Aquinas' alleged emphasis on divine substance to Rahner and Barth and their focus on God as absolute subject. 'Ever since Hegel,' he contends, 'the Christian Trinity has tended to be represented in terms belonging to the general

---

[2] Richard of St Victor, *The Twelve Patriarchs. The Mystical Ark. Book Three of* The Trinity, trans. and introduced G. Zinn, Classics of Western Spirituality (New York: Paulist Press, 1979), Ch. XIX, 392. For a fuller discussion of Richard's thought, see the first section of Chapter 4.

[3] Jürgen Moltmann, *Trinity and the Kingdom of God* (London: SCM Press, 1981), abbreviated as *TKG*, 19.

concept of the absolute subject: *one subject – three modes of being* (*TKG*, 17). The stress was on the unity of God at the expense of the diversity of the three persons. As a result the doctrine of the Trinity was reduced, he claims, to a form of 'patriarchal monotheism', whereas his social model thinks of God in terms of relationship, communion, and fellowship – a prototype for human community. Thus Moltmann wants to develop a more historically focussed and biblically based doctrine of the Trinity:

> In distinction to the trinity of substance and to the trinity of subject we shall be attempting to develop a social doctrine of the Trinity ... This trinitarian herme-neutics leads us to think in terms of relationships and communities ... [is] developed out of the doctrine of the Trinity, and is brought to bear on the relation of men and women to God, to other people and to mankind as a whole. (*TKG*, 19)

In his desire to leave behind the alleged patriarchal monotheism of the past, Moltmann highlights the threeness of the divine Persons as three centres of conscious activity linked together by the concept of *perichoresis*, their reciprocal indwelling or the 'circulation' of the eternal divine life. Rather than presupposing a unity, he begins with the divine plurality and then moves on to speak of a relational fellowship of unity. In his view, the term *perichoresis* 'links together in a brilliant way the threeness and the unity, without reducing the threeness to the unity, or dissolving the unity in the threeness' (*TKG*, 175). The unity is constituted by the reciprocal indwelling. The divine Persons are not subsistent entities in themselves (tritheist), nor are they three 'modes of being' of the one God (modalist). In other words, Moltmann wants to affirm both the different identities and the unity of the Persons.

Moltmann's trinitarian theology has been commended for its attempt to connect the doctrine of God with political and social concerns. He rejects interpretations of the Trinity that reduce the divine persons to modes of a single subjectivity, give rise to a disengaged trinitarian monar-chianism, and set God over against the world in a hierarchical manner.[4] Instead, the Trinity as a fellowship of equal persons serves as a critique of clerical and political monotheism and a paradigm for a mutually loving and interacting human society. The Brazilian theologian Leonardo Boff has largely followed Moltmann in this direction, particularly in his cri-tique of capitalism and its link with individualism, greed, and disparity between rich and poor. For him too, the Trinity as the archetypal open

---

[4] See Stanley J. Grenz, *The Social God and the Relational Self: A Trinitarian Theology of the* Imago Dei (Louisville, KY: Westminster/John Knox Press, 2001), 45. We noted how Moltmann creatively appropriated elements of Cappadocian thought in this direction in Chapter 3.

and egalitarian community provides a motive and inspiration to work towards a more equal human society.[5]

A number of other contemporary theologians have developed an ontology of persons in communion based on the social dimensions of personhood. Such a Trinity-inspired ontology views the three divine Persons fundamentally as relations, not substances or independent entities standing next to each other. The tendency had been to think of the three as isolated individuals who *have* relations. But 'relation, being related, is not something superadded to the person', but '*is* the person itself'. Specifically, the Father 'does not generate in the sense that the act of generating a Son is added to the already complete person, but the person *is* the deed of generating, of giving itself, of streaming itself forth. The person is identical with this act of self-donation.'[6]

The claim that the persons in God are nothing but the act of relating toward each other is not only a statement about the Trinity. For Moltmann, Ratzinger, LaCugna, Zizioulas, and others it opens up a perichoretic vision of human personhood which is at a remove from the insufficient and individualistic understanding as evidenced in the sixth-century Christian philosopher Boethius (a person is an individual substance of a rational nature), who influenced much of Western philosophy. In other words, God's self-revelation as triune illuminates the very nature of Being and of what it means to be a human person as the highest manifestation of Being. If the triune God is self-communicating, existing eternally in relation to another in an ecstatic process of self-communicating love, then, as LaCugna puts it, the 'ultimate source of all reality is not a "by-itself" or an "in-itself" but a person, a toward-another' (*GfU*, 14, 15). And this self-communication is inscribed into the heart of all beings – created as they are in the image of their triune source. Thus our understanding of the triune God informs our understanding of Being. It follows that to enquire or state what something is, we must ask who it is and how it is related (*GfU*, 248). Relationality, therefore, becomes just as important an aspect of the person as substantiality. In Chapter 3, following Zizioulas and LaCugna, we saw

---

[5] Leonardo Boff, *Trinity and Society*, trans. P. Burns, Liberation and Theology Series 2 (London: Burns and Oates, 1988), 236–7. There is the danger of an overly idealistic view of the relationship between theology and politics: the harmony, integration, and plurality of the Trinity may well ground similar patterns in society, but this is not to suggest that the latter will (or should) be free from tension and conflict.

[6] Joseph Cardinal Ratzinger, 'Concerning the Notion of Person in Theology', *Communio* 17 (1990): 444. God is 'not only *logos* but *dia-logos*, not only idea and meaning but speech and word in the reciprocal exchanges of partners in conversation ... [D]ialogue, the *relatio*, stands beside the substance as an equally primordial form of being.' Joseph Cardinal Ratzinger, *Introduction to Christianity* (San Francisco: Ignatius Press, 1990, 2004), 183.

how this ontology underlies Cappadocian theology. For the Cappadocians, Being itself originates in the personhood of God the Father; thus all of reality, since it proceeds from God, is personal and relational.[7] Zizioulas maintains that Being or substance does not precede relation. As one of his commentators puts it, 'it is not the case that something first is what it is, and then that it enters various relationships; rather *Being* and *relationship* are simultaneous'.[8]

Zizioulas, LaCugna, and Moltmann, then, argue for the priority of person over Being, and they see this exemplified in the communion that is the Trinity. This is a theology and ontology linked, as we have seen, to the ecclesial and eucharistic experience of the Greek Fathers, a tradition 'which lives and teaches its theology liturgically'.[9] But it is not an ontology that simply says persons *are* relations. Within the Trinity, of course, the Persons and the nature are the same and, with Aquinas, we can speak of the divine Persons as subsistent relations – existing or subsisting only in relation to one another. In sum, the interrelationship of the divine Persons constitutes the nature or substance of what God is.

Nevertheless, concepts such as 'Person' and 'relation' used in reference to the Trinity can only be applied to the human community in an *analogous* rather than in a univocal way. Yet today there is a tendency to almost exclusively define persons in terms of their relations to others partly in reaction to modernity's too individualistic outlook.[10] As William Norris Clarke puts it, 'the unique interiority and privacy of the person are wiped out ... and the person turns out to be an entirely extraverted bundle of relations, with no inner self to share with others'. The point is that 'relationality and substantiality go together as two distinct but inseparable modes of reality'.[11] There must be an 'in-itself' (*substantiality*) as the

---

[7] At the level of physical reality, the physicist and priest John Polkinghorne sees this 'relational and holistic' thinking resonating with what science has discovered of 'a deep-seated interconnectivity present in the fabric of the world ... [T]he general character of physical reality seems to correspond to a web-like character of interconnected integrity.' John Polkinghorne, *Science and the Trinity: The Christian Encounter with Reality* (London: SPCK, 2004), 74–5.

[8] Douglas H. Knight, ed., *The Theology of John Zizioulas: Personhood and the Church* (Aldershot: Ashgate, 2007), 2. For Zizioulas, following the experience of the Greek Fathers, the being of God can only be known 'through personal relationships and personal love. Being means life, and life means communion.' John Zizioulas, *Being as Communion: Studies in Personhood and the Church* (London: Darton, Longman and Todd, 1985), 16.

[9] Zizioulas, *Being as Communion*, 19.

[10] See Harriet A. Harris, 'Should we say that Personhood is Relational?', *Scottish Journal of Theology* 51 (1998): 214–34.

[11] William Norris Clarke, *Person and Being*, The Aquinas Lecture, 1993 (Milwaukee: Milwaukee University Press, 1993), 19, 14. Clarke comes to similar conclusions as Zizioulas and LaCugna about the nature of persons albeit by a different route.

necessary grounding for relationality (*towards others*). Relationship should not be at the expense of autonomy. Even within the perichoretic life of the Trinity where the divine persons mutually indwell each other, the distinct personal identity of each is preserved.

Notwithstanding these caveats and the critique of Moltmann in the previous chapter, the social analogy is an impressive and influential attempt to present the doctrine of the Trinity as a critical principle for theology. A trinitarian theology of the cross presents us with a God who has identified with the weak and the powerless. Faith in such a God will have an explicit practical and political dimension in its mission to transform the world. Secondly, the social Trinity opens up a new, more relational understanding of human personhood. Thirdly, the perichoretic relationship of the trinitarian persons – characterised by mutuality rather than lordship – provides the basis for a 'cosmic *perichoresis*' for 'a mutual indwelling of the world in God and God in the world'.[12] Biblically, this perichoretic theology is reflected in Jesus' high priestly prayer in John 17:21:

> May they all be one,
> just as, Father, you are in me and I am in you,
> so that they also may be in us.

Here the Trinity is a non-hierarchical community where, following the Council of Florence (1438–45), no person 'either precedes the others in eternity, or exceeds them in greatness, or supervenes in power'. This is not a closed unity, but an open Trinity: there is a longing in God arising not from any imperfection or deficiency in Being, but from God's superabundant and creative love which seeks internal and external form.

THE TRINITY AND POSTMODERNITY

The term 'postmodern' is a contested concept. On the one hand, it is presented as a radical break with modernity – and its faith in human reason, unbridled scientific progress, the autonomous human subject, and the divorce of the secular from the sacred. On the other hand, it has been described as a late form of modernity, an advanced or radicalised stage of the same historical process. For example, the postmodern focus on subjectivity and its concomitant distrust of authority and institutions can be traced back to modernity's 'turn to the subject'. More typically, however,

---

[12] Jürgen Moltmann, *The Coming of God: Christian Eschatology* (Minneapolis: Fortress Press, 1996), 295, 307.

postmodernism calls into question many of the so-called gains of modernity. Specifically, it is a reaction to the weaknesses and pretensions of modernity, despite its intellectual and societal advances, to what are perceived as totalising ideologies or political systems. If modernity and the Enlightenment project represented rationality, individual autonomy, and progress, postmodern theory denies that reason is absolute and universal, that individuals are autonomous and able to transcend their historical context and culture, and that unbridled scientific progress is the answer to humanity's ills.

The modern spirit placed great faith in human reason, in its desire for certitude and clarity, and in its search for a comprehensive explanation of reality – a master story or 'metanarrative'. The postmodern spirit, in contrast, is characterised by a scepticism and incredulity towards metanarratives.[13] Epistemological and religious foundations, timeless truths, and other forms of 'totalising' discourse are rejected. In place of 'total' explanations or epistemological foundationalism, the relative, perspectival, and contextual aspects of human knowledge are highlighted. Truth has a history.

'Thou shalt not believe in absolutes' is one way to describe the postmodern stress on provisionality, including the provisional nature of language. Language is not something neutral that directly and unproblematically represents an extra-linguistic reality, but is socially constructed. Meaning is related to context, or, more radically, the meaning of any text is unstable and flexible due to the changing contexts in which it is read. It is impossible to commit to any particular interpretation. In contrast to modernity's search for absolute truth, the postmodern quest is nomadic and wandering, convinced that nothing is simply 'true'.

The downside of this distrust of metanarratives, moral absolutes, and religious authority is a fragmentation of society, relativism in moral choices, and a loss of meaning and community. In the postmodern West this has left many with a sense of rootlessness and emptiness. The explosion of New Age spiritualities reflects a wish to develop an inner spiritual life in response to the harsher side of contemporary society and to Churches operating mainly out of a modern paradigm. Many Christians have absorbed, almost unconsciously, a consumerist, eclectic 'mix and match' approach to religious issues and practice, while some claim a multi-religious identity (e.g., partly

---

[13] Jean-François Lyotard, *The Postmodern Condition: A Report on Knowledge*, Theory and History of Literature 10, trans. G. Bennington and B. Massumi (Manchester: Manchester University Press, 1989), 37.

Christian, partly Buddhist). The resurgence of religious fundamentalism also constitutes a rejection of the values of modernity (including individual rights, democratic ethos, pluralism, etc.) and a return to pre-modern religious expression in sometimes aggressive and violent forms.

If the postmodern sensibility has done much to uncover or deconstruct the ambiguities of modernity, no single alternative is offered. Broadly speaking, there are at least three kinds of postmodern groupings, each of which has its advocates within the theological academy.[14] A first, more radical, stance exemplified in the work of Jean-François Lyotard and Jacques Derrida eschews all attempts to construct some grand narrative or overarching theoretical system. We are trapped in our own skin, as it were, in the immanence of our own experience; there is nothing more. There is no fixed meaning to anything – whether world, word, text, or human subject. This is a reaction to, and a protest against, any kind of system, any kind of pretence to totality. In place of classical foundationalist epistemology with its search for secure first principles (e.g., in Descartes), there is a celebration of the chaotic or heteromorphous dimensions of life and its otherness. Moreover, any system – religious, economic, political – purporting to structure our experience is said to be constituted and maintained through acts of exclusion and repression. The Jewish philosopher Emmanuel Levinas (1906–95) has also been particularly influential in this context. For Levinas, the thrust of Greek philosophy was a striving for totality, and Heidegger's fascination with it led to an ontology focussed on comprehension and assimilation.[15] The particular being is always already understood within the horizon of Being or, formulated differently, the other is perceived and accounted for by the metanarrative. For Levinas, on the other hand, the *perichoresis* of Being and knowing characteristic of the Western metaphysical tradition is displaced by the social relation, by the 'Other', the other human being, in a way that goes beyond comprehension. The abandonment of metanarrative enables an encounter with the repressed other of modernity. Rationality operates within an inter-relational context in which the other always has priority. The ethical encounter with the other person constitutes the proto-philosophical experience. This is to

---

[14] Postmodernism of course resists any easy categorisation. The suggested 'divisions' that follow should be seen as rather fluid and treated with a degree of caution. See Graham Ward, 'Introduction: "Where We Stand"', in Graham Ward, ed., *The Blackwell Companion to Postmodern Theology* (Oxford: Blackwell, 2005), xii–xxvii.

[15] Emmanuel Levinas, 'Is Ontology Fundamental?', in Adriaan T. Peperzak, Simon Critchley, and Robert Bernasconi, eds., *Emmanuel Levinas: Basic Philosophical Writings* (Bloomington and Indianapolis: Indiana University Press, 1996), 1–10.

acknowledge that the subject is not a self-enclosed totality; it is to awake to alterity. In relation to epistemology, the strong postmodern stance highlights the temporality of knowledge and the contingency of beliefs. To its detractors such a position leads down the slippery slope of relativism and radical scepticism. More positively, it is recognition of the indeterminacy of language and the elusive nature of ultimate meaning and truth. Derrida's linguistic deconstruction, for example, is essentially a reaction to the unequivocal domination of one mode of signifying over another. It is a rejection of a realist understanding of language that assumes our linguistic utterances have a fixed meaning. Meaning is never static. Texts have to be constantly re-read in new ways, against the grain, to disclose concealed or repressed meanings.

A second, more conservative, but equally radical postmodern stance critiques what it sees as theology's collusion with the project of modernity. It renounces the 'compromises' of liberal theology in its attempt to mediate religious thought to modern culture. The 'postliberal theology' of George Lindbeck and his colleagues at Yale University is one example, while the 'Radical Orthodoxy' movement, whose leading figures include John Milbank, Catherine Pickstock, and Graham Ward, is another. Lindbeck has reconceived religion and Christian doctrine, offering in effect a new vision of theology and Christianity.[16] Postliberal theology is suspicious of appeals to universal religious experience that reduce religions to a lowest common denominator as different expressions of the same thing. It espouses a strong anti-foundationalist stance: religions are not simply externalisations of a pre-reflective, pre-linguistic foundational experience. Rather, religions are like languages or cultures embedded in forms of life, and doctrines function as grammatical rules shaping and regulating a community's dispositions and discourse. Theological faithfulness is 'intra-textual' in that it refers to the theologian's primary commitment to the authority of the scriptural narrative. By locating themselves within this narrative, postliberals claim that it is the text which absorbs the world rather than the world the text. We will discuss shortly how recent trinitarian thought has engaged with these and other postmodern emphases.

Underlying the postliberal agenda is the view that theology, especially in its liberal or revisionist forms, in accommodating itself too uncritically to a secular and pluralist culture has undermined the specific content and identity of particular religious traditions. It is with the aim of combating

---

[16] George Lindbeck, *The Nature of Doctrine: Religion and Theology in a Postliberal Age* (Philadelphia: Westminster Press, 1984).

the 'acids of modernity' that postliberal theology wishes to absorb the universe into the biblical world.[17] Rather than 'translating' the language of the Bible into the speech and thought forms of modern culture, which leads to dissolution of the biblical witness and a loss of Christian identity, the postliberal approach highlights the assimilative power of the biblical text and its capacity to draw us into a particular framework of meaning. This is a plea to the Christian community to rebuild its particular, distinctive, biblical culture. A diaspora Church of communal enclaves of mutual support is envisaged living in the midst of a hostile and de-Christianised culture. The future of the Church will therefore require some kind of 'sociological sectarianism', some kind of standing apart in order to witness to and negotiate the challenges of a post-Christian society.

Another 'conservative' impulse within contemporary theology is the reform programme of the Radical Orthodoxy movement. Also rejecting what it considers modernity's questionable epistemological assumptions and its sharp separation of faith and reason, the radical orthodox perspective views faith not as alien to reason, but as its intensification and divine illumination. This position, inspired by Augustine and Aquinas, underlines how faith and reason involve a participation in the mind of God, a sharing in the mystery of the life of the Trinity. It also finds a resonance in *Fides et Ratio*, the Encyclical Letter of Pope John Paul II, where faith and reason are compared to 'two wings on which the human spirit rises to the contemplation of truth'.[18] Like the postliberals, the radical orthodox disavow any sphere, discipline or discourse, which is independent of God. This is a theology on the offensive: every discipline is framed from a theological perspective. Society, culture, politics, art, science, and philosophy – all are boldly critiqued with a view to establishing, or better recovering, a comprehensive Christian vision. It is the end of the master narrative of secular reason.[19] Theology makes a return to the public sphere and shapes the way we talk about everything.

Radical Orthodoxy has a particular and controversial view of the Christian theological tradition. It considers most Christian theology after the late Middle Ages as issuing in a fateful separation of philosophy from theology. Duns Scotus is presented as the main culprit, as a result of whom theology ceased to be concerned with the whole of reality and ceased to identify God with Being. Instead, philosophy claimed an autonomous

---

[17] Ibid., 127, 135.   [18] Translated as *Faith and Reason* (London: CTS, 1998), Introduction.
[19] Gavin Hyman, *The Predicament of Postmodern Theology: Radical Orthodoxy or Nihilist Textualism?* (Louisville, KY: Westminster/John Knox Press, 2001), 28.

knowledge of Being, while theology degenerated into a 'Protestant Biblicism' or 'post-tridentine Catholic positivist authoritarianism'.[20] Thus Radical Orthodoxy wishes to restore philosophy's pride of place in theology. Both terms are sometimes used synonymously. Philosophy is not about reason – understood in the scientific Enlightenment sense – but about wisdom. This is a mode of rationality where philosophical discourse is not separated from theological reflection, where faith and reason mutually support one another in the quest for a unified vision of knowledge. It is a vision which goes back to the Neoplatonism of Augustine. All knowledge of God, all search for truth, requires divine illumination. Radical Orthodoxy also, correctly, sees a similar harmony of faith and reason in Aquinas.

This pre-modern return to patristic and medieval roots is not meant as an exercise in nostalgia, however. While Radical Orthodoxy caricatures and dismisses whole epochs of the theological tradition, it does intend a new reading of this tradition. Against the postmodern backdrop of loss of faith in reason, it grounds truth and knowledge through a participation in the divine mind. Yet this Neoplatonic metaphysical outlook is unconvincing for those who claim Radical Orthodoxy only offers a one-sided reading of modernity, equating it with nihilism and violence, but overlooking its scientific gains, its sense of historical consciousness and legacy of critical thinking.

A third, more moderate stance recognises that just as there are many forms of postmodernity, so too modernity cannot be reduced to a single version. Prior to classical Enlightenment modernity there was the creative, influential culture of Renaissance humanism in the fifteenth and sixteenth centuries.[21] Modernity cannot simply be equated with the scientific achievements of the seventeenth century. Moreover, in this approach, modernity was not only entrapping; in its democratic and ethical ideals it was emancipatory. Hence political and liberation theologies have roots in modernity as do those who refuse to drive a wedge between faith and rationality. This approach, whose advocates include David Tracy, nevertheless acknowledges the limitations of modernity: its autonomous self-grounding subject, desire for totality, impoverished notion of reason, and its individualistic, idealistic, and Eurocentric perspective.[22] Postmodernity at its best challenges this

---

[20] John Milbank, Catherine Pickstock, and Graham Ward, eds., *Radical Orthodoxy: A New Theology* (London: Routledge, 1999), 2.

[21] Louis Dupré, *Passage to Modernity: An Essay in the Hermeneutics of Nature and Culture* (New Haven and London: Yale University Press, 1993).

[22] David Tracy, *On Naming the Present: Reflections on Catholicism, Hermeneutics and the Church* (New York: Orbis Books, 1994).

ambiguous tradition of modernity, not in a nostalgic, anti-modern hankering after a bygone era, but in its turn to the other and the different. By recognising and cherishing otherness and difference, particularly in groups marginalised or repressed by Enlightenment modernity – including the mystics, dissenters, and those from other religions and cultures – postmodernity inaugurates a new kind of theological self-consciousness. Those who are 'other' and 'different' return to challenge the dominant narrative of Eurocentric modernity.

The question of God also returns. As Tracy puts it, *theos* returns 'to unsettle the dominance of the modern *logos*' despite the fact that 'in modern theology the *logos* of modern intelligibility was the dominant partner in the conversation'.[23] This is an allusion to the analogies of knowledge and love, championed by Augustine and Aquinas and developed by Karl Rahner and Bernard Lonergan, which seek an insight into the triune nature of God on the basis of the operation of the human mind. A less prominent counter-current to this psychological trajectory is a strong apophatic strain – from Pseudo-Dionysius the Areopagite through John Scotus Eriugena, Aquinas, Meister Eckhart, and Nicholas of Cusa – that stressed the incomprehensibility of God. It should not surprise that a postmodern sensibility wants to recover this apophatic or mystical tradition against the systematising and speculative tendencies of traditional scholastic explications of trinitarian theology. Jean-Luc Marion, for example, inspired by Pseudo-Dionysius, wants to reclaim the tradition of God beyond Being, to name God anew as 'excess' and 'gift'.[24] This anti-idolatrous sensibility is essentially a claim that theology can never be reduced to or captured by a 'system'. Marion's project represents a deconstruction of attempts to name, grasp or control God. It points to God's alterity. The neighbour too is 'wholly other'. The work of Levinas and Derrida has also given rise to an ethics of alterity that retrieves responsibility for the other and faith in a justice to come.

We have seen how theology has been divided in its response to modernity. On one side are the 'mediating' theologians (e.g., Tracy, Tillich, and Rahner) who want to correlate revelatory claims with the demands of reason. Reason is valued but not overvalued. But there is the danger of domesticating the mystery of God and undermining the gratuity of revelation. On the other side are the postliberals and radical orthodox who reject all correlational strategies, and see theology's sole foundation

---

[23] Ibid., 37.
[24] Jean-Luc Marion, *God without Being: Hors-texte*, trans. T. Carlson (Chicago: University of Chicago Press, 1991).

in revelation. This is to distrust and ultimately to abandon an onto-theological approach that understood God in terms of Being. Marion, for example, challenges theology to leave behind modern theo-*logy* and become once again *theo*-logy.

What effect has this postmodern naming of God had on trinitarian theology? Certainly the renewed emphasis on the apophatic dimension of theology is a reaction and corrective to the excessive rationalism of modernity. It is not a question though of dismissing the possibility of any kind of affirmative theology or endorsing a simplistic fideism. Rather, following Gregory of Nyssa, it is to leave behind what we think we have grasped of God. This process of continual striving and straining on a never-ending journey towards God – Gregory's concept of *epektasis* (see Phil. 3:13) – challenges the theologian to a sapiential and participative knowing, as we have seen with the Cappadocians, Augustine, and the latter's medieval successors (Richard, Bonaventure, Aquinas, and Ruusbroec). It is to acknowledge that we do not speak of God unless we are first spoken to, or that theological speech is ultimately a response. Pointing to the ineffability of God is to say that the more we understand God, the *more* (not less) unknown God becomes.[25] This is the tradition of *docta ignorantia* or 'learned ignorance' already exemplified in Augustine and in the medieval period with Nicholas of Cusa (1401–64).

Postmodernity thus sees in the apophatic or contemplative tradition a critique of, and liberation from, absolute and definitive concepts of God. We have noted how it also critiques traditional metaphysics or any attempt to explain the totality of Being (onto-theology). Derrida, following Heidegger, discerns a closure to metaphysics by which he means the Western philosophical tradition of a metaphysics of presence – something *is* only if it is present or presentable – and turns to 'the *excessive* practice of language' in negative theologies.[26] Every predication applied to God has to be exceeded or crossed out in order to glimpse the Trinity beyond Being. In his deconstructive reading of Pseudo-Dionysius and Eckhart, Derrida, not unlike Balthasar and Milbank, has left behind early modernity's view of Being as a univocal concept applied to God and humanity and which placed both on the same level, with the effect that God's ontological transcendence

---

[25] Nicholas Lash, *Holiness, Speech and Silence: Reflections on the Question of God* (Aldershot: Ashgate, 2004), 76.

[26] Jacques Derrida et al., 'Original Discussion (1968) of La "Différance" [sic]', in David Wood and Robert Bernasconi, eds., *Derrida and Différance* (Warwick: Parousia Press, 1985), 132, as cited by Kevin Hart, 'Jacques Derrida: An Introduction', in Graham Ward, ed., *The Postmodern God: A Theological Reader* (Oxford: Blackwell, 1997), 163.

was denied. For Duns Scotus (*c*.1266–1308) 'Being' can be infinite (God) or finite (creatures). It is what each has in common and which reason can study without recourse to revelation. Balthasar reminds us, however (*GL*, 9–21), that for Aquinas Being subsists only in its emergence from God, thus highlighting the priority of God over Being. And following from this disproportionality between God and creatures, Aquinas claims that all language about God can only be predicated analogically. But at the same time, Aquinas also assumes a basic affinity and similitude between creatures and God. Otherwise it would not be possible (with Augustine, Aquinas, and the mystical tradition) to speak of participating in the dynamic life of the Trinity. God cannot be described in an unqualified manner as 'totally other'. Rather, theological discourse is an interplay of affirmation and negation, of purification and expansion, of revelation and concealment. Here is not the place to trace the history of the tempestuous relationship between God and Being. In an extensive reflection on Exod. 3:14, Paul Ricoeur has raised some of the issues at stake.[27] He traces how the conjoining of God and Being shaped our fundamental conception of Christianity in the West. It affected how we understand the relation between Hebraic and Greek culture, between theology and philosophy, and the role of development in tradition. His conclusion is a plea to preserve a balance between the affirmative way and its positive statements about God by way of analogy, and the negative way with its recognition of the limitations and inadequacies of all affirmations.

The apophatic way does more than liberate from conceptual idolatry; it invites to an epistemology of participation. It is linked to mystical speech. In place of the language of observation, representation, or objectification, mystical discourse is a failure of speech, a language of unsaying in the sense of a continual disciplining of language before the God who is always more than we can say. Throughout this book we have tried to show how personal language for the triune God, while used analogically, has participatory overtones in that Father, Son, and Holy Spirit are not so much nouns as verbs drawing us into the 'event of relationships' that God is.[28] This highlighting of the dynamic nature of the Being of God in terms of reciprocal movement or relationship underlies an epistemology of participation and illumination. Of course, such a position is far from a strong postmodern

---

[27] Paul Ricoeur, 'From Interpretation to Translation', in *Thinking Biblically: Exegetical and Hermeneutical Studies* (Chicago and London: Chicago University Press, 1998), 331–61. See also our discussion in Chapter 2.

[28] Paul Fiddes, *Participating in God* (London: Darton, Longman, and Todd, 2000), 36–46.

view, evidenced, for example, in Don Cupitt, who tends to reduce Christian mysticism to language, that is, to mystical texts.[29] Recognising that mysticism is mediated by language is not a warrant for restricting mysticism to a form of literature. Instead, following Bernard McGinn and others, we can point to a trinitarian basis for mystical speech. McGinn appeals to the distinction, for example, in Meister Eckhart between the Word unspoken and the Word brought forth, both in the Trinity and in the human person. This is to ground mysticism in the transcendent source of language, namely, 'in the *Verbum* within the dynamic consciousness of the Trinity – a Word that is *more* than language'.[30] As Eckhart puts it, 'the Word which is in the silence of the fatherly Intellect is a Word without word, or rather a Word above every word'.[31] And yet, it is only in and by this Word that the universe comes to be. The Creator God speaks and this creative speaking is in a real sense identical with God's self, 'a self-reproduction through a creative act of the will: language mediating the power and presence of God as God's word goes forth'.[32] The Father's speaking of the Word expresses the inner hidden divine silence, while the Spirit as the *nexus* or bond of love between Father and Son enables and is our point of access into this divine conversation, and so restores all things to God. Within Eckhart's Christian-Platonic framework of emanation and return, the soul returns to and participates in its divine ground. The mystical journey is conceived as an extension and prolongation of the trinitarian speech-event that unfolds in creation and incarnation – 'uttered' by God – as well as in the apophatic silence of the cross. Apophatic language tries to evoke something analogous to the path of union with God incorporating a more participatory and existential kind of knowing.

In some quarters of current trinitarian discourse there is an unfortunate tendency to play off a participative or contemplative approach against a more 'social' perspective as outlined in the first section of this chapter. More benignly perhaps, the former is advocated as a corrective to a model regarded as overly concerned with the functional relevance of trinitarian doctrine. Thus Matthew Levering, in his work on Aquinas as a resource for the renewal of trinitarian theology, concludes that rediscovering theology as

---

[29] Don Cupitt, *Mysticism after Modernity* (Oxford: Blackwell, 1998).

[30] Bernard McGinn, 'Quo Vadis? Reflections on the Current Study of Mysticism', *Christian Spirituality Bulletin* 6 (1998): 17. See also Mark A. McIntosh, *Mystical Theology* (Oxford: Blackwell, 1998), 123–36.

[31] Meister Eckhart, *Expositio Libri Genesis*, n. 77. English translation from Bernard McGinn, *The Presence of God: A History of Western Christian Mysticism*, vol. IV. *The Harvest of Mysticism in Medieval Germany (1300–1500)* (New York: Crossroad, 2005), 134.

[32] Oliver Davies, *A Theology of Compassion: Metaphysics of Difference and the Renewal of Tradition* (Grand Rapids, MI: Eerdmans, 2001), 255.

contemplative wisdom renders the quest for relevance 'less urgent'.[33] Similarly, though from a different angle, Karen Kilby critiques social trinitarians for using the doctrine to promote specific social, political, or ecclesiastical regimes.[34] This is to overstate the case, even if validly warning of the dangers of projecting our hopes and concerns onto God, and it reflects a regulative or 'grammatical' interpretation of doctrine along the lines of George Lindbeck. Trinitarian doctrine in this view does not have to be relevant or even the central focus of Christianity; it has a negative or regulative function, providing rules or guidelines about how to speak in a Christian way about God. More persuasive is David Ford's depiction of theology as wisdom that responds 'both to the cries of God and to the cries of the world', worked out 'in the complexities and ambiguities of history', all the time trying to discern the significance of doctrine for now.[35]

Another facet of trinitarian reflection in the context of postmodernity is the incipient development of a trinitarian ontology or metaphysics. Stanley Grenz, John Zizioulas, Colin Gunton, Oliver Davies, David Bentley Hart, and John Milbank have all made important contributions to this discussion. Grenz, for example, pursues a conception of Being that emerges from the narrative of the divine name, from the 'I am' of Exod 3:14 to the 'I am' sayings of Jesus. Against a backdrop of the demise and deconstruction of onto-theology – the attempt to connect the God of the Bible to the Greek concept of Being – he asks whether the revelation of the divine name as trinitarian could lead to an alternative 'theo-ontological' story more suitable for today. After tracing the historical development of the doctrine in its dialogue with the Greek Platonic and Neoplatonic tradition, Grenz concludes that both Eastern and Western theologies are concerned 'to speak meaningfully of the biblical experience of the God who is both hidden and revealed'[36] thus giving rise to the apophatic and cataphatic approaches to which we have referred. The apophatic aspects of biblical revelation can deconstruct 'and radically reconfigure prior conceptions of "Being" and "God"'.[37] This is to move beyond the God of onto-theology as the highest object of thought and beyond the vanity of logocentrism (Derrida). It is to

---

[33] Matthew Levering, *Scripture and Metaphysics: Aquinas and the Renewal of Trinitarian Theology* (Oxford: Blackwell, 2004), 240.

[34] Karen Kilby, 'Perichoresis and Projection: Problems with Social Doctrines of the Trinity', *New Blackfriars* 81 (2000): 444.

[35] David Ford, *Christian Wisdom: Desiring God and Learning in Love* (Cambridge: Cambridge University Press, 2007), 5 and 213.

[36] Stanley Grenz, *The Named God and the Question of Being: A Trinitarian Theo-Ontology* (Louisville, KY: Westminster/John Knox Press, 2005), 320.

[37] Levering, *Scripture and Metaphysics*, 200.

'remove "knowledge" from its place of ontotheological privilege, so that presence is always inflected with absence, selfhood is only constituted through radical otherness, and knowing is only possible in and through unknowing'.[38] This is more than simply a 'negative' theology; it entails a negation of the negations in order to attain some positive knowledge of God. Otherwise the suspicion that apophatic silence leads ultimately to agnosticism would be justified.

At issue is the connection between the God revealed as triune and the hidden God of apophatic theology. Grenz and others locate this in the notion of *otherness*. *Pace* Aristotle's God accepted within the matrix of Being and part of the world, Christianity postulates a fundamental distinction between God and the world. The world might not have been, but God's goodness and greatness would still remain undiminished. The Christian distinction insists that God is God even apart from any relation of otherness to the world. God transcends and is more fundamental than the distinction itself.[39]

From a trinitarian perspective the focus on the dimension of the otherness of God needs to be considered alongside its correlate, *communion*. As Zizioulas has noted, within the Trinity otherness is not simply consequent upon, but constitutive of unity: 'God is not first one and then three, but simultaneously one and three.'[40] Communion does not threaten otherness; rather it generates it in that Father, Son, and Spirit are names denoting relations, that is, relationships of distinction and alterity – relations of opposition as Aquinas would say – bound together by the Spirit as the love within the divine life. God is conceived neither as an individual nor as a collectivity, but as a communion-in-otherness, a unity of Persons in relation, where there is space for the 'Other'.[41] We have seen how Levinas' philosophy of alterity goes in a similar direction in his stress on the absolute responsibility of the self for the other, an ethical imperative that shatters the illusion of autonomy. His critique of traditional ontology was that it eradicated otherness and reduced it to sameness. There are echoes of this approach in much traditional theological discourse where the 'other', whether from an intra-Christian or extra-Christian perspective, was

---

[38] Mary-Jane Rubenstein, 'Unknow Thyself: Apophaticism, Deconstruction, and Theology after Ontotheology', *Modern Theology* 19 (2003): 393.

[39] Robert Sokolowski, *The God of Faith and Reason: Foundations of Christian Theology* (Washington, DC: Catholic University of America Press, 1982, 1995), 32–3.

[40] John D. Zizioulas, *Communion and Otherness: Further Studies in Personhood and the Church*, ed. Paul McPartlan (London and New York: T&T Clark, 2006), 5.

[41] Colin E. Gunton, *The One, the Three and the Many: God, Creation and the Culture of Modernity* (Cambridge: Cambridge University Press, 1993), 215–16.

presented more in terms of what was strange, different, and foreign. Neither is a model of the Church based on a communion ecclesiology immune from homogenising tendencies that reduce and undermine the alterity of the other.[42]

Another voice in the development of a renewed ontology is Oliver Davies, who holds that the (compassionate) self is best actualised in radical self-dispossession. He shows how the compassionate self is an image of the triune God by linking an ontology of compassion with the trinitarian being of the divine Persons. Here the relationality of Being is underscored: Being is the medium of relation between self and other, preserving the distinctness of each while facilitating their relation. In particular, the identification of Being and love defines the compassionate self, and it finds ultimate expression in the life of the Trinity that holds together 'the created order in dramatic tension with itself, in a compassionate dynamic of difference and identity'.[43] Davies points to the traditional formula *mia ousia–treis hypostaseis* as oppositional ontological terms devised to express the identity and preserve the distinctness of the Persons. The peculiar tension (or aporia) of this formula challenges us to think unity and distinction simultaneously within the immanent Trinity itself – and outside the space-time continuum – all the while taking our cue from the economic Trinity, God made visible in the world. The immanent Trinity exceeds all economic formulations. It is spoken of allusively, and its meaning is presented indirectly, analogically rather than literally. In this sense, trinitarian language is essentially 'negative' in that it critiques the various positive ways we speak about, and to, God in the Scriptures and in the liturgical tradition so as not to lose sight of God's essential mystery.

From an aesthetic perspective, David Bentley Hart offers an impressive trinitarian account of beauty that presents Being as primarily the shared life of the triune God: ontological plenitude and oriented toward another. The beauty of the infinite is reflected in the dynamic co-inherence of the three divine Persons, a *perichoresis* of love, an immanent dynamism of distinction and unity embracing reciprocity and difference. The triune God does not negate difference; rather, the shared giving and receiving that is the divine life may be compared to an infinite musical richness, a music of polyphonic and harmonious differentiation of which creation is an expression and variation.[44]

---

[42] Paul M. Collins, *The Trinity: A Guide for the Perplexed* (London: T&T Clark, 2008), 119–29.

[43] Davies, *A Theology of Compassion*, 23.

[44] David Bentley Hart, *The Beauty of the Infinite: The Aesthetics of Christian Truth* (Grand Rapids, MI and Cambridge: Eerdmans, 2003), 274.

Hart is deeply influenced by the dynamic or 'straining' (*epektasis*) onto-logy of Gregory of Nyssa, whose view of God as unanticipated beauty evokes desire in creatures who are drawn on in an unending pilgrimage to the source of beauty, to embrace the infinite. Once again, we have an ontology of participation: the soul thirsts for more of God's beauty, for participation in God's fullness. Participation is not simply noetic in the sense of discursive knowledge, but has to do with virtue, with assimilation to God. At the same time, the union of God with the creature is balanced by an awareness of the ontological difference or disparity between God and creation. For Hart, creaturely participation in the divine nature (2 Pet. 1:14) is always a contingent and analogical participation; the creature cannot become infinite. In a trinitarian context, it is to affirm 'that God is in himself a gift of distance', infinite yet not without form, and whose Being is always 'being given determinatively to the other'.[45] God gives Being to beings, while beings express God's infinite Being by being other than God. This is a reworking of the classical Christian position that God is the source of Being, the source in which every being participates. Being is God's good gift and we can speak of Being's kenotic self-donation in beings. Infinity is depicted not as negating human finitude but, more positively, as divine excess, as that fullness and fecundity that creates and sustains, taking on and transforming the contingent human condition. In sum, Hart offers a theological ontology drawn from patristic sources, including Augustine, Gregory of Nyssa, and Maximus the Confessor, which speaks of God as infinite Being or beauty who embraces all of Being in himself, and creatures as finite beings who exist by participation in this divine plenitude.[46]

Hart offers a persuasive theological vision of the beauty of God's infinity that lies at the heart of the Christian Gospel of peace and one that is grounded in analogical participation in the trinitarian life. Similar to Milbank, he contrasts this narrative of peace with a story of violence which he associates with much postmodern thought. In spite of the impatient and at times vituperative tone – one that ironically runs counter to a Christian rhetoric of peace – this vision shows how theology can never be reduced to the propositional and verbal, but begins with *philokalia* – the love of beauty. It is to acquire a taste for God's beauty enabling us, as Augustine would say, to imitate whom we worship. Theology, on this view, mediates between *theoria* (a contemplative knowing or 'seeing') and *logos* (an analytical knowledge).

---

[45] Ibid., 207 and 214.
[46] For a source book that treats of the intrinsic relationship of truth, goodness, and the vision of God, see Gesa E. Thiessen, ed., *Theological Aesthetics: A Reader* (London: SCM Press, 2004).

What is less developed in Hart is the role of the Spirit in the process of our participation in the divine nature. True, he acknowledges that the Spirit is not simply the love of Father and Son, not just the bond of love, but the one who breaks the bonds of self-love. The Spirit completes and perfects the love of Father and Son not only immanently, but economically as a kind of second intonation or second difference (Milbank) of that love. Echoes of Richard of St Victor are evident here – the love of two persons is never exclusive but always seeks a third to share that love. At stake is the personal character or distinct identity of the Spirit. If the Spirit is only depicted as the reciprocal relationality between Father and Son, we end up with a latent binitarianism or bipolarism. Yet our participation in God, as Rom. 8 attests, is effected by the indwelling Spirit. The Spirit is the means by which we are assimilated to Christ (see Chapter 2) and incorporated into the trinitarian life. It is through the Spirit, as Athanasius writes, that we are partakers of God, 'for inasmuch as we partake of the Spirit, we have the grace of the Word and, in the Word, the love of the Father' (*Letters to Serapion* 3.6).[47]

Moreover, following Augustine, the Spirit is the gift of God (*donum Dei*), the gift of our common participation in the Trinity (2 Cor. 13:13). The category of gift or donation is key in the trinitarian ontology of our final theologian in this section, John Milbank. Milbank, in dialogue with philosophers including Marion, Derrida, and Heidegger, as well as with the theology of Augustine, Gregory of Nyssa, and Pseudo-Dionysius, wants to show that there is 'a transcendental "giving" in all things' – we cannot assume that 'things are apart from their capacity to give themselves'.[48] The original, creative donation is that of God who 'gives to be', who gives Being out of his plenitude, while we receive (as a gift) and participate in Being. Creation is God's gratuitous giving of existence, including difference. God is a God who differentiates while encompassing and including every difference. But this difference or, more accurately, this harmony of difference applies firstly to the Trinity. The 'first difference' – a move from unity to difference – is the Son, the expressive articulation of God, while the 'second difference' refers to the Holy Spirit, the interpretation, reception, and response to this

---

[47] For a development of a participative or incorporative trinitarianism, see Sarah Coakley, 'Why Three? Some Further Reflections on the Origins of the Doctrine of the Trinity', in Sarah Coakley and David Pailin, eds., *The Making and Remaking of Christian Doctrine: Essays in Honour of Maurice Wiles* (Oxford: Clarendon Press, 1993), 29–56.

[48] John Milbank, 'Can a Gift be Given? Prolegomena to a Future Trinitarian Metaphysic', *Modern Theology* 11 (1995): 121.

expression.[49] The love between Father and Son is communicated through the Spirit and exceeds or overflows outwards into creation. Inspired by the 'musical' ontology of Augustine's *De Musica*, Milbank posits the Trinity as a '"musical" harmony of infinity', a community in process, within whose perpetual mutual exchange we analogically but actively participate 'such that the divine gift only begins to be gift to us at all ... *after* it has been received – which is to say returned with the return of gratitude'.[50]

Milbank has sought to establish Being as originally gift, a gift from God, reflected in creation. Moreover, he sees creation and redemption in terms of a trinitarian 'gift exchange'. There is reciprocity in that we receive God's gift of love while at the same time actively extending *agape* towards our neighbour. *Pace* Derrida for whom the gift is but the passing away of time, Milbank shows how Christian *agape* constitutes a purified gift-exchange. It transcends contractual obligations but neither is it unilateral: a good gift always elicits something in return, for example, gratitude and delight. *Pace* Marion, a gift is not constituted by distance alone – that would be too unilateral. Rather, gratitude, receptivity, and reciprocity constitute our being as creatures, are revealed in the life and death of Jesus, and are grounded in the giving and receiving of intradivine love, the inner-trinitarian exchange. Milbank's relational ontology of the gift is, therefore, rooted in the Trinity, specifically, in God's gift of the Spirit as *the* gift. Gift and relation are coincidental – the Spirit *is* the gift of relationship of Father to Son. The trinitarian circle of love is not self-enclosed, however, but is oriented outwards by the Spirit. The Spirit thus interprets or reshapes the dialogue of love between Father and Son. For our part, we too receive 'and receive through our participatory giving in turn ... This is the one given condition of the gift, that we love because God first loved us.'[51]

Milbank's ontology of participation holds that what most belongs to beings, namely, their very existence, is received as a gift. Yet this is not at the expense of the integrity and autonomy of creation. Inspired by the Christian metaphysics of Balthasar and the latter's development of the *analogia entis*, the relationship between God and creation is neither one of complete similarity nor complete dissimilarity. The human subject is a real partner in the God–human relationship. But this participation is more than simply a sharing in the Being and knowledge of God. Milbank extends it to

---

[49] John Milbank, 'Postmodern Critical Augustinianism: A Short *Summa* in Forty-Two Responses to Unasked Questions', in Ward, ed., *The Postmodern God*, 274. See also John Milbank, *Theology and Social Theory: Beyond Secular Reason* (Oxford: Blackwell, 1993), 423–4.

[50] Milbank, 'Can a Gift be Given?', 136.   [51] Ibid., 154.

language, history, and culture – the realm of human making.[52] Such *poesis* does not estrange us from God but constitutes our way of expressing and analogically participating in God's continuous creativity. This is an ontology that wants to show how it is possible to be both receptive and donating. It culminates in the liturgy where we receive the life of all three Persons in and through our worship – an 'active reception whereby in receiving we actively become what we receive: the triune God'.[53]

In Milbank's account of the Trinity and creation, differences are subsumed or drawn into an intrinsic divine harmony. This priority of harmony connotes a 'high' Trinity to which the created realm is 'lifted up' so as to participate in the trinitarian circulation of love. But this vision is also related to an explicitly anti-modern agenda. Not unlike Barth's condemnation of liberal theology, Milbank dismisses what he sees as the compromising strategies of correlation and mediation evident in 'modern' theologians including Rahner, Metz, and Gutiérrez. In effect, he is re-appropriating Augustine's *City of God* to the extent that the heavenly city, a harmonious community of love, is played off against the earthly city of conflict and strife. Two different worlds are irreconcilably and antagonistically set against each other. But such an agonistic portrayal is at odds with a Christian doctrine of creation, where reality is viewed as fundamentally good, while sin and evil are considered secondary realities. We might point out that Christians are 'citizens of both cities' (Vatican II, *Gaudium et Spes*, n. 43), and thus critics have seen in Milbank's project 'the danger of setting the common life of the Church too dramatically apart from the temporal ways in which the good is realized in a genuinely contingent world'.[54]

Milbank's depiction of the religious and secular spheres as competing hegemonic narratives reflects much of the tone of the Radical Orthodoxy movement of which he is part. Unfortunately, this exclusivist, oppositional, and ultimately dualist approach cannot acknowledge any value in secular or non-Christian discourse. These are dismissed as nihilistic. More positively, Milbank's ontological vision discloses a self-donating God, a first giver, who gifts reality to us, while the created temporal world, in its receptive and grateful response, participates in God's infinity. Yet the temporal implications of the notion of participation appear to be restricted to a kind of

---

[52] John Milbank, *Being Reconciled: Ontology and Pardon* (London: Routledge, 2003), ix.
[53] John Milbank, 'Gregory of Nyssa: The Force of Identity', in Lewis Ayres and Gareth Jones, eds., *Christian Origins: Theology, Rhetoric and Community* (London: Routledge, 1998), 105.
[54] Rowan Williams, 'A Theological Critique of Milbank', in Robin Gill, ed., *Theology and Sociology: A Reader*, new and enlarged edn (London: Cassell, 1996), 440. See also Fergus Kerr's chapter, 'Milbank's Thesis', 429–34, in the same volume.

aesthetic theological 'gaze' on history and society. But can aesthetics be isolated from *praxis*? Is a purely contemplative theology that gazes from the standpoint of eternity not in danger of becoming totally a-historical?[55] Milbank's repudiation of liberation theology, its social analysis 'from below', from the perspective of the victims, and its struggle for social justice is replaced by an idealised and romanticised notion of Church as the goal of salvation.

Both Milbank and Hart point to our participation in the Trinity, yet it is not always clear what this entails. Briefly, this metaphor, which has biblical and patristic roots in the terms 'deification' and *theosis*, refers to our gradual transformation (primarily by grace but also through ascetic effort) into likeness to God. Paul employed various expressions to describe this participatory union including 'in Christ' and 'with Christ', while the Johannine community had the idea of the incarnate *Logos* as the source of eternal life in which believers participate even now. Indeed, deification would be seen, particularly in the Alexandrian tradition, as the counterpart of the incarnation. Deification is the purpose or consequence of the incarnation. For their part, the Cappadocians connect the term with the imitation of Christ and the practice of virtue that transform and perfect the believer. The 'putting on' of Christ in baptism and the moral life deify. In the West, the main figure is Augustine, who presents the attainment of divine likeness, 'to become like God' (*City of God* 19.23.4), as the goal of the Christian journey. The purpose of creation is union with God. For the human person it is a participation in the Son's relationship with the Father.[56] Andrew Louth has shown how deification permeates the whole pattern of Orthodox theology, even if the term did not play a central role in the West from about the twelfth century. It is not a transcending but a fulfilment of what it means to be human. At the same time, creatures remain creatures; we cannot take on the nature of God.[57]

In sum, gift and participation, divine giving and human participatory response, comprise Milbank's theological vision. He depicts a triune God as pure giving and receiving in an eternal perichoretic communion or

---

[55] Georges De Schrijver, 'The Use of Mediations in Theology or, the Expanse and Self-Confinement of a Theology of the Trinity', in Jacques Haers et al., eds., *Mediations in Theology: Georges De Schrijver's Wager and Liberation Theologies* (Leuven: Peeters, 2003), 55.

[56] Modern writers also present participation in the divine nature as the goal of the Christian life. See Norman Russell, *The Doctrine of Deification in the Greek Patristic Tradition* (Oxford: Oxford University Press, 2004), 312–20.

[57] Andrew Louth, 'The Place of *Theosis* in Orthodox Theology', in Michael J. Christensen and Jeffery A. Wittung, eds., *Partakers of the Divine Nature: The History and Development of Deification in the Christian Traditions* (Grand Rapids, MI: Baker Academic, 2007), 32–44.

harmonious difference into which humanity is invited.[58] God's being is in giving, though Milbank also underlines that gift is a gift-exchange. God's superabundant donation promotes our responsibility for returning the gift, an active reception of self-giving love.

THE TRINITY AND RELIGIOUS PLURALISM

At first sight the Trinity appears an unlikely topic for dialogue with other faiths, especially the strongly monotheistic faiths of Judaism and Islam. Is it not the last piece of theological 'baggage' one would want to introduce into a dialogue between religions? Yet scholars working in this area consistently broach the question whether the Trinity can be a resource rather than a problem for inter-faith dialogue. Some hold that 'the Trinity provides the deep Christian grammar for relating particularity with universality'.[59] If the incarnation constitutes the particularity and apex of God's self-revelation in history, the divine self-communication is not exhausted by that historical appearance. Rather, the active and universal presence of the Spirit spreads and completes the effects of the Christ event throughout the world. Accepting the Trinity as a datum of Christian faith – with its concomitant claims of particularity and universality – is not to denigrate other faiths which do not share the doctrine. On the contrary, it is to see in the mutual interdependence and openness of the three divine Persons in the Trinity a basis and inspiration for interaction with 'the Other', with people of other religions. It is to assume that personal commitment to one's own faith and openness to the faith of others need not be mutually exclusive. This raises a more fundamental question whether the phenomenon of religious plurality is part of God's multifaceted plan for humankind, and, if so, how the religious traditions of others constitute for them a way of salvation.[60]

Traditionally Christianity did not consider inter-religious dialogue as an imperative, and such negative theological assessments of other religions persisted right into the twentieth century. Truth and grace in other faiths

---

[58] By arrogating the divine gift to the whole Trinity, however, the distinct identity of the Spirit, who traditionally in the West is the specific *hypostasis* of 'gift' and 'love', can be eclipsed.

[59] S. Mark Heim, *Salvations: Truth and Difference in Religion* (Maryknoll, NY: Orbis Books, 1995), 167–8. See also Gavin D'Costa, 'Christ, the Trinity, and Religious Plurality', in Gavin D'Costa, ed., *Christian Uniqueness Reconsidered: The Myth of a Pluralistic Theology* (Maryknoll, NY: Orbis Books, 1990), 16–29; and his *The Meeting of Religions and the Trinity* (Edinburgh: T&T Clark, 2000), 1–15, 99–142.

[60] Jacques Dupuis, *Toward a Christian Theology of Religious Pluralism* (New York: Orbis Books, 1997, 2000). See also Michel Barnes, *Theology and the Dialogue of Religions* (Cambridge: Cambridge University Press, 2002).

were, at most, reduced to 'seeds' or 'stepping stones' superseded by Christian revelation. The tendency was to repress difference, to predefine the other, to dismiss other religions as heresies or as a theological problem to be solved. This stance, at best one of tolerance, gradually gave way to more positive attitudes of openness and dialogue. With the revival of trinitarian theology the plurality and diversity inherent in the inner-trinitarian life can be seen as a support for such dialogue. At issue is whether the doctrine of the Trinity, by questioning the assumption that oneness and difference are mutually exclusive categories, or, more positively, by emphasising oneness and threeness as equally ultimate, can serve as a resource for dealing with the problems and challenges of religious diversity.[61] Before turning to this issue, we will discuss three approaches[62] to other religions as a context for the discussion, positions that cut across confessional boundaries. We will note the limitations of each and finally look at some recent trinitarian attempts that offer a way forward.

A first response has been termed 'exclusivist', and it stresses the explicit proclamation and confession of Christ. This conviction inspired the myriad missionary impulses of previous centuries and stressed the necessity of the Church for salvation. It emphasised the contrast and discontinuity between Christianity and other religions. The chequered history of Christian mission notwithstanding, the strength of the exclusivist position lies in its affirmation that salvation comes from Christ alone to a humanity estranged from God. It is not surprising to find advocates of this stance in Lutheran and Calvinist circles as well as in evangelical and Pentecostal churches. The other side of the basic incongruence between a sovereign God and sinful humanity is that salvation is an utterly unmerited and gratuitous gift. Some have labelled Karl Barth's attitude towards other religions exclusivist, though his position is actually more nuanced.[63] He offered a theology of religion rather than of religions. Barth's main critique of late nineteenth-century liberal theology was that it had put human religion on a par with divine revelation. To start with religion, he claimed, is to start with the human person and their grasping after truth. Thus he characterised religion

---

[61] Kevin J. Vanhoozer, ed., *The Trinity in a Pluralistic Age: Theological Essays on Culture and Religion* (Grand Rapids, MI: Eerdmans, 1997), x.

[62] This typology was introduced by Alan Race, *Christians and Religious Pluralism: Patterns in the Christian Theology of Religions* (London: SCM Press, 1983) and taken up by Gavin D'Costa, *Theology and Religious Pluralism: The Challenge of Other Religions* (London: Blackwell, 1986).

[63] J. A. Di Noia, 'Religion and the Religions', in John Webster, ed., *The Cambridge Companion to Karl Barth* (Cambridge: Cambridge University Press, 2000), 243–57; and Veli-Matti Kärkkäinen, *Trinity and Religious Pluralism: The Doctrine of the Trinity in Christian Theology of Religions* (Aldershot: Ashgate, 2004), 13–27.

as primarily a self-centred human construct, equating it with idolatry and contrasting it with divine revelation which is an act of divine justification or forgiveness of sins. Of ourselves we are unable to apprehend the truth or to reach God; hence the priority of revelation over religion or 'to let God be God and our Lord' (*CD* I/2, 302). In short, the grace of revelation, the yielding to the judgement of God and his saving power, leads to the sublation (*Aufhebung*) of religion. Revelation delivers a negative judgement on human religious endeavour, but only with a view to raising humanity up to a new level on the pattern of Christ.[64] Moreover, no religion is 'true', for Barth; it must become true. The Christian religion is true similar to the way we can speak of the 'justified sinner', that is, in virtue of the justifying grace of God. It is true to the extent that it listens to the divine revelation – God's gracious entry into human history – and finds its justification in its relationship to Jesus Christ. Again, this relationship is not something Christianity has chosen for itself but results from divine election.

If there is no basis for self-justification in religion, since religions fall not under human judgement but under the judgement of God, then neither can Christians denigrate or devalue other forms of human religiosity. Rather, their attitude will be one of reverence and tolerance, since 'there must always be a place for reverence for human greatness' (*CD* I/2, 301), while at the same time Christianity will not desist from proclaiming its conviction that Jesus Christ 'is the one and only light of life' (*CD* IV/3, 86). Alongside this Christological affirmation, Barth believed that Christ can speak outside the ambit of the Church. That no other words can be set beside the one Word of God 'does not mean … there are not other words which are quite notable in their way, other lights which are quite clear and other revelations which are quite real' (*CD* IV/3, 97).

While Barth's position is not one that dismisses the value of other religions, there is nevertheless a tension in his trinitarian theology between what has been termed his 'revelational restrictivism' or particularity and his 'soteriological universalism'.[65] In fact, the three theological responses to other religions that we are considering revolve around the weight of emphasis given to the *particularity* of Christian revelation on the one hand and the *universality* of God's grace and salvific will on the other.

---

[64] Trevor Hart, 'Karl Barth, the Trinity, and Pluralism', in Vanhoozer, ed., *The Trinity in a Pluralistic Age*, 132.

[65] Kärkkäinen, *Trinity and Religious Pluralism*, 14. Kärkkäinen's judgement (p. 20) is apposite here: 'Barth's restrictivism does not arise so much from the need to place Christianity in contradistinction to other religions, but rather out of his criticism of religions in general, especially the anthropocentric orientation of Classical Liberalism.'

Barth's theology is of course profoundly Christocentric – whatever lights exist outside Christianity must be measured against the definitive revelation given through Christ – yet he holds that the incarnation reveals a God of love and mercy who desires the salvation of all.

A rigorously exclusivist position, therefore, is hard to defend since, despite its insistence on the centrality of the Christ-event, this cannot be taken in isolation. In our view, there is a *trinitarian* rhythm to the divine economy: God's self-communication occurs through the Word and the Spirit. Recent writing in this area has thus focussed on a trinitarian Christology, including a Spirit Christology. Christology and pneumatology do not represent two separate economies of God's dealings with human-kind. Rather, the Father is known through Christ and the Spirit – the two hands of the Father's love.[66] Trinitarian Christology tries to reconcile the exclusivist emphasis on the particularity of Christ with an emphasis on God's universal activity in history.

At the other end of the spectrum of theological responses is what has been called the 'pluralist' position. In contrast to the exclusivist claim that only one religion or revelation can be true, the Christian pluralist puts all the major religions on a par with Christianity in that each contains an equal salvific potential for its adherents. There is more than one way to salvation. This, in effect, is to renounce any claims to the superiority of one's own religious tradition. All traditions are said to be relative and thus no one religion can claim privileged access to definitive truth. Two pioneers of this position are John Hick and, more recently, Paul Knitter. Though Hick's theological writings have focussed on the incarnation, these impact on his understanding of the Trinity and its significance (or otherwise) for inter-religious dialogue. Behind Hick's re-interpretation of the classical doctrines of the incarnation and Trinity is a wish to move away from 'religious absolutism' or, more specifically, 'the Christian superiority complex', towards an acknowledgement that salvation also occurs in other faith traditions.[67] Faced with competing claims to religious truth, the pluralist tries to promote tolerance, or better, mutual respect and appreciation among the different religious traditions. Allied to this vision of inter-religious harmony, however, is a revisionist theological and epistemological strategy. No longer are other religions to be regarded as revolving around

---

[66] N. A. Nissiotis, 'Pneumatologie orthodoxe', in F. J. Leenhardt et al., *Le Saint-Esprit* (Geneva: Labor et Fides, 1963), 93, cited by Dupuis, *Toward a Christian Theology of Religious Pluralism*, 207.

[67] John Hick, 'The Non-Absoluteness of Christianity', in John Hick and Paul F. Knitter, eds., *The Myth of Christian Uniqueness* (Maryknoll, NY: Orbis Books, 1987), 18.

Christianity and Christ, but around God or the Divine 'Real', marking a shift from Christocentrism and ecclesiocentrism to theocentrism. The many religious traditions, while having different ways of conceiving their relation to the ultimate divine Real, share a similar soteriological pattern which can be summed up in terms of a transformation of human existence 'from self-centredness to Reality-centredness'.[68] And given the assumption of a parity between the religions, it is not surprising that some pluralists advocate a 'world' or 'universal' theology of religions that takes its data from the various faith traditions.[69]

To offset traditional Christian claims about the uniqueness and centrality of the Christ event, Hick develops a metaphorical Christology that depicts Jesus as the embodiment of divine love. His counterparts are the religious founders, prophets and teachers in other religions. His divinity is to be understood in a mythological sense – as a kind of practical truth that evokes in us an appropriate disposition and response.[70] Critics have, not surprisingly, detected here a reductionist view of traditional Christological claims – Jesus is presented more in terms of a guru than a saviour.[71] What we have is an instrumentalist view of religious language and a functional view of doctrine that bypasses truth claims about the ontological reality of Jesus as divine saviour. Hick takes his epistemological model from Kant and the latter's distinction between the noumenal and phenomenal world. God, the 'Eternal One' or 'Ultimate Reality' belongs to the noumenal sphere beyond human comprehension – we cannot know the Real *an sich* or make any objective statements about it. Instead, the Ultimate Reality is manifested in different ways in the great world faiths: as Israel's Yahweh, the heavenly Father of Christian faith, the Allah of Islamic faith, the Hindu Krishna, and so on. This generic or pluralistic conception of God is not identified with any particular religion. It is a position outside or above existing religious traditions. But we might ask if this is not a 'flight from particularity', an attempt 'to occlude and erase the particularities of history and the uniqueness of religious traditions'?[72] When it comes to the Trinity, Hick's position is modalistic: there is no threeness in the Godhead. In his view we should not conceive the Trinity 'as ontologically three but as three ways in which

[68] John Hick, *Problems of Religious Pluralism* (London: Macmillan, 1985), 91.
[69] See N. Ross Reat and Edmund F. Perry, *A World Theology: The Central Spiritual Reality of Humankind* (Cambridge: Cambridge University Press, 1991).
[70] John Hick, *God and the Universe of Faiths* (London: Fount/Collins, 1977), 166–7.
[71] Stephen T. Davis, 'John Hick on Incarnation and Trinity', in Stephen T. Davis, Daniel Kendall, and Gerald O'Collins, eds., *The Trinity: An Interdisciplinary Symposium on the Trinity* (Oxford: Oxford University Press, 1999), 267.
[72] D'Costa, *The Meeting of Religions and the Trinity*, 28, 29.

the one God is humanly thought and experienced'.[73] From a Christian perspective we cannot rest content with a position that is finally agnostic, one that says very little about the ultimate transcendent Reality. One would want to go further to claim that the triune God is not one manifestation or appearance (among others) of ultimate Reality but is the ultimate Reality itself, an interpersonal communion. Or, in more familiar language, that the economic Trinity is the immanent Trinity. Not that we can penetrate the mystery of God, but the divine Trinity revealed through the Son and the Spirit is a true, though analogical, correspondence to the inner reality of God. Theology cannot bypass the structure of salvation history as revealed in the Bible and replace it with a more abstract theory based on a phenomenology of religions.

For his part, Paul Knitter is a supporter of Hick's project, tracing a similar autobiographical path from exclusivism to pluralism in his assessment of other religions. But he goes further in linking pluralism with liberation.[74] A theology of religions must be linked to a theology of liberation. Dialogue and liberation are part of the one agenda: the need for a new global ethic and the promotion of peace, for inter-religious cooperation in the face of the suffering of others, particularly suffering caused by religiously motivated violence. Knitter describes his approach as 'correlational' – a way of interacting with other religions that avoids the absolutisms of the past. It is in line with Hans Küng's plea for a dialogue among religions where the 'religious communities of the world ... come together to recognise a minimal basis of shared values, norms, fundamental principles, and ideals'.[75] Moreover, Knitter believes that any claim to religious superiority not only undermines dialogue, but fuels religious violence.

Like Hick, Knitter does not employ trinitarian categories in his discussion of religious pluralism but focusses on a re-interpretation of the uniqueness of Jesus. Briefly, Jesus is one saviour among other saviours; it is not necessary, therefore, to insist on Jesus as the *only* mediator of God's grace in history. Knitter does not deny that Jesus is truly a bringer of salvation, but he wants to endorse the probability that there are '*other* universal, decisive, indispensable manifestations of divine reality besides Jesus'.[76] Jesus defines

---

[73] John Hick, *The Metaphor of God Incarnate: Christ and Christology in a Pluralistic Age* (Louisville, KY: Westminster/John Knox Press, 1993), 149.

[74] Paul F. Knitter, *One Earth Many Religions: Multifaith Dialogue and Global Responsibility* (Maryknoll, NY: Orbis Books, 1995), 1–22.

[75] Hans Küng, 'Foreword', in Knitter, *One Earth Many Religions*, xi.

[76] Paul F. Knitter, *Jesus and the Other Names: Christian Mission and Global Responsibility* (Maryknoll, NY: Orbis Books, 1996), 79.

but does not confine God. Notwithstanding the merits of Knitter's correlational model of interfaith dialogue, his project reveals similar shortcomings to those of Hick. Again, there is a pragmatic or practical view of religious truth: religions that promote human well-being, conceived primarily in terms of socio-political engagement, are channels of salvation. But not all religious traditions (including Christianity) circumscribe their view of salvation in this way. Different religious traditions make conflicting truth claims and, while Knitter concedes religions may well be pursuing different ultimate ends, he wants to bring out 'that there is something common, something universal, something more than just our differences'.[77] Despite their differences, the world religions are more complementary than contradictory. Yet Knitter's struggle to incorporate traditional doctrinal claims about Jesus, such as his indispensability and uniqueness, is subordinated to his project of inter-religious dialogue and points up the limitations of his Christology. On the one hand, Jesus is indispensable in terms of a decisive message he brings that enriches our lives. He represents or embodies God's saving love; he is God's true but not only saving word.[78] But God can and does speak elsewhere in other saviour figures. This representative or functional Christology restricts Jesus to being God's representative. It overlooks the key Christian conviction that in Jesus God communicates God's very self. In this unique case the signifier is the signified.[79] An ontological Christology will want to affirm the personal identity of Jesus as *the* Son of God.

Knitter is to be commended, however, in calling for Christology and a theology of religions to be more informed by a theology of the Holy Spirit. A better balance is required between the economy of the Word in Jesus and the economy of the Spirit.[80] In the previous chapter we noted the Orthodox criticism of Western theology's subordination of the Spirit to the Word, sometimes called 'Christomonism'. Contemporary theology has seen an attempt to redress this imbalance: to affirm a real difference but also reciprocity between Word and Spirit. This leads us back to our original question, whether a trinitarian theology, with an emphasis on the universal

---

[77] Paul F. Knitter, 'Is the Pluralist Model a Western Imposition? A Response in Five Voices', in Paul F. Knitter, ed., *The Myth of Religious Superiority: Multifaith Explorations of Religious Pluralism* (Maryknoll, NY: Orbis Books, 2005), 39.

[78] Paul F. Knitter, 'Five Theses on the Uniqueness of Jesus', in Leonard Swidler and Paul Mojzes, eds., *The Uniqueness of Jesus: A Dialogue with Paul F. Knitter* (Maryknoll, NY: Orbis Books, 1997), 14.

[79] D'Costa, *The Meeting of Religions and the Trinity*, 36.

[80] Paul F. Knitter, 'Can our "One and Only" also be a "One among Many"?' in Swidler and Mojzes, eds., *The Uniqueness of Jesus*, 179.

presence of the Spirit who sows the seeds of the Word in various peoples and cultures, can in fact be a paradigm for a Christian theology of religions.

A third type of response, namely, 'inclusivism', needs to be mentioned before we address this issue. The inclusivist position can be seen as a kind of *via media* between exclusivism and pluralism. In its earlier versions it took the form of a 'fulfilment theory': non-Christian religions represent a kind of natural religion and have a propaedeutic value insofar as they are a *preparatio evangelica* to be superseded by God's (supernatural) revelation in Christ. But the challenge of a more positive construal of other religions' relationship to Christianity persisted, particularly with the increased knowledge and appreciation of the great religious traditions, including Hinduism, Buddhism, and Islam. Thus, a second version of the inclusivist position, more open to other religions, acknowledged that these continue to have salvific value 'by virtue of the operative presence in them ... of the saving mystery of Jesus Christ'.[81] It is this second version which influenced the emerging theology of religions in the second half of the twentieth century, with Karl Rahner's inclusivism and his controversial notion of the 'anonymous Christian' to the forefront.

Rahner's development of 'anonymous Christianity' stems not so much from an explicitly trinitarian basis but from his renewal of the theology of grace within Catholic theology using interpersonal categories. Not happy with the traditional dichotomy between nature and grace, where grace was viewed extrinsically, superimposed as a second (supernatural) level on human nature, Rahner reinterpreted grace as the immediate indwelling of God in the human person: God's self-gift. God does not confer merely human gifts as a token of God's love but communicates *God's self*.[82] One is enabled to share in the very nature of God. There is, moreover, a fundamental structure, a 'supernatural existential', built into humanity by God that orients every person towards accepting God's offer of grace, and yet one must receive this as free gift. As noted in the last chapter, Rahner developed a transcendental anthropology around this assumption that the desire for God is a constitutive element of every human person. In his view, 'there is no form of human living in which an encounter with God does not take place at least anonymously, non-thematically, and transcendentally'.[83]

[81] Dupuis, *Toward a Christian Theology of Religious Pluralism*, 132.

[82] Karl Rahner, 'Grace', in *Sacramentum Mundi: An Encyclopedia of Theology*, 6 vols. (New York: Herder and Herder, 1968–70), vol. II, 415.

[83] Karl Rahner, 'Theological Considerations on Secularization and Atheism', in *Theological Investigations*, vol. XVI (London: Darton, Longman and Todd, 1979), 176.

Rahner's reinterpretation of grace was also evident in his stress on the universality of God's saving will. No longer was grace scarce or seen as exclusively mediated through one religion; on the contrary, no sphere of human life was excluded from the saving presence of God. Such optimism about salvation led him to ask whether Christians could hope that the majority of humanity will, in fact, attain salvation. Rahner's work led to a more positive conception of the relationship between Christianity and other religions, paving the way for a Christian vision of a kingdom of grace beyond the Church. It would become an axiom of post-Vatican II Catholic theology that salvation is available to all people of good will (*Gaudium et Spes*, 22). Rahner claimed that when members of other religious traditions accept their transcendental openness to God and practise a radical and selfless love of neighbour, they are living out a form of anonymous Christianity. 'There are supernatural, grace-filled elements in non-Christian religions', and so 'it would be wrong to regard the pagan as someone who has not yet been touched in any way by God's grace and truth'.[84]

Not that anonymous Christianity has the final word. Rahner's theology of nature and grace oscillates between acknowledging an implicit, unthematic, and transcendental experience of God and the need for this experience to become more explicit, thematic, and historical. There is explicit as well as anonymous faith. Members of other religious traditions may well live out an implicit or anonymous Christianity, but Rahner insists such implicit faith carries an intrinsic dynamism towards full and explicit realisation. Anonymous Christianity is his attempt to portray the tension between the particularity of Christianity on the one hand and God's universal salvific will on the other. It is also connected with his 'searching Christology': humankind is searching history for a bearer of salvation and a genuine searcher may find what he or she is seeking in Christ. Rahner's anthropology, including his analysis of the transcendental orientation of the human person as a questioner, as oriented to mystery, issues in Christology. God's universal salvific will has a Christological referent: God's self-communication to humanity reaches its climax in the event of Jesus Christ, the definitive, irreversible, and eschatological revelation of God. In him, the transcendental openness to God is fully realised. Historical particularity converges with universal significance. Ultimately, for Rahner, anonymous Christianity remains a partial, unfulfilled reality that requires an explicit Christocentric, and ecclesial focus for its completion.

---

[84] Karl Rahner, 'Christianity and the Non-Christian Religions', in *Theological Investigations*, vol. v (London: Darton, Longman and Todd, 1966), 121, 131.

Rahner's theory has, of course, been criticised as presumptuous, as a form of Christian imperialism which sees the religious other only as an implicit reflection and lesser version of Christianity rather than as genuinely other. Other religions are viewed as stepping-stones, finding their fulfilment in explicit Christianity, while their saviour figures only anticipate or point to Christ. Moreover, in positing an underlying sameness to how various religions experience God, Rahner tends to downplay the real differences between the religions. As Francis X. Clooney has noted, Rahner's consistent attention to the nuances of the Christian tradition is not matched by a similar care for the nuances in other religious traditions.[85] Further, Balthasar and others claim that Rahner is insufficiently Christocentric, thus undermining the newness of the event of Jesus Christ and neglecting the biblical narrative that grounds the specific form of Christian disciple-ship. On the other hand, pluralists like Paul Knitter argue that Rahner is *too* Christocentric in stressing the singularity of Jesus to the detriment of other possible incarnations and saviour figures. If one set of critiques highlights the distinctiveness of Christianity in the face of a universalism that threatens to erase its particularity, another posits a plurality of 'true' religious tradi-tions, each with different concepts of ultimate Reality, yet each with moral and spiritual fruits similar to those of Christian faith and experience and with equal salvific value for their particular adherents.

In sum, Rahner's position is inclusivist in that all salvation comes through Christ. All people are 'included' in Christ's saving work. Christ's operative presence is concealed and implicit in non-Christian religions, explicit and conscious in Christianity. His starting with God's universal salvific will means he acknowledges a saving function to pre-Christian and non-Christian religions, while highlighting the significance of moving from an anonymous or transcendental experience of grace to a more explicit interpretation and appropriation in the context of Christian faith. Yet despite Rahner's distinction between transcendental and categorical reve-lation, what is less clear is the connection between his Christology and pneumatology. He often conflates the terms 'experience of God', 'experi-ence of transcendence', 'experience of the Holy Spirit', and 'experience of grace'. In conceding that 'Christ is present and efficacious in the non-Christian believer through his Spirit',[86] he is implying that the Spirit cannot

---

[85] Francis X. Clooney, 'Rahner beyond Rahner: A Comparative Theologian's Reflections on *Theological Investigations* 18', in Paul G. Crowley, ed., *Rahner beyond Rahner: A Great Theologian Encounters the Pacific Rim* (Lanham, MD: Rowman & Littlefield, 2005), 8.

[86] Karl Rahner, 'Jesus Christ in the Non-Christian Religions', in *Theological Investigations*, vol. XVII (London: Darton, Longman and Todd, 1981), 43.

be confined to Christianity. His is an attempt to combine the axioms of God's universal salvific will and the necessary mediation of Christ, while remaining conscious of Eastern criticisms of the 'Christomonism' of the West. Later theologians, including Jacques Dupuis and Gavin D'Costa, taking their cue from Rahner, Congar, and others, develop a more explicitly trinitarian theology of religions with a greater insistence on the role of the Spirit in the economy of salvation.

For Dupuis, Christology and pneumatology go hand in hand as complementary elements within the one economy of salvation. He affirms the unbounded influence of the Spirit, who 'blows where it wills', (John 3:8), while relating the Spirit's presence and action to Christ. 'The Spirit of God is, at one and the same time the Spirit of Christ, communicated by him by virtue of his resurrection from the dead. The cosmic influence of the Spirit cannot be severed from the universal action of the risen Christ.'[87] Yet just as the work of the Spirit in history did not begin with, nor is it limited to being given by, the risen Christ, neither is the *Logos* of God limited by its historical becoming in Christ. The Word made flesh in Jesus is not the only form of God's appearance in the world. In Chapter 2 we saw how God's Word or *Logos* operated prior to the *Logos* in the flesh as a personification of God's salvific will and action in the world. The hypostatic identities of, and order of relationships between, the Son and Spirit within the immanent Trinity must be respected and are mirrored in their distinct but related 'missions' in the economy.

If Christ and the Spirit cannot be separated, neither should Christ and God be set in opposition. Dupuis refuses to choose between the alternatives of Christocentrism or theocentrism, or between inclusivism and pluralism. The Christian tradition is Christocentric not in putting Jesus in the place of God, but in recognising that in him we reach the culmination of God's saving plan for humanity, the climax of God's engagement with the peoples of the world. But the revelation in Jesus does not exhaust the mystery of God. We have seen how the exclusivist stress on the particularity of Christ can be at the expense of the universality of God's grace, while pluralist positions run in the opposite direction. A trinitarian inclusivism or Christocentric trinitarianism will guard against 'an exclusive identification of God and Jesus' while acknowledging that it is through the Spirit *and* the Son that the Father is disclosed.[88]

---

[87] Dupuis, *Toward a Christian Theology of Religious Pluralism*, 197.
[88] Gavin D'Costa, 'Christ, the Trinity, and Religious Plurality', in Gavin D'Costa, ed., *Christian Uniqueness Reconsidered: The Myth of a Pluralistic Theology* (Maryknoll, NY: Orbis Books, 1990), 18.

Dupuis underscores the unity of God's saving action while also affirming a plurality in God's interaction with humankind, a way of acting that embraces all of human history.[89] His position is best described as 'inclusivist pluralism' – a *via media* between the opposing paradigms of inclusivism and pluralism. Christianity does not possess a monopoly on grace and truth and so ought to be able to acknowledge the salvific value of other religions. Dupuis moves beyond traditional fulfilment theories, where Christianity had nothing to receive but only to give, where so-called 'natural' religions found their fulfilment in 'supernatural' Christianity, to a position of reciprocal complementarity. On this view, dialogue between religious traditions can lead to mutual enrichment and deeper self-understanding. This does not mean putting all religions on the same level, or that there is something lacking in Christian revelation which is filled in by other religions. Rather, Dupuis does not see a contradiction between upholding the fullness of divine revelation in Jesus Christ as universal Saviour and the claim that other religions contain divine truth and grace from which Christians can learn. In this he is following the inspiration of Vatican II, which recognised 'seeds of the Word' enshrined in other religious traditions (*Ad gentes*, n. 11; *Lumen gentium*, n. 17).

Like Dupuis, Gavin D'Costa affirms God's trinitarian presence in other religions. In his opinion, we risk limiting or domesticating the Spirit if we refuse to recognise its presence and activity in other faiths or give non-Christians a narrative space within our theology. There may not only be 'seeds of the Word' in these religions, but shoots and branches as well. D'Costa has described his position as 'open inclusivist' though, latterly, he has expressed reservations about the threefold typology. By the former he means that when Christians say that in Christ they see the fullness of God's revelation, this is not a question of 'possession' but rather of 'being possessed'. There is an eschatological surplus to God's self-revelation in Christ. The claim to know God goes hand in hand with the realisation that this is always an imperfect perception (see 1 Cor. 13:12). D'Costa's reservation about the threefold typology of pluralism, inclusivism, and exclusivism is 'that what we are really dealing with are different forms of *exclusivism*'.[90] Pluralism, though claiming the high ground in its claim to openness and impartiality, conceals a liberal but intolerant agnosticism that erases the differences and particularities of various religions. Religions are *not* all

---

[89] Dupuis, *Toward a Christian Theology of Religious Pluralism*, 316–21.
[90] Gavin D'Costa, 'Theology of Religions', in David Ford and Rachel Muers, eds., *The Modern Theologians: An Introduction to Christian Theology since 1918*, 3rd edn (Oxford: Blackwell, 2005), 638.

saying the same thing. Inclusivism too, D'Costa maintains, shares traits of the exclusivists in finally requiring an explicit confession in the triune God. This description, however, does not square with the more nuanced inclusivism of Dupuis, or that of Rahner before him, and so, in our view, one should be wary of jettisoning the typology altogether as it helps to clarify many of the issues at stake in inter-religious dialogue.

Where D'Costa is on stronger ground is his use of the resources of trinitarian theology to engage with otherness and difference in a way that neither demonises nor assimilates the Other. A trinitarian Christology, where Christ is normative, but not exclusive or absolute, where 'the Spirit blows where it will', invites us to discover something of the Trinity in other religions. As D'Costa puts it, 'A trinitarian Christology guards against exclusivism and pluralism by dialectically relating the universal and the particular', while 'the Holy Spirit allows the particularity of Christ to be related to the universal activity of God in human history'.[91] The Spirit deepens and universalises our understanding of God's work in Christ. This trinitarian perspective is free from the a priori tendencies of pluralism and exclusivism, and calls forth a greater awareness of the active presence of the Spirit and the Word in the other religions. His point is not simply that God speaks outside Christianity, but that through recognising God's Spirit at work in other faiths, Christians penetrate more deeply into the mystery of Christ. Such committed openness will not avoid the complex issue of interpretation and assessment of a particular religion. The plurality of religions calls for a plurality of responses, yet these should always be a posteriori judgements resulting from specific encounters with other faiths. One cannot determine in advance what one will learn from the engagement and dialogue. Finally, D'Costa not only connects the Spirit with Christ, but also with the Church. His historical study of the traditional axiom *extra ecclesiam nulla salus* has shown how this was not intended to be applied indiscriminately to non-Christians but reflects an intra-Christian claim that salvation comes through Christ and his Church.[92]

Both D'Costa and Dupuis combine their commitment to the Trinity as a datum of Christian faith with an openness to the Spirit in other religious traditions. D'Costa, in particular, grounds religious diversity in a trinitarian understanding of God. Rephrasing Rahner's axiom, we could say that the

---

[91] D'Costa, 'Christ, the Trinity, and Religious Plurality', 18, and 'Toward a Trinitarian Theology of Religions', in C. Cornville and V. Neckebrouck, eds., *A Universal Faith? Peoples, Cultures, Religions, and the Christ* (Louvain: Peeters Press, 1992), 150.

[92] Gavin D'Costa, *The Meeting of Religions and the Trinity* (Edinburgh: T&T Clark, 2000), 101–32.

diversity of God's self-manifestations to humanity reflects the diversity within God. The triune God is a perichoretic communion of oneness and diversity, a communion that allows space for otherness and difference. Of course it could be objected that a trinitarian theology of religions is just another example of Christian imperialism. A genuinely trinitarian theology, however, does not elide or erase the differences between faiths, nor refuse to evaluate different narratives, while it also holds that the distinctively Christian identity of God has to be based on the triune God's self-revelation in history. It is convinced that fidelity to the particularity of the Christian tradition goes hand in hand with a respect and reverence for the 'otherness' of other religions, and that study and engagement with the beliefs and practices of other religious traditions contribute to the enrichment of one's own faith.

CONCLUSION: TOWARDS A TRINITARIAN VISION OF REALITY

In the last section we saw how theologians, reflecting on a global situation of religious plurality, explored how the Trinity might offer an appropriate theological framework to engage such religious diversity. Their hope was to remain faithful to the specific claims of the Christian tradition, while valuing the truth and integrity of other faith traditions. While Dupuis and D'Costa have pointed out the challenges and pitfalls of such an undertaking, other pluralist-oriented theologians have forged trinitarian approaches of their own. Thus S. Mark Heim maintains that the communion-in-difference that is the Trinity is reflected among human beings who are likewise constituted for relation to what is other, to what is different. The challenge is to mirror in our human relations something of the Trinity, where relations of asymmetry exist alongside equality. This is similar to D'Costa's position, as is Heim's claim that Christ is not an exclusive or exhaustive source for our knowledge of God.

If there is something in God's revelation in Christ that we will not receive until persons have lived it *through* the contexts of these other religions, then there must be something intrinsically valid about those religions themselves, some providential role for them ... Christ ... is not there only for the salvation of others ... Christ has a mission to the church out of and through the world religions.[93]

---

[93] S. Mark Heim, *The Depth of the Riches: A Trinitarian Theology of Religious Ends* (Grand Rapids, MI: Eerdmans, 2001), 145 and 147.

But Heim goes further in positing a plurality of religious ends or fulfilments for various religious traditions. These different ends are possible because a variety of distinct relations with God is possible. They are grounded in the diversity within the Trinity and providentially ordained by God. 'The plenitude of the universe and of human possibilities within it offer a reflection of its triune source.'[94] That the religions conceive of their particular aims, ends, or fulfilments in quite diverse ways is not in question. Christianity typically presents its end in terms of salvation – communion with, and participation in, the triune life of God – while the ends of other religions, though lesser goods, according to Heim, stand alongside the Christian end. However, Heim's proposal does not tally with the biblical vision of a *common* end intended by God for *all* of humanity in Christ (Eph. 1:10; see also Rev. 21 and 22). It is one thing to say that God's providential purpose for creation works itself out in various ways and to view other religions within such a framework; it is quite another to hold that, based on the diversity within the Trinity, there is a multiplicity of religious ends. Moreover, as Paul Knitter has pointed out, the major religions make not only particular but universal claims: '"Allah", "Brahman", "Nirvana", – as different as they are – are understood by their respective religions to embody the goal not just of one's own community but of all persons.'[95] Heim's somewhat idiosyncratic approach, while eager to respect the distinctiveness of various religious traditions, does not ultimately succeed in linking multiple religious ends with the idea of diversity within the Trinity.

What is intriguing and implicit in Heim's project, however, is a particular trinitarian reading of reality. We have noted a similar dynamic among the variety of theologians discussed in this chapter: from Moltmann's working out of the social implications of the trinitarian concept of *perichoresis*, to Milbank's incipient trinitarian ontology of participation and gift. This trinitarian intuition is reflected in an understanding of personhood and Being grounded in the rhythm of the triune life where communion and relationality are paramount. It suggests a relational anthropology and respect for the alterity of the other, where communion is not at the expense of difference. The shift from the self to the other is similarly evident in an understanding of Being as self-communicating love: to be is to relate – an ontology of reciprocity and mutuality inspired by the Trinity.[96] It is to see

---

[94] S. Mark Heim, *Salvations: Truth and Difference in Religion* (Maryknoll, NY: Orbis Books, 1997), 166.

[95] Paul Knitter, *Introducing Theologies of Religions* (Maryknoll, NY: Orbis Books, 2002), 230–1.

[96] Walter Kasper, *The God of Jesus Christ* (London: SCM Press, 1983), 156. See also Thomas J. Norris, *Living a Spirituality of Communion* (Dublin: The Columba Press, 2008), 120–59.

'person' as constituted by relationship with others, and the nature of God's Being as the communion of Persons. It reflects a social view of the Trinity to the extent that it is not so much the threeness that is stressed as the communion among the three.[97] Following Zizioulas, God's Being is in communion: to be and to be in relation are the same for the divine life. Or in the words of Irish theologian Thomas Norris, 'God is not only being-in-himself, "substance" to use the language of Greek philosophy. He is above all relation. Relation is no longer the weakest of the accidents, but rather expresses something essential – the very life of the Trinity.'[98] This perichoretic emphasis invites a break from styles of thinking and living characterised by individualism and egocentricity. Both Heim and D'Costa would espouse such a trinitarian ontology where Trinity has the character of ultimate Being. For Heim, the Trinity 'provides a particular ground for affirming the truth and reality of what is different', while, for D'Costa, 'a Christocentric trinitarianism discloses loving relationship as the proper mode of being'.[99]

Pertinent here is the perspective of Raimon Panikkar, a leading voice in multi-faith dialogue over many decades, who also sees the Trinity as the ultimate foundation for religious diversity. It is not simply a question of looking for trinitarian patterns or analogues in other traditions, though Panikkar has traced parallels between the Hindu, Buddhist, and Christian faiths. Rather, it is to posit a trinitarian concept of reality where the Trinity is the paradigm for infinite diversity (given that the Persons of the Trinity are infinitely different) and to affirm that this trinitarian conception is not an exclusive Christian insight. Pannikar presents the differences between the religions as a reflection of the irreducible diversity of reality itself. His vision is of a 'mutual fecundation' among religious traditions, a trinitarian *perichoresis* where each religion is a dimension of the others.[100] He calls it a 'cosmotheandric' vision of reality: the divine, the human, and the earthly are the three irreducible dimensions that constitute reality. *Theos-anthropos-cosmos* are invariants of all religions and cultures. This is an 'intuition of the threefold structure of reality, of the triadic oneness existing on all levels of consciousness and of reality', while the Trinity represents the summit of this vision, the truth that 'permeates all realms of being and

---

[97] Heim, *The Depth of the Riches*, 171.

[98] Thomas J. Norris, *A Fractured Relationship: Faith and the Crisis of Culture* (Dublin: Veritas, 2007), 221.

[99] Ibid., 127; and D'Costa, 'Christ, the Trinity and Religious Plurality', 19.

[100] Raimundo Panikkar, *The Unknown Christ of Hinduism*, rev. and enlarged edn (Maryknoll, NY: Orbis Books, 1981), 17.

consciousness',[101] a position reminiscent of the *vestigia Trinitatis* of Augustine. The cosmos mirrors the interrelatedness at the heart of the Trinity. The Trinity is not simply the privilege of the Godhead but 'as pure relation epitomises the radical relativity of all there is'.[102] The radically relational and interdependent nature of reality is one aspect of Panikkar's cosmotheandric vision. Another is that reality is ultimately harmonious, neither a monolithic unity nor disconnected plurality. He points to the paradigm of music and the symbol of 'concord' to describe this triune constitution of reality (though he prefers the term 'theandric' to triune because of its less explicitly Christian connotations). His vision is of a more dialogical relationship between the one and the many: 'Concord is neither oneness nor plurality. It is the dynamism of the Many toward the One without ceasing to be different and without becoming one, and without reaching a higher synthesis.'[103] Applied to inter-religious dialogue, this implies that Christians should acknowledge other traditions in their own right. It is a 'discordant concord', a harmony of many discordant voices of other traditions without reducing them to one voice.[104] It is a departure from 'dialectical dialogue' (which is still a duet of two *logoi*) to 'dialogical dialogue', a process of mutual learning that considers 'the other a true source of understanding and knowledge', and yields a truth transcending *logos*.[105] Panikkar, not unlike Levinas, claims this harmony has been lost in Western theology because of its drive towards 'universal theory'. *Logos* has dominated and subordinated *Spirit*, yet rationality does not exhaustively define human being: 'If the Logos is the transparency of Being, the Spirit is, paradoxically, its opaqueness. The Spirit is freedom, the freedom of Being to be what it is.'[106] This, he believes, represents a non-dualistic (advaitic) attitude that

[101] Raimundo Panikkar, *The Trinity and the Religious Experience of Man: Icon-Person-Mystery* (New York: Orbis; London: Darton, Longman and Todd, 1973), xi. See also his *The Cosmotheandric Experience* (Maryknoll, NY: Orbis Books, 1993), 74.

[102] Panikkar, *The Trinity and the Religious Experience of Man*, xv.

[103] Raimundo Panikkar, 'The Invisible Harmony: A Universal Theory of Religion or a Cosmic Confidence in Reality?', in Leonard Swidler, ed., *Toward a Universal Theology of Religion* (Maryknoll, NY: Orbis Books, 1987), 145.

[104] Ibid., 147. Panikkar also developed the notion of the 'Christic principle', where Christ stands for all humanity and which can be potentially present in any human being. It reiterates his claim that Christ does not belong only to Christianity and that no historical form can be the full and final expression of the universal Christ. The tendency with Panikkar, however, as Kärkkäinen and others have pointed out, is to accentuate the universality of the Christic principle at the expense of the historical particularity of Jesus. Kärkkäinen, *Trinity and Religious Pluralism*, 129.

[105] Raimundo Panikkar, *The Intrareligious Dialogue*, rev. edn (Mahwah, NJ: Paulist Press, 1999), 31.

[106] Raimundo Panikkar, 'The Jordan, the Tiber, and the Ganges: Three Kairological Moments of Christic Self-Consciousness', in Hick and Knitter, eds., *The Myth of Christian Uniqueness*, 109.

better accords with the pluralist nature of reality and allows our convictions to be fecundated by the insights of the other.

Panikkar's remarks about the neglect of the Spirit, especially in Western trinitarian theology, are well taken. Eastern Orthodox theology, in particular, has highlighted the danger of subordinating the work of the Spirit to Christ, accusing Western churches of a faulty 'Christomonism' (partly due to the unilateral addition of the *filioque* clause to the Creed) and a juridicism that jeopardises the freedom of the Spirit. We have already seen how the relationship between Christ and the Spirit is a reciprocal one and how the Spirit in the New Testament always has a 'christological stamp' (Wainwright), yet when the identity of the Spirit is absorbed into that of Christ, it loses something of its distinctiveness. As Rowan Williams puts it in his discussion of Panikkar's work, 'the endless variety of imitations of Christ … is where we recognize the divine action as *spirit* … The fullness of Christ is always *to be* discovered, never there already in a conceptual pattern that explains and predicts everything.'[107] In Panikkar's imaginative language, if the Son is 'the River who flows from the Source, then the Spirit is, as it were, the End, the limitless Ocean where the flux of divine life is completed, rests and is consummated'.[108] For Panikkar, the Spirit represents, firstly, divine immanence by which he means the Ground of Being, the depth of God, the deepest level of the Divinity. Secondly, the Spirit is a mediating and relational term passing from Father to Son and from Son to Father – bringing together while keeping distinct – in the *perichoresis* or dynamic circularity of the Trinity.

It has been further suggested that by starting with the Spirit, with a pneumatic trinitarianism, we can transcend the traditional subordination of the Spirit in the economy of salvation and open the way for a 'Spirit-centred theology of religions'.[109] Such a Spirit-centred theology overcomes the limitations of an overly Christocentric theology by emphasising how the Spirit not only continues the work of Christ but, more generally, represents the creative and redemptive power of God at work in the world – both before and after Christ. In short, the Spirit points to the universality of God, to a God who cannot be neatly captured or domesticated.[110]

---

[107] Rowan Williams, 'Trinity and Pluralism', in D'Costa, ed., *Christian Uniqueness Reconsidered*, 8.

[108] Panikkar, *The Trinity and the Religious Experience of Man*, 63.

[109] Michel Barnes, *Christian Identity and Religious Pluralism: Religions in Conversation* (Nashville: Abingdon Press, 1989), 154.

[110] 'It is the work of the Spirit to remind Christians that the *Logos* makes God's meaning concrete and tangible for the world; but it does not exhaust that meaning.' Barnes, *Theology and the Dialogue of Religions*, 227.

A Spirit-centred theology is open to other mediations of God throughout the great religious traditions. At the same time, this is not a Spirit of merging or assimilation, as Colin Gunton has pointed out, but of 'relation in otherness', that respects particularity.[111] It also means that an insistence on the particularity of Christianity is not at odds with a genuine appreciation of the particularities of other religions. Christocentric inclusivism tended to limit the unbounded action of the Spirit rather than indicating the Spirit's dynamic activity, beyond the ecclesial realm, in bringing about and promoting new life.

Finally, the Spirit as gift or the *donum Dei* offers a resource for an ontology of mutuality grounded in the reciprocal giving and receiving of the divine life.[112] God's giving and human giving are (analogically) related. All forms of human self-giving find their ultimate meaning and inspiration in this divine mutuality. It is not going too far to claim that 'in the Holy Spirit the intimate life of the Triune God becomes totally gift, an exchange of mutual love between the divine Persons and that through the Holy Spirit God exists in the mode of gift'.[113] Throughout this chapter we have referred to the category of receptivity or gift in all Being, rooted in the gift exchange at the heart of the Trinity: each divine Person gives, receives, and returns, or in the more traditional formulation, they have all things in common except that which distinguishes them.[114] This trinitarian dynamic should determine Christian living, since to be created in the image of the triune God is to be created for interpersonal communion. In sum, the relations in the immanent Trinity are paradigmatic for human relationships in that we reach authentic selfhood through giving to the other thus imaging the self-giving God.

SUGGESTED READINGS

Collins, Paul M., *The Trinity: A Guide for the Perplexed* (London: T&T Clark, 2008).

Dupuis, Jacques, *Toward a Christian Theology of Religious Pluralism* (New York: Orbis, 1997, 2000).

Grenz, Stanley J., *The Social God and the Relational Self: A Trinitarian Theology of the* Imago Dei (Louisville, KY: Westminster John Knox Press, 2001).

---

[111] Gunton, *The One, the Three and the Many*, 182.

[112] For a development of what she calls 'Donum Theology' or a 'Theology of Gift', see Mary Timothy Prokes, *Mutuality: The Human Image of Trinitarian Love* (New York and Mahwah, NJ: Paulist Press, 1993), 34–7.

[113] Pope John Paul II, *On the Holy Spirit in the Life of the Church and the World* (1986), Vatican trans. (Boston, MA, n.d.), No. 10, 18.

[114] Miroslav Volf, 'Being as God Is: Trinity and Generosity', in Miroslav Volf and Michael Welker, eds., *God's Life in Trinity* (Minneapolis: Fortress Press, 2006), 9.

Grenz, Stanley J., *The Named God and the Question of Being: A Trinitarian Theo-Ontology* (Louisville, KY: Westminster John Knox Press, 2005).

Gunton, Colin E., *The One, the Three and the Many: God, Creation and the Culture of Modernity* (Cambridge: Cambridge University Press, 1993).

Hart, David Bentley, *The Beauty of the Infinite: The Aesthetics of Christian Truth* (Grand Rapids, MI/Cambridge: Eerdmans, 2003).

Kärkkäinen, Veli-Matti, *Trinity and Religious Pluralism: The Doctrine of the Trinity in Christian Theology of Religions* (Aldershot: Ashgate, 2004).

Lash, Nicholas, *Holiness, Speech and Silence: Reflections on the Question of God* (Aldershot: Ashgate, 2004).

Vanhoozer, Kevin J., ed., *The Trinity in a Pluralistic Age: Theological Essays on Culture and Religion* (Grand Rapids, MI: Eerdmans, 1997).

Zizioulas, John D., *Communion and Otherness: Further Studies in Personhood and the Church*, ed. Paul McPartlan (London & New York: T&T Clark, 2006).

Epilogue

The reader who has persevered thus far will have gained some insight into the wide diversity of trinitarian theologies, past and present, particularly in the Western Christian tradition. We say this conscious that what has been presented is, of course, selective and not a comprehensive overview. Nevertheless, our hope is that readers are encouraged to delve more deeply into the primary sources and so come to a critical appreciation of the richness of the Christian trinitarian tradition. We have traced the routes taken by some of the leading trinitarian theologians West and East, past and present, Catholic and Reformed. At the same time, we have drawn attention to a number of perennial problematic issues with a trinitarian conception of God, including: how God can be considered simultaneously one and three; how the category 'Person' can be appropriately applied; and how the soteriological implications of the doctrine are to be worked out.

Throughout the book we have alluded to the significance of a participative and sapiential understanding of theology. This kind of sapiential approach, of central importance for approaching the doctrine of the Trinity, comprises two key aspects.

First, it will resist any separation of faith and reason. From Augustine to the medieval schoolmen, theological thinking about the doctrine of the Trinity assumed that reason and faith are not mutually exclusive, but complementary. Purely autonomous reason (Descartes) is a fiction. Michael Polanyi and others have highlighted the fiduciary nature of rationality. Not even the most strictly 'rational' of all disciplines – logic – operates without presuppositions, axioms, or premises (e.g., the principle of non-contradiction). Theology is an exercise in 'holy reason': its first basic act is prayer, where reason looks to God confessing its inadequacy yet daring to speak.[1] This is to underscore

---

[1] John Webster, *Holiness* (Grand Rapids, MI: Eerdmans, 2003), 9–12 and 24. See also Denys Turner, *Faith Seeking* (London: SCM Press, 2002), 135. 'They [e.g., Augustine, Aquinas, and Bonaventure] knew of intellect as a longing impossible to satisfy except in an infinitely beautiful truth.'

a rapprochement of faith and reason, but reason no longer conceived in purely autonomous or universalist terms.

Closely associated with the critique of autonomous reason and the notion that theology should not be subjected to extra-theological authorities is the issue of how to read the Scriptures. We have explained how Luther's *Sola Scriptura* principle led to the problem as to whether the doctrine of the Trinity, as traditionally conceived, was a legitimate interpretation of the biblical witness. In particular, when historical-critical methods (which do not presuppose a faith perspective) were applied to the biblical text, this question became especially pressing. We argued for inclusivist reading strategies, which accept the findings of historical-critical scholarship, without wanting to exclude other, more spiritual, interpretations which can also be accepted as legitimate readings. A text can have multiple layers of legitimate meaning not all of which have to coincide with the authorial intent of the (human) writer. Such hermeneutical pluralism is both pre-modern and postmodern and permits readers to re-engage with the Scriptures, to read the Bible not only as a historical but also as a spiritual and theological book. It should result in a rapprochement of theology and spirituality (including the liturgy and its use of the Scriptures), with the Bible at the centre.

This brings us to a second key aspect of sapiential theology, namely, its close link with spirituality. We have discussed how the early theologians (e.g., the Cappadocians, Augustine, and his medieval successors) placed the mystery of the Trinity at the heart of their spiritual vision. The much maligned 'psychological analogy', we suggested, was a valuable resource for exploring the biblical claim that we have been made in the image of the Trinity. Augustine's trinitarian theology and his relentless probing of human interiority was the first real development of this psychological analogy. The analysis of human interiority, and what it reveals about human and divine subjectivity, would be further developed by Aquinas (albeit in a different philosophical and theological context). For Aquinas, the human person is a *capax Dei*: in knowing and loving the rational creature reaches God's self (*ST* 1a.43.3). The 'assimilation' to the Trinity occurs by way of 'the enlightenment of the mind' and 'the enkindling of the affections' enabling the person to know God. But this cannot come about by one's own resources – the indwelling of the Trinity is the graced presence of God to the human person.

We have also discussed criticisms of the psychological analogy: that it was too speculative, too unrelated to experience and to the economy of salvation. Interpersonal or social models of the Trinity (e.g., Moltmann, and the insights of feminist theology) are now more in favour, and offer a rich resource for drawing out the practical ramifications of trinitarian theology. Here the principles of communion, equality, inclusion, and reciprocity are paramount. Moltmann, Boff, LaCugna, and others intend a trinitarian *orthopraxis*. In short, faith in the Trinity has ethical consequences. We also showed how the Trinity – as a communion that allows space for otherness and difference – can be a resource for inter-religious dialogue.

The psychological and social models of the Trinity reflect complementary, but not contradictory, ways of articulating the trinitarian mystery. Such theological pluralism and diversity has accelerated in the last thirty years, as our discussion of the postmodern context indicated. Many postmodern thinkers question the alleged autonomy of reason and are deeply suspicious of metanarratives, arguing that every interpretation and all truth claims are always perspectival and deeply contextualised. Christian theologians do not have to espouse all aspects of the postmodern analysis to appreciate that the critical questioning of a number of key presuppositions of modernity may create new intellectual scope for Christian theology.

In our final chapter we explored how contemporary theologians (e.g., Bentley Hart and Milbank) have developed a trinitarian ontology of participation by re-engaging with leading figures from the tradition (e.g., Augustine and Gregory of Nyssa). The postmodern celebration of otherness is also an invitation to rediscover the otherness and plurality *within* the Christian tradition. Throughout this book we have attempted to steer away from crude characterisations or stereotyping of this tradition. Thus we distanced ourselves from the oft-repeated contrast between Western Christianity (supposedly more unitarian) and Eastern Christianity (supposedly more genuinely trinitarian). The picture is more nuanced.

To conclude, we hope the reader will have discovered something of the vibrancy and creativity of trinitarian thinking in the West throughout the centuries and gained some insights into current trinitarian thinking. Of course, not all aspects of these debates could be treated. There is significant trinitarian reflection taking place not only in Europe, America, Latin America, and Asia but also on the African continent, even if the latter context is not represented here. Notwithstanding such lacunae, the aim of our volume has been to develop a constructive and participative trinitarian theology, and to show how the Trinity is not a conceptual puzzle but a living reality related to the whole of human existence.

Index